GERHARD RICHTER

FORTY YEARS OF PAINTING

GERHARD RICHTER

FORTY YEARS OF PAINTING

ROBERT STORR

THE MUSEUM OF MODERN ART, NEW YORK
DISTRIBUTED BY D.A.P., NEW YORK

This volume is published on the occasion of the exhibition **Gerhard Richter: Forty Years of Painting**, organized by Robert Storr, Senior Curator, Department of Painting and Sculpture, The Museum of Modern Art, New York.

Tour of the Exhibition:

The Museum of Modern Art, New York
February 14–May 21, 2002

The Art Institute of Chicago
June 22–September 15, 2002

San Francisco Museum of Modern Art
October 11, 2002–January 14, 2003

Hirshhorn Museum and Sculpture Garden, Smithsonian Institution, Washington, D.C.
February 20–May 18, 2003

The exhibition is sponsored by Jo Carole and Ronald S. Lauder.

Generous support is also provided by Mimi and Peter Haas.

An indemnity has been granted by the Federal Council on the Arts and the Humanities.

This publication is made possible by the Blanchette Hooker Rockefeller Fund.

Additional support is provided by Leila and Melville Straus and The Contemporary Arts Council and The Junior Associates of The Museum of Modern Art.

Produced by the Department of Publications, The Museum of Modern Art, New York
Edited by Harriet Schoenholz Bee
Design and composition by Gina Rossi and Antony Drobinski, Emsworth Design, Inc.
Production by Marc Sapir
Printed and bound by Dr. Cantz'sche Druckerei, Ostfildern, Germany
Printed on 150 gsm PhoenixMotion Xenon

Library of Congress Control Number: 2001099460
ISBN: 0-87070-357-9 (clothbound MoMA, T&H)
ISBN: 0-87070-358-7 (paperbound MoMA, T&H)
ISBN: 1-891023-37-X (clothbound D.A.P.)
ISBN: 1-891024-39-6 (paperbound D.A.P.)

Published by the Museum of Modern Art, 11 West 53 Street, New York, New York 10019
(www.moma.org)

Distributed in the United States and Canada by D.A.P., New York

Distributed outside the United States and Canada by Thames & Hudson, Ltd., London

Front cover: Gerhard Richter. Detail of *Abstract Picture [Abstraktes Bild]*. 1992. Oil on aluminum panel, 39½ × 39½" (100 × 100 cm). GR 778-4. Private collection

Back cover: Gerhard Richter. *Reading [Lesende]*. 1994. Oil on linen, 28½ × 40¼" (72.4 × 102.2 cm). GR 804. San Francisco Museum of Modern Art. Purchased through the gifts of Mimi and Peter Haas and Helen and Charles Schwab, and the Accessions Committee Fund

Frontispiece: Gerhard Richter. Detail of *Abstract Picture [Abstraktes Bild]*. 1999. Oil on aluminum panel, 21 ¹¹⁄₁₆ × 18 ¹⁵⁄₁₆" (55 × 48 cm). GR 857-4. Private collection

Page 12: Gerhard Richter. Detail of *Stag [Hirsch]*. 1963. Oil on canvas, 59" × 6' 6¾" (150 × 200 cm). GR 7. Private collection

Page 96: Gerhard Richter. Detail of *Himalaya [Himalaja]*. 1968. Oil on canvas, 6' 6¾" × 63" (200 × 160 cm). GR 181. Collection Gilberto Sandretto

Printed in Germany

CONTENTS

FOREWORD

The Museum of Modern Art is on the verge of a thoroughgoing physical and organizational transformation that will greatly increase its overall size, diversify its sites of operation, and substantially expand and innovate its programming. Nevertheless, its mission remains fundamentally unchanged: to bring the best of the art of our times to the widest possible public. In the case of the present retrospective of paintings by the distinguished German artist Gerhard Richter, the Museum is once again doing what it has traditionally done on behalf of contemporary art and the artists who challenge our ideas and perceptions: namely, provide an opportunity for engagement with the work to a wide public audience. This retrospective makes the case that exploring the development of advanced art beyond our own borders fundamentally alters and enhances our understanding of work that is better known to us. The purpose of such an exhibition, then, is to make this extraordinary body of work as familiar as that which has originated closer to home.

No artist of the postwar era merits this kind of attention more than Gerhard Richter. No other artist has placed more intriguing and rigorous demands upon specialists, interpreters, followers, and average viewers alike—nor upon himself. Richter is the author of pictures so different from one another that at first glance they seem to be by different hands. He has defined a vast pictorial and conceptual territory for himself, and has given it specific dimensions in canvases that vary from Photo-Realist figuration to total abstraction, from snapshot and postcard banality to transcendence, and from serene or pyrotechnic beauty to brooding austerity. Approaching this maze of paintings can be confusing at first, but the more one looks and the more the overt contradictions and subtle continuities of Richter's oeuvre take on substance, the more enlightening the experience becomes. In Richter's work there is pleasure and pain, sly wit and high seriousness, but above all there is a demonstration of the ways in which painting's resources are constantly replenished by the very problems it seems to pose, both for the painter and the viewer. Nobody in our own time has posed them better or solved them more inventively than Richter.

The problems of mounting such a retrospective are daunting at best, and these are surely not the best of times. Under present circumstances, we are all the more thankful for the generosity and faith in The Museum of Modern Art shown by individual collectors and institutions who have made their works available for inclusion in the most comprehensive overview of Richter's career in North America to date, and, almost certainly for years to come. Their commitment to the artist and to the continued free exchange of works of art is exemplary. The lenders to the exhibition are listed in this volume. We are also deeply grateful for the unwavering support provided for this exhibition by its sponsors Jo Carole and Ronald S. Lauder, by Mimi and Peter Haas and Leila and Melville Straus, and for an indemnity granted by the Federal Council on the Arts and the Humanities. This volume has been made possible by the Blanchette Hooker Rockefeller Fund.

On behalf of the Trustees, I would also like to express my appreciation for the extraordinary efforts of the Museum staff at every level to guarantee that this show meets the standards we have always maintained in situations of less upheaval. In particular, I would like to acknowledge the curator of the exhibition, Robert Storr, Senior Curator in the Department of Painting and Sculpture at the Museum, who has brought to this project his tremendous intelligence and insight into contemporary art as well as a deep understanding of Richter's work.

This retrospective of art works by one of the seminal painters of the second half of the twentieth century and the start of the twenty-first is on view at the Museum concurrently with an exhibition devoted to Russian avant-garde books from 1910 to 1934. Together, these shows bracket much of modern art and an important chapter in this Museum's own history; as such, they represent a fitting punctuation for what is both the end of one era and the start of the next.

Glenn D. Lowry
Director
The Museum of Modern Art

ACKNOWLEDGMENTS

An exhibition of this magnitude is the work of many hands. It also reflects the combined determination of many people to make that work possible.

First of all, I would like to thank those who have cleared the path for this project to go forward. Foremost among them is Glenn D. Lowry, Director of the Museum, who has strongly supported this exhibition from its inception and has offered indispensable help along the way to maintain its integrity and find solutions to the unexpected problems of such a large undertaking. Like his commitment to the 1995 acquisition of Richter's great cycle of paintings *October 18, 1977*, his commitment to this retrospective underscores The Museum of Modern Art's overall intent to collect and exhibit contemporary art of the highest order internationally and with the same seriousness with which it has historically pursued classic modern art throughout its history. I owe a huge debt of gratitude to Kirk Varnedoe, former Chief Curator in the Department of Painting and Sculpture at the Museum, who gave me the best job I ever had and has supported me unstintingly in my efforts to fulfill his faith in my work. His steadfast, straightforward insistence on the highest scholarly and professional standards has been a model for me; and his friendship both in hard times and in good has been a great personal boon. In the Department of Painting and Sculpture I also want to thank my esteemed colleague Kynaston McShine, Acting Chief Curator, and grand master of the Modern, whose knowledge, wise counsel, and professional support have been invaluable; Paulo Herkenhoff, Adjunct Curator, whose enthusiasm for and imaginative response to art is the perfect antidote to the bureaucratic blues; Anne Umland, Associate Curator, whose recent peerless Giacometti exhibition, organized with Carolyn Lanchner, former Curator of Painting and Sculpture at the Museum, inspired many thoughts for the present exhibition; Cora Rosevear, Associate Curator, whose diplomatic skills considerably eased the logjam of loans; and Mattias Herold, Manager, and many others in the department who have borne the various pressures generated by this endeavor with good grace. I would also like to acknowledge the curatorial intervention of my colleague Gary Garrels, Chief Curator of Drawings and Curator in the Department of Painting and Sculpture.

The essential contributions of Catharina Manchanda, Curatorial Assistant, have been in every way critical to the research and organization of this retrospective and publication. Her in-depth understanding of the artist and his work, her intellectual gifts, and her forthright character in dealing with lenders, colleagues at this Museum, other institutions, galleries, and all the many people who have contributed to this exhibition have been exemplary. She has my sincere gratitude. Elizabeth Grady, Research Assistant, has devoted herself with admirable skills and astute attention to art-historical accuracy and administrative detail in the preparation of the exhibition and catalogue. My assistant Cary Levine has kept careful watch, in my stead, over the ongoing demands of the department, over all the exigencies and details involved in the preparation of the exhibition, over my difficult schedule, and miraculously has kept his sense of humor while doing so. I would also like to acknowledge the invaluable assistance of numerous interns, translators, and research assistants: Christina Margenfeld, Lynette Roth, Judith Raum, Carmen Alvarado, Philip Glahn, and Stefan Altevogt. All have my sincere thanks.

Outside my own department, the professional staff at the Museum responsible for seeing to it that exhibition and loan contracts are negotiated, works of art are secured, cared for, and properly installed have performed with customary but extraordinary zeal and the utmost regard for the technical and aesthetic demands of such a retrospective. Moreover, with the present turmoil in the world and the complex preparations for moving the Museum to a temporary site as soon as the exhibition has ended, they have managed to do so admirably under difficult circumstances. First among them, I would like to acknowledge Jennifer Russell, Deputy Director for Exhibitions and Collections Support, New York's doyenne of exhibition practice and diplomacy. I am also greatly in debt to Maria De Marco Beardsley, Coordinator of Exhibitions; Jerome Neuner, Director of Exhibition Design and Production, and Mari Shinagawa-Thanner, Production Manager; Peter Omlor, Manager of Art Preparation and Handling, and the Preparators, with whom I share the challenge and pleasure of actually getting the show onto the walls.

A special thanks also goes to Ramona Bronkar Bannayan, who, prior to becoming Director of Collections Management and Exhibition Registration, served as Manager in the Department of Painting and Sculpture, and in that capacity smoothed the way for much of the organization of the exhibition. In the Registrar's Department, she has been ably supported by Jennifer Wolfe, Senior Assistant Registrar, and Seth Fogelman, Assistant Registrar. James Coddington, Chief Conservator, Anny Aviram, Conservator, and Michael Duffy, Associate Conservator, have attended to the condition and protection of the artist's works with their usual care.

This volume is the second book on the artist produced by the Museum within the past year and half, and with its companion volume, *Gerhard Richter: October 18, 1977*, it represents an exceptional effort on behalf of all concerned. I owe an enormous amount to Michael Maegraith, Publisher, for having supported both books to the limit of his resources and with his own critical perspective on the subject at hand. Gina Rossi, Senior Book Designer, and Antony Drobinski, of Emsworth Design, Inc., have worked tirelessly, patiently, and imaginatively to arrive at a design format that shows Richter's work to best advantage. As in the past, Marc Sapir, Director of Production, has supervised the book's production with the hand of a craftsman and the eye of a painter, and it was as one artist talking to another that he and Richter sat down to correct proofs and review layouts. Harriet Schoenholz Bee, Editorial Director, made it possible for me to write this book by reading and editing it section by section with such patience and such attention to sound and sense that the harried author was able to maintain his concentration and keep moving forward. I have been fortunate in my editors before, but never luckier, or more grateful, than in the case of the two Richter books.

There are many others at the Museum I will want to thank in person, but publicly I would like to acknowledge Patty Lipshutz, General Counsel, Stephen Clark, Associate General Counsel, Nancy Adelson, Assistant General Counsel; Mary Lou Strahlendorff, former Director of Communications, Kim Mitchell, Acting Director of Communications; Josiana Bianchi, Public Programs Coordinator; Ed Pusz, Director, Graphic Design, Claire Corey, Production Manager, Graphic Design; Cassandra Heliczer, Associate Editor, Publications, Chris Zichello, Production Manager, Publications; Mikki Carpenter, Director of Imaging Services, Kate Keller, Chief Fine Arts Photographer, Tom Griesel, Fine Arts Photographer, John Wronn, Fine Arts Photographer; Milan Hughston, Chief of Library and Museum Archives, Janis Ekdahl, Senior Librarian, and Jenny Tobias, Associate Librarian. Finally, and most importantly, I would like to express my deep appreciation for the strong support this project has received from Michael Margitich, Deputy Director for External Affairs, and Monika Dillon, Director of Development. Without their knowledge and foresight, none of the foregoing would have been possible.

Assistance has come from many quarters outside the Museum as well. In particular, I am indebted to Marian Goodman and the staff at her gallery, which represents the artist in this country, for many crucial contributions to this project. I would also like to thank Anthony d'Offay, who until recently represented the artist in London. Thanks are also extended to David Zwirner and Massimo Martino for their kind assistance with loans. Richter's assistants Frank Wickert and Doris Lohmann have been patient and thorough in answering our constant questions, and Hubert Becker has also been of real help during our visits to the studio. Among many to whom we owe a debt of gratitude for their generous assistance with research are René Block, Manfred Bolz, Hubertus Butin, Dorothée Fischer, and Bernd Lutze.

On the art historical side, I want to acknowledge the work of the many writers who have taken on this artist as their focus. It had been our intention to publish a book of readings that would gather some of these texts together in order to give voice to diverse views and to show the overall breadth and depth of Richter criticism in English as well as other languages. Compilation of this volume was nearly complete when the economic consequences of the events of September 11, 2001, began to be felt, and publication had to be deferred. We hope that this book will eventually see the light, but I would simply like to say, in this context, that I have learned much from the fine essays of my fellow critics and historians, even and perhaps especially those with whom I respectfully disagree, and I wish to recognize their contributions to my own thinking.

On a personal note, I wish to acknowledge publicly my aunt Gabriele Vawter, who experienced many of the events described or alluded to by the artist in our many conversations and in his art. My understanding of Germany before, during, and after World War II has been deeply enriched by the stories she told to me from my childhood onward; sometimes harsh, sometimes funny, those stories introduced me early on to the idea that oral history contains all the ideological, psychological, moral, and imaginative complexity of the written kind. Combined with the testimony of other German expatriates in whose company I grew up, her vivid descriptions of the ambiguities of that place and those times began my "research" for this book long before I could read.

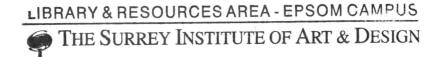

In closing, I gratefully acknowledge the immense debt owed by the Museum and its public to the lenders to the exhibition, listed in this volume, without whose generosity this show would not have been possible. Also, it bears reiterating the gratitude expressed by our director Glenn Lowry to those whose magnanimity made this show happen: I second his thanks to Jo Carole and Ronald S. Lauder, Mimi and Peter Haas, and Leila and Melville Straus, as well as the Federal Council on the Arts and the Humanities for the indemnity it has granted the exhibition, and the Blanchette Hooker Rockefeller Fund for its support of this book. And last but not least, I want to offer my special thanks to the artist Gerhard Richter and his wife Sabine Moritz for having welcomed a stranger into their midst with such warmth and for having cooperated so completely in a project that surely complicated life and just as surely carried with it all the worries that attend any close scrutiny of an artist's career. I hope that the results vindicate their trust, but even more than that I hope this endeavor expresses the extraordinary regard in which The Museum of Modern Art holds Gerhard Richter's achievement.

Robert Storr
Senior Curator
Department of Painting and Sculpture

GERHARD RICHTER

FORTY YEARS OF PAINTING

ROBERT STORR

INTRODUCTION

The present retrospective of paintings by Gerhard Richter is long overdue. As the first comprehensive exhibition of the work of the seventy-year-old German artist to appear in New York, it follows two previous surveys held over a decade ago in other parts of the country. The first was a synoptic overview consisting of only twenty-two paintings, organized in 1987 by John T. Paoletti for the Wadsworth Atheneum in Hartford, Connecticut, as part of its Matrix series, a program usually focused on emerging artists. That Richter was fifty-five when the show opened indicates the lag in recognition his paintings have met in the United States, although on that occasion the art critic Roberta Smith, in *The New York Times*, hailed the artist as "one of the most important West German painters of the postwar period." [2]

Close on the heels of the Hartford show, the Art Gallery of Ontario in Toronto widened the public's view of Richter in 1988 with an eighty-painting survey of his career that traveled to the Museum of Contemporary Art in Chicago, the Hirshhorn Museum and Sculpture Garden in Washington, D.C., and the San Francisco Museum of Modern Art, organized by Roald Nasgaard and I. Michael Danoff. In the fifteen years since that exhibition, Richter has become an increasingly visible figure in American galleries, group or thematic shows at museums, and exhibitions devoted to one or another aspect of his work, such as the presentation of Richter's cycle of canvases *October 18, 1977*, at The Museum of Modern Art in 2000, and *Gerhard Richter in Dallas Collections*, which opened the same year, and which, along with a selection of paintings, also included a complete set of the artist's multiples recently acquired by the Dallas Museum of Art.

The fact remains, however, that compared to American contemporaries of comparable achievement—Jasper Johns and Robert Ryman, to name two—Richter is relatively unfamiliar to the general American public, and still insufficiently known or understood by the dedicated audience for modern art. Only two years older than Richter, Johns (who was born in 1930), has had three full-scale retrospectives in New York, not counting exhibitions of his drawings and his prints; still other exhibitions elsewhere in the country have concentrated on particular series of pictures. Ryman (also born in 1930) has had two large New York retrospectives and one moderately sized one. If one were to add to this list somewhat older artists, such as Roy Lichtenstein—whose early Pop images helped spur Richter to make paintings of equal radicality within months of seeing them—or Robert Rauschenberg, who, along with Lichtenstein, had a powerful impact on Richter's friend Sigmar Polke—the discrepancy between the attention given American artists of the post-Abstract Expressionist generation and that paid to leading painters on the opposite side of the Atlantic (not to mention other parts of the world) becomes more glaring.

Things have not been much better—and sometimes have been worse—for European artists who came of age before Richter. Joseph Beuys, Richter's mercurial colleague on the faculty of the Art Academy (Kunstakademie) in Düsseldorf, and among the most influential experimental artists of his period, has had only one American retrospective (at the Solomon R. Guggenheim Museum in New York in 1979) and one large survey of his drawings (at the Philadelphia Museum of Art and The Museum of Modern Art in 1993–94). Lucio Fontana, a vital link between prewar and postwar Italian avant-gardes, who helped open Richter's eyes to modernism, has had only one retrospective in New York (at the Guggenheim in 1977); and Marcel Broodthaers, a cryptic but essential counterforce to Pop art and a seminal figure in Conceptual art, with whom Richter collaborated in the early 1970s, was given a retrospective by the Walker Art Center in Minneapolis in 1989, which never made it to New York. Finally, two artists in whom Richter has expressed scant interest but who helped set the stage for him and his contemporaries, Yves Klein and Piero Manzoni, have found even less favor. A Klein retrospective was held at The Jewish Museum in New York in 1967, after which none has been mounted in the United States; and Manzoni has had only two gallery exhibitions and no American retrospective.

The motive for compiling this fragmentary and admittedly argumentative list is merely to point out the most obvious evidence of America's, and in particular New York's, cultural nearsightedness. This myopia is not the fault of the American artists who have benefited from it but, rather, the consequence of dramatic shifts in power. After 1945 the United States experienced an unanticipated, largely unchallenged, expansion of its economic, political, and military might—along with an extraordinary, often glorious, fulfillment of its untapped artistic potential. This was not a Renaissance, since it came without precedent, but rather a convergence of creative energies and social circumstances whose explosive effect sent shock waves across the nation and abroad. From roughly 1945 to 1975 there were as many good reasons to think that New York City was where advanced culture "happened," as there were ambitious artists working in downtown apartments and lofts—and there were a lot of them. Widespread opinion had it that Paris had ceded its status as the capital of modernism to New York, but this consensus was predicated on the assumption that modernism had always had such a capital, and that, failing one, it was bound to have another. Although contested, the transfer seemed clear enough: from the mid-nineteenth up to the mid-twentieth centuries it had been France's turn, this time it was America's. Fueled by quantities of art (much of it truly innovative) and by intense debate (much of it ideologically narrow but all the more compelling), Americans, with New Yorkers in the lead, soon got used to the idea that anything and everything of real consequence in contemporary art either originated there or would find its way there soon enough.

The alternative model of a polycentric art world in which far-flung, relatively small but genuinely cosmopolitan regions or cities were connected to one another by loose networks of artists, dealers, critics, and curators nurturing divergent but vigorous strains of avant-garde art had dawned on relatively few people caught up in the feverish, demonstrably fertile activity of the Tenth Street or SoHo art scenes. However, this was exactly the model that was developing all over Europe: in Austria, Denmark, Belgium, the British Isles, France, Italy, and, most dramatically, in Germany. There, in Düsseldorf, Cologne, Berlin, and other pockets of ferment the first modernist German art to appear since Adolf Hitler came to power in 1933 was being made. Although some individuals and tendencies were able to attract attention for more-or-less brief periods of time, it was not until the early 1980s that the overall dynamism of the German art scene was generally acknowledged in the United States. The work that captured the spotlight first—and held it—was work that fit the conventional American idea of what authentic German modernism had always looked like, which is to say Expressionist, with all that the term connotes: full-bore emotionalism and gestural and chromatic violence. Typical of this perspective, in many ways, was a 1983 exhibition at the Saint Louis Art Museum, *Expressions: New Art from Germany*, which featured the work of Georg Baselitz, Jörg Immendorff, Anselm Kiefer, Markus Lüpertz, and A. R. Penck, among others. This revival of painting dovetailed with the resurgence of painterly figuration in New York, which despite the disparate work of its star performers, Jean-Michel Basquiat, Eric Fischl, David Salle, and Julian Schnabel, was labeled, neo-Expressionism, along with that of Baselitz and his cohorts. It came after almost a decade of art making and art discourse preoccupied by forays into new media and out-of-the-studio territory—installation, site-specific sculpture, land art, video, text art, photo-documentation, performance art—carried on under the aegis of new aesthetic paradigms heavily influenced by Marxism, feminism, linguistics, and the social sciences; and it stirred a powerful backlash among the advocates of the suddenly overwhelmed and no longer youthful post-Minimal avant-gardes of the 1970s.

The resulting side-taking and polemical shortcuts employed by critical adversaries made it almost impossible for anyone to concentrate on the obvious differences among the diverse representatives of this reborn—or retread—German variant of Expressionism. This caused some people to overlook or hastily acknowledge in passing the conceptual component of Kiefer's early photo-based work, in order to linger over his grand-manner tableaux and neo-Gothic woodcuts, and led others to ignore the political thrust of Immendorff's otherwise broad-brush Café Deutschland paintings, not to mention the agit-prop and neo-Dada work that preceded them. [3] Above all, this lumping together of everything German into the "Expressionist" basket made it hard to see and virtually impossible to reckon with paintings that simply would not fit this description. Both Richter and Polke fell into this category, which goes a long way toward explaining why neither one of them fully emerged in his own right until the 1980s were almost over. [4]

Granted, Richter had by that time been making brightly colored gestural abstractions for a decade, examples of which had been included in a number of exhibitions that framed the public's understanding of the "new spirit in painting," to borrow the title of one such show. But the strange deliberateness of these canvases did not conform to the heated spontaneity that was the basis of the Expressionist myth: in particular, the earliest works of this kind in which what appears at a distance to be a bold slash of heavy pigment or a shimmering wash of color reveals itself up-close to be a flat illusionistic rendering of expressionist painter-liness. Moreover, those intrigued enough by what Richter called his Abstract Pictures to look further into his work might have found landscapes, still lifes with skulls, wine bottles, burning candles, and the occasional portrait—all of which bore dates similar to those of the abstractions. Additional investigation would have revealed that Richter's work could be traced back to 1962 and that, almost from the outset, it was character-ized by the same kinds of simultaneous stylistic contrasts that were found in his most recent paintings.

In the 1980s confusion about what was recent and what belonged to the past was prevalent in a context where the "newness" of the new German art often meant that people took little or no account of the facts that the artists they were encountering for the first time were actually in mid-career, and the work they were dis-covering had quite possibly been made ten or even twenty years before. In short, this was art without an art history. As familiarity with it grew, the need for a substantial rewriting of existing histories of European art in the second half of the twentieth century—histories previously dominated by famous survivors of the pre-war avant-gardes and postwar eminences such as Jean Dubuffet and Francis Bacon, with a nod to British Pop art and varieties of hard-edge abstraction in France, Switzerland, and Germany—had become even more imperative, as had a fundamental rethinking of American art history in the same period.

The multifaceted nature of Richter's output posed an especially daunting challenge to the received aes-thetic wisdom of an American public educated to the idea that modernism consisted of the linear progression of movements propelled by individual talents struggling to make their distinctive contribution to "mainstream" painting and sculpture. Criticism of this kind presupposed a logical and, in hindsight, necessary evolution of styles—from figuration to abstraction, or at least from realism to more interpretive forms of depiction—advanced by artists whose reputations for creative rectitude were consolidated around readily identifiable bodies of work. After World War II the cult of authenticity rested upon artists' sincere efforts to match their work with their experience; and the cult of formal integrity rested upon the consistency of their intentions with regard to the larger scheme of their medium's predicted development. Inauthentic, insincere, or incon-sistent art—signaled by stylistic zigzags and about-faces as opposed to uninterrupted forward motion—were a matter of existential bad faith or aesthetic fickleness.

The positive role models for this ethos are legendary: Vincent van Gogh's agonizing self-transformation from provincial amateur working in a stilted, already old-fashioned naturalist manner to a pioneering Post-Impressionist; Piet Mondrian's solitary pilgrimage from a similarly conservative naturalism through Symbolism to the earthly paradise of pure nonobjective art; and Jackson Pollock's desperate battle against his demons and technical awkwardness leading to the invention of a psychologically charged but pictorially unfettered allover abstraction. Conveniently bypassed in the construction of this archetype was the always pluralistic Pablo Picasso, who reveled in changing artistic directions as well as in raiding art history and the work of his contemporaries for anything he could use; and Francis Picabia, who was as stylistically promiscu-ous as Picasso (though not as seductive), and even more brazen in his indifference toward aesthetic idealism of the sort that produced the intertwined narratives of the modern artist as a uniquely purposeful being and modernism as an ever more concentrated force unswervingly targeted on wholeness or on irreducible essences. Although Picasso defined high modernism in the public imagination, consensus taste often treated him as if he were heroically beyond it, while that same consensus dismissed Picabia—especially the peek-a-boo, decorative neoclassical pictures and pastiches of pulp pinups he painted after abandoning Cubism and Dada—as if he were ignominiously beneath it.

By the 1960s few artists in Europe or America thought, as Pollock and Willem de Kooning had twenty years earlier, that Picasso was "the man to beat," but in Europe, as distinct from America, the idea that Picabia's multifariousness might open paths through the unified-field theory of modernism had taken hold. [5] When asked in 1979 about the superficial slickness and apparent detachment of his photo-based painting, Richter replied: "I would say that my behavior is a little comparable to Picabia, wouldn't you?" [6] The inter-viewer reporting Richter's remark added that it was delivered coyly, but that is unlikely. Rather, the positive invocation of Picabia's name marked the line separating observers who were wedded to the notion that important artists set themselves apart by the creation of a signature style (and who, therefore, could not believe that anyone serious would opt for eclecticism) and practitioners who were increasingly impatient with the demand that they invent and then stick to such a style as proof of their absolute "originality," since it was indicative of the kind of imposed value that their free appropriation of images and mimicry of established styles had called into question. The unexamined expectation that artists do one thing—their thing—gave traction to painters like Richter who were gifted with the ability to do many things but doubtful of the inherent validity or necessity of any single way of working.

Richter's technical facility coated the pill he offered those with doctrinaire modernist taste, but it also heightened suspicion. The virtuosity he demonstrated—a virtuosity he has been at pains to play down for this very reason—reinforced the belief of some detractors that he was a trickster or, worse, an opportunist ready with good-looking pictures to suit every sensibility and every turn of the fashion wheel. [7] But if that were really the case, why did Richter show his work in mixed batches when it would have been more efficient, as well as less easily subject to antagonistic scrutiny, for him to funnel each genre's examples to its receptive public? Instead, Richter has deliberately muddied the waters and opened himself up to attack by insisting that appreciation of any given aspect of his production is contingent on an awareness of its overall multiplicity of aspects.

Speaking at a round table convened in 1994 to consider the problem of Richter's many guises, the writer Diedrich Diederichson argued: "The paintings don't only stand for themselves. They are, so to speak, stage directions for viewing other paintings." [8] A more sympathetic view was taken at the time of Richter's first New York exhibition in 1973 [9] by Peter Frank: "As Richter's art is dependent on his own history...the Onnasch Gallery correctly showed Richter in retrospect." [10] Frank was the first American critic to recognize the impact on Richter of Fluxus—a neo-Dada tendency to which Frank was also close—and based on that association pronounced him "a conceptual painter" whose "paintings are statements about ideas for paintings—almost tautologies but more evasive and unsettled." [11] Early on, then, Frank's commentary set the tone for the supportive response to Richter's deft, cool, and hermetically multifarious picture making.

That presumption that the artist was a Conceptualist in studio garb was the jumping-off point for Nasgaard's essay in the catalogue of the 1988 Richter retrospective. Noting that he was the only painter in The Art Institute of Chicago's Europe in the Seventies: Aspects of Recent Art, a 1977 exhibition he described as the "most dramatic rejection of conventional media ever observed in an art exhibition that purports to survey both a decade and a continent," Nasgaard said: "Here Richter's paintings kept company with Arte Povera artists and other European counterpoints of Minimal and Conceptual Art. And, indeed, this has been the more critical context for his work: where what is addressed is the conceptual basis of his painting, or its deconstructivist program. The discussion therefore has often led away from painting—an orientation also supported by Richter's own ventures into other kinds of work—performance, collaboration, inventories, photographs, objects, books." [12]

When Nasgaard wrote this, the war between neo-Expressionism's defenders and its adversaries had reached its climax, and was settling into a stalemate. Chief among the latter were critics who, having cut their teeth on Minimal, Process, and Conceptual art in the 1960s and 1970s, set about to construct artistic teleologies that drew direct connections between those tendencies and more recent varieties of postmodern art, even as they used that ostensibly radical new art and the psychoanalytic, linguistic, and political underpinnings in which it was entangled to deconstruct the existing teleologies of modernism. With few exceptions, this self-consciously anti-aesthetic school of thought took it as a given that painting had been rendered historically obsolete by new media—in particular by photomechanical means that permitted the mass reproduction of words and images. If painting were to serve any credible function, they maintained, it would be as an instrument to hasten the demolition of the formal and ideological foundations that had previously held painting up and guaranteed its preeminence among other art forms. [13] From this vantage point, for example, David Salle's overlaying of pirated fragments from Picasso, Max Beckmann, Reginald Marsh, advertising, and the comics (a procedure derived from the work of Polke) was seen as canceling one order of image with another, until all—"high" as well as "low"—were marked null and void.

While pioneers of reductive abstract painting such as Ryman and Frank Stella were regarded as saving remnants of the modernist avant-garde and granted special dispensation from the sweeping declaration that painting was dead by those dedicated to the proposition that painting was a social and aesthetic anachronism, Richter the postmodern polymath was accorded a special—and especially—problematic role as the unrivaled anti-master of his craft who could demonstrate once and for all that painting had exhausted its formerly protean possibilities—possibilities which could never be revived no matter how skillfully they were evoked.

And so when the German-born, American-based art historian, and Richter's longtime friend, Benjamin Buchloh, told the artist that critical commentators had "started to see you as a painter who knows all the tricks and techniques, and who simultaneously discredits and deploys all the iconographical conventions.... At the moment, this makes you particularly attractive to many viewers because your work looks like a survey of the whole universe of twentieth-century painting, presented in one vast, cynical retrospective," he was inverting the hostile view that Richter was a gifted jack-of-all-trades and offering the repolarized condemnation as a compliment. [14] In sum, doctrinaire exponents of Marcel Duchamp's conceit that "retinal," or perceptual, forms of art had been permanently eclipsed by conceptual ones cast Richter as the man who could thoroughly undo painting precisely because he could do it so well.

Richter's own complex, intermittently gloomy feelings about painting's prospects are by no measure so categorical or so extreme. Acutely conscious of his own limitations and those of his medium, Richter responded to Buchloh by saying that he saw "no cynicism or trickery or guile" in his practice. Pressed by the critic to admit that the tension in his work between depiction and self-reflection—in other words, the making of images and the critical examination of them—was set up in order "to show the inadequacy, the bankruptcy of both," Richter replied, "not the bankruptcy, but always the inadequacy," after which he took care to stipulate that he meant this "in relation to what is expected of painting." [15]

He might just as well have said what *he* expected of painting, by which we may understand "everything" shadowed by the fear of "nothing." The existential misgivings about the medium Richter harbors as a practitioner are fundamentally different from the rhetorical certainties his postmodernist supporters have ascribed to him in their desire to make him a standard-bearer for their overdetermined brand of endgame speculation. If Richter has managed to straddle the divide between conceptual and perceptual art—art as analytic method and art as the material expression of intuitions and emotions—it has not been a matter of hedging his bets, and it has certainly not been the easy way out. Instead, Richter has persisted in bridging the gap—a dichotomy which, in the hands of those who most rigidly stress it, raises the schizophrenic separation in our culture between thinking and doing to the level of a supposedly "progressive" principle—because the alternative of stepping to one side or the other in order to contemplate the opposite cliff in greater comfort and with diminished risk of being misunderstood was untenable. Looking back from the fenced-in promontory of an ideologically secure position at the articulate but nonverbal means by which he had groped toward truths or partial truths, was inconceivable to him. And so, conversely, was a retreat into the safety of artistic tradition with an occasional glance over his shoulder toward the brink of philosophical doubt to which the daily practice of painting had brought him.

Although critics have spoken his name—and the most attentive have spoken well, with the result that there is a rich and rapidly growing body of commentary on his work—no one has set forth the terms of Richter's dilemma more cogently than the artist himself. In interviews, letters, and private ruminations, the leitmotifs of Richter's thought have been clearly stated from the very beginning: faith versus skepticism; hope versus pessimism; engagement versus neutrality; self-determination versus fatalism; imaginative freedom versus ideology. In the work itself these dialectical binaries and the ramifications they have engendered take on a visual, and, beyond that, material reality: impersonal iconography versus delicacy of facture; veiled intimacy versus formality of presentation; chromatic austerity versus rich tactility; optical splendor versus physical remoteness; gestural exuberance versus strict self-censorship; resistance to easy pleasure versus exquisite hedonism; somberness versus playfulness; forthright assertion of image as object versus mistrust of the image as representation.

These attitudes and qualities are manifest throughout his career and across his artistic production, and, as cited above, their scope has included everything from performance, artistic collaboration, and installation to sculpture, drawings, watercolors, photographs, multiples, and books. Nevertheless, with the exception of a graphic variant of his first mature painting, *Table* (1962), and Richter's portrait busts of himself and Blinky

Palermo, the present retrospective is exclusively focused on paintings. Several considerations have determined that decision; some are practical, others cut closer to the heart of the debate over Richter's accomplishment and his place among the leading artists of his day. First, Richter has been enormously prolific, and any exhibition attempting to deal in depth with his work in all mediums would surpass the current spatial capacities of The Museum of Modern Art (as well as most other museums). At over 113 works, this exhibition is already among the largest the Museum has ever devoted to a contemporary artist. Second, three recent exhibitions lessen the immediate need (and opportunity) for an extensive coverage of Richter's work on paper: the Dia Center for the Arts' yearlong New York presentation of the complete *Atlas*, organized by Lynne Cooke in 1995–96; *Gerhard Richter: Drawings 1964–1999*, organized by Dieter Schwarz for the Kunstmuseum Winterthur, Switzerland, in 1999, which, though it did not travel to the United States, has been documented in a scholarly catalogue in wide circulation; and the previously mentioned Dallas Museum of Art exhibition, comprising all of Richter's multiples, organized by Charles Wylie in 2000.

The third, and overriding, criterion in deciding to concentrate on Richter's work on canvas is simply to acknowledge that painting has always been his primary concern and for appreciable periods his *only* concern. Although Richter began, as many young artists do, by drawing and painting in watercolors, the body of drawings produced in the early 1960s and mid-1970s is relatively small, and it is only in 1982 that drawing became a major, though still fitful, part of his studio regimen. Moreover, between 1952—when he entered the Art Academy (Kunstakademie) in Dresden, where the curriculum centered on oil painting—and 1977, Richter did not take up watercolors again, and then, after a brief flurry of activity lasting through 1978, he once more abandoned the medium before returning to it in earnest in 1984. Meanwhile, better than half of Richter's multiples were produced between 1965 and 1974, and, with the exception of the 1978 artist's book *128 Details from a Painting*, it was not until 1991–92 that he began to make graphic and photographic work that significantly altered the parameters of his larger aesthetic project.

The interpretative maze that has grown up around Richter's oeuvre has at times distracted viewers from the fact that the pictorial maze he has built within that critical outer structure is made not merely of pictures—images subject to the kind of semiotic analysis that would treat them all as essentially the same regardless of their material presence—but of paintings whose meaning can only be grasped, if fleetingly and with difficulty, by the fully alert senses in tandem with an agile, rather than dogma-bound, mind. Furthermore, one would have hoped, a dozen years after the 1980s, that even the most hard-line opponents of painting's resurgence would concede that there is little left to gain and perhaps something of significance to be lost by continuing to use painting as a rhetorical whipping boy. Painting is no longer the dominant medium it once was. There is no urgent need to topple it from its pedestal when other practices have begun to crowd painting on an equal, or nearly equal, footing. Moreover, the new art forms championed at its expense have begun to show their age and accumulate the burdens that come with tradition in any medium. And, insofar as special political and social status was accorded those art forms because they were ignored by the market or otherwise escaped the corrupting effects of commodity capitalism, which had supposedly compromised painting beyond redemption, recent expansion and diversification of the market have deprived them of that virtue.

The moment is ripe, then, to reexamine Richter at one remove from these increasingly dated and preemptive ways of looking, and to see his work more clearly from all the many angles from which it begs to be seen. Whatever has been or may be said about his contribution to the medium—be it as lethal parodist, dour undertaker, dry-eyed mourner, systematic debunker of clichés, demystifying conjurer of illusions, or as tenacious seeker of ways to make visible the longing and queasy uncertainty inherent in our hunger for pictures—Richter has, paradoxically or stealthily, demonstrated painting's resiliency. Fifty years after Richter found his vocation and forty years after making his first distinctive mark, the accumulated evidence selectively presented in this exhibition vindicates his faith in an art form fewer and fewer of his closest supporters have believed in, and much of the general public has taken for granted at high cost to painting's ability to convey fresh meaning. In any event, it is a medium that has come to depend on Richter's severe scrutiny—and it has survived and thrived in large measure because of it.

I: BEGINNINGS

Gerhard Richter was born in Dresden in 1932. Three years later his family moved to the small town of Reichenau in Saxony, where his father was employed as a school teacher. It was the first of two relocations that would keep the young Richter, for the most part, out of harm's way during the upheavals of the twelve-year Third Reich and the early years of the Soviet occupation that followed. The second move was to the still smaller village of Waltersdorf in 1942. His father Horst Richter was an affable but, in many respects, ineffec-tual man; he was also a staunch Protestant and, like most functionaries, a member of the National Socialist Party. Mobilized after the outbreak of war, as were Richter's maternal uncles Rudi and Alfred, he first served on the eastern front in Russia, though not on the front lines, and later on the western front, where he was taken prisoner by the Americans. Released in 1946, he made his way back to Waltersdorf but was never able to find his footing again; as an ex-Nazi he was not allowed to return to his teaching post, nor did he ever fully reintegrate himself into the family. "He shared most fathers' fate at the time.... Nobody wanted them."[2]

Before her marriage, Richter's mother, the former Hildegard Schönfelder, had been a bookseller in Dresden, and when she reluctantly moved away from that cultural center she brought with her a passion for music and for the classics of German literature. The daughter of a gifted concert pianist who had given up his career to manage the family brewery business (only to superintend its collapse), she had a sense of her own special status within the community and passed this on to her son.

Although Richter's parents were a mismatched couple, family life before the war was typical of the provincial *petit-bourgeoisie* or, as Richter summed it up, "simple, orderly, structured—mother playing the piano and the father earning money."[3] With the father absent during war, family life was more eventful than before. Like all boys, Richter was drummed into the Hitler Youth. "I was very impressed by the idea of sol-diers, of militarism, maybe Hitler, that was impressive," he recalled, but the Hitler Youth, "was too tough for me. I don't like fighting games, I wasn't very sporty."[4] Besides that: "They were all a bunch of pompous asses. When you are twelve you're too little to understand all that ideological hocus-pocus, but even though this might sound funny now, I always knew I was something better than they were. Hitler and soldiers, and all of that was for plebeians, whereas my mother always kept me close to 'culture,' to Nietzsche, Goethe and Wagner."[5] Nevertheless, the disruptions of war broke the pall of small-town life, and Richter seems to have welcomed them with curiosity and a certain relish. He and his friends would scout the woods with an army rifle and take pot shots at the trees, while military trenches were dug behind his house, squadrons of American planes dropped propaganda leaflets from on high, and Russian MiGs flew low overhead hunting for German army trucks. Richter recalled: "There were weapons and cannons and guns and cigarettes; it was fantastic."[6]

There was also fear and terrible, though distant, destruction. In February 1945, Allied bombers unleashed a firestorm over Dresden that ranks as the most devastating aerial assault in history prior to the first use of atomic weapons in Hiroshima and Nagasaki later that year. Although details have been lost to memory, Richter's recollections of being alerted to the Dresden attack in nearby Waltersdorf are vivid enough: "In the night, everyone came out into the street in this village 100 kilometers away, Dresden was being bombed, 'Now, at this moment!' We knew because of the radio, and you could hear it, [though] I can't remember whether I really heard it, whether that was possible...but maybe over the radio."[7] His grand-mother and aunt had been in Dresden at the time and survived the raid. While he remembers exploring a "totally damaged" city when he went there five years later and knew that it had "been very awful there," he also recalls having listened excitedly to descriptions of people walking through the burning wreckage of buildings.[8] It was as if his grandmother and aunt were telling a picaresque story. More likely, however, it was the boy's adolescent spirit, reveling in the turmoil nearer to home, which caused him to hear their account in that way; and perhaps it was his instinct for deflecting trauma that turned catastrophe into adventure.

Although Richter had prepared to flee the Russian advance by making a small cart, in the end he remained in Waltersdorf. The first phase of the Soviet occupation was chaotic and at times brutal (looting was widespread and rapes were common), but before long relative order was reestablished and with it came some mixed blessings. According to Richter: "It was very nasty, [but] when the Russians came to our village and expropriated the houses of the rich who had already left or were driven out, they made libraries for the people out of those houses. And that was fantastic. We could get all the books: [Hermann] Hesse, [Ernst] Wiechert, [Lion] Feuchtwanger. All that stuff was suddenly there. Later it was forbidden. You could almost not buy a Thomas Mann. But at the beginning everything was there."[9]

In 1945, having failed math, Richter left grammar school and enrolled in a trade school where he studied accounting, stenography, and Russian (required by Soviet authorities). Among his friends in those days were a slightly older local painter, of little talent but a mentor of sorts, and a photographer whose father had a dark-room where Richter briefly worked as an assistant. It was under his tutelage that Richter took the snapshots that fill his photo albums of this period. In 1948 Richter left home, and settled in the nearby town of Zittau, where he took up residence in a hostel for apprentices. During this period he read avidly his mother's beloved philosopher Friedrich Nietzsche, but also Karl Marx; boldly breaking with his parents' stern faith and firm in his new materialist convictions, he renounced religion. "By the age of sixteen or seventeen I was absolutely clear that there is no God—an alarming discovery to me, after my Christian upbringing. By that time, my fundamental aversion to all beliefs and ideologies was fully developed."[10]

By the time he was fifteen Richter had also begun to draw on his own with some dedication, his first success in this medium being a nude that his parents discovered with a combination of embarrassment and pride. At sixteen he attended a summer camp, where he continued to draw and fell in love for the first time. Asked when he decided to be an artist he has said: "I didn't know when I was fourteen or fifteen, but from age sixteen on I knew it."[11] At seventeen he started experimenting with watercolors, but his professional prospects did not yet include a career as a painter. Instead, he thought about being a forester (but he was small and not physically rugged enough for the job), a dental technician (a visit to the local dentist's office scared him off), and a lithographer (a visit to a printing plant likewise put an end to that idea).

Richter's first art-related job was as a member of a team that made Communist banners for the government of the German Democratic Republic. However, during his five-month stint he never actually painted any slogans, having been assigned the task of washing them off old banners to make them ready for newly mandated exhortations. This unpromising start, plus friendships formed at night school, led to his positions as a sign painter and theater set painter. The latter of the two, in addition to the classes he attended, helped fill in gaps in his education, inasmuch as the company produced plays by Johann Wolfgang von Goethe, Friedrich von Schiller, and other classic authors, along with operas and operettas. Richter plunged into this bohemian milieu enthusiastically, but his refusal to do more menial painting jobs for the theater resulted in his being fired. With that experience behind him and hoping to set out in earnest on his chosen path he applied to the Dresden Art Academy but was turned down in part for lack of preparation and in part because he was viewed as being "too bourgeois."[12] Advised to try to solve that problem by associating himself with a state-run Socialist organization, Richter took another job producing propaganda, for which he painted posters of Stalin among other approved subjects. Using this position as a way back into the system, he reapplied to the Dresden academy in 1950 with a portfolio of drawings and watercolors—including a semiabstraction that puzzled his examiners, who gave it the title "Volcano" to allay their discomfort—and was accepted.

Prior to the bombings, which destroyed the heart of the city and many great masterpieces in the world-renowned Zwinger Museum, Dresden had been one of the cultural centers of Germany. While it had formerly been the home of the Expressionist painter Ernst Ludwig Kirchner and the base for *Die Brücke* (The Bridge), the artists' group he founded in 1905, its academy, like that of Munich, was a longstanding bastion of conservatism. When Richter entered the academy as a student, it still retained some of that distinction, but its curriculum had been radically changed to accommodate the Communist Party's policies of Socialist Realism. While still on his own, Richter had steeped himself in the old and modern masters—Albrecht Dürer, Diego

Gerhard Richter. **Self-Portrait.** 1949. Watercolor on paper, dimensions unknown. Private collection

Velázquez, Rembrandt van Rijn, the Impressionists, and Lovis Corinth—whose work he could find reproduced in books and albums that represented consensus taste in the 1930s and 1940s. However, the hardening of the party line as the cold war set in meant that Impressionism—considered a "bourgeois" movement—was soon out of official favor. German Expressionism and other modernist tendencies that had been banned by Hitler after the famous *Degenerate "Art" (Entartete "Kunst")* exhibition of 1938 were largely unknown because of censorship and in any case completely off-limits. Richter's personal pantheon at that time included Velázquez, Édouard Manet, Caspar David Friedrich, and Max Beckmann. "[Adolf] Menzel I knew," Richter said of the nineteenth-century German realist and history painter, "but I was not so impressed." Also included in his field of awareness were Pablo Picasso and the Italian artist Renato Guttuso, both of whom were prominent Communists whose formal and expressive deviation from realism was therefore tolerated by the Soviet leadership.[13] Although information about modern art filtered in through magazines and newspapers, Richter and his fellow students were largely cut off from developments in the West, and Richter's only direct contact with a representative of the prewar avant-garde left him suspicious. Early in Richter's years at the academy Otto Dix, the Expressionist painter of the first decades of the twentieth century and a leading exponent of the socially critical *Neue Sachlichkeit* (New Objectivity) movement of the 1920s, visited the school. But by then his painterly manner had become decorative and his subject matter blandly humanist. Moreover, with his large floppy hat, he dressed like an old-fashioned artistic dandy. Richter's encounter with him triggered a response that would be characteristic thereafter, namely his "mistrust of people who are very flamboyant . . . this seductive side that people are taken in by. I don't even know if Dix had that, but he appeared to because he came from the West, as if he were coming from a different planet."[14]

The five-year curriculum at the academy was strictly traditional—drawing followed by painting in oils—with portraits, nudes, still lifes, and set-piece figurative compositions providing the basic pictorial program. Curiously enough, though, the mural department in which Richter chose to study, was well known as a sanctuary from the most rigid application of the Socialist Realist model because it was assumed that the demands of wall decoration would permit a measure of otherwise unacceptable "formalism." Given the choice between the grim class-struggle narratives of André Fougeron (a French painter then in vogue at the academy) and the sophistication and pictorial verve of the muralist Diego Rivera (like Guttuso and Picasso, an internationally renowned ornament of the Stalinist Left), Richter chose the model represented by Rivera, even though his own style and methods owed nothing to the Mexican's. Heinz Lohmar, the professor in charge of the mural department, had been a minor Surrealist in Paris before the war, and, although a loyal Communist Party member, remained a comparatively well-informed and cosmopolitan figure, in Richter's words, "a very interesting type, a little gangster."[15] In this context, Richter completed the four years of mandatory painting exercises and for his fifth and final year, was given a studio of his own and a major commission for a mural in the German Hygiene Museum [Deutsches Hygienemuseum] in Dresden.

As a composition, Richter's painting there is true to its type and period: solidly modeled figures of healthy men, women, and children engaged in life-enhancing activities. None of the figures has any individuality, but despite this and its other formulaic qualities the painting as a whole has a certain graphic energy resulting from a simple design, lack of rhetorical overkill, and general ease of execution. In short, it offers the pleasures of a well-made thing that accepts its own conventions and operates unpretentiously within them. Although Richter says he "always tried" to believe in the content of his commissioned work he and his comrades could not muster any real fervor for the cause they ostensibly served.[16] Nevertheless, a hint of conviction couched in the political code words of the time or, at least, the suggestion of genuinely mixed feelings, enters into his published statements on the subject of muralism. Thus, in a 1958 article, Richter cautiously but firmly pushes for rationalizing the bureaucratic process that governed commissions, refers to pressures he "never took seriously" to adhere strictly to Socialist Realism, and mentions the dangers of "stupid dogmatism."[17] In an earlier article of 1956, he wrote at length about the promise and problems of painting's "reorientation toward architecture"; argued for the merits of seeking stylistic "originality and freshness"; described his own technique of building up the image by blocking it in equal perpendicular strokes; but emphasized his awareness that "this last is not to be confused with 'painterly' carelessness," when instead, "cleanliness and clarity of the total painting and every individual form is the tendency of our efforts in mural painting."[18]

Furthermore, he called "for an art that steps outside of the private sphere and represents the absolute general good," and spoke of his ambition to make a painting that is "festive-bright, cheerful, at the same time calming, clear and rational."[19] At face value, Richter's comments might read as an adroit accommodation to an imposed aesthetic doctrine, but signs of his own independence and of his desire to open up creative room within that doctrine are plainly evident. More striking, on reflection, are the implicit contrasts and correspondences these texts set up. On the one hand, the work for which Richter later became known was the antithesis of "cleanliness and clarity of the total painting and every individual form."[20] On the other hand, his abiding distrust of self-dramatizing or overtly introspective painting as well as his belief in art as a moral undertaking echo his advocacy of "an art that steps outside the private sphere and represents the absolute general good," even as his interest in painting's "reorientation toward architecture" is reflected in the various public commissions he accepted after coming to the West and in the unrealized projects for rooms constructed around mirrors or large-format canvases.[21] These unexecuted works are documented in *Atlas,* Richter's ongoing archive of sources for his work begun in 1969.

Although Richter remembers completing only a couple of murals, there is evidence of others, some of them in a heroic socialist mode. One of his outdoor political pictures shows a bare-chested man distributing official newspapers; another large indoor painting features muscular men and women wielding sledge-hammers and paving stones, and waving banners as they confront mounted troops swinging truncheons. Richter's later condemnations of ideological art are something more than the opinions of a man who simply lived under authoritarian regimes; they are those of someone who had participated in the creation of a state culture. That said, Richter's apprenticeship and journeyman years in the East constitute a substantial preamble to his career in the West, and not just a uniformly and transparently negative experience against which to react. Indeed, they represent a struggle to answer serious aesthetic challenges, but one pursued on terms that made any artistically satisfying answers impossible. Like all real struggles they left scars, but they also clarified and strengthened his basic inclinations.

Although Richter had already shown a rebellious streak, one can hardly fault him for trying to find his niche, or for being naive in gauging the long-term hopes for greater artistic freedom. In 1953 Stalin died, and the Korean War—one of the cold war's many hot wars—came to an end. The East–West stand-off seemed to relax for a moment, although by 1956, following uprisings in Czechoslovakia, Hungary, and Poland, it locked-in even more rigidly than before. For a young painter who had barely made it out of his small-town setting and into the academy, the relatively comfortable life he led had much to recommend it. The circle of friends with whom he associated included Marianne [Ema] Eufinger, a textile design student he met around 1951 and married in 1957.[22]

Moreover, the success that greeted Richter's initial public projects must have been gratifying no matter how restless he felt about having their parameters dictated to him. Those successes increased the demand for his work and brought certain "perks": a steady income, a motorcycle, then a small car, and travel abroad. Richter's first such trip was in 1955 when he toured West Germany to study mural painting there and took a week-long excursion to Paris. Of the visit to Paris Richter remembered: "I went to galleries and museums, but I don't remember any of that. [And] I tried to find the existentialist hangouts with music and literature, but I never found them. You had to know the addresses and I couldn't speak French."[23] The second trip was also to West Germany, where Richter saw Documenta 2, one of a series of omnibus exhibitions brought into being by Professor Arnold Bode, whose aim was to reintroduce Germany to international modernism and to its own avant-gardes after the long darkness of the Nazi era. Strategically located in Kassel, a city close to the border between the German Democratic Republic and the German Federal Republic, the show was also a deliberate enticement to East Germans whose cultural horizons were still blocked. Having missed the first exhibition in the series in 1955, Richter took full advantage of the second four years later, photographing virtually all the work he saw for reference when he returned home. It was the turning point of his artistic life, and two painters in particular were responsible: "I... was enormously impressed by [Jackson] Pollock and [Lucio] Fontana.... The sheer brazenness of it! That really fascinated me and impressed me. I might almost say that those paintings were the real reason I left the GDR. I realized that something was wrong with my whole way of thinking.... But that is what I mean, I lived my life with a group of people who laid claim to a moral aspiration, who wanted to bridge a gap, who were looking for a middle way between capitalism and Socialism, a so-called Third Path. And so the way we thought, and what we wanted for our own art, was all about compromise."[24]

Gerhard Richter. Study for **Skull.** c. 1956. Ink on paper, approx. 11¹³⁄₁₆ × 15¾" (30 x 40 cm). Preparatory sketch for a mural in the Deutsches Hygienemuseum, Dresden. Whereabouts unknown

Gerhard Richter. **Mural**. 1956.
Deutsches Hygienemuseum, Dresden.
Installation view, late 1950s; mural
now covered.

The nerve that Pollock and Fontana hit had already been sensitized by Richter's unavailing attempts to adapt a variety of existing styles to his own needs. Other than the (now overpainted) mural at the Hygiene Museum, the only surviving record of Richter's work prior to 1962 are the albums of photographs he took of murals, paintings, and drawing before the work itself disappeared or was destroyed. These efforts include moody watercolors of the countryside of his native Saxony, made when he was in his teens, commissions, work done at the academy, and work done independently. Among the independent works are life studies, many with the generalized features and full volumes of his murals (two paintings of women reading are reminiscent of David Alfaro Siqueiros's heavy modeling); and face and figure compositions with the abstraction and graphic filigree of works by Picasso of the late 1940s and early 1950s (a drawing of a tractor in a field, pastiches of Picasso's drawing *Knight and Page Boy* and the murals, *War* and *Peace*, he created for a Cistercian chapel in Vallauris, France, in 1951–52), heads that mimic Picasso's peace-movement posters and his prints and sketches of Françoise Gilot, and several sheets devoted to skulls. While the skulls clearly seem inspired by Picasso's treatment of the same subject (for example, *Still Life with Skull, Leek, and Pottery* 1945), they also presage Richter's return to the subject in paintings of 1983 (page 193) and in drawings of 1986. It is worth pointing out that when Richter began painting skulls and candles in the 1980s, some observers assumed that he was ironically invoking the memento mori of neo-baroque or neoclassical painting, then in fashion. Rather, it appears that he was going back to a motif from the earliest chapters of his own development and, indirectly, resuming his "conversation" with Picasso by offering his uncanny but impersonal rendition of the image as a lasting riposte to Picasso's ceaselessly inventive but too often facile stylizations. Richter had once imitated such stylizations in the hope that they might solve his problems; but in the final analysis they offered him nothing except a reminder of his own lack of invention.

Mixed into this miscellany (which encompasses self-portraits, portraits of Ema, copies from Dürer, quasi-abstract scenes in a delicate Lyonel Feininger-like mode, and schematic landscapes and still lifes with muted expressionist color) are a handful of undated paintings and drawings influenced by Art Informel painting, or Abstract Expressionism. Their energy is confined by their small format, but is still palpable. For the rest, Richter's documented work of the mid- to late 1950s is competent or more than competent, seldom distinctive, often sentimental, and occasionally pretty. Richter's predicament was compounded in his own mind by what he saw as a temptation to regard any opposition to the meretriciousness of official art as an inverse guarantee of aesthetic quality: "For an artist the situation in Dresden was unreal. They [the cultural bureaucracy] by calling you a formalist could deny you the opportunity to exhibit. This gave you a false sense of your own importance. [It] made you think that you were a great artist, when really you were nothing."[25] Richter was in a double bind, and one can readily appreciate his frustration and well imagine the shock the sight of works by Pollock and Fontana engendered. But there is one further thing to note; unlike some artists who trained in the Eastern

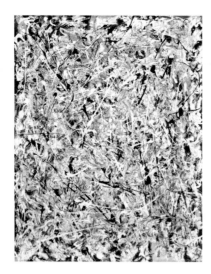
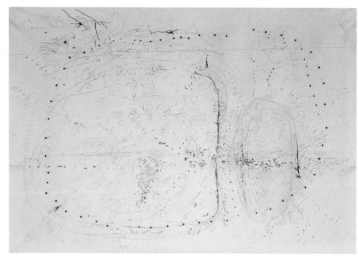

bloc (Eric Bulatov and the team of Vitaly Komar and Alexander Melamid, for example), Richter was not a master of academic illusionism when he left Dresden. Quite the contrary; nothing in his work foreshadowed the extraordinary proficiency of his photo-based paintings. Richter the virtuoso was a product of his own re-education as a painter once he arrived in the West rather than the strange reincarnation of an accomplished but conservative technician schooled in the East.

Although the impact of Documenta 2 was immediate, Richter did not pull up stakes for another two years. Coming back from a trip to Moscow and Leningrad in 1961, his train unexpectedly went directly through East Berlin to West Berlin, where he disembarked and put his luggage in safe storage. He then returned to Dresden, hurriedly sold his car, gathered a bare minimum of possessions, and arranged for a friend to drive him and Ema to Berlin (to avoid the closely watched East German trains). From that point, pretending to be day-trippers, they crossed over from the eastern into the western zone on the subway.

Richter and his wife first stopped at the home of her parents, who had emigrated some years before; but with a small allowance granted refugees by the West German government in their pockets, their initial destination was Munich and the highly regarded art academy there. However, a friend from the Dresden academy whom Richter visited in Düsseldorf, encouraged him to look instead at the academy in that Rhineland city, whereupon Richter changed his mind. With a two-year scholarship, he enrolled in the class of the uninspiring painter Ferdinand Macketanz, but before long he switched into that of Karl-Otto Götz, an exponent of Art Informel, or gestural abstract painting, whose work had been included in Documenta 2 and who was an active presence in the local art scene. That scene, in particular, and the German art world in general were in the throes of a dramatic transformation.

The vision of modernism advanced at the first Documenta by Bode and his colleague, the art historian Werner Haftmann, was that of a varied but essentially integrated tradition defined by a succession of "isms." These tended toward abstraction but retained a strong "humanist" aspect through their anthropomorphic or natural imagery or in their emphasis on rationality as an expression of progress. The first Documenta gave precedence to avant-gardes that had come into being just before or after World War I—Fauvism, Expressionism, Orphism, Cubism, metaphysical painting, and de Stijl—and then leapfrogged to contemporary post–World War II work by representatives of Art Informel, by artists pursuing geometric abstraction, and by an assortment of figurative painters and sculptors of a more-or-less existentialist bent. Conspicuously absent from this lineup was any significant representation of Surrealism—only Joan Miró and Max Ernst were accounted for—nor, with the exception of a single work by Kurt Schwitters, was Dada acknowledged. In 1959 Documenta 2 partially made up for these lacunae—Kazimir Malevich stood in for the Russian Suprematists and Constructivists, who had been wholly overlooked in the previous exhibition, while Matta, René Magritte, and Yves Tanguy weighed in for Surrealism. The biggest change was the influx of Americans, a shift in orientation facilitated by the advisory role of Porter A. McCray, Director of the International Program of The Museum of Modern Art.

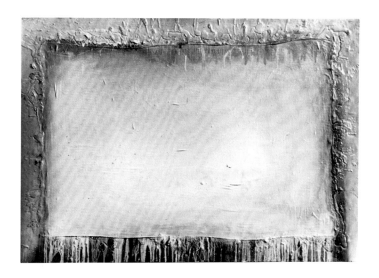

Gerhard Richter. **Wound 16
[Wunde 16].** 1962. Oil on canvas,
27⁹⁄₁₆ × 39⅜" (70 x 100 cm).
Whereabouts unknown

In the same year, under his aegis, the Museum had also mounted the first survey of the New York School to
tour Europe—*The New American Painting*. The second Documenta exhibition focused on many of the same
Abstract Expressionist and Color Field painters, among them Sam Francis, Helen Frankenthaler, Adolph Gottlieb,
Franz Kline, Jackson Pollock, Mark Rothko, Clyfford Still, and Barnett Newman, who subsequently became
one of Richter's favorite artists. Almost lost in the shuffle at Kassel was one of the most innovative painters of
them all, Robert Rauschenberg.

If Pollock, who had been dead for three years, still symbolized the New American Painting in 1959, then
Rauschenberg, only thirty-four, was the harbinger of things to come. It is one of the ironies of history that
Rauschenberg's neo-Dada aesthetic should have come to the attention of the German art world before that
world had fully reacquainted itself with its own Dada artists, although a 1958 survey of their work had been
mounted by the Kunstverein für die Rheinlande und Westfalen in Düsseldorf, and a retrospective of the work
of Kurt Schwitters, Rauschenberg's most important precursor, had been held in Hannover in 1956. In 1960
Rauschenberg and Cy Twombly were paired in a show at Galerie 22 in Düsseldorf, run by Jean-Pierre Wilhelm,
a dealer who represented Götz, Emil Schumacher, and a number of other artists associated with Art Informel.
Theirs was the last exhibition Wilhelm presented, and in a sense it not only marked the end of an era for his
gallery but signaled a decisive change in the direction contemporary art would take. Having come from the
East, where he had been shut off from information about Germany's avant-garde past, Richter remembers
that he learned about Schwitters and his contemporaries "by way of Rauschenberg." [26] But, he concluded: "I
don't think it's that bad. And I don't regard Schwitters as the innovator and Rauschenberg as the exploiter." [27]
Furthermore, Rauschenberg offered new technical solutions to the problems of image appropriation and
image grafting. At Galerie 22 he exhibited his *Thirty-Four Drawings for Dante's "Inferno,"* all of which had
involved transferring newspaper and magazine images to another paper surface by soaking them in solvents;
and although Richter had not yet arrived in Düsseldorf when the Rauschenberg-Twombly show went up, the
method Rauschenberg used found applications in Richter's work two years later.

It is a further historical irony that Fluxus, the most radical and, for many people in Richter's circle as well
as Richter himself, the most influential of resurgent Dada's many forms should have owed its existence to the
United States Army, acting as its unofficial patron. Already, with the G.I. Bill paying for the education of veter-
ans, the armed forces were responsible for shipping a number of cutting-edge artists overseas. And so Al Held,
Ellsworth Kelly, and countless others flocked to Europe after 1945 with government stipends, which made the
G.I. Bill the second most important example of federal sponsorship of the arts after the Depression-era Works
Progress Administration. Following a parallel path, George Maciunas, the New York–based founder of the
anarchic Fluxus movement, traveled to West Germany in 1961 on the promise of a job working as a graphic
designer for the United States Air Force. Upon his arrival, he made contact with future collaborators Ben
Patterson, who sold encyclopedias to the families of American servicemen stationed there, and Emmet Williams,

Gerhard Richter. **Untitled (One of
Many Efforts to Paint Abstractly).**
1960. Mixed mediums on cardboard,
approx. 7⅞ × 7⅞" (20 x 20 cm).
Whereabouts unknown

George Maciunas. **"In Memoriam Adriano Olivetti."** Festum Fluxorum Fluxus performance at Düsseldorf Art Academy, 1961. Photographed by Reiner Ruthenbeck.

who wrote for the Army newspaper, *Stars and Stripes*, where the Fluxus phenomenon was written up for the first time, by Williams. Together with Patterson, Williams, and Nam June Paik, a Korean composer who had studied in Freiburg and made connections with the avant-garde music scene in Darmstadt and Cologne, Maciunas proceeded to establish a beachhead for a multipronged assault on the existing artistic order. "To establish [the artist's] nonprofessional, nonparasitic, non-elite status in society," Maciunas argued, "he must demonstrate his own dispensability, he must demonstrate [the] self-sufficiency of the audience, he must demonstrate that anything can substitute [for] art and anyone can do it." [28] Not so much anti-art as anti-institutional, Maciunas further characterized Fluxus as "a fusion of Spike Jones, Vaudeville, gag, children's games and Duchamp," all with a dash of revolutionary Marxism.[29]

The postwar ascendancy of Marcel Duchamp, an artist famously inactive since the 1920s—or so he wanted people to believe—was signaled in America by the interest in the composer and Fluxus inspiration John Cage and the artists who gathered round him, principally Rauschenberg and Jasper Johns. In Europe, Duchamp, who traveled frequently to France and Spain, also captured the imagination of the younger generation, in particular Jean Tinguely, Daniel Spoerri, and others associated with the proto-Pop Nouveaux Réalistes in Paris. Having twice been left out of Documenta, Duchamp was first seen in depth in Germany in a 1965 exhibition in Krefeld, by which time he had already made a deep impression on artists in the Rhineland, not least of them Joseph Beuys. However, as much of a touchstone as Duchamp's work became for a rising group of European painters, sculptors, conceptual, and performance artists, some of them and their critical supporters were at the same time anxious to dissociate themselves from the anti-art, or as they perceived it, primarily nihilistic thrust of early Dada. The French critic Pierre Restany thus sought to transform the negative reading of Dada generally and of Duchamp's work in particular—an interpretation he blamed on the Surrealists—into a positive one. Speaking for the Nouveaux Réalistes in 1961, he wrote: "Dada is a farce, a legend, a state of mind, a myth. A badly behaved myth whose subterranean survival and capricious manifestation upset everyone.... The esthetic of absolute negativity has been changed into methodical doubt, thanks to which it will finally be able to incarnate new signs. The new realists consider the World as a tableau, the Great Work from which they appropriate fragments invested with universal significance. They present us the real in all the diverse aspects of its total expressivity.... In the present context the ready-made of Marcel Duchamp takes on a new sense. After the No and the ZERO, there is a third position for the myth; the anti-art gesture of Marcel Duchamp has been charged with positive energy. The Dada spirit identifies itself with a method of appropriation of exterior reality of the modern world. The ready-made is no longer the height of negativity or of polemic, but the basic element of a new expressive repertoire. Such is the new realism: a direct means for getting one's feet back on the ground but at 40 degrees above Dada zero, at that precise level where man, if he succeeds in reintegrating himself with the real, identifies his own transcendence, which is emotion, feeling, and finally poetry."[30]

For his part, Beuys, after having appropriated the Readymade, as well as strategies for cultivating his artistic persona from Duchamp, would eventually disown him, ascribing responsibility for Dada's supposed failure to Duchamp's elegant abdication. Rather than affirm Dada's anti-art stance by refusing to make any more art, as Duchamp had apparently done, Beuys sought to explode traditional aesthetic categories with an expanded definition of art whereby everyone was an artist insofar as they approached their lives creatively. Against that messianic dream Beuys declared: "The silence of Marcel Duchamp is overrated." [31]

Prior to Beuys's attempts to overthrow the father of Dada, Maciunas's interest in Duchamp and in Paik's links to Cage consolidated the Dada legacy in Germany and, quite literally, put it into action. In this regard, Maciunas took his cue from the Zero Group. Founded in Düsseldorf in 1957 by Heinz Mack, Otto Piene, and Günther Uecker, Zero had mixed monochrome painting, technological forms such as kinetic and light art, and utopian musing about beginning modernism over again from "zero," and drew attention to itself by organizing a number of public spectacles. In much the same spirit, Maciunas put together a series of Fluxus Festivals to promulgate his ideas. These became the first Happenings or, as the Fluxus artists preferred, "events" to hit Germany, and they made a huge impression. That Richter should have been attracted to Fluxus at all, much less been as liberated by it as he had been by Pollock and Fontana, is surprising given Fluxus's hostility toward traditional studio practice. To understand why, it is necessary to consider the new context in which Richter found himself.

With their burgeoning museum and gallery scenes, Cologne and Düsseldorf jointly became the center for experimental art in Germany. In addition to the artists and tendencies mentioned above, these cities also felt the impact of Wolf Vostell, Yves Klein, Piero Manzoni, and Lucio Fontana. A German neo-Dadaist, Vostell was a painter, sculptor, and experimenter with mixed mediums whose theories of de-collage—or the deconstruction of images by tearing and recombining—followed the example of the French artists François Dufrêne, Raymond Hains, Jacques de la Villeglé, and the Italian Mimmo Rotella, whereas Vostell's early video work paralleled that of Paik. The brother-in-law of the Zero artist Uecker, Klein was the dandified forerunner of Beuys's special blend of conceptualism and mysticism. In 1958–59 Klein had worked on and off in Gelsenkirchen, in the Ruhr valley, creating a large sponge mural for a theater there; and in 1961, a year before his death, he was given a major exhibition at the Museum Haus Lange in Krefeld. A monochrome painter with ties to Zero, Manzoni was a whimsical demythologizer of aesthetic pieties whose conceptual and performance work overlapped with those of Klein, and whose early death in 1963 followed that of his French counterpart. Fontana, Manzoni's mentor, was also a ubiquitous presence in Germany around this time. Starting in 1960, he exhibited frequently in Cologne, and in 1962 the Städtisches Museum, Leverkusen, organized an important retrospective of his work.

For Richter, who knew nothing of Duchamp and Dada when he had arrived, it was a heady environment, and in order to assimilate the contradictory mass of information he had to start over again from scratch. Still bound by the ideal he had brought from Dresden of finding a "third way," a path between capitalism and socialism, between tradition and the avant-garde, Richter identified with Jean Dubuffet, Jean Fautrier, and Alberto Giacometti—role models that he called "transitional figures." [32] More than the impact of these figures, however, the early works he made at the Düsseldorf academy with cardboard, stiffened fabric, and heavily laid-on paint show the influence of Fontana's slashed canvases and Alberto Burri's pigment-caked torn-burlap assemblages: "I painted through the whole history of art toward abstraction," Richter said of his first year there. [33] "I painted like crazy, [and] I had some success with all that, or gained some respect. But then I felt that it wasn't it, and so I burned the crap in some sort of action in the courtyard. And then I began. It was wonderful to make something and then destroy it. I was doing something and I felt very free." [34]

Although the Art Informel movement was almost spent, it did leave a residue. Putting together the remarks made on different occasions, the nature of its effect on his thinking is clear: "It was no accident that I found my way to Götz at the time. This 'Informel' element runs through every picture I've painted, whether it's a landscape, or a family painted from a photograph, or the Color Charts or a Gray picture. And so now it is a pursuit of the same objectives by other means. . . . As I now see it, all my paintings are 'Informel' . . . except for the landscapes, perhaps. . . . The 'Informel' is the opposite of the constructional quality of classicism—the age of kings, of clearly formed hierarchies." [35]

In other words, through exercises in a style he quickly discovered was psychologically and formally unsympathetic, Richter nonetheless grasped the lessons that Abstract Expressionism had taught his American counterparts regarding the allover quality of gestural abstraction and a process-determined distribution of painterly incident. The resulting equalization of the surface was such that no area within a painting had

Gerhard Richter. **Party**. 1962. Oil on canvas, 59¹/₁₆ × 71¹¹/₁₆" (150 x 182 cm). GR 2-1. Collection Frieder Burda

greater importance than another, regardless of what one's assumptions about the inherent priorities of a given image might have been. Compositional diagramming fleshed out by schematic figuration was the foundation of his Dresden work, and although the early Düsseldorf work was inspired by allover painting, the more profound implications of this treatment of painterly effects was its potential for subverting gestural showmanship and self-dramatization. Whatever existential angst Richter may have felt, he was determined not to make a spectacle out of it. In order to avoid that, he had to contradict the expressionist readings to which postwar-era painterliness so readily lent itself. Banality gave him the means. Thus, he defaced an apparently sincere Art Informel picture with an image appropriated from a magazine. He explained: "My first Photo Picture? I was doing large pictures in gloss enamel, influenced by [Winfried] Gaul. One day a photograph of Brigitte Bardot fell into my hands, and I painted it into one of these pictures in shades of gray. I had had enough of bloody painting, and painting from a photograph seemed to me the most moronic...thing that anyone could do."[36]

More photo-pictures promptly followed. Several show the same contrariant grafting of styles in reverse. For example, the third image in Richter's catalogue raisonné of paintings, *Party* of 1962, is a crudely delineated image of a group of women and a man "on the town," but the canvas has been pierced or sliced with a knife and in places stitched back together, as if, with red paint splattered over the surface, the cuts were open or sutured wounds. The most obvious reading is that the scene portrayed is the prelude to a sex murder—distantly linking it to *Neue Sachlichkeit* images of *Lustmörder*—but the formal joke is directed at Fontana and his elegant perforations of abstract space.

Other paintings from early in Richter's catalogue raisonné have similar though less overtly satirical dissonance in them. Based on a news photograph that appears in *Atlas: Panel 9* (page 102), just opposite the squared-off clipping used for *Party*, the painting titled *Coffin Bearers* of 1962 (page 109) combines a fairly straightforward rendering of the original black-and-white image heightened by color in the face of one of the undertakers, with loose scumbling of slate gray paint in the upper middle section and a drizzle of light gray paint to the left, over which two number-filled text balloons have been inscribed in white near the mouth of the man furthest to the left. Even more so than the letters scratched into the mottled wall next to the figure in a work such as Jean Dubuffet's *Wall with Inscriptions* (1945), Richter's painterly washes and graffiti balloon are at once gestural enhancements of the image and an impish aggression against naturalism.

The fact that the sources for the third and sixth paintings in Richter's recorded oeuvre appear in the ninth panel of *Atlas*, after more than two hundred images, would suggest that other works had been painted by this time but were destroyed. Indeed, a number were documented by the artist, and some were even exhibited prior to his discarding them; two examples are *Firing Squad* (1962), a composite of an image of men with their arms raised, embellished with a broad-brush vertical skein of paint to the left, and five identical upside-down head shots of a smiling blond beneath; and *Pope* (1962), a white silhouette of Pope John XXIII. Interestingly, neither of these paintings has a source in *Atlas*, although many images that do appear were never painted and others may have been. Meanwhile, sources for works painted after *Party* and *Coffin Bearers* have been inserted into the sequence *before* their source photos, for example, Richter's portrait *Horst and His Dog* of 1965 (page 122) and *Eight Student Nurses* of 1966 (pages 134–135). Furthermore, we have it from the artist that the thirteenth canvas in his catalogue raisonné, *Mouth* of 1963 (page 108)—a disconcertingly large and morbidly hued picture of Brigitte Bardot's lips—was actually made before *Table* of 1962 (page 107), the first work in the catalogue.

Plainly, neither the numbering system for paintings, which Richter established in 1963 and upon which his catalogue raisonné is based, nor the order of images in *Atlas*, which the artist began to assemble in 1969, is entirely chronological. In some cases, the image groupings in *Atlas* are thematic or taxonomic; panels 1, 2, 3, and 6 are snapshots of family and friends, while panel 4 consists of landscape photographs (pages 98–100). In others, the associations are jarring; panel 11 (page 103) features several pictures of wild and domestic animals, juxtaposed with the pictures used for *Kitchen Chair* of 1965 (page 114) and another of vultures watching over emaciated corpses on a street somewhere in the "third world." Further on in *Atlas* whole panels devoted to concentration-camp pictures are set against others devoted to pornography, an incommensurable pairing Richter once considered as the possible basis for an exhibition of paintings but abandoned when he found the concentration-camp photographs "unpaintable." Still later, in panels 131, 132, and 133, Richter contrasts press photos of Adolf Hitler speaking or visiting with supporters—a series immediately preceded by mountain views that recall the Nazi cult of the Alps—with news photographs of a lion devouring a tourist that were the basis for *Tourist (with 1 Lion)* of 1975 (page 177) and related paintings. The editorial mind at work in forming these ensembles seems as determined to disrupt patterns as to create them, as eager to draw attention to certain pictorial equivalencies or disjunctions as to nestle the most personal or shocking items or clusters of items in settings that obscure their meaning to the artist and stymie interpretation based on conventional attitudes regarding intrinsic significance. At once a vast index of primary material and a device for reviewing and rethinking the many possible relations of one image to another as icons in their own right, as image-types, or as entries in his intellectual and artistic autobiography, *Atlas* is a mechanism for simultaneously organizing and disorganizing information, a way of showing the artist's hand and of camouflaging his intimate connections to the contents on display.

The rearrangement of pictures in the catalogue raisonné, meanwhile, corresponds to a related habit of gathering and sorting images in an effort to take stock and identify latent qualities or previously unrecognized possibilities in the work that piled up around him in the studio.[37] If *Atlas* represents a critical use of collage technique on a massive and open-ended scale, then, in the initial phases, the catalogue raisonné, following up on the albums of photos he brought with him from Dresden, is less a literal history of his production than an empirical narrative construct internally adjusted to account for the importance paintings had for him after he had studied them in the context of others of their generation.

Table was not the first photo-based painting he painted—nor was it even the first in which the superimposition of Art Informel gesture over realist subject appears. *Firing Squad* and *Coffin Bearers* came before. Nevertheless, *Table* was the first painting in which the opposition or layering of incompatible styles transcended a polemical use of contradiction and became something tense but whole. Simultaneously austere and assertive, *Table* was the paradigm for which Richter had been waiting, the tuning fork that would set the aesthetic tone of his work for years thereafter, work whose scope would embrace an astonishingly wide variety of images but whose painterly mood was to remain consistently reserved. In this one work, based on a photograph of a modernist table he had found in the design magazine *Domus*, Richter became himself as an artist by applying the lessons learned from his ongoing experiments in wiping out reproductions of architectural photographs with turpentine or benzene applied directly to the inked page (experiments similar to procedures Rauschenberg employed in his transfer drawings). Paradoxically, this aesthetic self-discovery meant disappearing into the haze of photographs reincarnated as paintings.

Richter's growing antagonism to the stylistic tendencies taken most seriously at the academy—Art Informel, Zero, and various kinds of conservative abstraction—was shared by his closest student friends,

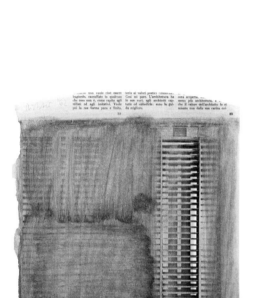

Gerhard Richter. **Untitled.** 1962. Oil and solvent on printed paper, approx. $9^{15}/_{16} \times 8^{7}/_{8}$" (25.2 x 22.5 cm). Busch–Reisinger Museum, Harvard University, Cambridge, Mass. Patrons of the Busch–Reisinger Museum Fund

Gerhard Richter, his wife Ema, and Sigmar Polke's family, c. 1965.

Sigmar Polke and Gerhard Richter in a bathtub. From *Polke/Richter, Richter/Polke* (Hannover: Galerie h, 1966).

Konrad Lueg, Sigmar Polke, and Blinky Palermo, the last two also having come from East Germany. In the beginning, Lueg was the most crucial to Richter's artistic re-departure: "He was very well informed and he had this cool manner, like Humphrey Bogart. He knew what was going on and how things worked. He knew the mechanisms. He was more arrogant than the other students because he knew more and wasn't so sentimental. It was his advantage and disadvantage at the same time. You have to be a bit sentimental to stay alone in your studio. That was too much for [Lueg]. He needed a public." [38]

These qualities were recognized by the art-world types with whom Lueg hung out. One day the art dealer, Alfred Schmela, who later showed Richter's work, introduced the two companions to one of his professional colleagues, saying of Richter, "He'll be a very good painter," and of Lueg (to Lueg's dismay), "He'll be one of the best gallerists." [39] The author of paintings that were bright, patterned, and pleasingly Pop, Lueg eventually abandoned his modestly successful career as an artist, changed his name to Konrad Fischer, and did become one of the most important gallerists in Germany, representing, among others, Carl Andre, Lothar Baumgarten, Hanne Darboven, Gilbert & George, Sol LeWitt, Bruce Nauman, Robert Ryman, and, intermittently, his former classmates Richter, Palermo, and Polke.

Polke was wilder and more sardonic than Lueg: "He was very different, he was not cool…He had irony. He was very funny. The things we did together were a kind of craziness." [40] Both Polke and Richter felt like outsiders to the art scene: "We thought everything was so stupid and we refused to participate. That was the basis of our understanding," but Lueg was an insider; the art scene was "his family." [41] Notwithstanding Polke's wild streak, Richter was impressed that "he was able to paint those little dots in his raster paintings by hand with such patience while he was living with his two children and his wife in a small subsidized apartment.…We both had apartments like that." [42] In addition to sharing what seems to have been a sibling bond, complete with sibling rivalry, a powerful aesthetic current passed between the two from the time of their meeting in the early 1960s until they went separate ways in the mid-1970s. This led to a two-person exhibition at Galerie h, in Hannover in 1966, to collaborative texts (one of them for that exhibition) in which the artists tease the reader from behind literary masks, to collaborative prints, and to photographs of the pair that amount to performance pieces. Moreover, attention to the scraped red and yellow paint to the left of the couple in Polke's *Lovers II* (1965) reveals an aggressive painterliness prefiguring Richter's own scraped and smeared abstractions of the mid-1970s onward.

For a rough, but possibly useful, comparison to the Richter-Polke friendship one might turn to the aesthetic dynamic between the young Rauschenberg and the still younger Jasper Johns at the outset of their careers. In that relationship Rauschenberg was an omnivorous extrovert with astonishing gifts of improvisation combined with a remarkable capacity for assimilating whatever pictorial resources came his way. The more reticent Johns applied his mastery of paint on canvas to mine the iconic power of each image he addressed and to extract the full measure of its inherent uncanniness. Although six years younger than Richter, Polke was extroverted and inventive in ways not that dissimilar from Rauschenberg, while Richter distilled images with a gravity and rigor not unlike that of Johns, albeit in a style that owes nothing to the Cézannesque tradition to which Johns belongs. [43] Historically, the reciprocal influence of Georges Braque on Picasso and Picasso on Braque during the creation of Cubism comes to mind. Of course, Richter and Polke did not join forces to start a movement, nor has Richter been outstripped in the long run by Polke's always wide reach, but the sparks thrown back and forth between the two men, sparks generated by their temperamental differences as well as by their mutual attraction in an art world where both felt themselves to be alien, was, so long as it lasted, one of the closest and most beneficial exchanges between two first-rank artists in modernism's history.

Of Palermo, the third member of this triumvirate, there is more to be said later, since Richter's greatest involvement with him came in the 1970s after he and Polke had parted company. For now, it is enough to mention two things. First, Palermo's idiosyncratic paintings and objects with its subtle color and lyric sense of shape and line had relatively little to do with the Pop sensibility that Richter, Lueg, and Polke shared. Second, Palermo's dependency on his mentor Beuys held him in an orbit that Richter assiduously avoided. When Richter arrived at the Düsseldorf academy, Beuys had just been appointed Professor of Monumental Sculpture, and his juggernaut through the academy, the Cologne–Düsseldorf scene, and the European art world had barely begun. As Richter remembered it: "In 1962 I saw a young man in the Düsseldorf academy

Konrad Lueg. **Mr. and Mrs. S. [Herr und Frau S.].** 1965. Casein on canvas, 39⅜ × 51³⁄₁₆" (100 x 130 cm). Private collection. Courtesy Galerie Konrad Fischer, Düsseldorf

wearing jeans, a waistcoat, and a hat. I though he was a student, and discovered that he was the new professor."[44] Eventually, when Richter joined the academy faculty in 1971, he and Beuys became colleagues, and, later, after Beuys was dismissed from his teaching position for allowing unauthorized students into his class as a part of his campaign for educational reform, Richter supported him (along with the novelist Heinrich Böll and others) to the extent of lending his name to the roster of participants in Beuys's alternative "Free International College for Creativity and Interdisciplinary Research." All the same, Richter had reservations about Beuys and his activist view of art, and the degree to which those ideals and Beuys's larger-than-life persona loomed over everyone working in his vicinity, posed an ongoing challenge to Richter's own more skeptical, and decidedly anti-utopian, outlook. In the final analysis, however, Richter appreciated "the dangerous quality Beuys had," and in a double-edged and self-deprecating memorial statement summed up his feelings: "This phenomenon . . . took us by surprise 25 years ago, and soon appalled us, unleashing admiration, envy, consternation, fury . . . which, for all our rebelliousness, gave us a framework in which we could 'carry on' in relative security."[45] It was Beuys who brought Fluxus to the academy, where he arranged for and participated in the two-day Festum Fluxorum Fluxus on February 2 and 3, 1963. By then the friendship of Richter, Lueg, and Polke had already formed. "Contact with like-minded painters—a group means a great deal to me: nothing comes in isolation. We have worked out our ideas largely by talking them through. . . . One depends on one's surroundings. And so the exchange with other artists—and especially the collaboration with Lueg and Polke—matters a lot to me," wrote Richter.[46] Witnessing Fluxus galvanized the group, Richter recalled: "Shocking absolutely shocking—they pissed in the tub, sang the German national anthem, covered the audience with paper, poured laundry detergent into the piano, attached microphones to fountain pens."[47] "It was all very cynical and destructive; it was a signal for us and we became cynical and cocky."[48] Within months the three painters were staking out their own territory.

That year, Richter and Lueg had traveled to Paris, where they paid a call on Iris Clert, who represented Klein and other artists, and also visited Ileana Sonnabend, whose Paris gallery was linked to the New York gallery of her husband Leo Castelli (together they represented most of the leading neo-Dada and Pop artists). Clert showed no interest at all in the Cologne delegation, but Sonnabend received them, whereupon they declared themselves to be "German Pop artists." Richter particularly remembers being struck by a Roy Lichtenstein painting he saw in the back of Sonnabend's gallery, confirming an interest in Lichtenstein that had been triggered by a reproduction in the magazine *Art International* earlier that year (shortly after which he staged the destruction of his Art Informel work).

The timeliness of these encounters is significant. Like Richter, Lichtenstein had been painting for a decade before he found his own identity; his very first Pop pictures date from 1961, only a year before Richter came upon them. Although Polke, rather than Richter, engaged most directly with Lichtenstein's work from a stylistic point of view, both were inspired by its cool detachment and by its confident "anti-painterliness." And

Sigmar Polke. **Lovers II [Liebespaar II].** 1965. Oil and enamel on canvas, 6'2¼" × 55" (190 x 140 cm). Courtesy Michael Werner Gallery, New York and Cologne

Invitation to Gerhard Richter's first exhibition in Düsseldorf, with Manfred Kuttner, Konrad Lueg, and Sigmar Polke, at the Ladengalerie, May 1963.

both responded to the new art and took off in their own directions from it before Pop art was a fully developed tendency. Thus, while the reflex conclusion might be that Richter, Polke, and their generation simply absorbed a codified style, it is closer to the truth to say that the Germans recognized the potential of a still evolving phenomenon and altered its course by extending it further through their own efforts and in accordance with their own talents and intentions. They were not one step behind the Americans or, if so, not for long; whatever catching up they needed to do was over almost as soon as they became aware of what had already been accomplished—first in London by Richard Hamilton, Eduardo Paolozzi, and others, and then in New York by Lichtenstein, Andy Warhol, Claes Oldenburg, and their cohorts. From then on Richter and Polke were making fresh sentences in a thoroughly international idiom.

Lueg, whose own work was never the equal of that of his friends', contributed an indispensable entrepreneurial gift. Convinced, as Polke and Richter later wrote, that, "We cannot assume that good pictures will be painted one day: we must take matters into our own hands," [49] Lueg and the others arranged to show their work in an abandoned building controlled by the municipal government of Düsseldorf. This exhibition, which opened on May 11, 1963, was advertised by an announcement that listed the welter of currently fashionable styles in concentric lines of type around the names of the three principal artists plus that of a fourth member of the group, Manfred Kuttner: "This exhibition is not a commercial undertaking but purely a demonstration, and no gallery, museum or public exhibiting body would have been a suitable venue. The major attraction of the exhibition is the subject matter of the works in it. For the first time in Germany, we are showing paintings for which such terms as Pop Art, Junk Culture, Imperialist or Capitalist Realism, New Objectivity, Naturalism, German Pop and the like are appropriate.... Pop Art has rendered conventional painting—with all its sterility, its isolation, its artificiality, its taboos and its rules—entirely obsolete.... Pop Art is not an American invention, and we do not regard it as an import....This art is pursuing its own organic and autonomous growth in this country."[50]

This hit-and-run exhibition garnered little attention, but it posted notice that for those involved anything was fair game. Among the isms cited was a previously unheard-of entry, Imperialist Realism, which in the context of Richter's remark about Pop art not being "an import," nevertheless lends a political cast to the Pop aesthetic for the first time. The second exhibition organized by Lueg and Richter (Polke's absence indicates the internal competitiveness of the artists' alliance) sharpened that political edge. Like the first show, it made use of borrowed space—this time the Berges furniture store in Düsseldorf where the artists were given permission to hang works on the walls in the display areas—and it was titled *Life with Pop: A Demonstration for Capitalist Realism*. Partially inspired by Oldenburg's *The Store*—a 1961 exhibition on the Lower East Side of Manhattan where the artist sold sculptural caricatures of food and dry goods from the rented shop in which they were made—Lueg and Richter orchestrated an evening-long event in which the entire Berges store was conceptually annexed, including fifty-two bedrooms, seventy-eight living rooms, kitchens, and

Gerhard Richter and Konrad Lueg. **"Demonstration for Capitalist Realism,"** Berges Furniture Store, Düsseldorf, 1963. Photographed by Reiner Ruthenbeck.

nurseries. [51] Visitors were greeted in an upstairs waiting room by thirty-nine chairs, each with a copy of the daily newspaper, fourteen pairs of antlers (which had, according to the artist's post mortem report, come from roebuck shot between 1938 and 1942), and two life-sized papier-mâché figures in the style of Carnival effigies, one of the gallerist Schmela, the second of John F. Kennedy. [52] Lueg and Richter appeared in the first exhibition room wearing suits and ties as "living sculptures." Lueg sat in a chair mounted on a white plinth, Richter lounged on a couch—also on a white base—reading a detective story. Other elements of the installation included designer magazines, a set of the complete works of Winston Churchill, a television tuned to the news and to a special on the Adenauer era, which had just ended in 1963, assorted coffee cups, glasses and bottles of beer, and in a wardrobe by the door the "official costume of Prof. J. Beuys (hat, yellow shirt, blue trousers, socks, shoes; to which 9 small slips of paper are attached, each marked with a brown cross…)" and beneath which, in a box, was a wax and margarine sculpture by Beuys. [53] Although Beuys was not yet the figure he would become, his Fluxus activity had broken the ice for Richter and his contemporaries, and his presence in the exhibition made that connection, particularly to the performance aspect of the show—guided tours by the artists, music, dancing, liquor—which quickly got out of control. In just over an hour and a half the whole event was over.

Despite Richter's efforts to downplay it, much critical attention has been paid to the label *Capitalist Realism*, and a good deal of confusion has arisen as a result. Within a year of the Düsseldorf "Demonstration" the Berlin dealer René Block picked up on the term and used it for his own purposes in connection with exhibitions and editions he sponsored, grouping Richter with artists with whom he had little in common, among them Wolf Vostell, K. P. Brehmer, and K. H. Hödicke. Moreover, the Fluxus-oriented dealer underscored the political sense of the term, and would later attack Richter for wanting nothing more than to paint beautiful pictures. [54] For his part, Richter certainly never intended Capitalist Realism to be understood as a political movement, nor was there ever anything more than a catch phrase for a one-shot show in his mind. That said, Capitalist Realism is rich in provocative meanings. As a play on Socialist Realism, it turns the tables on the eastern-bloc aesthetic dogmas in which Richter had been schooled, but it has an even more satirical effect when applied to the commercial culture of the West as a substitute for the label *Pop*.

In the definition of Richard Hamilton, the English polymath: "Pop Art is: / Popular (designed for a mass audience) / Transient (short-term solution) / Expendable (easily forgotten) / Low cost / Mass produced / Young (aimed at youth) / Witty / Sexy / Gimmicky / Glamorous / Big business." [55] For Warhol, Pop was a question of "liking," with all the emphasis on excess and novelty implied by Warhol's deadpan delivery. [56] However, the context in which English and American Pop art arose was fundamentally different from that in Germany, where the devastation and shortages of the recent war were fresh in memory despite the relative plenty of the "Economic Miracle," where the new consumerism stirred deep misgivings in many people's minds, and where the ideological battle between "big business" democracy and "big brother" egalitarianism

Gerhard Richter. **Neuschwanstein Castle [Schloss Neuschwanstein].** 1963. Oil on canvas, 6'2¹³⁄₁₆" × 59¹⁄₁₆" (190 x 150 cm). GR 8. Collection Frieder Burda

Gerhard Richter and Konrad Lueg. **John F. Kennedy.** 1963. Papier-mâché over wire mesh, 70⅞ × 22⅞ × 10⅝" (180 x 58 x 27 cm). Private collection, Germany

was being fought along a militarized frontier partitioning the country. Socialist Realism heroicized its subjects in the reflection of a distant but radiant utopia; Capitalist Realism turned the glare of the mass media and bright, shiny modern packaging back on themselves to highlight the encroachments of a seemingly limitless new materialism. Richter's own attitude was plainly laid out in a note dated 1962: "I did not come here [West Germany] to get away from 'materialism': here its dominance is far more total and more mindless. I came to get away from the criminal 'idealism' of the Socialists." [57] Unquestionably, Richter shared much of Hamilton's enthusiasm for things young, witty, and sexy, and his affinity with Warhol is likewise indisputable; but his view of the postwar paradise of the 1960s was clouded by his experience of its antithesis, which gave his work, like Polke's and unlike Lueg's, a dark quality from the very start. On one level, then, the equation established between the two economically determined realisms is a throwaway line by a group of cheeky young painters; on another, the symmetry underscores the ideological similarities between two world views vying for dominance in an all-or-nothing game of power politics that made no allowance for the ambivalence felt by those same artists. For Richter, making this point once was enough; however, the semantic judo involved is impossible to forget and its full ramifications hard to escape.

Richter exhibited four works in the Berges furniture store "Demonstration." Only one of them, *Mouth* (page 108), would have struck most people as typically Pop. The others, *Neuschwanstein Castle* and *Pope* (1962) and *Stag* of 1963 (page 110), were images that fell outside the normal run of advertising, cartoon, and movie graphics that were Pop's tap roots; and two of them, *Neuschwanstein Castle* and *Stag*, were essentially Photo-Realist, albeit less so than several contemporaneous pictures. At the time he painted these canvases there was as yet no such category. Indeed, there was virtually no one testing the waters Richter had already entered. Malcolm Morley's rough grisaille battleships, generally acknowledged as the first Photo-Realist paintings, were painted in 1964, although Richter very much admired the perfection of Morley's full-color ocean-liner paintings of a year later. Only Richard Artschwager's acrylic on Celotex photo-based portraits and cityscapes date from the same year as Richter's first essays in the genre; Artschwager's work of that kind was not exhibited until 1964 when Leo Castelli gave the artist a show at his New York gallery. [58] When Photo-Realism became a full-fledged movement in the 1970s, Richter was at pains to distance himself from it, even though he was thrown together with representatives of the tendency in Documenta 5 in 1972, including the American Chuck Close and the French painter Jean-Olivier Hucleux. While many Photo-Realists used photography primarily as a means of achieving feats of trompe l'oeil magic (although a technical wizard, Close was the leading exception to this rule), Richter was more concerned with the problematic reality of photographs than in the reality photographs ostensibly recorded.

Malcolm Morley. **Boat.** 1964. Liquitex and ink on canvas, 36" × 6' (91.4 × 182.9 cm). The Museum of Contemporary Art, Los Angeles. Partial gift from the Collection of Laura-Lee and Robert Woods. Courtesy Sperone Westwater, New York

For Richter, photography's greatest virtue was what it was not. It was not fine art. At any rate not the kinds of photography that had stuck in his mind and to which he was now attracted. "As a boy I did a lot of photography and was friendly with a photographer, who showed me the tricks of the trade," he explained. "For a time I worked as a photographic laboratory assistant: the masses of photographs that passed through the bath of developer every day may well have caused a lasting trauma." [59] Those pictures were ordinary snapshots without aesthetic pretensions. Yet, whatever they lacked in compositional sophistication, they made up for in raw information; and whatever they lacked in expressiveness, they made up for matter-of-factness. Up to this point, painting had meant subordinating vision to aesthetic principles, things seen to predetermined formats, and the uncertain truth of appearances to the authority of the artist's will-to-style. Removing the filter of creative identity allowed the painter to recognize the disembodied objectivity of the camera image: "The photograph reproduces objects in a different way from the painted picture, because the camera does not apprehend objects: it sees them. In 'freehand drawing,' the object is apprehended in all its parts.... By tracing the outlines with the aid of a projector, you can bypass this elaborate process of apprehension. You no longer apprehend but see and make (without design) what you have not apprehended. And when you don't know what you are making, you don't know, either, what to alter or distort." [60]

Richter's epiphany that "the photograph is the most perfect picture," allowed him in a single stroke to have done with the problems of reconciling his artistic taste, talents, and ideas with the demands of an art world obsessed with originality and overdetermined meaning. "It does not change," he said. "It is absolute, and therefore autonomous, unconditional, devoid of style." [61] A certain Fluxus-inspired defiance attended this realization. "I consider many amateur photographs better than the best Cézanne," Richter wrote in 1966. [62] But this declaration also contained an element of humility or at least an escape from the expectation that he "foreground" the maker of the work, allowing him, instead, to pursue a deliberate self-effacement in which the unresolved particularities of the subject painted took precedence over the subjectivity of the artist. When he does speak about himself—with quiet humor—it is as one of a class of things that has asked to be taken more or less at face value: "I like everything that has no style: dictionaries, photographs, nature, myself and my paintings. (Because style is violence, and I am not violent.)" [63] The violence at issue is not merely the overt distortion of reality to which modern art is prone, but the very notion of imposing the self on things as they are, or as they seem to be in a given instance.

The impersonal image Richter sought to make—or remake—through the use of photography corresponds in some respects to those kinds of art produced in response to Cage's theory of chance operations, and, through the agency of Fluxus, Cage was very much a presence in Germany in the early 1960s. After the socially committed art of the 1920s, 1930s, and 1940s, the influence on Surrealism of Sigmund Freud and his concept of the ego, combined with the impact of Existentialism's celebration of the self-made man of thought and action in the 1940s and 1950s, the desire to leave things alone rather than transform them into something else or place them at the service of a larger goal was pervasive. Cage's embrace of randomness was perhaps the most radical version of this tendency in that it cheerfully shrugged off all social, political, and moral imperatives. His famous "Lecture on Nothing" took a word that was rich in Sartrean anguish and gave it

Richard Artschwager. **Portrait I.** 1962. Acrylic on wood and Celotex, 6'1¼" × 26" × 12" (186 × 66 × 30.5 cm). Collection Kasper König, Cologne

back to the reader as a term signifying a liberating, but always attentive, equanimity. "I have nothing to say," Cage wrote, "and I am saying it."[64] Richter, who has quoted that phrase, was plainly impressed by Cage; but there is a brooding quality to Richter's work—as well as an obvious, if vague, moral dimension—that departs from Cage's more optimistic disengaged model. Nevertheless, before delving into the much-vexed question of photography's special status as a modern medium, it is important to say that its initial value to Richter seems primarily to have been the opportunity it gave him to turn Cage's formulation around and talk about—or represent—everything without stepping forward to say anything and, by that means, to access many of the same artistic freedoms, beginning with the freedom from self that Cage preached.

The philosopher Roland Barthes offers other essential points of reference. He observed that the temporal reality of the photograph arrests life in the click of the shutter and reconstitutes it as "the that has been," making the viewer aware that "Death is the *eidos* of that Photograph."[65] This may be taken as axiomatic with regard to Richter's work, especially insofar as it frequently alludes to or depicts death and thus puts the mortal subject of the painting and the implicitly morbid condition of photography in tension with the immediate presence and sublimated corporeality of the painted picture. Moreover, Barthes's distinction between what he calls the photograph's *studium* (its dominant image and overall scope) and the photograph's *punctum* (the unique, even incidental detail that stops the eye, pricks the mind, and captures the imagination) is also provocative insofar as Richter's brushy re-presentation of photographs tends to obscure the dominant characteristics of the image (studium) or render it generic—a portrait, a landscape—even as it exaggerates existing anomalies (puncta) within the image. The latter occurs often (as an awkward gesture or a byproduct of painterly accents and erasures) and we may take Richter at his word when he says that he turned to photography "not to use it as a means to painting but use painting as a means to photography"—not, that is, to imitate photographs but to remake them in paint. [66] Richter's discovery that photographs freed him from the "conventional criteria . . . associated with art"—from style, from composition, from judgment—and "from personal experience," leaving" nothing to it: it was pure picture" that he wanted to "have" and "show,"[67] can be more vividly understood by attention to Barthes's elliptical intellectual self-portrait, in which he wrote of his own struggle against the entrapments of expression. Barthes said: "He is troubled by any image of himself, suffers when he is named. He finds the perfection of a human relationship in the vacancy of the image: to abolish—in oneself, between oneself and others—adjectives; a relationship which adjectivizes is on the side of the image, on the side of domination, of death." [68] Although Richter seemingly had sided with the image, and many of his images were death-haunted, his motivation and reasoning essentially parallel those of Barthes, resulting in a pictorial language at "degree zero," one that, eschewing domination and violence, had been stripped of adjectives.

"I had very little interest in any critique of packaged culture or the consumer world," Richter said.[69] This sets him apart from his Pop art counterparts, although it might well be argued that given their ambivalences Richter's favorites, Lichtenstein, Oldenburg, and Warhol, had little interest themselves in what is now—with Frankfurt School Marxism in the background—called cultural critique. Instead, Richter's preoccupation was with the iconography of the everyday. Implicit in this was the pathos he saw both in the photograph as object and the image it contained, a pathos indelibly marked by use. Rather than emphasize the photograph's lowliness or meagerness, Richter sought to dignify it, not by making it more glamorous or more aesthetic, but by respecting it for what it is and showing that. "Perhaps because I'm sorry for the photograph," he explained, "because it has such a miserable existence even though it is such a perfect picture, I would like to make it valid, make it visible." [70] Behind this declaration is a commitment to the visible from one of the most demanding of contemporary artists—and, beyond that, a belief in the shared experience of the visible—which should not be taken lightly in a context where attacks on "visuality," "opticality," and the very possibility of communicating directly through the senses are staples of postmodernist discourse. As to the images in the paintings themselves, it was not the chair in the Berges showroom that mattered to him—one of many on display, as in Warhol's Campbell's soup cans or Coca-Cola bottles—but the one in a hundred that sits in the corner and acquires the patina of all things lived with, while emitting the cold aura of all things devoid of innate vitality. Asked by an interviewer what function the subjects of his realist paintings had, Richter simply said, "sympathy."[71] Caught off guard by the answer, the interviewer inquired about his painting of a common chair, and he replied: "It is our chair, which we use. It is really pitiable and very banal, but it has a mood."[72]

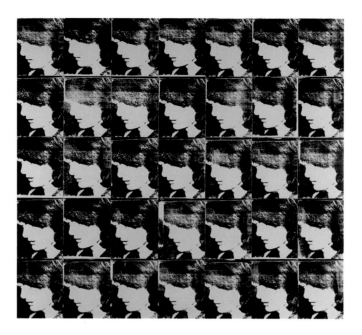

Andy Warhol. **Multiplied Jackies.** 1964. Acrylic and Liquitex silkscreen on canvas; 35 panels, each 20¹⁄₁₆ × 15¹⁵⁄₁₆" (51 x 40.5 cm); overall 8'4⅝" × 9'4¹³⁄₁₆" (255.5 x 286.5 cm). Museum für Moderne Kunst, Frankfurt am Main, previously Ströher collection, Darmstadt

The mood or ambience of *Kitchen Chair* of 1965 (page 114) is stark and cold, but it is also haunting. Had Richter set out to make a ghostly object he might fairly be accused of having cheated on his commitment to remove Expressionism, Symbolism, and other aesthetic overlays from his work. In actuality, however, there are no obvious stylistic interventions to account for this effect. Richter says: "Even when I paint a straightforward copy, something new creeps in, whether I want it to or not: something that even I don't really grasp."[73] On several occasions, Richter has not only copied photographs but made several versions of the same image, or very similar images, and the unanticipated or only partially anticipated differences can be striking. There are, for example, three versions of Richter's laconic, scatological, vanity-defying *vanitas* paintings titled *Toilet Paper* of 1965 (pages 112–113). [74] The first one depicts bold, nearly abstract volumes. The second and third, based on another source, are bathed in a penumbral light that catches more detail than does the harsher chiaroscuro of the first version, even as it makes the toilet-paper roll seem more remote. The first is forceful and objective in a semi-Pop manner; the second and third literally foreshadow the quasi-romantic glow that often suffused Richter's paintings starting in the early 1970s. It is a light that Richter withholds from *Flemish Crown* of 1965 (page 128) precisely, it seems, because the subject conventionally calls for it, and the artist is generally loathe to satisfy such expectations, but also because he regarded the kind of bourgeois interior that such chandeliers supposedly ennoble with palpable horror.

The iconography of the everyday also includes things in the environment that refer to situations outside it or realities that routinely intrude on quotidian existence through the media. From that perspective, paintings such as *Stag* and *Neuschwanstein* are simultaneously manipulated reproductions of other images and citations from the "dictionary" of cultural archetypes. The first evokes the traditional German fascination with the wild (symbolized by the forest and deer) which comes down from Nordic legend by way of Dürer and Romanticism. The second involves the most decadent manifestation of that archaizing tendency, a travel-poster or postcardlike image of Ludwig II of Bavaria's last great architectural folly. It would be a mistake, however, to regard either of these canvases as examples of pictorial camp. Of *Neuschwanstein* Richter said: "The real-life castle is a hideous monstrosity. But it does also have this other, seductive side to it, that of the beautiful fairytale, the dream of sublimity, bliss, happiness—and that's the dangerous part; that's why it's a very special case of kitsch." [75] And of *Stag* he remarked: "It's not the stag's fault if he's been badly painted— 'Stag Roaring' over the sofa. For us Germans, in particular, relating to forests as strongly as we do, the stag does of course have a symbolic quality. I wanted to be a forester when I was young, and I was really excited when I found a real stag in the forest and took a photograph. Later I painted him, and the painting was a bit less romantic than my youthful photograph." [76] Insofar as such paintings invite the critical scrutiny of "kitsch" they first acknowledge its genuine—therefore problematic—appeal, and the tug of fundamental poetic and philosophical possibilities they so poorly embody. When Richter quotes from debased sources, it is never merely for the purposes of mocking them, nor is his regard for them (no matter how they trouble or dismay him) ever contemptuous or cynical.

Stag is the second work in Richter's oeuvre in which the artifice of painting is laid bare. In the first, *Table*, this is accomplished by superimposing two styles of painting; in *Stag* it is done by separating areas of the composition from one another with different gray tints—something that would not occur in the faithful transcription of a black-and-white photograph—while the smearing of the stag against the crisply delineated but unfilled contours of the trees displays the skeleton of drawing against the abraded flesh of paint. *Dead* of 1963 (page 111) simultaneously emphasizes and destroys the illusionism in which Photo-Realism traffics by reproducing a printed image in a vastly enlarged scale and cropping it so that white margins and oversized type are visible while parts of the picture itself are lost. Such cropping and fragmentation are typical of modernist collage, and from one historical angle, *Dead* might resemble a huge excerpt from a tiny Schwitters. Such a comparison may seem farfetched, but it is plausible considering the extent to which Richter was surrounded by artists actively pursuing neo-Dada collage or decollage practices, in particular, Polke, who learned as much from Rauschenberg's pictorial elisions as from Lichtenstein's dot matrices, while contributing far more to those techniques than he borrowed. Inasmuch as both Richter and Schwitters trim or fracture images and break words or parts of words away from their linguistic contexts, both are engaged in a graphic dismantling of the established semantic and pictorial order. Nevertheless, with the exception of the destroyed *Firing Squad*, and the seamless composite *Spanish Nudes* (1967), Richter has rarely pieced disparate pictures together in the same painted format. And, even when he draws attention to the incompleteness of the image—as in the obviously reframed *Dead* or *Ferrari* of 1964 (page 125) or in *High Diver I* of 1965 (page 126)—the relation of figure and ground within the carefully proportioned rectangle achieves equilibrium and reasserts a sense of pictorial wholeness.

Whereas the *Coffin Bearers* presents the reverential but awkward ceremonies that attend death, *Dead* depicts it as almost comically incidental. Based on a newspaper clipping, it portrays a hapless man felled by a chunk of ice. Painted with a cartoonish economy, the work shows the prostrate man's body lying next to the huge white block. White margins, and one mottled gray one to the right, surround this image, and above, in crisp black letters is the word *tote*, or *dead*. Image and text are equally blunt: the first shows a disastrous encounter of the inert truncated corpse and a mysterious mass; the second, a pictorially truncated word, confirms its fate. However, in order to read the word, the viewer must supply the missing pieces just as he or she must connect the cold finality of the text to the nearly slapstick image; and this simple but jarring leap of the imagination drives the metaphor home. Throughout Richter's early career—and there are major examples later, as well—consciousness of death is, explicitly or implicitly, the defining characteristic of numerous works. Like Warhol in his Disaster paintings, Richter picked up on the public's horrid fascination with suffering and the media's exploitation of it. On the front page, murder is at once spectacular and banal, raising the ordinarily unfortunate to the level of celebrities, and bringing celebrities down to the level of common people. Seizing upon this macabre permutation of the law of supply and demand, Richter understood, as did Warhol, that the tabloids were modern-day variants of the hierarchy collapsing tradition of the Dance of Death.

At one extreme of this social equation is *Woman with Umbrella* of 1964 (page 131). Based on a news photograph of Jackie Kennedy after the assassination of her husband, President John F. Kennedy, it is notably discreet by comparison to Warhol's many treatments of the same subject—her hand covers half of her face and her name does not appear in the title—and more subtly emotional than Warhol's high contrast, grainy silhouettes of the bravely tearful first lady.[77] Taking advantage of the iconic nature of the source as his foil, Richter turns things around to give us a respectfully distant, gently brushed, almost tender likeness of a grieving woman.

At the other extreme are the two paintings of a murdered prostitute who briefly caught the attention of Germany—*Helga Matura* and *Helga Matura with Her Fiancé*, both of 1966 (pages 132–133)—and individual portraits of the victims of American serial killer Richard Speck: *Eight Student Nurses* of 1966 (pages 134–135).[78] The photographs from which Richter worked show Helga Matura seated in the grass, smiling, and as a smartly dressed woman with her arm around an equally happy and well-turned-out but oddly boyish young man. The first image includes her name in a caption signaling its origins in a newspaper or magazine, the second has none.

However, both belong to the genre of before-and-after photographs that the press uses to sentimentalize lurid stories, in which "before" is normality (which upright citizens can snicker over since they know what's coming, particularly when the victim violated their codes) and "after," with the ghastly twist that brings it about, is annihilation. Richter's painterly transposition of the photographs removes this sentimentality, and in the later painting especially, introduces a genuine poignancy that comes with the awkward mix of formality and informality in the couple's pose, her almost overbearing presence in relation to him, and the focus on their two feet touching, which Richter's treatment of the image turns from a corny gesture to a believably affectionate one.

Eight Student Nurses bears some resemblance to Warhol's *Thirteen Most Wanted Men* (1964), a group of portraits of criminals based on police mug shots that was commissioned for the 1964 World's Fair in New York. Perhaps mindful of that correlation, Richter explained: "I would rather paint the victims than the killers. When Warhol painted the killers, I painted the victims. The subjects were of . . . poor people, banal poor dogs."[79] Indeed, *Eight Student Nurses* alters and recycles pictorial conventions in delicate and emotionally charged ways, similar to those found in the Helga Matura paintings. Although consisting of eight separate paintings, it is one work. Its standardized format (based on nursing-school class pictures) and an even greater degree of blurring than in the Helga Matura paintings (which reduces each face to an almost, but not quite, schematic of eyes, nose, mouth, and helmet of hair), tend toward homogenization, as does the title which identifies the subjects as a group rather than as individual women.

The collective identity begins with institutional photography and professional regimentation (the nurses are in their uniforms), and is rendered definitive by the arbitrary, media-reinforced circumstances of their deaths. However, the faintly registered peculiarities of one victim's expression, another's permanent wave, or yet another's tilt of the head work against these averaging parameters and open up a shallow space in which these unprepossessing phantoms assume a measure of uniqueness. This, in turn, reminds the viewer that no matter how they have been presented to us before, their deaths, like all deaths, were the ultimate statement of their individuality and solitude. Painting brings these qualities to the surface in ways that photography and photomechanical means cannot—and which each generation of reproduction only exacerbates. "In the age of reproduction," Bernard Blistène has written, "Gerhard Richter, like Warhol or Lichtenstein, is the deviation of the multiple into the original, the successful passage of the plural into the singular." [80] Substituting the handmade mark for the consistent reaction of light on chemical emulsions or the consistent impression of dot screens on paper—the canvas object for the serially printed sheet—Richter's paintings restore a sense of finitude to the human form that had seemingly been superseded by the potential infinity of reproductions. When Richter said that his aim was "not to use [photography] as a means to painting but use painting as a means to photography," he was not looking for a way out of painting but describing a quality—minimum aesthetic intervention—that he wanted *for* painting. In paintings such as *Woman with Umbrella* and *Eight Student Nurses*, Richter was nevertheless able to show what could be done within that minimum to inject feeling into images that had seemingly been emptied of it by overexposure.

In contrast to these public images, although painted in more or less the same manner, are the many private portraits in Richter's work. Conceptually speaking, their prominence and ubiquity in his oeuvre is a paradox. After all, Richter had always shied away from painterly emotionalism and other forms of first-person expression. As early as 1966, he was on record as having said: "I believe the painter mustn't see or know the model at all, that nothing of the 'soul,' the essence, the character of the model should be expressed. Also a painter shouldn't 'see' a model in a particular, personal way . . . because one certainly cannot paint a specific individual but only a painting, which, however, has nothing to do with the model." [81] Yet insofar as people expected accessible "humanistic" subject matter and overt displays of artistic feeling, it is easy to understand Richter's vehemence and his apparent self-contradiction. Before it came to his own family photographs, Richter was interested in the latent psychological content of family photos as a class. If chairs and other household objects had the status of skulls in classical *vanitas* pictures, then the equally banal snapshot was an icon for the contemplation of, and futile battle against, mortality. Describing photography's historical usurpation of painting's function of representing reality, Richter wrote: "At the same time, photography took on a religious function. Everyone has produced his own 'devotional pictures': these are the likenesses of family and friends, preserved in remembrance of them."[82]

The usually artless, awkward, or deadpan qualities of such icons were a barrier against sentimentality, although sentiment was the reason they were taken. For Richter, this generic aspect was a mask behind which he could conceal himself while inserting numerous images of this type into his lineup of pictures appropriated from the media. For example, in 1965, Richter painted *Woman Descending the Staircase* (page 129), a sleek grisaille image of a fashionable woman striding briskly down a flight of steps that was based on a photograph that he clipped from a magazine and juxtaposed in *Atlas: Panel 13* (page 104) with a sharply contrasting picture of a decidedly unglamorous secretary walking past the camera, an image he also painted. A year later, Richter painted *Ema (Nude on a Staircase)* (page 137), a subtly tinted color portrait of his wife. The titles, of course, refer to Marcel Duchamp's notoriously iconoclastic *Nude Descending a Staircase* of 1912. But the painting of Ema, with its lovely diffuse naturalism, may be taken as an act of counter-iconoclasm. Indeed, Richter seems never to have been wholly convinced of the radicality of Duchamp's work in the first place. "A very beautiful painting, and utterly traditional," he said, and in the strict technical sense of its being an old-fashioned easel painting executed in the old-fashioned way, he was correct. [83] An inversion of the Readymade, in that it is based on a photograph Richter took for the purpose rather than a found image (it was the first time he had done so), it was the most classical pose the artist had yet painted despite its having been explicitly inspired by an anticlassical Cubist masterpiece. To the degree that it is a witty gesture of defiance directed toward the neo-Dada practices in favor among his peers, the work is an argumentative entry into public discourse, but not the least part of that argument consists of the artist's tender portrayal of his own private reality. It is not just the depiction of any nude descending a staircase, it is Ema.

Nothing like it can be found in American Pop art of the period or, for that matter, in American Photo-Realism. [84] Nor are there equivalents to Richter's paintings of other family members, the most exceptional among them being *Uncle Rudi* of 1965 (page 121). A full-figure small-format likeness of one of his two maternal uncles, the picture portrays the subject posing stiffly in his army uniform and smiling for the camera. On the one hand, *Uncle Rudi* is, for Germans, an immediately recognizable but, after the war, seldom discussed type: "The Nazi in the family." [85] He is not a monster but the average, ordinarily enthusiastic soldier. On the other hand, he was the apple of Richter's mother's eye. "He was handsome, charming, tough, elegant, a play-boy, [and] he was so proud of his uniform," recalls Richter, who, as a boy, seems to have been impressed by this paragon of manly virtues, but of whom he adds, "He was young and very stupid, and then he went to war and was killed during the first days." [86] In short, *Uncle Rudi* represents a generation that willingly participated in its own destruction and the destruction of the millions it tried to dominate. The painting's final destination underscores this point. Included in an exhibition in Berlin organized by Block and dedicated to the memory of the victims of Lidice—an infamous atrocity committed by German troops at Lidice, Czechoslovakia—it was eventually donated to the Czech Museum of Fine Arts by the artist. [87]

A companion painting is Richter's portrait of his aunt Marianne, who appears hovering in the photographic shadows above the artist, a baby at the time the picture was taken. Committed to a mental institution from the age of eighteen Marianne was, in family lore, the antithesis of Rudi and her sister, Richter's mother. Richter said: "Whenever I behaved badly I was told you will become like crazy Marianne." [88] She, too, died during the time of the war—killed by Nazi doctors who organized a large-scale system of "euthanasia" to deal with the chronically ill, the mentally retarded, and the insane.

In the catalogue essay for a 1986 retrospective of Richter's work (by far the best biographical and critical overview of the artist's career until that time), Jürgen Harten asked rhetorically what should be made of these two pictures and others that tell incomplete stories linking Richter's family life to history. A partial answer can be found in another work made the same year as *Aunt Marianne* of 1965. A small, atypically ocher-tinted picture of two men with their backs turned—one wearing a Homburg, the other a policeman's cap—and simply titled *Mr. Heyde*, it is, in essence, a portrait of Marianne's executioner. As a neurologist working under Hitler's mandate, a Doctor Heyde had established a program for the extermination of the medically undesirable. In that capacity, Heyde had pioneered the gassing techniques employed in the "Final Solution." After the war, he continued to practice medicine under an alias, with the knowledge of local officials in Schleswig-Holstein, until he was exposed in 1959. The resulting furor ended with his suicide five days before he was to stand trial. The discovery that Dr. Heyde had succeeded in evading prosecution while living comfortably in Germany broke the spell of postwar

Werner Heyde im November 1959, als er sich den Behörden stellte.

Gerhard Richter. **Aunt Marianne [Tante Marianne].** 1965. Oil on canvas, 47¼ × 51¹⁄₁₆" (120 x 130 cm). GR 87. Private collection

Gerhard Richter. **Mr. Heyde [Herr Heyde].** 1965. Oil on canvas, 21¹¹⁄₁₆ × 25⅝" (55 x 65 cm). GR 100. Private collection

amnesia and helped prompt a concerted effort to locate "the murderers among us," to quote the title of a ground-breaking 1946 film about hidden war criminals. [89] Israel's 1961 conviction of the former administrator of the concentration camps, Adolf Eichmann, accelerated the process; and in 1962 the Federal Republic of Germany tried a group of Auschwitz guards, in the first major case of its kind prosecuted under West German jurisdiction.

Painted a few years after these events, *Mr. Heyde* points a finger at the accused with calculated discretion. Rather than strike a dramatic tone or take a position outside the reality to which it refers, Richter treated the matter as an ordinary enigma of the sort that would prompt viewers to wonder, in the same way that they might wonder about any person on the street in the custody of a policeman, Who is Mr. Heyde? What has he done? He looks as if he could be anyone's neighbor, and nothing about the man's demeanor or that of the officer escorting him indicates the enormity of his actions. Together with *Uncle Rudi* and *Aunt Marianne*, *Mr. Heyde* closes the gaps between personal experience and public reality, between a painful guilt-laden past and a present predicated on selective memory—gaps in the fabric of German society and culture kept open by denial and reticence. Richter breaks that silence, quietly but unmistakably. There is nothing in German painting of the time that presents the continued Nazi penetration of daily life so matter-of-factly, so unflinchingly, or from so many sides of the German experience.

Nor is there anything quite like Richter's paintings of military aircraft. The first of these—and only the thirteenth work in his catalogue raisonné—*Bombers* of 1963 (page 117), shows a flight of American B-52s methodically dropping explosives from the clouds. *Mustang Squadron* of 1964 (page 116) depicts low-flying American fighter planes in action. Meanwhile, *Phantom Interceptors* of 1964 (page 119) portrays a group of modern jets. The first two are scenes from World War II, similar to things Richter saw or heard about as a boy; the third depicts a commonplace sight—and media image—in the 1960s when NATO planes were stationed at bases in Germany. In the past, Richter has fended off the suggestion that there was any antiwar message in these paintings: "Pictures like that don't do anything to combat war. They only show one tiny aspect of the subject of the war—maybe only my own childish feelings of fear and fascination with war and with weapons of that kind." [90] Nevertheless, the specific choice of planes and their associations resonates in ways that outstrip these narrow criteria. Although there are two paintings featuring German planes—one of diving Stukas from World War II, one of a modern fighter—it is hard to ignore the fact that the rest are not, and that, in turn, reminds us not only of allied saturation bombing during World War II but of cold-war pressure on Germany

Roy Lichtenstein. **Blam.** 1962. Oil on canvas, 68" × 6'8" (172.7 × 203.2 cm). Yale University Art Gallery, New Haven, Conn. Gift of Richard Brown Baker, B.A. 1935

after the war to host NATO forces and eventually rearm against the Warsaw Pact. These pressures deeply disturbed many Germans, especially as the confrontation with the Soviet Union worsened and American involvement in the "third world" intensified in the 1960s. In a strict sense, these paintings are neutral, in keeping with Richter's intentions, but the political and ideological tensions to which they allude are tangible.

Richter's cityscapes of 1968 are similarly loaded. *Cathedral Square, Milan* (page 145) is the first of his aerial views. The subject is one of the most ornate Gothic churches in Europe and a symbol of feudal civilization in all its grandeur and vulnerability, and, to the left, the portal of a nineteenth-century shopping arcade, a symbol of bourgeois power in all its monumental self-assurance. Brushed in generally thin, gently seismic vertical and horizontal hatchings, the image wobbles optically, and the perspective shifts and torques as if it were emanating from a giant black-and-white television set with bad reception. With its deep perspective contradicted by shallow volumes and its abundance of detail—spires, arches, pedestrians, lamps, and cars—barely discernable in the fuzzily interlocking lights and darks, the canvas is, in terms of painterly tradition, the antithesis of Antonio Canaletto's work. In comparison, *Townscape Madrid* (page 146), with its meaty, *alla prima* slabs and dabs of black, white, and gray, is solidly modeled and neatly laid out, as if Manet had been at Richter's elbow. Bracketing these two large pictures at either extreme are two smaller ones of 1969–70: *Townscape PL* (page 148), which resembles the Madrid picture but seen from a higher angle and painted as if the buildings below had been pummeled, and *Townscape SL* (page 147), a lateral view of squared-off housing or office blocks anchoring a rigidly planned setting. On one level, the four paintings are demonstration pieces that show how the allover quality of the composition and paint handling associated with gestural abstraction can be put at the service of representation. On another level, they and others like them—as well as the earlier *Administrative Building* of 1964 (page 115)—are reflections on the new face of Europe and on the other surviving remnants of the old one. The contrast between the woozy splendor of *Cathedral Square, Milan* or the sunny boulevards of *Townscape Madrid*, and the immaculate high-rises of *Townscape SL* or the dreary contemporary facade of *Administrative Building*, is the difference between the prewar and postwar urban context, with the bombed-out *Townscape PL* in the middle.

Viewing his work as a multifaceted, constantly expanding aggregate, it is tempting to accept Richter's early declaration: "I have no favorite pictorial themes."[91] This position is elaborated upon by the statement: "I pursue no objectives, no systems, no tendency; I have no program, no style, no direction. I have no time for specialized concerns, working themes, or variations that lead to mastery. I steer clear of definitions. I don't know what I want. I am inconsistent, non-committal, passive; I like the indefinite, the boundless; I like continual uncertainty."[92] However, other remarks significantly qualify these sweeping dismissals of purpose or preference. Most vivid, is his playful anti-Duchampian assertion: "For me there really exists a hierarchy of pictorial themes. A mangel-wurzel and a Madonna are not of equal value, even as art objects."[93] Another explanation for his recourse to photographs is even more revealing: "Do you know what was great? Finding out that a stupid, ridiculous thing like copying a postcard could lead to a picture. And then the freedom to paint whatever you felt like. Stags, aircraft, kings, secretaries. Not having to invent anything any more, forgetting everything you meant by painting—color, composition, space—and all the things you previously knew and thought. Suddenly none of this was a prior necessity for art."[94]

If read one way, this list of possibilities has an averaging effect, as though the principal benefit of photomechanical technology were the equivalency it established between stags and aircraft, kings and secretaries. Read another way, the list evokes Richter's excitement at the prospect of these secondhand images giving him the raw data with which to paint the world. To a considerable extent, that is precisely what he did. More so than any Pop artist or Photo-Realist of the time, Richter used the working premise of the inventory to assess contemporary reality from top to bottom, revamping the traditional genres—figure composition, still life, landscape, portraiture—while exploring wide-ranging subject matter: the look and speed of cars in *Ferrari* of 1964 (page 125); the advertised pleasures of the "good life" in *Motor Boat* of 1965 (page 141); pornography in *Student* of 1967 (page 140); the allure of exotic places as packaged by the travel industry in *Egyptian Landscape* of 1964 (page 124); the oppressiveness of the urban landscape in *Administrative Building*; and the comfortless furnishings of home in *Kitchen Chair*.

A century before, Charles Baudelaire, writing about a minor painter, Constantin Guys, while in the back of his mind thinking about a major one, Manet, had described what he called "The Painter of Modern Life," whose task it was to catch the "transient, the fleeting, the contingent," that is modernity and give it the immobility of art, to "extract from fashion the poetry that resides in its historical envelope." [95] Transposing the frozen action of the photograph into the enduring but temporally ambiguous realm of painting, Richter fastened on the emblems and ephemera of postwar life and distilled their often bitter essence in tonal pictures whose poetry is a combination of matter-of-fact watchfulness and unrelieved uncertainty.

Given the latitude Richter permitted himself to paint anything, and given his belief that not all subjects have the same degree of importance, there is a cumulative meaning in his choosing to paint family members caught up in the war, menacing airplanes, and cities that recall the bombings of World War II. They do so because they remind us of treasures that were destroyed in whole or in part—in that sense Richter's views of Milan and Madrid are metaphorical counter-images of Cologne or Dresden in rubble after the war—because they look like they actually had been hit or, finally, because they are examples, in Richter's words, of the "horrible, newly built housing developments, so inhuman, so revolting," that were being erected on the ruins of damaged towns or constructed on vacant land in the postwar expansion of the "Economic Miracle." [96] Almost from the moment that Richter began to elaborate his labyrinth of disparate images and styleless styles, he left a trail of crumbs connect paintings imbued with added dimensions of sadness, foreboding, violence, and stifled anger that derive from or refer (often obliquely but sometimes with startling directness) to the dangers and upheavals of his age. As Manet had shown when he ventured into the streets to draw the bloody aftermath of the Commune of Paris, or when he restaged the execution of Maximillian I of Mexico, the Painter of Modern Life may retain his composure and, for the sake of his art, the appearance of neutrality; but he does not avert his eyes at the sight of modernity's horrors. Instead, he is determined to depict the cruelty and absurdity that engender them and the suffering they cause as objectively and as unforgettably as possible. When, in 1988, Richter turned to the subject of the lives and deaths of young German Leftists known as the Baader-Meinhof group, commentators were surprised that he would try his hand at "history painting," the most problematic and least practiced of traditional academic genres. But while *October 18, 1977* (pages 207–223), the cycle of fifteen canvases that resulted from that effort, radically alter the meaning of that term, precedents for the decision to make them had existed in his work almost from the beginning. Whether painting Jacqueline Kennedy or Uncle Rudi, bombers or urban reconstruction, all along Richter had been painting pictures saturated with history.

Engaged in a balancing act, Richter established a system for maintaining his and the viewer's distance from the subject, no matter how provocative it might be; it rested on one of two painterly decisions, and frequently on both. The first was to obscure the image by feathering the paint or by dragging a spatula or hard edge across the surface and smearing it while it was still wet. The second was his reliance on grisaille. Almost immediately, blurring the image came to be seen as a trademark of his work—the signature device he had tried to avoid. Consequently, Richter went to some lengths to play down its importance: "I don't create blurs. Blurring is not the most important thing, nor is it an identity tag for my pictures." [97] However, even if he was unsuccessful in convincing people of this, they could not help but notice that the methodical, even mechanical, way he achieved this effect was the antithesis of the forceful and heartfelt expressionist gesture that declares itself and proclaims the painter's involvement. In fact, for Richter, this indirect way of working back into a partially painted picture served to eliminate lesser details without any editorial judgment being made, to elide forms and ease transitions, unifying the surface in a more-or-less even spread of pigment and sealing the whole image under a skin that gave it the look of something "technological, smooth and perfect"—like a photograph. [98]

The variety of blurrings, or unpainting techniques, Richter deploys is actually considerable. In some pictures, in *Horst with His Dog*, for example, or *Small Nude* of 1967 (page 143), the results are of an exquisite refinement, in others, such as *Student* and, even more so, *Olympia* of 1967 (page 142) they are comparatively broad or loose. In *Cathedral Square, Milan*, meanwhile, the blurring present from the start of the process is made up of complex patterns of repetitive strokes, which, fitted together, give off a destabilizing shimmer. By contrast, in others, such as *Townscape Madrid*, the overall slightly out-of-focus impression of the image is arrived at by the application of boldly contrasting but abbreviated strokes none of which was later modified by the swipe of a wider brush or tool. Thus, for all the emphasis that can and has been placed on the homogenized appearance of particular paintings, the truth is that the painterly license he spurned when it was granted only on the condition that it be used to evoke specific kinds of strong emotion, Richter reissued to himself when the same viscosities and frictions, the same drawing, scumbling, erasing, wiping, blending, smearing, and reworking of the surface were harnessed to the detached realization of an apparently generic image. Within those self-imposed limits however, Richter came into his full powers as a virtuoso in oils.

Although Richter painted several monochrome canvases in blue, green, magenta, and other tints, most of his early paintings were gray. Of his decision to work in grisaille, Richter has said: "It makes no statement whatever; it evokes neither feelings nor associations: it is really neither visible or invisible. . . . It has the capacity that no other color has, to make 'nothing' visible. To me, gray is the welcome and only possible equivalent for indifference, noncommitment, absence of opinion, absence of shape." [99] "But," he was quick to add, "gray, like formlessness and the rest, can be real only as an idea. . . . The painting is then a mixture of gray as a fiction and gray as a visible, designated area of color." [100] Of course, full color entered into the equation from the start in his paintings such as *Mouth* and *Egyptian Landscape*, but it was color without vitality or atmosphere, the washed out, artificial color of magazine reproductions and faded snapshots. Instead of creating the illusion that the thing represented and its environs are within our reach, such color made them seem doubly remote. Gray does this even more insistently. Moreover, in the aesthetic context of the time, where vibrant color was the common currency of expressionism, depleted color or the colorless colors of the tonal spectrum operate as a rhetorical rejoinder, which is to say they retain an expressive function by announcing their expressionlessness. For an artist eager to portray himself as "inconsistent, noncommittal, passive," gray strongly recommended itself. As is true of the variousness of Richter's paint handling, so too his palette of grays is surprisingly wide in scope and subtly calibrated, from blueish, purpleish, and earthen tints to untinted shades that span the black-to-white scale, from dense shiny anthracites to pale dry eggshell tones.

The limited vocabulary of critical discourse tends to betray such perceptual distinctions, and the consequences have seriously affected the ability of many observers to see what Richter has really done. For those whom the artist tried to address when he denied that the blurring or his use of gray were an "identity tag for my pictures," the problem is a fairly straightforward, but in the long run probably insurmountable, one of getting people accustomed to looking at a painting only for so long as it takes to register its stylistic hallmarks to spend more time with a work, and thus become aware of the formal nuances that loosen the constraints of style. [101] But those inclined to forget that "gray, like formlessness and rest, can be real only as an idea," that is, can exist absolutely only at the level of abstraction, must nevertheless come to terms with qualifications that "gray as a visible designated area of color," lends to such an abstraction. In the history of modern art, the ambiguities embodied in the painterly cancellation or obscuring of the image and in the transformation of full natural hues into unnatural twilight tones range as greatly as differences between the intentions and the technical modes of execution of Alberto Giacometti and Jasper Johns. What can be said about each of them conceptually or philosophically is worth saying, but what the paintings themselves tell us one by one amplifies, rather than tidies up, the ambiguities that prompted the artist to make them. No matter how persuasive the generalizations applied to his work can be, Richter has further complicated the already complex traditions into which he projected his own contradictions and his own painterly solutions.

II: OPENINGS AND CULS DE SAC

Art historians write, for the most part, with the benefit of hindsight. Basically, they are encouraged by the commonplace predicates of retrospection to think that things turn out the way they did because they had to. Otherwise, of course, they would have turned out differently. This tendency to align all the facts with the outcome—and to choose which ones matter and which do not accordingly—is compounded if the writer is operating from a theoretical model that says, This is how things should have happened. In such a case, he or she will choose not just the facts that suit the end of the story, but the artist who fits the preconception of what the story should be and how it should conclude. In this context, *modernism* is an empty category, which compet-ing schools of thought have sought to fill. It is an idea awaiting substance but one that, if the various contenders are accepted on their own terms, cannot accommodate all the proposals for what its substance should be. Or, if modernism is understood as a construct that does indeed encompass all of these mutually exclusive hypotheses, then it is understood on the condition that modernism is and always has been the name for a certain class of assertions and arguments about the aesthetic, political, social, and cultural content of modernity.

Some artists have participated directly in these debates by offering their own predictions or models for how society and art ought to or must inevitably develop. These teleologically minded practitioners have reinforced the tendency of like-minded critics to treat all art as if it explicitly or implicitly foresaw an ultimate goal, a definitive statement of the way things will be in the future. When events fail to follow the prescribed course then the fall-back position is that a misunderstanding or mistake has detoured history from its true path or, worse, that some monolithic negative force has steered humankind away from its proper destiny. In the first decades of the twentieth century, manifesto-driven art of this kind was rife, and ideological forms of criticism that spoke in the name of modernism grew out of it. Such criticism survives today long after the vanguards it championed have ceased to produce innovative work. Postmodernism in art and postmodernism in criticism, to the extent that they exist at all as currents outside of modernism's ongoing debate about what modern culture will be, are all too frequently exercises in nostalgia or Monday-morning quarterbacking, and often both. Between reactionary postmodernism (with its dreams of restoring the old aesthetic order by dressing art up in thrift-store styles retailored for the carriage trade) and radical postmodernism (refighting battles lost and revolutions gone wrong in an attempt to stave off full recognition of the dangers and futility of apocalyptic or utopian thinking) stretches an almost unbreakable chain of conservative assumptions and emotions. Reactionaries want the past back; aging vanguardists guardedly extrapolating from history want a present and future consistent with the past, as they have conceived it.

The position of most artists is different from that of critics, even for those artists given to concocting their own theories. For them, possibility takes precedence over reasoned necessity. For artists who must start over each day without any assurance that the success or failure of the previous day's work will reliably indi-cate what comes next, possibility is the product of intuition, trial and error, and an instinctive trust in the voice that says Yes or No to each option that presents itself. This voice does not address art in general, but the artist in that moment of decision. Against this tentative sense of what can be done stands the constant threat of options suddenly being closed. This may happen as a result of misuse by others or of a restrictive codifica-tion of formerly productive uses, or it may be the consequence of the artist having used them well but, at the same time, having temporarily exhausted the freedom of maneuver they initially afforded. But while aes-thetic prognosticators are prone to declaring certain artistic practices obsolete based on their waning power in a given period, artists, whatever their public positions might be, seldom write off any possibility once and for all. On the contrary, the ability to see fresh opportunity in neglected or abandoned models is one of the basic

Konrad Lueg, Sigmar Polke, Blinky
Palermo, and Gerhard Richter outside
Galerie Heiner Friedrich, Cologne, 1967.

ingredients of innovation. No serious artist downs his or her tools because historians and critics have deduced
that nothing remains to be done; instead that he or she may pick them up to probe for previously ignored open-
ings. Moreover, such practitioners know that inasmuch as the value of any chosen convention cannot be dis-
proven logically, neither can it be proven; the only thing that finally matters is whether its imaginative potential
can be shown and whether the works it engenders supersede the paradigm and assume a life of their own.

The drama of Gerhard Richter's artistic life has consisted of repeated encounters with totalizing systems
of thought that dictated how he should conduct himself and what his painting should be. First, these ideological
mandates were issued by authoritarian political regimes. By the time he had achieved art-world recognition
in the late 1960s, they issued from the avant-garde in whose midst he had landed. Those pressures have yet to
abate, but insofar as they have sometimes exacerbated his deep-seated doubts and made it hard for him to
proceed, his responses to them—from direct defiance and verbal dodging and weaving to transforming the
tension they generate into a source of energy—have had a profound impact on the outward appearance and
inner dynamics of his work.

Between 1962, when Richter was still a student at the Düsseldorf academy and painted his first mature
paintings, and 1971, when he was appointed to the academy faculty in recognition of the place he had carved
out for himself in the burgeoning German art scene, much changed. By the mid-1960s Pop art and neo-Dada
had ceded their positions on the cutting edge to Minimal, Process, and Conceptual art. When, in 1967, the
painter Konrad Lueg became the dealer Konrad Fischer, the artist whose work he selected to open his gallery
was the American sculptor Carl Andre. The choice was indicative of the new temper of the times. The year
before, Alfred Schmela—who in 1964 hosted Richter's first one-man show in Düsseldorf, closely followed
by another mounted by Heiner Friedrich in Munich—had temporarily closed his doors. To mark the occasion,
Schmela gave each of his artists a one-day one-man exhibition; for his, Richter made an installation "honor-
ing" one Volker Bradke. It consisted of wallpaper with Bradke's name emblazoned on it, a portrait banner, a
pointedly large portrait canvas of a person Richter remembers as a nondescript "small-time" art-world
hanger-on, and a fifteen-minute black-and-white film in which the images were blurred.[2] Meanwhile, the
two-year contract Richter had signed in 1963 with Heiner Friedrich, ensuring his basic living expenses, had
expired. Friedrich continued to exhibit his work until 1974, but like Fischer, who did not show Richter until
1970, he was drawn into the orbit of the new reductive art. For several years before securing his professorship
at the academy, Richter taught in secondary school to make ends meet. Although he was a recognized member of his generation of artists, the market for contemporary German painting was still small.

For his own part, Richter felt more at home with much of this new work than he did with that of other
painters then on the rise, for example Georg Baselitz, another East German come to the West, whose meaty
figurative works of early 1962–63, and Hero paintings of 1965–66 were harbingers of neo-Expressionism.
Although they would eventually exhibit together in 1981, in an attempt to reconcile warring camps in the

Georg Baselitz. **The Great Friends [Die großen Freunde].** 1965. Oil on canvas, 8'2⁷⁄₁₆ × 9'10⅛" (250 x 300 cm). Museum Ludwig, Cologne

German art world, nothing could have been further from Richter's sensibility or way of thinking than Baselitz's and Eugen Schönebeck's intentionally scandalous "First Pandemonium Manifesto": "We have blasphemy on our side. . . . In my eyes can be seen the altar of Nature. In me the brewers of poison, the annihilators, the degenerates have attained a place of honor. Euphoria deep-ends abysses." [3] Richter had a greater affinity with the rigor and reserve of Andre, Walter de Maria, Dan Flavin, Sol LeWitt, Bruce Nauman, Robert Ryman, and Lawrence Weiner. With the exception of de Maria, all of these American artists showed sooner or later at Fischer's gallery. Feeling once again as if he were on the outside looking in, as he had been when he and Polke first met—and all the more so because the worldly third member of their group, Fischer, was responsible for bringing these internationally renowned exponents of Minimalism and Conceptualism to Düsseldorf—Richter appreciated the willingness of some of these artists to meet their local counterparts. Recalling the opening of Andre's show, Richter said: "I was sitting with Polke and Palermo, apart from the main group, and Carl came to our table and said 'Hello, I'm Carl.' And I thought this is a good artist, this is a nice guy." [4]

Richter's and Polke's most intense collaboration occurred in 1966–68. This first manifested itself in the joint exhibition at Galerie h, Hannover, in 1966, which was also the first major presentation of Polke's works. There were photographs of the two painters clowning around; their 1968 print, *Hotel Diana*, showing Richter and Polke in separate beds in a shared room, and another, *Transformation*, in which a mountain mutates into a moonlike ball. There was also a sardonic mock interview with Richter by Polke from 1964, which gives insight into their relationship; it was based, in some measure, at least, on the stigma attached to being a German artist in the postwar era, the alienation from mainstream art they both felt, and the taboos they dared each other to break. Responding to a question about his work from his interlocutor, Mr. Thwaites (Polke), the character representing Richter is quoted as saying: "And if you saw my new pictures, Mr. Thwaites, you would collapse! . . . Because they are so good! You've never seen such good pictures in your life, No one has ever seen such good pictures, and I can't show them because everyone would collapse. So in the first place I hung clothes over all the pictures, and then in due course I overpainted them all white. And now I don't paint anymore, because I don't want to have the whole human race on my conscience. It was more interesting earlier on, when the big death camps in Eastern Europe were using my pictures. The inmates used to drop dead at first sight. Those were still simple pictures, too. Anyone who survived the first show was killed off by a slightly better picture. I haven't done at lot [of drawings]. Buchenwald and Dachau had two each, and Bergen-Belsen had one. Those were mostly used for torture purposes." [5] Thwaites then asks: "And the Russians?" Richter replies: "Stalin mounted his reign of terror with two pictures. After killing millions of Russians, it is said that

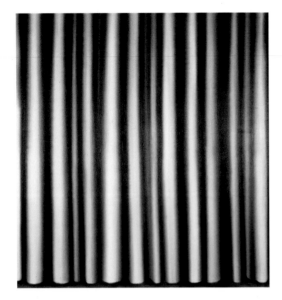 

Gerhard Richter. **Curtain IV [Vorhang IV].** 1965. Oil on canvas, 6'6¾" × 6'2¹³⁄₁₆" (200 x 190 cm). GR 57. Kunstmuseum Bonn. Permanent loan from the Grothe Collection

Gerhard Richter. **4 Panes of Glass [4 Glasscheiben].** 1967. Glass and steel, each, 6'2¹³⁄₁₆" × 39⅜" (190 x 100 cm). GR 160. Collection Anton Herbert

he caught an accidental glimpse of one of your pictures, just for a fraction of a second, and immediately dropped dead."[6]

Although the words are not Richter's own, the inclusion of this text in his collected writings lays at least partial claim to the sentiments they express. It would be difficult to come up with a more perverse way of explaining Richter's reasons for blurring or painting over his pictures. Nevertheless, this exchange offers a glimpse of the anxiety and bravado with which both artists approached their work and the world.

Less extreme, but similarly satiric qualities appear in the explanatory note for *Transformation:* "The mountain was transformed into a ball on April 26, 1968, for a period of two hours. Well aware that the power of the picture is no greater than the faith that moves mountains, the artists conceal the misery of their never ending powerlessness by imagining a temporary dematerialization, as if to say, at long last reality did us the favor of excelling itself."[7] The collaborative work had been intended as a lampoon of the much-touted Conceptualist dematerialization of art and, simultaneously, according to Jürgen Harten, as a send-up of the euphoria of the "revolutionary" year, 1968. By that time, longstanding tensions arising out of student unrest over the war in Vietnam, the conservatism of government policy generally, and of the educational system in particular erupted into confrontations between the authorities and the young across Germany, elsewhere in Europe, the Americas, and in Japan. It was the simultaneous collapse of the old independent socialist, labor, and antiwar coalitions, and the hardening of the traditional Right that lay the groundwork for this crisis, which produced the new Left. This, in turn, gave rise to armed bands of militants, such as the Baader-Meinhof group, and the hard-line response of officials. That polarization precipitated Joseph Beuys's full transition from an aesthetic agitator to an activist for all seasons. In 1968 he declared that art *was* life and, in the spirit of that declaration, stepped up the campaign to turn the academy into a laboratory for testing his utopian theory of "social sculpture."

Richter's and Polke's skepticism toward such fantastic notions of global change is apparent in *Transformation,* and although Beuys loomed ever larger on the national and international scene from this time onward, both kept their distance from his anarchic mystical proselytizing. As a refugee from the Communist German Democratic Republic, Richter felt even less sympathy for the political radicals who began to influence discourse in the art world and academic circles around the same time: "I had a big shock coming to West Germany and finding that every intelligent person was on the Left."[8] Richter can be quite caustic on the subject of dogmatic Leftism, and he became more rather than less so as the Soviet bloc fell apart and whatever threat orthodox Communism had posed all but vanished. In notes to himself of 1992, when *October 18, 1977* (1988) was still a topic of intense debate (pages 207–223), Richter wrote: "Because Marxist intellectuals refuse to own up to their own disillusionment, it transforms itself into a craving for revenge. And so they turn their own ideological bankruptcy into the utter bankruptcy of the whole world—mainly the capitalist world, of course, which they vilify and poison in their hatred and despair."[9] However, Richter was neither inclined to starry-eyed views of Western-style free-market democracy, nor had he been tempted by doctrinaire anti-communism. Instead, he has been the odd man out between two opposing ideological forces, and while crucial friendships were sealed with the "intelligent" people on the Left, he remained in fundamental, sometimes anguished, disagreement with them on basic political and artistic questions.

Well before these changes in his immediate situation and the convulsions in the culture at large, Richter had been trying out new ways to make a picture. In 1965, he made a series of five paintings of rippling curtains, and one installation work on the same motif consisting of freestanding cylinders on which were brushed the same gradations of gray that gave volumes to the folds in the paintings. They were the first of his mature works that did not have a specific photographic source. In 1967 he experimented in much the same way with the related theme of rows of doors open or ajar in which one-to-one scale representation and schematic formatting competed. The largest of his curtain paintings also dates from that year, as do two polyptychs of corrugated metal in which he used the simple technique of shading to suggest low relief in what are nevertheless essentially abstract, almost Op-art, compositions.

Also in 1967 Richter created *4 Panes of Glass*, a sculptural installation in which four vertical sheets of glass framed in metal swing on a central axis between four floor-to-ceiling poles. Unique in his oeuvre, the piece is a precursor of subsequent paintings on glass and framed mirrors. In one respect, this work is a deft critique of the truthfulness of realist painting, insofar as what one sees behind the glass is not a representation but reality itself. At the same time, however, it stands as a backward compliment to painting, since, as Richter explained it, looking through the glass the viewer is able to "see everything but grasp nothing,"

Michelangelo Pistoletto. **Man with Yellow Pants.** 1964. Paper collage with oil and pencil on polished stainless steel, 6'6⅞" × 39⅜" (200.3 x 100 cm). The Museum of Modern Art, New York. Blanchette Rockefeller Fund

although it must be conceded that Richter's paintings often hold the image so tenuously that in the end it escapes our grasp as well.[10] In his later mirrored paintings on glass, the problem is given a tautological twist in the sense that the subject of the image is a reflection of the subject who looks, and that subject is in a position to recompose the picture by moving or by shifting the focus of his or her eyes. This annexation of ambient space has a precedent in Michelangelo Pistoletto's work, beginning in 1962, in which the Italian artist painted life-size Photo-Realist figures on mirrors and polished steel. Richter, in effect, removed the depictive element and therefore the obvious conflict between illusion and reality, leaving only the literal but contingent likeness of the person standing in front of the mirror. In that respect, he turned the tables on painting yet again, intending this visual trap as a "polemic: devaluing of all other pictures; [a] provocation of the viewer, who sees himself instead of a picture."[11] Rather than gratify the viewer's desire to see something artful, fixed, and pictorially complete, he provided a void for the viewer to fill in however he or she could.

On the other hand, in *Gray Mirror* of 1992 (page 237) the reflective surface of the tinted glass is split in two, and the separate halves are hinged so that they can be rotated. When the paired panels are turned toward each other they double the image of the spectator, and when they face away from each other the spectator, in effect, disappears into the crack between them and sees only the surrounding room. Thus Richter creates a revolving-door effect in which the absence of the painted image one expects to see when approaching the work from a distance perceptually and psychologically alternates with the narcissistic presence of a self-image, but one which, with a simple repositioning of the mirrors, may vanish into a smoky gray void. Like the Curtains and Doors that preceded them, and the window paintings that follow, *4 Panes of Glass* and the mirrors that came after them play with the idea of the relation between the architecturally or structurally implied figure and the actual perceiving body. All have a disquieting emptiness or, in the case of the curtains, a hidden quality; and all pose oblique unresolvable questions about the limits of human perception or apperception. Looking back on them in 1971, Richter wrote: "Perhaps the Doors, Curtains, Surface Pictures, Panes of Glass, etc. are metaphors of despair, prompted by the dilemma that our sense of sight causes us to apprehend things, but at the same time restricts and partly precludes our apprehension of reality."[12] It is a common trick of traditional painters to check for distortions in their work by looking at it in a mirror trained over their shoulder. Richter's use of mirrors amounts to something close to this; however, his aim was not to eliminate distortions but to draw attention to them and to the discrepancy between what one sees firsthand and what happens to that image when it is re-created pictorially. Not that Richter privileged the real over its

Frank Stella. **Getty Tomb (first version).**
1959. Enamel on canvas, 6 × 8'
(213.4 × 243.84 cm). Los Angeles
County Museum of Art,
Contemporary Art Council Fund

representation; to the contrary, his whole enterprise is intended to undermine the belief that we have direct access to truth by any means: "I don't mistrust reality, of which I know next to nothing. I mistrust the picture of reality conveyed to us by our senses, which is imperfect and circumscribed. Our eyes have evolved for survival purposes. The fact that they can also see the stars is pure accident."[13]

As much as 4 Panes of Glass posed a challenge to painting, it was also a shot across the bow of neo-Dada. Comparisons between Richter's spare sculptural ensemble and Marcel Duchamp's intricately etched, inlaid, and symbolically encoded The Bride Stripped Bare by Her Bachelors, Even (the Large Glass) of 1915–23 came quickly after the work was shown in Heiner Friedrich's Cologne gallery. Richter seems to have courted the association only in order to push off from it: "Something in Duchamp didn't suit me—all that mystery-mongering—that's why I painted those simple glass panes and showed the whole windowpane problem in a completely different light."[14] He reinforced this in his comments to Benjamin Buchloh: "I can say that my Panes of Glass, like the Nude on the Stairs, involve something of an anti-Duchamp attitude, because they are so plain and deliberately uncomplicated."[15]

Inspired and irritated by Duchampian conceptualism, Richter felt a corresponding ambivalence toward the neo-Platonic aspects of Minimalism. Adopting the supposed pure conventions of the grid, he made a series of pictures that, for the most part, resemble window frames with cast shadows. In some instances, the positive white of the frame, which optically advances, is in actuality the primed canvas, while the negative space behind the frame and the offset fretwork of the frame's shadow are layered between these unpainted bars. In Shadow Painting of 1968 (page 139) Richter blocked in heavy seams and rectangles of pigment, but the pictorial pun is the same. Reductive as they may at first appear, by virtue of their tonal shifts and structural overlaps, such paintings retain their representational aspect, wreaking havoc both on the Renaissance notion of painting as being a window on the world—in the case of Richter's work, it is a window on a window on nothing—and on the high formalist pursuit of a type of painting detached from any referent outside itself. Pushing the point still further, Richter addressed himself to Frank Stella, whose adamantly anti-illusionistic Black Paintings had been based on the positivist axiom, "What you see is what you see."[16] Richter, of course, had no such faith in the self-evidence of visual phenomena. Appropriating one of the nested arch forms found in such works by Stella as Getty Tomb and The Marriage of Reason and Squalor (1959), he bled the contrasts of black enamel and white canvas out of it and gave the gray result a vertiginous wobble, as if Stella had been dizzyingly reinterpreted by Bridget Riley.

Of all Richter's redepartures in the uncertain interval of the mid- to late 1960s, the one that produced the largest number of paintings over the longest period of time was his Color Charts. Once again, it would seem, he had modernist precedents in the back of his mind: the abstract work of the Bauhaus color theorist Josef

Albers (for whom he professed little regard), the Constructivist tradition of the 1920s and 1930s, postwar neo-Constructivists such as Max Bill and Richard Paul Lohse, the monochrome canvases by Yves Klein, the high-polish planks and boxes of California sculptor John McCracken, and the striped paintings and installation pieces of the conceptually oriented French artist Daniel Buren. It appears, however, that Richter was unaware of the randomly arranged color-swatch paintings made by Ellsworth Kelly between 1951 and 1953, or that artist's spectrum panels of 1968 and after; nor was he consciously responding to the color bars that were a feature of Jim Dine's work in 1963–64 and of Jasper Johns's in 1964–65.

If Richter's approach closely corresponded to that of any of his contemporaries, it was to Sol LeWitt's, not so much in the sense that his paintings resembled LeWitt's work but, rather, in the manner in which they parallel LeWitt's use of systems to discipline sensibility, preempt taste, and sublimate the artist's drive to assert himself. Although LeWitt published his seminal essay "Sentences on Conceptual Art" in 1970, five years after Richter embarked on the Color Charts, one can profitably read them for insights into Richter's own working premises. LeWitt wrote: "The artist's will is secondary to the process he initiates from idea to completion. . . . His willfulness may only be ego. . . . The process is mechanical and should not be tampered with. It should run its course."[17] Even more thought-provoking in this context, however, are the first three sentences, which are rearranged here to form an aesthetic syllogism: "3. Rational judgements repeat rational judgements. 2. Irrational judgments lead to new experience. 1. Conceptual artists are mystics rather than rationalists. They leap to conclusions that logic cannot reach."[18] By this definition, Richter was and is a Conceptual artist not merely by virtue of method, but by poetic aspiration.

Color Charts preoccupied Richter three times during this period, beginning in 1966, then again in 1971, and finally in 1973–74. At first he approached the problem much as he had the use of photographs—by reproducing a standard commercial paint sample card on a vastly enlarged scale. Circumventing spiritual notions of color as epitomized by Vasily Kandinsky's theories and the more scientific methods of Albers and the Constructivists, Richter's new use of the ready-made also set aside the issue of composition, and contained and suppressed gesture in favor of a blandly impersonal facture, even more so than in his photo-based paintings.

Executed in glossy pigments, each rectangular element had sharp, taped edges and each was filled with a consistently blended hue. Of the eighteen works in the 1966 group, there are three gray-scale paintings, two large-format pictures composed of only six color blocks, and the rest are made up of at least nine color squares and at most of one hundred tinted bands. Of the large pictures, the first is all shades of yellow, and the second, *Six Colors* (page 138), includes the three primaries plus a muted green, brown, and pale tan. The 1971 group consists of only five large works, four of them the same size with the same 180 units fitted into a white grid, and the fifth a mural-scale work made up of twenty sections with nine color units each. This time Richter abandoned the sampler as a pretext, along with the improvised changes he had rung on that formal given, and replaced them with a mathematical system for mixing the three primary colors in graduated amounts so as to dramatically expand the number of combinations and refine the distinctions among them.

Taking that system to extremes in the Color Charts of 1973–74, Richter added a fourth, fifth, and sixth component—a light gray, a dark gray, and later a green—and multiplied the admixtures exponentially while arriving at chromatic nuances that were at times nearly impossible to differentiate from each other. In his final burst of activity in this mode, Richter further sublimated his hands-on involvement as a painter by hiring assistants to participate directly in the process. The twenty-six canvases that grew out of these technical and procedural adjustments—which in some cases also included the elimination of the white grid—range in size from the 4-color canvas or the 16-color canvas to, in arithmetic progression, the 64-color, the 256-color, the 1,024-color, and finally the 4,096-color canvas. In a text explaining the project, Richter teasingly declared: "If I had painted all the possible permutations, light would have taken more than 400 billion years to travel from the first painting to the last," but what interested him more than this science-fiction speculation was what he described as the paintings' "artificial naturalism."[19]

In light of this comment, it is best perhaps to look at these pictures as the painted equivalent of one of Carl Andre's variegated metal plate carpets— Richter's "idea of a powerfully realistic work"—because like them his painting represents neither a physical nor a metaphysical entity outside itself.[20] The difference, of course, is that no matter how many pieces might conceivably go into their creation, Andre's checkerboards are

Ellsworth Kelly. **Colors for a Large Wall.** 1951. Oil on canvas, mounted on sixty-four wood panels, overall, 7'10¼" × 7'10¼" (239.3 x 239.3 cm). The Museum of Modern Art, New York. Gift of the artist

symmetrically patterned, whereas the arbitrary arrangement of part to part in Richter's paintings distributes his tonally uneven color and chromatic contrasts of adjacent units irregularly across the field. Only the white armature retains a uniform surface tension throughout, and it is optically destabilized where the lines intersect, resulting in a black retinal pop (much like staring at a red spot and then seeing green when your eyes move to an empty space), a phenomenon that, in reverse, first became a factor in Piet Mondrian's modernist black-gridded paintings. However, Mondrian's work was, for the most part, based on pure primary colors plus black and white. By contrast and in keeping with his general avoidance of absolutes, virtually all of the colors in Richter's paintings of this type are modulated by the traces of others or by grays located in the intervals between black and white. Thus, for example, *256 Colors* of 1974 (pages 180–181) is a feast for the sharply discerning eye, but each of the "flavors" is a melange, and each consists of ingredients whose exact proportions are known to the maker but can only be guessed at by the viewer.

Between the first and second group of Color Charts Richter's work manifested a previously uncharacteristic disparateness; indeed, it is from this time (1966 to 1971) that his habit of tacking from format to format against the main currents of contemporary art really can be dated. Casting about for subjects for his photo-based paintings, he turned to pornography, producing *Student* and *Olympia* of 1967 (pages 140, 142) along the way, as well as his townscape and mountain pictures, among them *Himalaya* of 1968 (page 149). In the meantime, Richter also painted the Door and Shadow paintings and the last of the Curtains, although in the final analysis, he professed his dislike for these exceptions to the use of ready-made motifs.[21] In the midst of these big projects, he also made four small landscapes based on his own snapshots, three taken on vacation in Corsica, and a fourth, *Bridge (by the Sea)* of 1969 (page 152). There had been intimations of Richter's affinity for landscape before—for example, *Egyptian Landscape* of 1964 (page 124), and the mountain paintings and two moonscapes (1968)—but nothing quite like these delicately brushed, overtly picturesque scenes had thus far appeared. They were the seeds of what later was to become a dominant strain in Richter's output.

As modest as these landscape canvases may have seemed, at first glance, they could not have been more provocative. After all, who else in vanguard circles at that time dared to paint a holiday souvenir, much less one so enchanting or with such a picture-postcard allure. From this juncture, Richter had to deflect critics of his new direction from applying the label neoromantic to his work. Some of them, like the dealer René Block, were former supporters hostile to what he was doing, and some were critics who welcomed the new style, often out of a naive desire for the return of romanticism, which Richter had no intention of reviving. Nevertheless, even his opening the door to a reassessment of romanticism offered a serious challenge to the antipictorial, antipainting factions that dominated art discourse in the late 1960s and early 1970s, especially given the fact that Richter's landscapes themselves lacked even a hint of the kind of irony to be found in Morley's crystalline Photo-Realist renderings of tourists and ocean liners. Nor had Richter's *sfumato* been manipulated in the obvious manner of Richard Hamilton's beach scenes, similar as those were to Polke's raster dot pictures. Instead, Richter caused a disturbance by quietly making paintings that resisted every attempt to fit them into existing categories or to explain them away as deliberately insincere exercises in formal and pictorial anachronism.

Part of the difficulty Richter built into these works stems from the fact that *as* pictures they were not anachronisms but, rather, thoroughly contemporary photographically impersonal views of the land, sea, and sky. In some, for example, *Bridge (by the Sea)*, the setting is plain and plainly modern, with the sparest detail in the description of the viaduct, flat countryside, still water, and hazy horizon of nowhere in particular. This feeling of having looked out the window of a car—or airplane—in motion or of having stopped on the road between points of interest is fairly common in Richter's landscapes. It is as if what has caught his attention are the anonymous places where roads are engulfed by nature, but nature, in turn, is implicitly bracketed by the cities, towns, and urban infrastructures the roads connect. No matter how sublime the vista, the highway or the airport are near. That said, the vistas are frequently sweeping. Devoid of any human element—except for the presence of the viewer—and absent any *repoussoir*, or visual break, in the foreground, the waves in *Seascape (Cloudy)* of 1969 (page 157) advance toward the edge of the canvas as the horizon disappears into a bank of menacing clouds. The subject is potentially melodramatic, but with its off-key prestorm aspect and suave paint handling, the treatment is almost meteorological. Another work, *Cloud* of 1970 (page 153), part of a triptych, almost dares viewers to project their sentiments onto the image—this time, for example, the hope of transcendental release—but offers nothing in the way of painterly inflection to which such sentiments might attach themselves. These pictures are as beautiful as are their natural subjects and beautiful as painted artifacts, but they withhold any invitation to empathy. Whereas romantic paintings generally meet viewers halfway—usually by means of a surrogate figure in the landscape that intensifies their associations and emotions while offering to lift them out of themselves—Richter's paintings of this type are indifferent to the viewer's needs, acknowledging by that pointed indifference that the viewer and his or her needs exist. Thus they portray natural phenomena without symbolic amplification. In *Seascape (Sea-Sea)* of 1970 (page 154) Richter goes out of his way to denature nature by hinging two images of choppy water to a glowing horizon line, one in its proper position and one inverted above it, so that where the sea meets the sky, the sea meets itself. Seen across the room, it could well be mistaken for a conventional seascape, triggering all the responses customarily experienced in looking at such a sight. But the viewer is brought up short when the calculated artificiality of its symmetry reveals itself, breaking the thrall of reflex awe just as it takes hold. But not entirely, for the desire to lose oneself in the image remains, and the radiant light and the subtly rendered flux of the waves continue to beckon and lull, leaving one caught between the trick question that has been asked and the longed-for answer. If Richter had truly been intent on burning out all the circuits connecting the image to traditional landscape, it would have been sufficient to diagram the reversal upon which it rests. That he went further in order to evoke an impossible reality suggests that he had reasons for keeping those circuits in operation.

Interspersed with Richter's landscapes of 1970–71, and recurring on a grand scale in 1973 and 1979, were paintings based on photo-enlargements of brushstrokes or whirling pools of mottled pigment. This is the only case in which the artist's early interest in Roy Lichtenstein's work seems to have had a direct bearing on his own. But whereas Lichtenstein's translation of the Abstract Expressionist gesture into heavy cartoon outlines and static Ben Day dots contradicts the impetuous thrust of the marks depicted, Richter's handling of closeups of similar marks puts them under the microscope and lends them added dazzle predicated on a flat,

meticulous, blatantly illusionistic rendering of what in the presumed original was a quick, viscous, physically assertive swipe of paint. Some of these blown-up simulations of the bravura gesture are opulent in color and texture. However, *Detail (Brown)* of 1970 (page 151), for all its disproportionate size, tactility, and succulence is comparatively austere. In essence, it is a one-shot monochrome or, insofar as the horizontal ridges of dead brown suggest a specific correspondence, a giant Manzoni-like "Achrome" with a blush of earth tones. In all of these paintings the actual brushmarks that create the effect are blended away leaving the macrocosm of the image to represent their microcosmic actuality. Over the years Richter has returned to this idea more than once. In 1978, he documented 128 details of the surface of a painting in raking light. The model for the project would seem to have been Man Ray's famous photograph of dust collecting on Duchamp's *Large Glass,* but the resulting black-and-white images published as an artist's book resemble moonscapes or topographical studies of a desert.

Having taken color charts and photo-enlargements as his first two jumping-off points on the way to abstraction, Richter then tried a third, which he called *Inpainting.* The process originated in several paintings of trees and a meadow or park where the verdure is laid in via bundles of relatively thick impasto strokes that obscure the shapes where they run together. Previously, Richter had painted over landscapes with similarly blunt, greasy marks. The Inpaintings themselves consist of thickets of such lines with no apparent image underneath them. Some are in shades of gray, others in shades of shoe-polish brown; the largest of the series is a grid composed of 120 separate panels painted this color. The rest are made of the three primary colors mixed together on the canvas much as children do when finger-painting. And, as anyone knows who has watched a child at work in this way, the pure hues with which the child started soon turn to mud. In the same fashion, Richter's three-into-two-into-one fusions vary from the lustrous Rubens-like skeins of crimson, gold, burnt umber, and burnt sienna in *Red-Blue-Yellow* of 1972 (page 179) to almost sickening combinations of dirty reds, yellows, and blues with greens, grays, and violets in between. Where the clash among the colors is most localized, one is reminded of Johns's mottled and deliberately mislabeled spectrum paintings and in others of the curlicue paint application of some of Robert Ryman's work of 1961–62, but there are no specific debts to them. Rather, the Inpaintings are the often uningratiating, purposely muddled extensions of the clean and orderly Color Charts. They are paintings about painting by an artist aware that the walls were closing in around him.

Richter's arrival at complete abstraction coincided with the almost total eclipse of painting as contemporary art's dominant medium. "I was out of fashion for a long time after the early 1960s work, and painting itself was unfashionable too," he told an interviewer in the 1990s.[22] Elsewhere, he ascribed the decline in painting's importance to the broad cultural tensions of the period: "At the end of the 1960s the art scene underwent its great politicization. Painting was taboo, because it had no 'social relevance' and was therefore a bourgeois thing."[23] The exception to this consensus among advocates of emphatically material Minimal and process sculpture, and of dematerialized Conceptual art was the special status accorded artists such as Alan Charlton, Robert Mangold, Brice Marden, Agnes Martin, and Robert Ryman, most of whom at one time or another showed at Konrad Fischer's gallery and many of whom, along with Richter, were included in the 1975 survey *Fundamental Painting* at the Stedelijk Museum in Amsterdam. Employing the word *fundamental* to describe this type of work is preferable to labels like *reductive* (which presumes that the new art involved boiling down an existing model of painting rather than starting from scratch) or *minimal* (which suggests that the point is "lessness," while also confusing an intuitive approach to painting with systems-based sculpture). But the term *fundamental* still conflated the divergent intentions and achievements of individual artists under a loosely formalist rubric. It lumped together Marden, the precocious exponent of a tradition-minded gesturalism subsumed by the monochrome; Martin, a puritan mystic for whom diluted tonality, and exquisitely imperfect mark-making created a meditational field; and Ryman, an empiricist of delight for whom paint in all its variety opened up new visual territory where only a void has been thought to exist.

Richter fits none of these descriptions, although his first abstract paintings sometimes display skidding surface currents similar to those in Marden's most heavily worked encaustics, and his sensibility has deep affinities with Ryman's dispassionate pursuit of objective beauty. But whereas these two painters—and many others associated with this long-standing tendency—chose categorically nonrepresentational painting, and approached the problems it posed as an affirmation of painting's essential self-sufficient and open-ended future, Richter backed into abstraction. Initially, it wasn't even his aim to paint monochromes as such. Rather, they seem to have resulted from two discoveries, one positive and the other negative. First came the realization that the transitional intervals in the paintings on which he was working—the zones of ambiguity within or around the image—were of greater importance to him than the image itself. Thus, as early as 1965 he wrote: "All that interests me is the gray areas, the passages and tonal sequences, the pictorial spaces, overlaps and interlockings. If I had any way of abandoning the object as the bearer of this structure, I would immediately start painting abstracts."[24]

Saying this, Richter had already characterized the kind of abstraction toward which he was heading, and it was not the realm of pure formalist painting (clear-cut constructs, consistent gesture, well-defined color, with a preference for black, white, or primary hues) but a murkier painterly dimension where none of the compositional elements of a work fully declares itself, no matter how schematic the design or systematic the paint application might be or how evenly blended the varying shades of gray being used. Richter's second discovery was overpainting or, as he also referred to it, inpainting or un-painting.

As previously mentioned, cancellation plays a large role in postwar art, from the erasures and redrawing of Alberto Giacometti, to the scraping-down and repainting of Willem de Kooning. And as these examples suggest, cancellation has often been a combination of subtraction and addition. Richter's method is basically additive or at least cumulative, the covering up of one layer by another, although this frequently involves the deliberate skinning of a painting's surface with a hard-edge tool, smearing the top coat, and mixing it with the still-moist undercoat, which is kept that way by the liberal use of carnation oil and other mediums that retard drying. In that sense, Richter nearly always paints *a la prima*, or wet into wet, with the result that the sometimes heavily sedimented canvases seem all of a piece because they "cure" slowly, ensuring that the enriched pigment retains a uniform freshness. Thus, even his most subdued gray paintings possess a palpable immediacy that qualifies their austerity and remoteness and, ultimately, their intimations of depression and despair.

The earliest all-gray painting in Richter's oeuvre is a small-format townscape of 1968 in which the usual chiaroscuro contrasts have been reduced to a middle tone that suffuses the whole image, leaving only the brushstrokes to distinguish the shapes of what might be buildings. That same year, Richter painted two more all-gray abstractions, one in which the pasty oil color is stirred by looping marks and another in which similar marks crisscross the rectangle and overlap in the middle, giving the impression that they are all radiating from a common source. The title of one of them, *Gray Beams*, suggests that it is a light source, but the painting absorbs or reflects light rather than emits it, as if it were a gray, rather than black, hole. In 1970 Richter embarked on a suite of four large-scale gray monochromes with fleshy, gestural surfaces, and also painted eleven other gray pictures in different, mostly smaller, formats. Then in 1972–73 he painted a group of still larger gray canvases; those completed in 1972 belonged to his Inpainting series, while the subsequent works

128 details from a picture (Halifax 1978)

THE NOVA SCOTIA PAMPHLETS 2

Gerhard Richter. Cover of **128 Details from a Picture (Halifax 1978).** (Halifax: Nova Scotia College of Art and Design, 1980).

were simply titled *Gray*. The next and largest group of gray paintings was made in 1974, and the final group—painted on aluminum and wood panels rather than stretched canvas—was completed in 1976.

Not counting image paintings—townscapes and star pictures—that are almost but not quite abstractions, or the baked-enamel-on-glass mirror paintings, Richter has, to date, painted over one hundred gray monochromes. That is roughly one tenth of his entire production; and most recently he has gone back to making gray, or nearly gray, abstractions in significant numbers. However, within the larger body of work, the gray monochromes of 1970–76 represent a distinct and critical episode in Richter's development, a period in which he struggled against active hostility to painting on the part of many of those around him and, on his own part, a fear of diminishing returns and the ultimate failure of his own efforts to keep painting going.

Since the first decades of the twentieth century, when Kazimir Malevich created *Composition: White on White* (1918–20), along with his black squares, crosses, and circles (often interpreted as paradigmatic of painting's terminus) and Aleksandr Rodchenko made his triad of monochromes *Pure Red Color, Pure Yellow Color, Pure Blue Color* (1921), shortly thereafter setting easel painting aside for the sake of more radical Constructivist practices, painting had been thought to be nearing the end of its usefulness—or past it. A decade later the Surrealist, soon-to-be Stalinist poet and critic Louis Aragon argued in *Challenge to Painting* (1930) that collage and montage had preempted painting's representational functions as well: "Painting has not always existed. . . . Absolutely nothing in the world will be changed if one ceased to paint altogether, although such a view cannot be advanced without alarming the conservative spirit of art lovers. Let them be reassured; we are not so optimistic as to assert that the day will come when no one paints any longer, but what one can propose is that painting, with the ensemble of superstitions it carries with regard everything from the subject to materials, from the decorative sensibility to the illustrative one, from composition to taste, etc., will in the near term certainly pass for an anodyne diversion reserved for young girls and elderly provincials, as is the case today with verse, and tomorrow with the writing of novels."[25]

The rebellious ferment of the late 1960s and early 1970s revived these attitudes toward the medium and further entrenched their totalizing assumptions in art historical and theoretical discourse, sometimes phrased with the dripping sarcasm of the young Aragon. Parenthetically, it should not go unremarked that such attitudes persist to this day even though the apocalyptic changes once predicted have not come about, and the predictions themselves are seventy to eighty years old—in other words, antique visions of the new. Nor should it be forgotten that, in addition to becoming a champion of the most aesthetically *retardataire* forms of Socialist Realism in his capacity as spokesman on cultural affairs for the French Communist Party, Aragon also devoted considerable energy to writing about Picasso, Matisse, and other leading painters of the School of Paris. Depending on one's perspective, this may be seen as a betrayal of his previous, unimpeachably avant-garde position or a tacit admission that painters had proven him wrong. In any event, Richter found himself immersed in a climate of opinion in which it was more or less taken for granted that *this* time around painting could no longer avoid revealing that its aesthetic reserves were spent.

Under these circumstances, the path of least resistance—and the one most likely to secure his reputation in avant-garde circles—would have been to reenact the painting of what Ad Reinhardt once called, "the last painting anyone can make."[26] Unsure of how long he could sustain the effort of postponing painting's predicted demise but equally unwilling merely to illustrate it, Richter set his course between the symbolic absolutes available to him in the Manichean world of all-white nothing or all-black nothing. Gray was the obvious, but also surprisingly broad, middle term. "I just went on painting," Richter recalled, but it was never a question of going through the motions out of mere stubbornness, as the scope and variety of his gray paintings show.[27] For example, *Gray* of 1973 (page 175) is distinguished by an implacable opacity and surface regularity reminiscent of the enervating interiors of institutional buildings. With its horizontal slabs of grained pigment, another work called *Gray* of the same year (page 174) has a density and solidity that exude the oddly comforting feel of masonry. Others, such as *Un-Painting (Gray)* of 1972 (page 173), display a furious animation, as if the painter had been thrashing about inside a gunny sack or a sealed tent. Employing a roller in the first work, a heavily loaded brush in the second, and repetitive gesture in the third—as well as using different tones of gray in each—Richter represents the tonal range and even greater diversity of painterly effects encompassed by these otherwise somber monochromes.

Blinky Palermo. **Pillow with Black Form [Kissen mit schwarzer Form].** 1967. Oil, fabric, and foam rubber, 20¼ x 16⅚₆ x 3¹⁵⁄₁₆" (52 × 42 × 10 cm). Private collection, Germany

Except initially, Richter was not actually obliterating representation with abstraction but, rather, starting with an empty canvas he was simultaneously attempting to picture negation and fullness, trying to give them substantial definition in the hope of forestalling entropy. The fact that the paintings are manifestly different from one another—not only in the most obvious aspects of format or technique but also in the nuances of their individual facture—vindicated Richter's strategy, although it took a while for him to be fully confident that this was true. The fact that separately and collectively they carry the emotional weight of his anxious neutrality proves that they are more than simple holding actions. With some distance, Richter gradually came to appreciate their distinctive qualities, and reevaluated their psychological content. Speaking to the critic Coosje van Bruggen, he invoked John Cage's "Lecture on Nothing," to explain how the nihilistic motive turned into something positive, even beautiful: "It was the ultimate possible statement of powerlessness and desperation. Nothing, absolutely nothing left, no figures, no color, nothing. Then you realize after you've painted three of them that one's better than the others and you ask yourself why that is. When I see eight pictures together I no longer feel that they're sad, or if so, they're sad in a pleasant way."[28] This is the voice of a maker rather than a theoretician, someone more committed to the particular than the general; but had Richter not been half-persuaded that the theoreticians were right and that his own frustrations supported the charges brought against painting, then his attempts to elude the predicted outcome of the crisis that confronted him would have had far less meaning. Ultimately, though, he won more than a reprieve for his medium, he won a judgment against those who had condemned it on flawed and insufficient evidence.

Richter's isolation from the rest of the contemporary art world during the late 1960s and early 1970s was alleviated by his friendship with Blinky Palermo. It was a friendship that grew as the distance between Richter and Polke increased, a distance partially accounted for by the comparatively rapid recognition that had come Richter's way, while the response to Polke's protean output of paintings, sculptures, installations, photographs, and conceptual projects had been much slower. Their rift was further exacerbated by a crisis and pause in the work of the extravagantly talented but erratic Polke. Like Richter and Polke, Palermo was East German in origin. Born Peter Schwarze in Leipzig in 1943, he was almost immediately adopted and given the surname of his new parents, Wilhelm and Erika Heisterkamp. In 1952 he moved with his family to West Germany, and in 1962 he enrolled at the Düsseldorf academy—the same year Richter did. In 1963 he entered the class of Joseph Beuys who treated him as a favorite and in effect became his artistic father. Beuys suggested the pseudonym Blinky Palermo (the moniker of a minor gangster and boxing promoter associated with Sonny Liston), which his protégé assumed in 1964. Gifted with the subtlest of artistic sensibilities, but emotionally volatile and self-destructive—he died at thirty-four while in the Maldives after years of hard drinking and drug abuse—Palermo was something of a romantic figure, but his art was resolutely contemporary,

Installation view of Gerhard Richter's first American exhibition at Reinhard Onnasch Gallery, New York, 1973.

and the lyricism that infused it was the product of a keen sensitivity to materials and a deft, matter-of-fact touch. In addition to working in oil, enamel, and acrylics on canvas, wood, and metal, Palermo drew extensively, made watercolors, wall reliefs, graphic architectural interventions, and so-called *Stoffbilder,* or cloth-paintings, in which fabrics were stretched over wood stretchers with the harmonious juxtaposition of dyed colors recalling the chromatic "zone" compositions of Mark Rothko or Ellsworth Kelly. In Beuys's words, Palermo was "very permeable."[29] Although quiet and not given to debating ideas, he was alert to what was going on around him, as Lueg was. Unlike Lueg, he was able to absorb it and make it his own. Richter's bond with Palermo was predicated on this combination of refinement, reticence, and openness. And yet, commenting on his affinity with Palermo, Richter explained that it was in part based on the differences in their inclinations and abilities. Speaking to the Swiss curator Dieter Schwarz, Richter said: "His constructive pictures have remained in my memory because they particularly appeal to me, because I can't produce such a thing. I always found it very good how he made it and that he made it—this astonished me. There was an aesthetic quality which I loved and which I couldn't produce, but I was happy that such a thing existed in the world. In comparison, my own things seemed to me somewhat destructive, without this beautiful clarity."[30] It was Palermo who brought postwar American abstraction back to Richter's attention, including the work of Rothko, Willem de Kooning, Morris Louis, and especially Barnett Newman, who came to occupy a prominent place in Richter's mind. Comparing Rothko to Newman in 1998, Richter recalled the mood of that early moment: "I only identified with [Rothko's] seriousness, which was absolutely to be admired. At that time, in the 1970s, Barnett Newman, with his nonhierarchical structures, his nonrelational Color Field painting, seemed more interesting because his work was less pretty."[31] It was with Palermo that Richter made his first trip to New York in 1970. Taking a room in a tourist hotel on Forty-second Street while doing the rounds of jazz bars, galleries, and parties, they stayed ten days and left, "feeling we were Europeans, and we were a little bit proud. We have the right to exist, [we were] not afraid of this superpower."[32] In subsequent years, Richter returned to New York many times, and in 1973, Palermo moved there. Yet, even after Richter's first American exhibition at the Reinhard Onnasch Gallery in Manhattan in 1973, when James Rosenquist toured him around in an open convertible and he met other artists, Richter has always regarded New York with a mixture of amazement, distaste, and wariness. In notes written during a 1984 visit, he purged that ambivalence, which is the mirror-image of a deeper ambivalence toward his own country: "This city of the elect and the privileged, of wielders of power and decision-makers, which implacably raises up and destroys, producing superstars and derelicts; which is so merciless and at the same time so beautiful, charming, dream-like, romantic, paradisal. The city that exerts such a deadly fascination; the city that killed many others besides Palermo. . . . I envy the New Yorkers, and I think with discontent of Germany, the stifling fug of its society, its affluent philistinism, its all-smothering, oppressive ugliness. I shall rebook tomorrow and fly home early."[33]

Sigmar Polke. **Polke's Collected Works [Polkes gesammelte Werke].** 1969. Lacquer on canvas, 15 × 56" (40 × 150 cm). Collection Lise Spiegel Wilks

Gerhard Richter and James Rosenquist at the opening of Rosenquist's exhibition at Galerie Ricke, Cologne, 1970.

Richter's relationship with Palermo—more so than that with Polke—was based on a common approach to the problems in their work: "We could really just speak about painting. The main thing was about the surface of color or the proportion of color. It was impossible for me to talk to Polke about the opacity of color. With Palermo, yes. We supported each other, we comforted each other a little bit. We thought this really could not be true that everything was supposed to be over. Art had to be relevant, and our art was not relevant."[34] "Of course, Richter added, "we remained strangers to each other, but we shared the same judgments."[35] Richter's collaborations with Palermo were also more direct than those with Polke. The simplest of these projects is a beautiful print of 1971 in which two abutting photographs chosen by Richter—a telephone and a closeup of a lightbulb—are set into a wide field of mustard yellow chosen by Palermo. The most important project they undertook together was the creation of a room in 1971 at the Cologne gallery of Heiner Friedrich, where the walls were covered with a dark yellow ochre, and at the center of which were two busts with tall pedestals facing each other several feet apart. The walls were painted by Palermo, the busts, full plaster casts of the two artists' heads painted gray, were by Richter.[36]

The layered meanings of the piece depend more than usual on the specific cultural experience brought to it, the consequent assumptions made, and the social, political, and aesthetic context within which it is finally located. For many reasons, the Pop sensibility of Richter and his cohort differed considerably from that of their English and American counterparts. These differences were not confined to attitudes toward consumer society and the mass media—the givens of Pop—but also toward the emblems of the artistic past. While Johns, Lichtenstein, Rauschenberg, and others quoted works by everyone from Picasso and Léger to Rubens, the household gods and civic monuments to tradition familiar to Europeans played no part in their thinking because, as a rule, Americans do not grow up surrounded by such tokens of established culture. Germans, however, are more likely to have lived in a world where writers, composers, and philosophers are commemorated in garden sculptures, and where uniform editions of the works of eighteenth- and nineteenth-century authors fill a shelf or two in someone's house. Thus, it was not just commercial goods, advertising, and movie images that attracted the eye of the German Pop artists but also the mass-produced, or at least ubiquitous, icons of the bourgeois, aristocratic, and bureaucratic ideals of *Kultur*. For example, no American would have thought to paint a row of leather-bound books with the painter's name in gilt letters on their spines, because almost no one in the United States in the 1960s had the collected works of Sir Walter Scott or Charles Dickens next to the fireplace in their high-rise apartments or suburban ranch houses. But in 1969 Polke painted just such a set of books with his name on each volume because the collected work of Goethe or Schiller had recognizable symbolic value, and virtually any German could understand the humor of the ploy—and the provocation. If the essence of Pop art is to objectify the commonplace or standardized things that clutter modern life so as to interrupt passive acceptance of them and hold them up to fresh scrutiny, then to the extent that high culture appears in the contemporary environment as if it were just part of the furniture, it too can be re-presented with the critical irreverence used in the Pop appropriation of low culture.

Richter and Palermo's simulation of neoclassical interior design and decorative sculpture is of the same order. Busts like those made by Richter are a familiar sight in the parks around old official buildings and stately houses of the eighteenth and nineteenth centuries just as they are in the drawing rooms where the walls are often painted colors similar to the one Palermo used. For Richter and Palermo to have insinuated themselves into these conventions is, at one level, both a parody of good taste, and a joke at their own expense insofar as they have assumed the demeanor of artist-heroes in a spiritual or poetic trance—the antithesis of the revolutionary role-playing of vanguard artists like Jörg Immendorff (another Beuys favorite) in that period.

A basically political reading of this ensemble has been offered by Benjamin Buchloh, who sees it as a critical "restaging of the myth of the hero and the leader" in the neoclassicist manner promoted by Hitler and Stalin. Pointing to Richter's own experience of those regimes, while acknowledging the artist's "claims not to have worked with any particular model in mind," Buchloh argues that "it is rather evident," that the uncanny similarity between *Two Sculptures for a Room by Palermo* of 1971 (page 159) and certain fascist prototypes—Arno Breker's bust of Hitler, in particular—involves a reprise of totalitarian tropes that points toward Germany's incapacity to address its Nazi past and mourn the devastation it caused.

Buchloh is not wrong in making these connections insofar as the neoclassical impulse does account for a cultural continuum stretching from the late eighteenth century to the Third Reich and the consolidation of the Soviet empire. But, why, one asks, would Richter—who has made very few self-portraits—use his own visage or that of an artist he admired to recapitulate the rhetorical falsehoods of authoritarian art? The answer must be: that was not what he and Palermo had in mind. Instead, it would seem that they were cautiously, but seriously, hinting at the possibility that this perennial style might not be a permanent hostage to its most corrupt incarnations, and that it could still be re-created in its own semisatirical image. At odds with an increasingly radicalized art world, they chose to "immortalize" themselves at just the moment when their own place in history seemed most tenuous. Practitioners of so-called outmoded forms of modern art at the respective ages of thirty-nine and twenty-eight, they donned the conservative guise of venerated masters. Yet, even though they were plainly flirting with the tainted connotations such memorial sculptures had (and bearing in mind that the musty if not morbid atmosphere Palermo's ocher evoked is not far removed from the palette of his mentor Beuys, and in particular from Beuys's *Braunkreuz*, a homeopathic recycling of fascist brown), there is a calm and equipoise to the room and to the busts themselves that at least partially transcends the negative precedents Buchloh cites. This is evident even in the bronzes cast from the plasters, which are covered by a dark brown patina flecked by oxidization. They preserve the texture of the heavy gray brushstrokes of the original painted plasters, making them facsimiles of what amount to three-dimensional paintings as much as they are life masks—or premature death masks—of the artists. Symmetry and sculptural restraint account for the serenity these heads possess, but so too do the strange expressions on the faces of the two friends who confront each other, with eyes closed. They seem withdrawn into themselves and, at the same time, of one mind; the current that passes between them is not telepathic or mystical but rather an internalized exchange of sympathy and intelligence.

Another artist whose work and character struck a chord with Richter in this period was the Belgian Marcel Broodthaers. Broodthaers is too elusive a personality to deal with here in any detail, and his work is too important and too complex to encapsulate in simple formulas. Furthermore, Richter's contact with him, although significant, was relatively limited. Suffice it to say that Broodthaers, a former member of the Resistance, lapsed Marxist, dedicated bohemian, protégé of the Surrealist René Magritte, former poet, and Conceptual polymath, was the sly scourge of institutional aesthetics in every form. He turned his hand to art in 1963 after seeing an exhibition of Jim Dine's work in Brussels and one of George Segal's sculptures at the Sonnabend Gallery in Paris—the same year Richter saw work by Lichtenstein there. "I, too, wondered if I couldn't sell something and succeed in life," Broodthaers said. "For quite a while I had been good for nothing. I am forty years old. The idea of inventing something insincere finally crossed my mind and I set to work at once."[37] Broodthaers's mixed feelings about American Pop art in some ways echoed those of Richter, and their attitudes toward the widespread politicization of art also corresponded in many ways, as did their leeriness about the transformation of Beuys the neo-Dada agitator into Beuys the guru and activist. Indeed, in a characteristically oblique polemic Broodthaers compared Beuys to the self-aggrandizing Richard Wagner, while likening himself to the light-opera composer Jacques Offenbach. Such a deliberate anachronism was an essential part of Broodthaers's own neo-Dada strategy. Using nineteenth-century objects, texts, graphics, and typography in his drawings, prints, films, and installations, Broodthaers created a parallel universe in which the old mirrored the new in absurd ways, and antique kitsch mocked the certainties of modernity. This mockery had an implicitly political dimension; Broodthaers had not forgotten his Marx. But, rather than make tendentious progressive art that repeated the mistake of conservatives who assumed that visual and verbal language are a self-evident and reliable means of communication, he rested his anthropological reconstruction and deconstruction of bourgeois society on exhaustive inventories of its popular symbols and the adroit subversion of their formal and ideological codes. "All human action is political. That is false," Broodthaers affirmed, but went on to say: "It becomes true when the image of natural objects is constructed and guided by a social class that intends it to serve the preservation of its privileges. What is political in the profession of art or of other things is to reveal this way or in any case not to conceal it. The method I have employed is to introduce and establish falsehoods in (artistic) reality."[38]

Richter concurred with Broodthaers's mistrust of natural appearances, although he was disinclined to create semiotic "booby-traps" as Broodthaers called them, for the sake of exposing the social privilege implicit in such fictions.[39] Broodthaers's skeptical wit and his willingness to go against the tide of the times appealed to Richter: "He was an incredibly likable and fascinating man; we always greeted each other warmly . . . but to this day I still don't understand what he was doing."[40] When he was invited to contribute to Broodthaers's magnum opus, *The Museum of Modern Art, Department of Eagles, XIXth Century Section,* he readily accepted. The "museum" that Broodthaers had initially created in his apartment with a display of packing crates, signs, and postcards of nineteenth-century paintings consisted of a series of taxonomic installations that parodied museological, economic, and artistic systems. This then expanded at other locations to include "departments" of Cinema, Documentation, Figures, Finance, Publicity, and Modern Art, with the eagle representing the metaphorically exalted view of art enshrined in cultural institutions inherited from the past. At Broodthaers's prompting, Richter painted two eagles, one of which was added to the museum's collection of some three hundred examples. The first version, *Eagle* of 1972 (page 158) is blurry and relatively subdued, the second more painterly and well-defined. Both raise the same questions as *Two Sculptures for a Room by Palermo,* because they recall an idealized notion of the artist—this time as an all-seeing bird of prey—and both raise the specter of imperial power, if not the specifically Nazi use of such emblems. But like the two busts, *Eagle* is more than a device; it is a picture, which in its austere rendition of a majestic, if menacing, subject acknowledges the abiding potency of such images, even as it took its place in Broodthaers's exhaustive catalogue of similarly questionable emblems of authority. While Richter willingly offered the painting as a target for speculation on, and demystification of, aesthetic myths, he did not make it an easy target.[41]

Both *Eagle* and *Two Sculptures for a Room by Palermo* prefigure Richter's *48 Portraits* of 1971–72 (pages 161–171), the most sustained and unified series of painting the artist had so far undertaken. Richter planned the work to represent his country at the 1972 Venice Biennale and to fit the grand neoclassical spaces of the German national pavilion. The selection of Richter is a reminder that no matter how much he may have felt out of step with his contemporaries around this time, he was still very much an artist to reckon with in the minds of many people in the art world. Slightly smaller than *Eagle* but similar in format—a centered image with little space around it—each of the forty-eight heads that comprise the group was based on a photograph of a famous man found in an old encyclopedia. This was just the sort of "style-free" reference image for which Richter had earlier declared his preference, but which he had never before quoted so explicitly. While the organizational paradigm of the inventory suggests Broodthaers's influence, it is also true that Richter had already begun work on the paintings the year before he painted *Eagle.* His first essays in this format include two portraits of Sigmund Freud, one partially un-painted by a flurry of lines that blots out the psychiatrist's features like an uncontrollable eruption, the other a fuzzy but more faithful likeness. An additional five trial runs, or out-takes, from the final series of forty-eight are known to exist, among them a portrait of the French writer Henry de Montherlant, which is not listed in Richter's catalogue raisonné, and there are eight pages of *Atlas* containing 270 clipped images that were candidates for inclusion.

Much has been made of who was finally painted and who was not. In *Atlas* the subjects range from Gabriel García Lorca to Chou En-lai and from Niels Bohr to Jacob Burckhardt. The most historical figures are Edgar Allan Poe, Charles Baudelaire, Stephen Melville, Charles Darwin, Henrik Ibsen, Ivan Turgeniev, Richard Wagner, Giacomo Puccini, and Karl Marx; the most contemporary as of that time are Ho Chi Minh, Eugène Ionesco, Jean Genet, Truman Capote, and Samuel Beckett (who appears twice, as does Bohr), Jean Anouilh, Dag Hammarskjöld, and Bertrand Russell. Among prominent Germans not already mentioned are Bertolt Brecht, Hermann Hesse, Paul Hindemith, Thomas and Heinrich Mann, Ludwig Mies van der Rohe, and Richard Strauss. Notably absent, with the exception of the architect and painter Le Corbusier, are visual

Gerhard Richter. **Untitled (Portrait of Henry de Montherlant).** 1971. Oil on canvas, 27⅝ × 21⅞" (70.2 × 55.5 cm). The Museum of Modern Art, New York. Gift of Ronald S. Lauder

Gerhard Richter. **48 Portraits.**
1971–72. Oil on canvas; 48 paintings,
each, 27⁹⁄₁₆ × 21¹¹⁄₁₆" (70 × 55 cm).
GR 324-1 through 324-48. Museum
Ludwig, Cologne. Installation view at
the Venice Biennale, 1972.

artists. There are no women. Of those thus far named only Thomas Mann and Puccini take their place in the completed pantheon. The others are a curious assortment of the internationally renowned and the all but forgotten; starting with H. G. Wells and ending with Anton Bruckner, they proceed by way of Mikhail Sadoveanu, William James, Hans Pfitzner, Paul Claudel, Franz Kafka, Patrick Maynard Stuart Blackett, Isidor Isaac Rabi, Saint-John Perse, Graham Greene, and Karl Manne Siegbahn. If this sampling runs long, it still remains only a fraction of the people Richter considered painting or painted. If a pattern fails to emerge that, too, is characteristic of the whole, which, ultimately seems not to have one but instead is an arbitrary enumeration with the potential for willful editing or infinite expansion.

Judging from the results, Richter's most sweeping decision was to eliminate all political thinkers and leaders, although a collotype print of Mao Tse-tung, produced in a large unsigned edition in 1968, anticipates *48 Portraits* and represents that social sphere. (Besides Chou En-lai, Ho Chi Minh, Hammarskjöld, and Gustav Stresemann, the other readily recognizable statesmen in the *Atlas* group are David Lloyd George, V. I. Lenin, Mao, Mahatma Gandhi, and Leon Trotsky.) The absence of artists effectively constitutes Richter's refusal to provide any information that might be interpreted as an aesthetic genealogy (at least until the 1990s: a recent print titled *Survey* of 1998 features a markedly idiosyncratic selection of artists, architects, writers, composers, and philosophers who have contributed to Western culture from the Middle Ages to the present). After that, it is harder to divine Richter's motives for excluding certain possibilities, unless we assume that his overall purpose in the work—anonymity and indifference—would have been undermined if he had permitted his personal tastes or intellectual preferences to be discernable in the final array.

Richter has offered few clues about what he may have had in mind, but he has spoken several times of a need to identify father figures. In purely private terms, the issue of fatherhood is an admittedly unresolved one. Uneasiness about his own father is clear from remarks made about his family situation as he was growing up. "Why should I have painted only this photo of him?" he asked himself with reference to *Horst and His Dog* of 1965 (page 122), where his father appears as an amiable tipsy buffoon.[42] Moreover, three recent portraits of his own son, titled *Moritz* (2000–2001), have an uncanny atmosphere about them, while expressing a bewilderment seemingly at odds with the scrap-book cuteness of their subject (pages 276–279). Whatever Oedipal drama they foretell, Richter has acknowledged that "it wasn't until Moritz was born that I started to know what a father is."[43]

Nevertheless, in *48 Portraits* the psychological compulsion to establish a cultural paternity is inextricably connected to the historical disasters of National Socialism and Stalinism. This is true not just in the sense that such pictorial halls of fame are a staple of totalitarian art, and it is important to recall that Richter himself had once painted Stalin's likeness on banners, while serial portraits of Marx, Engels, Lenin, Stalin, and Mao were frequently seen on the mastheads of Communist newspapers published by the student Left in the West as well as in news photographs. (In his capacity as a Maoist agit prop artist, Immendorff painted such a line up

Ich wollte Künstler werden:

Ich träumte davon, in der Zeitung zu stehen, von vielen Ausstellungen, und natürlich wollte ich etwas "Neues" in der Kunst machen. Mein Leitfaden war der Egoismus.

Jörg Immendorff. **"I Wanted to Be an Artist" ["Ich wollte Künstler werden"].** 1971. Acrylic on canvas, 35½ × 31½" (90 × 80 cm). Courtesy Michael Werner Gallery, New York and Cologne

around 1973.) In other words, Richter had chosen a format that evoked not only the library but the assembly hall and the street. Then, reversing that model, Richter expelled all politicians and concentrated instead on writers, composers, scientists, and philosophers whose achievements in almost every case represented a humanist tradition intolerable to authoritarian regimes, even when, as in the case of Tchaikovsky or Bruckner, their works were co-opted by the Communists or the Nazis.

The word *humanism* is, of course, a suspect term in postmodern discourse; however, it is not being used ironically, nor did the artist intend his pictures to been viewed ironically. Richter's panorama of faces neither advocates any particular view of culture, nor condemns any. (The distance separating the world view of the deeply conservative Catholic poet and playwright Paul Claudel and that of innovative modern allegorist Franz Kafka could hardly be greater, as is that which lies between the composers Puccini and Hindemith.) In this context, rather than signaling the *pro forma* celebration of passively agreed upon values, the invocation of the Western tradition and the concept of humanism opens a debate about the content of those terms in relation to specific examples. Nevertheless, in the most antideclamatory way, *48 Portraits* makes intellectual and artistic endeavor its subject, and did so at a time when the cultural past was under widespread attack. Standing between his youthful experience of societies in which intellectual and artistic work were routinely denigrated unless it served the party in power and the ongoing culture wars of the 1960s and 1970s, Richter compiled a pictorial roster of the kind of men who had been or might be sacrificed to the imperatives of ideology.

The fact that they are *all* dead white males has exposed Richter's selection to criticism from several quarters. His less-than-satisfying justification has been that in the 1960s feminist—or for that matter multicultural—awareness was not so developed, and that in any case the inclusion of women—Virginia Woolf or Eve Curie, for example—would have broken the formal compositional unity of his parade of men in dark suits.[44] The more obvious explanation is that the cultural legacy of the West is or, until recently, has been overwhelming if not overbearingly patriarchal, and that aside from the fact that Richter is not a reformer, his purpose was to represent that heritage. His way of doing so—by projecting an aggressively neutral Pop, almost Warholian, appropriation of mass-produced imagery back into history (his frieze is unlike Warhol's multiple portraits of celebrities in every other respect)—is hardly reverential. (Warhol's *Thirteen Most Wanted Men* again comes to mind.) Nor was the initial installation of the piece in Venice, where the images were symmetrically arranged in a single row around the curved walls of the German pavilion, with Kafka in the middle staring straight ahead, and the heads to his left and right gradually turning as nearly frontal poses flowed into three-quarter poses. Since then, Richter has laid them out or ranked them in ways that avoid such visual gags, emphasizing instead the primitive system of the list or grid as a means of bringing order to the disorder of history.

Once again, Buchloh's interpretation focuses narrowly on the Nazi past and the psychological transference effected by "the destruction of the paternal image" and "the adulation of the image of the male *Führer*."[45] Using Freud as a stalking horse for his own antagonism toward any reconstitution of old hierarchies, Buchloh writes of the dilemma confronting Germans who came of age in the 1930s and 1940s: "For any subsequent construction of a paternal image or national legacy to be accepted, it would have to bear the marks of that traumatic experience and its subsequent secondary elaborations. That is, it would have to shift continuously between negating the 'natural' paternal image of the Germans as fascists and laboring to construct a radically different *paternal* legacy and a post-traditional *national* identity—while emphasizing at the same time the artificiality of any such retroactively constructed positive paternal identification. . . . (It is simply not possible to construct a cohesive cultural canon out of these figures. . . .) The resulting instability, if not actual breakdown of this fiction of a transnational liberal-humanist community was, then, as integral to its constitution as were the careful omissions that guaranteed its success as an acceptable fiction of paternal history. . . . Richter's pandemic collective functions simultaneously, then, as a secondary elaboration of the process of identity construction and as a manifesto of disidentification."[46] To some extent, Richter's own comments on *48 Portraits* confirm Buchloh's reading. Acknowledging the hostility with which some have responded to these enigmatic images, Richter has said: "In addition, you have the psychological or subjective moment of the father problem. This affects all of society. I am not talking about myself because that would be rather uninteresting, but the absence of the father is a typical German problem. That is the reason for such agitation, why it has such a disquieting effect."[47]

Moreover, Richter has spoken of the series as being emblematic of a break in tradition which cannot be mended. In that light, *48 Portraits* is "not a restoration. It is a reference to this loss. It is a question of whether or not we do something. I don't believe it comes back."[48] But the difference in tone between his commentary and Buchloh's is striking, representing a difference in generational experience and perspective. On the one hand, Richter lived through National Socialism and Communism and emerged with a longing to fill the gaps that totalitarian culture created. On the other, Buchloh looks back on history with unmitigated horror and an ineradicable antipathy toward anything that might be construed as a figure of authority. In that sense, Buchloh resembles Richter's characterization of "people [who] are always upset when confronted with something traditional and conservative. It's not considered to be part of our time . . . reactionary."[49] Whether or not that description fits Buchloh, it is obvious that Richter has neither painted a "manifesto of disidentification" nor a manifesto of any kind. He is not an ideologue, and Buchloh's essentially ideological cooptation of his work is too narrow to account for the regret and pessimism that cling to these otherwise impassive images— regret at having been deprived of the chance of identifying with any part of the cultural legacy that fascism and Communism suppressed or distorted, pessimism over the prospects of reconnecting with and extending that legacy in the context of reflex hostility to anything "traditional and conservative."[50]

For many postmodernists, the philosopher Walter Benjamin's ideas about "the work of art in the age of mechanical reproduction" and Theodor Adorno's critique of the "culture industry" have been rephrased to promote agendas that press the cause of artistic tendencies that capitalize on previous ruptures with the past and anticipate even more definitive ones, in the interests of theoretically post-traditional aesthetic practices. Anything short of this is dismissed as nostalgic, melancholic, and retrograde. Although Richter is in no sense a Marxist, his understanding of what has been lost to culture and his often melancholy, though never nostalgic, feelings about the predicament in which art now finds itself are closer in spirit to the Marxist writings of Benjamin and Adorno than those of many contemporary polemicists who selectively quote them. One might even go so far as to say that as phantoms they bracket *48 Portraits*: Benjamin's "loss of aura" being the vacuumlike anti-aura in which the series as a whole hovers and Adorno's insistence on difficulty being the demand that these works—like the whole of Richter's oeuvre—address in an equally uncompromising way to all who labor in the culture industry, including critics on the Left made uncomfortable by Richter's intransigent ambiguities.

The measure of Richter's ambivalences and of his determination not to succumb to the temptations of nostalgic pastiche—a major tendency in conservative postmodern art from Francesco Clemente to Anselm

Kiefer, to name only its most skillful exemplars—can be found in Richter's *Annunciation after Titian* of 1973 (page 183). There are five versions of this painting. The first, where the image is clearly legible but diffuse and overly saturated with warm tones, is the closest to the original. In the second, the image has been almost totally obscured by un-painting. The third, fourth, and fifth versions, uniformly larger than the others, are also un-painted, but the blurring is never so complete as in the second. Richter's motive for making a work based on the Titian was a common one among artists with a gift for copying: the wish to live with a favorite painting. It should also be remembered that copying has long been a basic component of traditional studio education and, prior to the twentieth century, was a means of disseminating unique images by the masters. Richter undertook the anachronistic project of reproducing the Titian, he recalled, "simply because I liked it so much. I saw it in Venice and thought: I'd like to have that for myself. To start with I only meant to make a copy, so that I could have a beautiful painting at home and with it a piece of that period, all that potential beauty and sublimity."[51] But the act of painting quickly made the change in historical circumstances apparent, and not because of any technical deficiency on his part, but because of changes in the artist's relation to the process of painting and to the presumed inviolability of the perfect model. "Then," Richter said, "my copy went wrong, and the pictures that finally emerged went to show that it just can't be done any more, not even by way of a copy. All I could do was to break the whole thing down and show that it's no longer possible."[52] In hindsight, one might assume that this "failure" was a foregone conclusion, or that Richter in some way set out to demonstrate the impossibility of reviving the paintings of the glorious dead, but the truth is that Richter had to arrive at this impasse. Moreover, his point of departure was unselfconscious admiration, and his desire was to possess a work manifesting certain qualities that he wanted to introduce into his art, if only by overt emulation.

Two additional factors enter in. "The central problem of my painting is light," Richter wrote in the early 1960s.[53] Although he had already painted light sources—a lamp, a chandelier, the morning or evening sky— Richter had never before chosen an image whose *theme* was light. Furthermore that theme was metaphorical and the light divine. This is the first of his pictures with an unequivocally religious iconography. Given the results, Richter's decision to copy an Annunciation was unexpectedly, or perhaps intuitively, appropriate. A standard medieval explanation of the Immaculate Conception was that God's insemination of the Virgin resembled the passage of the sun's rays through clear glass. It was in the literal sense an act of pure inspiration, akin to the inspiration artists were said to receive from powers higher than they. Not only are reports of virgin births rare in our day, such direct transmissions of creative energy are similarly uncommon. Communication between divinity and genius has ceased, and communication between the demiurges of art history and contemporary artists is tenuous at best. The vessel of painting has clouded and the images projected into it are refracted, fragmented, and dissolved. Richter, thus, looked at Titian's Annunciation "as through a glass darkly," and we, looking over his shoulder, contemplate the once radiant masterpiece in the same smudged lens.

Richter's apparent detour into art history or art-historical ways of seeing earned him the enmity, or at least the suspicions, of a number people in the contemporary art world. Even the portrait he made in 1971 of the burnt-out Warhol superstar *Brigid Polk* (page 176) has a remoteness that is warm and atmospheric rather than coolly technological, especially in contrast to Warhol's gratingly intense silkscreen pictures of denizens of the Factory such as Polk. Nevertheless, this new-old dimension to Richter's painting found favor with some, notably the English Conceptual artists Gilbert & George, whose "living sculpture" performances had been anticipated by Richter and Lueg in their "Demonstration for Capitalist Realism." Avowedly "reactionary" artists who affected out-of-date bourgeois clothes and proper manners and, in 1970, had depicted themselves in bucolic settings with a text that archly declared, in the age of anti-aestheticism, "To be with Art is all we ask," Gilbert & George were the first to take a positive interest in his landscape paintings.[54]

Although he began painting landscapes for his own pleasure, much as he had tried to copy Titian, Richter was well aware that this "subversive attempt to paint beautiful pictures" represented something more than a private digression from avant-garde practice. It was, instead, a quiet act of defiance directed at those who traditionally claimed a monopoly on "subversive" means and ends.[55] Richter's explanations of why he did the "unthinkable" can be disarmingly straightforward. Asked about his interest in a genre that many of his contemporaries were certain was a thing of the past or, worse, a pastime, Richter answered: "Just because landscape is beautiful, it's probably the most terrific thing there is. . . . I felt like painting something beautiful."[56] His refusal to be pigeon-holed has further stymied those who have pressed hard to question his motives. "By using so many Romantic motifs—clouds, water, infinite spaces without a foreground or background—are you deliberately inviting the suspicion that you're a neo-Romantic," one incredulous interviewer inquired. "No, certainly not," the artist replied. "To do that, I would have had to think things out before I painted, and that's just not possible."[57]

There is an evasiveness to these responses, perhaps, but they are essentially truthful. Richter knew what he was doing and knew that it had broad implications, yet he was not about to fall into the trap of discussing of his work in terms that immediately consigned it to pre-defined aesthetic categories. Undoubtedly the German Romantics of the eighteenth and nineteenth centuries—the Dresden-born Caspar David Friedrich, in particular—had a profound impact on Richter when he was still a student, but the Romantic influence goes deeper than surface resemblances between Friedrich's scenic views and Richter's. The differences between the two have less to do with how the paintings look than with what we are encouraged to read or discouraged from reading into them. Friedrich's works are sharply focused, linear, almost brittle and usually contain a stand-in for the viewer, whereas Richter's are diffuse and seldom portray such surrogates for the viewer. The crucial distinctions, therefore, rest on assumptions the artist and the public make about the worlds these paintings ostensibly depict and about humanity's possible place in them. Thus, when Richter says, "A painting by Caspar David Friedrich is not a thing of the past. What is past is only the set of circumstances that allowed it to be painted. . . . It is therefore quite possible to paint like Caspar David Friedrich today,"[58] he is simultaneously defending his right to paint as he sees fit and preparing the way for a fundamental reinterpretation of the type of painting he has seemingly resuscitated.

On occasion, Richter can sound very much like his Romantic antecedents: "I believe that art has a kind of rightness, as in music, when we hear whether or not a note is false. And that's why classical pictures which are right in their own terms are so necessary for me. In addition to that there's nature which also has this rightness."[59] Left unstated in this equation, however, is an important aesthetic possibility: the *intentional* wrongness of an image that apparently strives toward rightness, the false note deliberately struck to disrupt a prevailing harmony. Thus, where Friedrich and the artists of his era imbued nature with human emotions—indulging in what John Ruskin called the Romantic fallacy—Richter stresses a simultaneous and disconcerting awareness of nature's inherent beauty and its complete disregard for human needs, desires, and fears.

Tourist (with 1 Lion) of 1975 (page 177) is the most graphic expression of this implacable indifference—one of a group of pictures based on published film stills of a person being killed by a lion at a French safari park. One can barely make out the legs and torso of the victim and the head and shoulders of the lion in the hazy off-key, off-register reds, yellows, and greens. We are watching death at work, but not cruelty, since the predator is doing what comes naturally, attacking the unfortunate individual who has crossed the line designed to protect people from a dangerous reality. The artificiality of the color effectively highlights the catastrophic falseness of the circumstances. Nothing in the manner in which the image is rendered invites pity, or exploits horror. What is disturbing is how reasonable and unstoppable the mauling seems to have been under the circumstances.

Likewise, when Richter painted a man killed by a block of ice in *Dead* of 1963 (page 111), no special emotion was attached to the image, nor does ice symbolize anything specific in the evocative but still straightforwardly photographic *Iceberg in Fog* of 1982 (page 189), despite the degree to which it recalls Friedrich's famous painting of a sailing vessel sundered by mounding ice floes, *The Sea of Ice* (1923–25). And yet that parallel contributes much to the aura and meaning of Richter's work. Such was Richter's fascination with that canvas, he said, that in 1981: "I even went all the way to Greenland, because C. D. Friedrich painted that beautiful picture of *The Wreck of the 'Hope.'* I took hundreds of photos up there and barely one picture came out of it."[60] Richter's inability to capture the essence of that scene photographically is indicative not only of differences in technical approach but of the discrepancies between Friedrich's aesthetic expectations and his own. Friedrich's theme was awesome forces greater than humankind, but it is a human presence that gives them scale and imbues them with meaning. The emotional power of Richter's treatment of the same situation derives from the mesmerizing lifelessness—the total un-humanity—of the subject. Whatever feeling we may try to invest in these inanimate objects is returned to us intact, like a shout or cry without

Caspar David Friedrich. **The Sea of Ice.** c. 1823–25. Oil on canvas, 38½ × 50½" (96.7 × 126.9 cm). Hamburger Kunsthalle, Hamburg

a transforming echo, making the inappropriateness of our attempt to link those objects to psychological states unnervingly manifest.

Thus, no matter how picturesque an image may be, a barrier imposes itself between the scene depicted and the viewer's longing to make himself or herself a part of it and at home in nature. To a lesser extent this also holds true for the bucolic *Barn* of 1984 (page 200) and *Meadowland* of 1985 (page 201), the beckoning remoteness of *Davos S.* of 1981 (page 188), or even the miragelike *Venice (Staircase)* of 1985 (page 202). The *Davos S.* canvas is a seamlessly illusionistic reprise of the iconography of Richter's mountain paintings of 1968. Perceptually, the image involves a photographic flattening of volumes and perspectival depths, and the smoothing out of the painted surface so that we can neither enter the space nor visually grasp painterly details within it. Conceptually, Roland Barthes's definition of the photographic condition as "the that has been" of experiential reality is once again germane. These vistas never were and never will be there for us; they were there for the artist just as long as it took to snap the picture and are only available to him now through the combination of that imperfect documentation and his equally imperfect memory.

In traditional landscape painting, as in traditional still life or portraiture, duration becomes a salient part of the image, which embodies evidence of the time it took the artist to see and record his impressions. Losing oneself in painterly time is the sensuous and imaginative catalyst for losing oneself in painterly space, be it the naturalistic landscapes of Friedrich and Camille Corot or the stylized ones of Vincent van Gogh and Georges Seurat. For Richter, where the camera intercedes, one reality is incrementally synthesized into its facsimile by traditional procedures and telescoped into an instant. The execution of the painting itself is subordinated to that mechanical abbreviation of the process of looking. This temporal implosion of the image and the psychological interruptions that accompany it were precisely what Richter wanted when he initially turned to snapshots and media clippings; but his subjects also tended to be easily recognizable as inherently photographable. This was also the case with his postcardlike landscapes in which the gap between two pictorial situations—the photographic and the painterly—is maintained but accentuated in the later landscapes. There, the tensions increase between the desire for one thing (a beautiful imaginary place to which the viewer might escape) and the actuality of another (a beautiful painting that checks that escape and makes the viewer acutely conscious of its impossibility).

The viewer is thus left in a state of perpetual limbo bracketed by exigent pleasures and an understated but unshakable nihilism. Those who approach Richter's landscapes with a yearning for the exotic or the pastoral are greeted by images that first intensify that desire and then deflect it. This is by design: "Of course, my landscapes are not only beautiful or nostalgic, with a Romantic or classical suggestion of lost Paradises, but above all 'untruthful.'. . . By 'untruthful' I mean the glorifying way we look at Nature—Nature, which in all its forms is always against us, because it knows no meaning, no pity, no sympathy, because it knows nothing and is absolutely mindless: the total antithesis of ourselves."[61] Still, the yearning persists, and the more lovely the painting the more likely it is to touch sophisticated viewers who already take nature's uncaring for granted but seek comfort in art. Richter anticipated that response, as well. Speaking for his audience as well as himself, the artist has said: "What I lack is the spiritual basis which undergirded Romantic painting. We have lost the feeling of God's omnipresence in Nature. For us, everything is empty. Yet, these paintings are still there. They still speak to us. We continue to love them, to use them, to have need of them."[62] Under these conditions, painting does not attempt to re-create the sense of divine or transcendent order upon which centuries of art were based but, rather, provides aesthetic solace for those it simultaneously disabuses of all metaphysical hope.

For critics or observers of the scene still convinced that modern art is a sequence of ruptures, each one more radical than the last, Richter's landscapes may seem at best a kind of fence-sitting between the old and the new, and at worst an intellectually adroit and technically masterful form of backsliding. However, these paintings are no more a throwback to lapsed aesthetic conventions than they are an ironical recapitulation and then dismantling of them. The Janus-like position Richter occupies, recognizes that those who work fully in the present always enter history in medias res. Looking both ways from such a position affords us a clearer perspective on the continuities and discontinuities of artistic practice than those available to anyone craning his or her neck to see the present from a vantage point in the hypothetical future or the reconstructed past. Richter's unwillingness to sacrifice tradition to the new is therefore based on an appreciation of the uses tradition retains and those it acquires in the here-and-now, rather than on a desire to emulate or hold onto a former understanding of it. Furthermore, his refusal to turn his back definitively on tradition is explicitly qualified by the knowledge that what has been done in one time cannot be repeated in another. On the contrary, as Richter made plain in notes to himself in 1983, the aesthetic proximity of the past stands as a challenge to living artists to respond on their own terms: "Traditional, supposedly old works of art are not old but contemporary. So long as we 'have' them, in the broadest sense of the word, they will never be outworn: neither are we setting something of equal stature alongside them, nor shall we match or surpass their quality. Their permanent presence compels us to produce something different, which is neither better nor worse, but which has to be different because we painted the Isenheim Altar yesterday. . . . This is not to say that it would be pointless to produce something similar to traditional work. But the better we know tradition—i.e., ourselves—and the more responsibly we deal with it, the better things we shall make similar, and the better things we shall make different."[63]

If Titian and Friedrich represented two models for painting that haunted Richter in the mid-1970s and drove him to test the limits of their actual viability, then modernist abstraction represented the third. From 1968 through 1976 the monochrome preoccupied him, but by the latter part of the decade it became apparent to him that there was no way he could paint himself out of the gray corner he had been led into by the example of minimalism and his own anti-expressive inclinations. As frequently happens in art history, the only alternative for an artist caught in such a *cul de sac* is to permit himself to do all or some of the things previously proscribed by creative habit, temperament, or aesthetic ideology. Willem de Kooning said it best. Confronted with a theoretical ban on figuration in the 1950s, de Kooning, having already spent several years painting pure abstractions, reasoned: "If you take the attitude that it is not possible to do something, you have to prove it by doing it."[64] Richter's dissatisfaction with the *grisaille* world in which he had lingered and his frustration with the orthodoxies that grew up around reductivism pushed him at first tentatively and then forcefully in the opposite direction. According to him: "The gray monochromes were the most complete ones I could imagine. The welcome and only correspondence to indifference, to a lack of conviction, the negation of commitment, anomie. After the gray paintings, after the dogma of 'fundamental painting' whose purist and moralizing aspects fascinated me to a degree bordering on self-denial, all I could do was start all over again. This was the beginning of the first color sketches."[65]

These sketches consisted of subtly brushed renderings of sections of richly textured Art Informel paintings that have not survived. The hues are generally saturated, the value contrasts extreme. Working from photographs in between sessions devoted to his last gray abstractions, Richter called these canvases and those that followed Abstract Pictures. The choice of title is significant in that it reinforces the impression conveyed by the illusionistic description of shoals, riptides, and cresting waves of pigment that these are pictures of gestural paintings not of the spontaneously eventful real thing. To spectators enthralled by formalist notions of pure opticality here were paintings that unabashedly lured the eye—and unapologetically deceived it. The first of these canvases, *Abstract Picture* of 1976 (page 184) demonstrates this bait-and-switch technique in a small format, while *Abstract Picture* of 1977 (page 185), which reproduces a detail from the top part of the former picture in greatly increased scale, shows how the same technique operates on a large one, with almost Rothko-like expanses of harmonious reds and browns. Another *Abstract Picture* of 1977 (page 186) introduces further complications, as Richter incorporates a collage technique in these nonobjective works that he had generally avoided in his figurative images. In it he has pieced together painterly passages, shapes, layers, perforations, and shadows from several photographic sources much as James Rosenquist had done in his billboard-inspired Pop paintings of the 1960s but without the mass-media referents. Late that same year and into the next Richter turned in his spare time to watercolors for the first time since his youth, and the floating quality of the forms in his oils and the seemingly translucent depth of the intervals between them reproduce the effects of that aqueous medium.

As with his landscapes, Richter was initially reluctant to exhibit the new Abstract Pictures (Beuys was among the few colleagues to have seen and approved of them), and finally did so in 1978 at a place as remote from the art world he knew as could be imagined, the Nova Scotia College of Art and Design, in Halifax, on the northeast coast of Canada, where he had been invited to teach on the recommendation of Buchloh, who was also an instructor there. During the late 1970s through the 1980s Richter's association with Buchloh (combined with his ongoing relationship with Konrad Fischer) brought him into contact with a wide group of conceptually oriented artists among whom he was the only painter. They included Lawrence Weiner, Dan Graham, Jeff Wall, and Isa Genzken whom he had met briefly through Buchloh in the early 1970s when she was a student. Richter and Genzken met again in 1977—in the final days of the "German Autumn" that saw the deaths in prison of three members of the Baader-Meinhof group, a subject Richter would return to a decade later when he painted *October 18, 1977*—and in 1982 they married.

The tension between Richter's sensibility and that of his circle of friends coupled with his own uneasiness about "showing his hand" in painting, informed his new work in essential ways. Speaking of his figurative works, Richter said: "Painting is the form of the picture, you might say. The picture is the depiction, and painting is the technique for shattering it."[66] While his Abstract Pictures were also based on ready-made images, painterly affect engendered by the history and mythology of modernism clung to them; and he was determined to detach it. In contrast to his other works, Richter recalled: "I didn't quite dare to consider them regular paintings. I looked at them as purely subjective. That is why I copied them to objectify them."[67] For eyes accustomed to emotionally heated Action Painting or exultant Color Field abstraction, Richter's masterful but abrupt cooling down of the rhetoric of postwar art can be even more disconcerting than Pop or Minimalism because it seemed at first glance to have employed that rhetoric. But Richter had, in effect, removed the body as the agency of the psyche or spirit, and confined its duties to that of image maker in a puzzling iconoclastic enterprise, which exploited reflex feelings of existential or transcendental identification only to quell them with a dazzling display of painterly ability conspicuously free of any drama, struggle, or ecstatic abandon. In contrast to Pollock, the painter was never "in" his painting nor, given Richter's opinions on the matter, did he ever think of himself as "nature." In contrast to Rothko, the absolute was not merely veiled by Richter, it had retreated beyond reach—into painting.

In conversation with Buchloh, Richter described his abstractions as, "An assault on the falsity and the religiosity of the way people glorified abstraction, with such phony reverence."[68] "Devotional art," he called it, "all those squares—Church handicrafts."[69] But despite these scathing remarks, Richter was, as always, of two minds about the fundamental issue of abstraction's capacity to represent the unrepresentable. Furthermore, his thinking on the subject evolved even though some critics, stuck in the period when Richter took a hard line, have been loath to acknowledge that evolution. Thus, in response to questions about Rothko from the art historian and curator Mark Rosenthal he explained his simultaneous admiration for Rothko's "seriousness" and his earlier distrust of his work, which Richter had considered "both too holy and too decorative," although he also confessed that, "I am less antagonistic to 'the holy,' to the spiritual experience, these days. It

Gerhard Richter at work on "Detail" ["Ausschnitt"]. 1971.

is part of us, and we need that quality."[70] In short, Richter is prepared now, as he was not then, to entertain the idea that the sentiments abstraction awakens need not be judged on logical grounds, but rather on their psychological resonance. Abstraction cannot claim to embody the absolute as it did from Kandinsky, Malevich, Mondrian, to the Abstract Expressionists, but it can lend substance to otherwise elusive aspects about our makeup. In the late 1970s and early 1980s, however, Richter remained uncomfortable with Rothko's transcendental approach. "While I certainly prefer that to cynicism," he said, "there was a kind of science fiction coming from Rothko's darkness that was Wagnerian or had a narrative side, which bothered me."[71] His answer was to further fictionalize this science fiction, and thereby make all the artifice and suspension of belief involved explicit.

In this regard, Richter made a distinction between Newman and Rothko that hinged on the comparative austerity and materiality of Newman's canvases—their ability to comprise both aesthetic fact and metaphysical fiction. He said: "Barnett Newman was always important. . . . Newman was an ideal, because he created these big, clear, sublime fields that I could never have managed. He was my complete opposite."[72] Nevertheless, in 1979 Richter painted two huge mural-sized canvases—*Brushstroke (in Blue)* and *Brushstroke (in Red)* , as well as two smaller but by no means small sketches for them—that resemble the "zips," or painted lines, of the kind Newman used to bifurcate his paintings. Like the "Detail" painting of 1971, though, Richter's two Brushstrokes are vastly enlarged representations of oil paint traveling across the surface rather than the gargantuan marks they appear to be, simulacra of a stripped-down Abstract Expressionist gesture that amaze by their sweep and their impossible trompe l'oeil effects but do not—and were not intended to—inspire awe in the manner of Newman's mammoth painting *Vir Heroicus Sublimis* (1950). Indeed, the orientation and scale of the strokes—horizontal rather than vertical—reverses the equation set by Newman's anthropomorphic play of upright bands against a horizon of color. Richter's exaggerated blow-up of a seam of pigment violates the classical ideal of the sublime as an experience of the infinite because it is impossible to imagine this line going on forever. Once again Richter's paintings constitute a deliberate contradiction in terms that simultaneously energize and lock those terms into a perplexing but evocative stalemate.

Before Richter began painting Abstract Pictures most people would not have thought of him as a colorist, although his grays were finely calibrated and sometimes blushed with pale blue, violet, or earth tones. Since then, it is hard to think of him as anything other than one of the great colorist of late twentieth-century painting. Whatever resistance to that designation there might be may be explained by the *kind* of color Richter favors and the role it plays in enhancing the disquieting psychological effects of his work. When Richter talks about the relation between music and painting he has two extremes in mind, Bach and Mozart on the one hand, and on the other, Schönberg and more unexpectedly the "noise" composer Glenn Branca. For anyone predisposed to judge musicality by harmony, and an artist's gifts for color by soothing optical chords, Richter's preferences among composers stand as a warning. None of the available precedents or labels—most obviously Fauvism and Expressionism—account for the stridency of Richter's combinations of chlorophyll greens, sulfuric yellows, ice-cool blues, raw vermilions, and all the ragged and gritty combinations they achieve when dragged across one another, or when slate grays and dirty whites are dragged over them. For Americans habituated to French color, from Impressionism to Henri Matisse, Richter's clashing hues sting the eye, but you will not really find them in works by Ernst Ludwig Kirchner or Franz Marc either. The painter and critic Stephen Ellis hit the mark when he drew a connection between Richter's palette and the "luminous, acid color of Dürer, Altdorfer and Grünewald,"[73] masters of the German Renaissance in all its uneasy, frequently violent, and occasionally somber glory. In that context and particularly in the abstractions of the 1980s and 1990s, Richter's clear, corrosive Danube School colors are often called upon to cut through the dense, chromatically saturated curtain of paint that sometimes mimics the thickness and light absorbency of fuel oil or tar. The light in Richter's painting is northern rather than Mediterranean, complete with the heavy darkness that alternates with crystalline brightness during the long nights and short days of Northern European fall and spring. In the 1970s, the art historian Robert Rosenblum argued that Abstract Expressionism had its origins not only in the School of Paris, but also harkened back to the German Romantics. If so, then Richter's response to Newman, Pollock, and de Kooning may be seen as that American strain of the Northern Sublime repatriated by photographic and painterly means that further mutate Romanticism's generative poetic and pictorial traits.[74]

By 1980, the technique in Richter's Abstract Pictures had shifted from rendering alone to the direct application of paint with a brush or hard edge over rendered passages, and from there progressively toward paintings whose visible layers were almost entirely gestural or pigment loaded. This gradual obliteration of the illusionistic underpainting can be seen in the sequence of works that begins with *Clouds* of 1982 (pages 190–191) and continues on through *Marian* of 1983 (page 199), the two Abstract Pictures of 1984 (pages 192, 196), *Bush* of 1985 (page 197) and *AB, St. Bridget* of 1988 (pages 204–205). The atmospheric quality of these paintings ranges from summery pyrotechnics and autumnal tempests to a crepuscular winteriness. Some, like *Marian*, are ravishingly beautiful; others, like *Bush*, are almost off-putting in their churning brushmarks and turgid contrasts of green and violet, as if Richter had set out to demonstrate that compelling "ugliness" was not only within his grasp, but a condition that painting and lovers of painting must accept in exchange for the more easily digested products of his new way of working.

"Constructions, not expressions," was how Ellis described Richter's abstractions, and the distinction holds, especially in the context of the "New Wild," or neo-Expressionist, work that flooded the galleries in Europe and America in the 1980s. Richter's engagement with expressionist-type painting antedates this movement by several years, but he was doubtless aware of this current as it began to well up around him and as he was lumped together with its exponents in a number of exhibitions as the tendency crested. As ever, his reactions were at once self-protective and laissez-faire, caustic and understanding: "I'm no 'wild one.' [I] find it irritating when the most obvious stupidity too is washed high on the 'wild' wave . . . but it has always been that way in times without orientation. One thing will still be visible in the 'wild' paintings even in Kassel; that they have broken out of something that was totally ossified. With an audacious stroke of the hand, they have destroyed dogmas that appeared to be internationally unshakeable. I certainly think that's very good. And seen in this way, I regret the process of domestication of the wild ones that sets in now, and promotes so much harmlessness."[75] Thus, Richter discreetly nodded to the rising generation in the process of brushing aside the settled aesthetic wisdom of Minimal, Conceptual, and other "progressive" postmodernisms. If he did not care for the work they produced—indeed, he found most of it distasteful—he at least acknowledged its appearance as a vital sign, though one that was unlikely to survive the embrace of art world institutions.

But while the atavistic "wild ones" ostensibly mined raw feeling, Richter's paintings were not only well "cooked" but carefully prepared. Richter never simply went at the canvas, brush in hand. For him spontaneous invention always required a foil. To explain his method he contrasted it to that of Pollock, Newman, and company: "The Abstract Expressionists were amazed at the pictorial quality of their productions, the wonderful world that opens up when you just paint. . . . But the problem is this: not to generate any old thing with all the rightness and spontaneity of Nature, but to produce highly specific pictures with

Gerhard Richter. Work in progress: an early state of one of the Abstract Pictures of 2000.

highly specific messages (were it not for this, painting would be the simplest thing in the world, since in Nature any old blot is perfectly right and correct). Even so, I have to start with the 'blot,' and not with the new content."[76]

Lest anyone suppose that Richter's blots are kernels or spontaneous eruptions of new content, it should be underscored that many are painted in styles categorically different from the final image, and some are painted this way in anticipation of radical changes. In numerous cases, for example, Richter has sacrificed fully developed figurative works on his way to making abstract pictures. In most instances overpainting of the original image is complete, promising that art historians, conservators, and forensic aestheticians of the future will have a field day X-raying Richter's canvases in search of what lies buried under their heavy sediment of pigment. In *Blanket* of 1988 (page 224), however, one can clearly make out in the margins of the predominantly white painting the shadowy forms of the second version of *Hanged* (1988) from *October 18, 1977*—a picture of the Baader-Meinhof group member, Gudrun Ensslin, as she was found dead in her cell. The sheet of white paint that has been pulled across the surface functions as a shroud, and in that sense contributes new meaning to the appropriated photographic subject matter. But more often than not, additional layers have no such metaphorical relation to what lies beneath, as Richter obliterates the original image in successive sweeps of his scraper.

In other instances, photographic documentation of Richter's studio shows him boldly blocking in abstract compositions keyed to the brightest hues that, by turns, resemble Al Held's dynamic perspectival pictures; the patched-together compositions of contemporary artists such as Jerry Zeniuk (who exhibited with Konrad Fischer in the 1980s); or hard-edge color grids reminiscent of Bauhaus and Constructivist art that represent the next phase of Richter's Color Charts. None of these styles is characteristic of Richter's own finished work, and it is impossible to tell whether direct or indirect references to them at this stage in his process are the expression of an affinity for the diverse modes of abstraction represented or of a competitive drive to do and then undo various types of contemporary painting. Richter's motives may well have involved a little of both, but in the end these schematic preliminaries disappear under progressively denser coats of dragged paint that eliminate virtually all traces of improvisatory form building, for which they served as pretexts in the artist's creation of homemade modernist ready-mades.

Richter's laconic explanation of this procedure does not emphasize the destruction of what is there for destruction's sake so much as the erasing of something overly familiar and dissatisfying in the hope that erasure will open the way toward problematic painterly phenomena with unforeseen and unforeseeable consequences. And it bears repeating that anti-art is not his vocation. Richter's former comrade, Polke, has for many years capitalized on the mistakes photomechanical devices make, and in recent years he has taken to manipulating Xerox copiers to create distortions that are analogous to the warping effects of Richter's scraper. But whereas Polke's approach is akin to that of the Surrealists in privileging stylized transformations of the known, Richter is on the lookout for visual anomalies that free him from stylization while raising the stakes attached to recognition and acceptance.

A severe judge not only of the clichés of his metier but of his own facility, Richter effectively crosses out anything that pleases too easily or fails to match the highest historical standards of whatever manner he is pushing off from. As he put it: "People speak of my work in terms of virtuosity. That is an absolute exaggeration. Unfortunately I am not a virtuoso at all. I have a little taste. I have an eye for bad things."[77] In effect, Richter's practice rests not so much on skill as on connoisseurship and rigorous editing. And while it is untrue that he "mindlessly" copies photographs, or is "clumsy,"as he has said, the standards he has set for himself are impossibly high, and his inability to meet them results in violence aimed not at the image itself but at his inability to capture it.

The more exquisite the paradigm and the more vulnerable the subject, the more alarming this violence can be. The portraits Richter has recently painted of his wife Sabine and their child Moritz are perhaps the most striking examples of this. The paintings are tender images of a babe in arms in generally delicate tints; however, all but two of them have been skimmed or scored by a blade. "They are a little damaged," he said. "I really want to make beautiful paintings, [but] I couldn't quite hold it; they're not as beautiful as Vermeer."[78] And so he attacked them with a palette knife: "I had no choice. I didn't want to."[79] One might argue that under these circumstances stripping away or smearing paint is a studio expediency, but something other than gimmicks are at issue.

Elsewhere, Richter has described beauty as being a quality of "uninjured" things. In this case, the inadequacy of the image as it was originally painted was hidden by surface appeal that could not equal that of Richter's ideal, Vermeer—making that appeal a kind of inverse blemish that could only be corrected by explicitly wounding the picture and thereby exposing the anxiety that went into its creation and the pathos that attends any painful discrepancy between an imagined perfection and a flawed reality. In these examples that pathos is intensified by the intimacy of the theme and Richter's relation to the two people—sometimes naked—to whom the injury is done.

Richter's frustration must be taken seriously, not only when it comes to paintings of those near and dear to him but to paintings of others as well, and to abstraction. In this light, Richter's comments about Jasper Johns and the painterly tradition to which he belongs are revealing, as is his greater sympathy for Warhol. When Buchloh asked Richter about Johns, he answered: "Johns retained a culture of painting, which also has something to do with Paul Cézanne, and I rejected that."[80] The something that connects Johns to Cézanne is painterly touch. Richter's work does not depend on what Cézanne called his "little sensation" by which he meant the translation of increments of perception into discrete marks; nor does it exploit the nuances of superficially similar but subtly dissimilar brushstrokes as Johns's paintings do. Moreover, Richter is not, as he himself has been the first to admit, a virtuoso in this sense. As noted, the early phases of most paintings are quite broad or schematic. But every positive application of paint awaits its invigorating negation, a seemingly arbitrary adjustment that pulls the edges of the alternately meticulously or perfunctorily laid-in, but never completely resolved, forms together while throwing globs and viscous strings of oil color off like mud from the window of a car whose windshield wipers battle against muck spit up from the road. That same arbitrary action also sheers ridges of oil color in staccato patterns and opens up crevices in still-wet pigment; it trims the margins of the primed canvas to reveal the layered accumulation covering it and drags solid particles that cut channels into the moist paint; it skips over hollows accentuating the edges surrounding them, and lends a washboard roughness to other areas. In myriad ways it thus creates material and visual events that substitute themselves for the effects achieved by an artist whose work is based on touch without the intrusion of the self as the embodiment of such a talent or such methods. Warhol's silkscreening techniques did much the same for his work, and the squeegees Richter uses are rigid variants of the pliable ones Warhol employed. In that regard, both have brought to painting the kind of metamorphic alterations of the image that traditional printmakers calculate into their work. For painters who rely on touch, everything that matters happens as the paint goes down; for Richter as for Warhol, the transforming moment is when the second stage of the process selectively reinforces or diminishes details of the first stage, while giving rise to pictorial by-products that instantaneously become part of the final result (unless they are revised by yet another pass of the squeegee). In Warhol's oeuvre these procedural dividends provided grist for a keen graphic sensibility intent on dominating viewers with unavoidable, unforgettable yet disturbingly vacant emblems of visual power. In the work of Richter, who possesses perfect pitch for controlled accident, they can be lavish, hyperkinetic, harrowing, or lyrical. In any form they are the stuff of visual poetry.

From 1977 through 1987, Richter concentrated his efforts on Abstract Pictures, interspersed with occasional landscapes or clusters of landscapes. Between 1982 and 1983, two other subjects preoccupied him: candles singly, in pairs, or in groups of three, and skulls, always one at a time and once in combination with a candle. The candles, with one exception cropped above the candle-holder, burn against a muted background in two tones of brown or gray. The skulls, bathed in what appears to be natural light that is alternately warm and cool, sit on a barren table top or sill, right-side up or upside down. The ambience of both subjects is still and austere. The skull has an alabaster or ivory sheen. The flames seem to tilt ever so slightly, and the molten wax below the wick glows. Although the candles might have come from a restaurant table, neither they nor the skulls seem contemporary, yet they are not obviously of any other time either. One hesitates to state the obvious logical conclusion because it sounds so trite, but in the most problematic ways possible Richter has made them timeless, as if the only way to achieve that point without sentimentality (while simultaneously suggesting the brevity of life) is to seem to be quoting the old-master *vanitas* painters such as Georges de La Tour and Francisco Zurbarán yet to side-step exact correspondences. Different from his landscapes, in their iconic emptiness as well as in the accent they place on motion (the flickering taper) or its absence (the shell of bone), they are the antithesis of his agitated abstractions of the period. The candle and skull paintings are serene, meditative, overtly classical, and eerie. Richter has said little about these works—although it is perhaps telling that he began painting them as he turned fifty—and they garnered little attention when they were first exhibited in Germany.[81] However, in retrospect they were plainly forerunners of the much darker reflection on mortality that comprises the *October 18, 1977* cycle.

The date from which this cycle of fifteen paintings takes its title marked the mysterious end of a prolonged struggle between a small group of student radicals turned armed revolutionaries, and the police, courts, political establishment, and large parts of the population of the German Federal Republic. It was, in the word of the German novelist and Nobel laureate Heinrich Böll, a war of "six against sixty million." The six stood for a loose confederation of youthful activists—mostly anarchist and Communist—who in turn represented a much larger segment of their disaffected generation, a generation for the most part born after the war and at odds with that of their parents who had acquiesced to, if not supported, Hitler. Alienated by their society's refusal to come to terms with the Nazi past, by the rampant materialism of the booming postwar German economy, by the specter of another hot war on European soil brought on by the cold war being waged between the Soviet Union and the Warsaw Pact and the United States and NATO, and finally by Germany's involvements with the Shah of Iran and with the escalating American campaigns in Southeast Asia, students and others began to organize and protest with increasing fervor and effect in the late 1960s. Their initially peaceful actions soon triggered a violent response from authorities, which pushed parts of the Left toward violent countermeasures and finally toward a decade and more of underground urban guerilla attacks. Of the many who participated in such tactics, the Red Army Faction (RAF) became the most notorious. Its principal members were a rebellious street hustler with a streak of bandit-like bravado named Andreas Baader and a morally severe radical journalist and former pacifist, Ulrike Meinhof. Added to this mismatched pair, for whom the Baader-Meinhof group was named, were another antiwar organizer and sometime publisher Gudrun Ensslin (Baader's lover and Meinhof's ideological adversary), a sociologist of the counter-culture and filmmaker, Holger Meins, and two others who shared their fate, Jan Carl Raspe and Irmgard Möller. In varying degrees and capacities, all were involved in a two-year string of robberies, shootings, escapes, and bombings, which ended in 1972 with their arrest and imprisonment and eventual trial, a five-year-long battle of wills between the German legal system at its worst and the radicals at their worst. Over the course of their incarceration, Baader, Meinhof, Ensslin, Meins, and the others resisted the state in every way possible; the state broke or rewrote its own laws to pursue their prosecution while maintaining a police presence in the Federal Republic that was in many respects uncomfortably similar to that of Germany's authoritarian past.

Meanwhile, outside Stammheim prison near Stuttgart, where the radicals were kept in virtual isolation, other members of the RAF and allied groups of European and Middle Eastern terrorists kidnapped hostages, hijacked planes, invaded embassies, sequestered high government officials, exploded bombs, and retaliated for the deaths of their comrades-in-arms. Inside Stammheim, among the methods of protest followed by the prisoners were hunger strikes, the longest of which physically and emotionally exhausted Meinhof and claimed the life of Holger Meins. On May 9, 1976, Meinhof was found hanged in her cell; the official and probably accurate verdict was suicide but circumstances bred widespread suspicion that she had been murdered. On the night of October 18, 1977, the last and most desperate attempt to free the prisoners in exchange for hostages on a plane hijacked by terrorists and flown to Mogadishu, Somalia, ended in a raid that killed all but one of the hijackers, and released the passengers. The following morning, Baader was found dead in his cell with a bullet wound in his head; Raspe was found dying, also of a bullet wound; Ensslin was found dead in her cell hanging from a grate; and Möller, the only one of the core group to survive, was found with stab wounds in her chest. Once again, the official verdict was suicide, but the situation was even more fraught with suspicion and more mysterious than at the time of Meinhof's death. The question of whether the three who died took their own lives as a last act of revolutionary defiance or out of despair, or whether they were executed by agents of the state has never been settled, although some combination of the first two explanations is the most probable answer. In any event, the "civil war" started by the Baader-Meinhof group continued to flare into violence as late as the 1990s.[82]

October 18, 1977 of 1988 (pages 207–223) consists of fifteen paintings depicting people or scenes from the Baader-Meinhof story. With one exception—*Youth Portrait* (page 207), based on a studio photograph of Ulrike Meinhof taken shortly before she abandoned her career as a political essayist and public spokesperson for the Left and went underground—all are based on video footage, press images, and evidentiary pictures from the police archives, which Richter clipped from news magazines, or copies of which were made available to the artist by friends. *Arrest 1* and *Arrest 2* (pages 208–209) show Meins surrendering to an armored car whose gun is trained on him while he strips to prove that he is unarmed. *Confrontation 1, Confrontation 2,* and *Confrontation 3* (pages 210–211) follow Ensslin as she passes in front of the camera on her way to or from her cell. *Hanged* (page 213) centers on Ensslin's corpse as it was discovered the morning of October 18. *Cell* (page 215) reveals the book-lined corner of Baader's quarters in Stammheim; and *Record Player* (page 214) zeros in on the phonograph that was supposedly the hiding place for a smuggled gun with which police claimed Baader shot himself. *Man Shot Down 1* and *Man Shot Down 2* (pages 216–217) are two versions of the same forensic image of Baader dead on the floor of his cell. The three versions of *Dead* (pages 218–221) are likewise based on a single photograph of the hanged Meinhof, cut down and laid out, with the ligature still around her neck. The final and largest canvas, *Funeral* (pages 222–223), depicts a procession of three coffins containing the remains of Baader, Ensslin, and Raspe as they moved through a crowd of thousands of sympathizers—interspersed with and surrounded by a thousand armed police officers—on their way to a common grave in a cemetery on the outskirts of Stuttgart.

Episodes from a much longer narrative, the paintings Richter completed and preserved make use of only a handful of the dozens of pictures he had amassed. (At least two, a portrait of Meins on his deathbed and the second version of *Hanged,* which became *Cover,* were overpainted.) Moreover, he bypassed all documentation of the RAF's terrorist acts as well as all pictures of their victims, their trial, and the secondary members of the RAF such as Raspe. Instead, Richter concentrated on the terrible denouement of their destructive, self-destructive, and ultimately futile efforts at toppling the German power structure and transforming Germany.

Although Richter had implicitly painted history when he tackled the subjects of Allied war planes in action—*Bombers* of 1963 (page 117) and *Mustang Squadron* of 1964 (page 116)—and probed his own relation to events in such works as *Uncle Rudi* (page 121) and *Herr Heyde* (both 1965), and, on a more abstract level, *48 Portraits* of 1971–73 (pages 161–171), nothing in his oeuvre had fully anticipated *October 18, 1977*. Neither its topical nature nor its ambitious reappraisal of the reliability of photomechanical imagery in relation to the problems of representing what we know about the past and what we believe about its significance had any precedent. Not only did Richter, in effect, inventory photographic genres in selecting sources for the imagery, he also examined the nature of the elusive "facts" the camera records and memory ostensibly preserves as well as make use of the classic painterly genres (portrait, still life, interiors, and figure composition). Additionally, he reprised history painting, a lapsed genre but once the most celebrated in Western tradition; he invoked and then utterly reconceived it in the cycle as a whole. Further, he pushed to new expressive limits his use of *grisaille,* which he had set aside a decade before and had not expected to take up again.

Thus, the gradual dissolve of the three images of Meinhof's head and the two of Baader's body suggest the simultaneous fading away of life and memory, just as the equally cinematic progression of images of Ensslin traces the fleeting smile of an all but condemned woman spontaneously responding to the regard of another person, only to record her final turning and the hardening of her face as she prepares to walk out of view and out of time. In *Hanged* the vapors surrounding Ensslin's faint, husklike form gently hold her in suspension as they envelop her; in *Cell,* the striated pigment reinforces the feeling of being immured by books—metonymic symbols of ideological possession—while they also create the vertiginous impression that the floor has fallen away like a trap door. In *Arrest* the pull of Richter's brush across the wet surface mimics the lateral breakdown of a picture on a television screen, while in the chiaroscuro lighting of the formally composed *Youth Portrait* Richter appropriates a manifestly artificial likeness of the thirty-six-year-old Meinhof taken at the fatal moment of decision when she joined Ensslin in springing Baader from jail and became an outlaw herself. This effect renders the image more artificial while rejuvenating the subject and conjuring up an innocence for Meinhof that was long since lost when she sat for this picture. Finally, in the large panoramic *Funeral* the artist amalgamates individuals within the crowd as if they formed a human tide bearing the coffins along. In the upper margins of the canvas he adds a subtle horizontal bar to the top of a tree, discreetly introducing into the composition a crucifix not present in the source photograph.

In sum, the painterly alterations—of size, proportion, tonal nuance, properties of pigment, manner of application, manner of revision or un-painting—of the photographic source call into doubt the pretense that such documentary sources can be trusted to testify to the truth of the situations or events they ostensibly register faithfully and without visual distortion or bias. At the same time, these alterations edit out nonessential details and add pictorial accents to those that remain, leaving us with inflections that tap into uncertainties about overly familiar ready-made images and the intense, contradictory feelings that may be absent from the original but are deeply rooted in the media-saturated consciousness of the viewer who recalls seeing the pictures before, yet is suddenly confronted with the ambiguity and instability of the information they contain, and, by extension, with the gaps in the stories they purport to tell.

The impulse for painting the series came some ten years after the events it describes. By that time, the wounds inflicted on Germany by both sides in the conflict had scarred over, leaving a dull throb. Richter reopened and probed them at just about the time that summaries of what had happened had been fully codified by the main ideological camps (those of normalizing order and those of stalled dissent) threatened to overtake firsthand recollection and become contending versions of the "official story." At the heart of the project was Richter's own ambivalence toward the opposing parties involved. Having left the East after living for thirty years under crusading dictatorships, Richter was thoroughly disenchanted by the apocalyptic romance that had seized the Baader-Meinhof group and so many people in his milieu; but he had equally few illusions about the stultifying self-satisfaction of West German society with its old hierarchies, new materialism, and dispiriting conformity. On the one hand, Richter admired the RAF for its naively hopeful convictions, but rejected the philosophical and social premises upon which those convictions were based and the violence that was their consequence. On the other hand, he sided with capitalist democracy as the lesser of political evils but scorned its inertial smugness and philistinism: "I was impressed by the terrorists' energy, their uncompromising determination and their absolute bravery; but I could not find it in my heart to condemn the State for its harsh response. That is what States are like, and I have known other, more ruthless ones."[83] In this regard, Richter's position is neither one of Olympian detachment nor one of unquestioning partisanship. Rather, the paintings speak from a confusion that more accurately defined the reality of the situation than any view that presupposed an unclouded perspective, a logical or moral high ground, or individual view of the contested field that did not inherently limit or skew one's understanding.

The truth suffusing the shadows of *October 18, 1977* is that truth is fragmentary, that its enemy—ideology—is ultimately murderous, and that history is irremediable and, for the most part, irretrievable.

Good does not necessarily rise from the ashes; it more likely evaporates into them and is blown by the wind leaving behind a damaged consciousness that must endure not only the sharp pain of specific losses but the constant ache that reminds us of the self-deception and error that are the origins of tragedy. Contrary to the critics who attacked Richter's commemoration of the lives and deaths of the members of the Baader-Meinhof group on the grounds that it celebrated them as martyrs to Leftist causes, and contrary also to commentators who questioned Richter's right as a "bourgeois" artist to address himself the issue of revolution, or to those who took him to task for failing to point an accusing finger at German authorities whom they were sure had executed the prisoners in Stammheim, Richter never intended to lay a wreath at the tomb of self-sacrificing heroes nor play the part of a Zola and condemn official injustice. Indeed, few critics seem to have troubled themselves to read Richter's unequivocal dismissal of Communism and the disastrous folly of radical adventurism, nor did they ever come to terms with the fact that Richter thought the Baader-Meinhof group was desperate and deluded, not heroic.

Richter's aim was more complex than hagiography and by far harder to achieve. First, he sought to make a series of modern paintings that would do the work of traditional history painting in a period when photography, film, and television had taken over as the chroniclers and preservers of public memory, and to do it in a way that instilled critical doubts about the memories we harbor and those that are handed down to us by professionals in the media, government, and academy. Second, he wanted to give a human face to the victims of ideology who, for ideology's sake, created victims of their own, and to free the suffering they experienced and caused from reductive explanations of their motives and actions, and from political generalizations and rigid antagonisms that triggered the events in the first place. Richter's third purpose in painting *October 18, 1977* was to mourn.

Identifying with the idealism but not the ideals of the RAF, Richter painted a lament for the mesmerizing, unrealistic, and potentially ruinous visions to which critical reason gives rise. "The deaths of the terrorists, and the related events both before and after, stand for a horror that distressed me and has haunted me as unfinished business ever since, despite all my efforts to suppress it." Richter wrote in preparation for a press conference held when the cycle was first exhibited.[84] "It is impossible for me to interpret the pictures. That is: in the first place they are too emotional; they are, if possible, an expression of a speechless emotion. They are the almost forlorn attempt to give shape to feelings of compassion, grief and horror (as if the pictorial repetition of the events were a way of understanding those events, being able to live with them)."[85] This reckoning runs directly counter to the assumption of many postmodern critics that painting had once and for all forfeited its claims to speaking to the public on public matters but, even more, had given up on doing so in ways that could bring about genuine catharsis, which is the culminating effect of tragedy. By word and deed Richter insists that this cathartic function, though not a symbolic resolution to social and political dilemmas, remains within painting's scope. He wrote: "Art has always been basically about agony, desperation and helplessness. (I am thinking of Crucifixion narratives, from the Middle Ages to Grünewald; but also of Renaissance portraits, Mondrian and Rembrandt, Donatello and Pollock.) We often neglect this side of things by concentrating on the formal, aesthetic side in isolation. Then we no longer see content in form. . . . The fact is that content does not have a form (like a dress that you can change): it *is* form (which cannot be changed). Agony, desperation and helplessness cannot be represented except aesthetically, because their source is the wounding of beauty (Perfection)."[86] The utopian dreams of the 1960s and 1970s were emblematic of an impossible perfection. The wounding of their beauty was both inevitable and in large measure self-inflicted, but such knowledge does not diminish the "agony, desperation and helplessness," to which Richter responded in spite of himself and to which he gave morally disquieting and profoundly moving artistic expression.

Many Americans have never heard of the Baader Meinhof group, just as many will have forgotten their nearest equivalent in this country, the Weather Underground, and the angry period in our own history that produced it and other violent splinter groups of the new Left. However, the reality of terror and its dynamics are anything but remote. Quite the opposite: the September 11, 2001, attack on the World Trade Center in New York has made terrorism horrifically of the moment and chillingly promises that it will also be a part of our future. In light of recent events, then, the reflex response to paintings of terrorists from another time and place may be to withdraw in fear or hurt or contempt and refuse to engage with such images on the premise that to do so would show compassion toward people who would seem to have lost all claim to it. If the choices were so simple and the people who perpetrated such acts were essentially alien to us, such a turning away would be understandable. However, the lesson of the Baader-Meinhof group and its rebellion is that men and women who make war on the society from which they come are not driven by demons or individual perversities but, rather, by soul-destroying despair over the perceived evils of the world into which they were born and the irrational hope that symbolic violence can remake that world anew. This is no less true of Timothy McVeigh who struck out at the U.S. government and killed hundreds of his fellow citizens or of the foreign kamikaze who imploded an icon of the system they abhor, killing innocent individuals from countries around the world, including their own.

The day the World Trade Center was destroyed a journalist noted that in the dust on a car near the site someone had traced the words: "Oppression produces monsters." Wittingly or unwittingly, this is a paraphrase of the legend on the first image of Francisco Goya's phantasmagorical suite of etchings, the *Caprichos*. It reads: "The sleep of reason produces monsters." In the *Caprichos* and in Goya's other masterwork, the *Disasters of War*, antirational forces are embodied by superstition, religion, and the oligarchy of Spain, while oppression is personified by the armies of Napoleon, which invaded Spain in the name of revolutionary enlightenment. Whatever the cause in modern times, oppression or the sleep of reason, the fact is that monsters are not freaks of nature, they are created in our midst out of destructive inclinations we subliminally share, misguided beliefs to which we are also susceptible, and extreme pressures we experience. Richter's paintings do not excuse and certainly do not glorify the things the Baader-Meinhof group did, nor do they presume sympathy for the people portrayed, but powerfully and inexplicably they draw such sympathy from the depths of the viewer's conflicted being. They are not pictures of an absolute political, psychological, or cultural other but of an otherness that we can recognize if only we look inward as long and hard as the paintings themselves demand to be looked at. An avid reader of Nietzsche throughout his life, Richter knows that what is there to be seen in either direction is "all too human." Our recent experience with terror on a truly appalling scale makes such knowledge imperative.

While working on *October 18, 1977*, Richter made a color portrait of his daughter. The photograph on which *Betty* of 1988 (page 225) is based shows her facing away from the camera and staring into a dense amorphous expanse of gray. The source image dates from the late 1970s when the Baader-Meinhof drama was still unfolding and Richter was grappling with avant-garde hostility and the dwindling hope for painting that the monochrome represented to him. In short, he was confronted on all sides by orthodoxies. Returning to this photograph while in the process of painting the October cycle was a delayed response to that earlier moment of desperation. At the center of the RAF were two women—Meinhof and Ensslin—who impressed Richter the most among all the other members of the group. An alternating psychological current of anxiety and vitality runs through *Youth Portrait*, the *Confrontation* triptych, and *Betty*, connecting Richter's thoughts about one generation to those about another. The grim reality faced by two women—one of them, Meinhof, having been his near contemporary—is reflected in the murky horizon that lies over the shoulder of a young girl becoming a woman. *October 18, 1977* was painted in tones of death; *Betty* is comparatively lifelike, but grayness threatens to engulf her; an implicit competition in one's mind between optimism and pessimism fills the image with a gentle pathos.

A year later, Richter made another series of paintings, this time abstract and on a heroic scale. They are three diptychs titled *November*, *December*, and *January* (pages 226–231), the months following October. It is as if, after a hiatus, Richter had shifted gears aesthetically to record the rising anguish of the "German Autumn" of 1977 as it passed into a long dark winter of discontent. Heavily encrusted with anthracite black and cold white pigment that has been raked so that in spots reds and yellows crackle like embers, these raw but masterful canvases suck up all the oxygen in the rooms they occupy and occlude any view of the world beyond. Punctuating a decade that began with painterly fireworks, and heralding a new generally harsher variety of allover abstraction, these paintings are a coda to *October 18, 1977*, a majestic dirge for a bitter era.

III: PERMISSION GRANTED

"SINCE THERE IS NO SUCH THING AS ABSOLUTE RIGHTNESS AND TRUTH, WE ALWAYS PURSUE THE ARTIFICIAL, LEADING, *HUMAN* TRUTH."

—Gerhard Richter[1]

Since the late 1980s Gerhard Richter's work has assumed a fairly steady rhythm, oscillating between photo-based pictures and abstractions. Virtually all of the former are in color, *October 18, 1977* having been the climax and summary statement of his prolonged ambivalence, after which gray ceased to be the metaphorical noncolor of choice. When grays reappeared as the dominant hues of Richter's abstractions of 1998 to 2001, they are generally suffused with other hues and sometimes—as in *Abstract Picture* of 2000 (pages 284–285)—achieved a purely tonal vibrancy unprecedented in his lead- and pewter-gray paintings of the late 1960s and early to mid-1970s. Richter's new subject matter reflected this same shift in emphasis. Previously the proponent of an impersonal and dispassionate art, Richter began to produce works of startling intimacy, although, in the past, he had frequently scattered images of family and friends among the facets of public modernity he chose to paint. Thus, *Betty* of 1988 (page 225) had been preceded by another portrait of his daughter, *Betty* of 1977 (page 187). She is roughly the same age in both works, since the photograph used for the later painting was taken around 1977. But the hard, almost Flemish old-master quality of the earlier full-face picture contrasts strikingly with the softer turned-away head that came after it. This contrast is also seen in *Ema (Nude on a Staircase)* of 1966 (page 137), Richter's portrait of his first wife and Betty's mother, painted the year their child was born. Before that, in 1965, there were portraits of Richter's uncle in a soldier's uniform, *Uncle Rudi*; of his clowning father, *Horst with His Dog*; of himself as an infant with his aunt, *Aunt Marianne*; and numerous other pictures, which, although not specified as scenes from his own domestic life, resonate subliminally with private feeling. However, Richter's paintings of his second wife, the sculptor Isa Genzken, of his present wife Sabine Moritz, whom he married in 1995, of Sabine with their son Moritz, of Moritz by himself, and, most surprisingly perhaps, two self-portraits (one of which includes his critical supporter and aesthetic sparring partner, Benjamin Buchloh), which collectively represent a new, psychologically charged, though still psychologically ambiguous, direction in his work.

Altogether, Richter seems to have made seven portraits of Isa Genzken: two frontal head-and-shoulders images dated 1990 that are atypically brushy in their un-painted portions were published in a 1996 book on Richter's work, but do not appear in his catalogue raisonné, and five half-length nudes of 1993 simply titled *I.G.*, of which the last two are the most striking and the most severe in the series (pages 242–243). In them, Genzken's pale bare shoulders and close-cropped black hair set up a sharp tonal contrast that is echoed in the semiabstract arrangement of gray panels and black molding in the background and what appears to be the black frame of the photographic print in the foreground. Against this stark setting, Genzken's lean body softens, even when, in the first of the pair, she stretches her arms laterally as if she were exercising and in so doing presses outward against the picture's edge. Facing away from us in both paintings, she is as inaccessible as she is exposed, as lost in her own reality as she is vulnerable to the objective gaze of the camera that captured her likeness and the reticent but hardly objective hand that transcribed it onto canvas. Here, the very detachment Richter assumes becomes the inverse sign of emotion, of a distance between two people that is not just aesthetically imposed but rather the expression of two solitudes.

Of Sabine alone, Richter has thus far painted three paintings. Two are titled *Reading* and are from 1994. The first, seen here, is an exquisitely diffuse view from the back of a young woman looking down at the page of a magazine. Her hair is bound in a tight bun by a dark cloth or fastener at the apex of the pyramid of light and shadow that is her neck, while her ear and the side of her face blush orange-red, and her cheekbone and jaw are silhouetted by a delicate violet. The image floats before the eyes in space and time, having nothing about it that identifies the place or period from which the woman comes and with only the subtlest stylistic

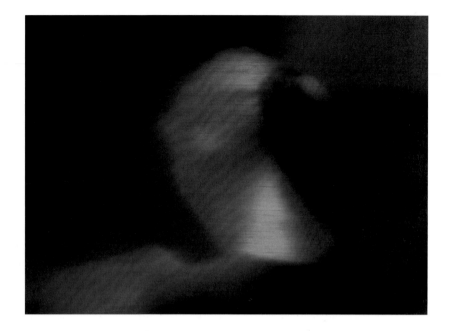

Gerhard Richter. **Reading [Lesende].**
1994. Oil on canvas, 20¼ × 27¾"
(51.4 × 70.5 cm). GR 799-1. High
Museum of Art, Atlanta. Purchase in
honor of John Wieland, Chairman of
the Board of the High Museum of
Art, 1994–97, with funds from Alfred
Austell Thornton in memory of Leila
Austell Thornton and Albert Edward
Thornton, Sr., and Sarah Miller
Venable and William Hoyt Venable,
1996

indicators of when it was made. Equally refined but in sharper focus, the second version is a full profile of a
singularly beautiful person unconcerned by her beauty and wholly engrossed by the text in her hands (page 255).
Although frustrated in the past by his inability to paint like Vermeer (to the point of mutilating his own
pictures), the fact of the matter is that in this instance Richter came astonishing close to that model, but no
closer than he should have for it to still be his own work and one that is unmistakably of its moment. The
same holds true for *Small Bather,* his third portrait of Sabine of that year (page 254). This diminutive, pastel-
like oil on paper recalls turbaned odalisques in the seraglios of the French painter Jean-Auguste-Dominique
Ingres, but the turban is a towel and the nude wearing it appears to have just stepped out of the shower. She is
lovely, to be sure, but also pensive and modest in her nakedness, not the explicitly alluring eternal female in
Oriental garb but something closer to Mme Bonnard just out of the tub, as seen through the consolidating
lens of Richter's subdued neoclassicism.

The eight 1995 paintings of Sabine that make up the series of works titled *S. with Child* (pages 246–253)
revert to Richter's earlier practice of defacing his pictures for reasons previously discussed. Here, the primary
ones are his insistence on artifice in opposition to assumed realism, his preference for ugliness over mere
attractiveness, and for anti-facture over the easy resolution of conventional pictorial finish. However, despite
the more-or-less radical erasures that mark all but one of the series, the motif itself remains shocking in the
context of his work as a whole and in that of late twentieth-century painting. After all, what other major
artist of the last fifty years has dared to paint anything so overtly suggestive of a Madonna and Child? For
that matter, who has painted anything so like family-album baby pictures as the three versions of *Moritz* that
Richter completed between 2000 and 2001 (pages 276–279). In the world of gendered perspectives that we
have inherited from feminist critical discourse beginning in the 1970s, Richter's paintings of Sabine are
plainly examples of the male gaze at work, albeit the gaze of a man experiencing love and mature content-
ment of an almost palpable tenderness. By the same token, it may take a father's eyes to read these pictures
accurately, or the capacity to appreciate how a new but older father who had little involvement with his own
father might look at his first-born male child. From that vantage point, Richter's response embraces an elusive
mix of fascination, bemusement, and uneasiness, which is an adult manifestation of the devoted, puzzled, and
wary gaze a child might direct at its parents. Even for someone like Richter, who places little stock in Freudian
ideas, but whose familiarity with the German Romantic painter Philipp Otto Runge's race of moon-faced children
should be taken into account, the specter of the Oedipal other hovers over this plump cherub, whose cheeks are
smeared with food as if he were an uncanny poster boy for baby food. And if the first version of *Moritz* is the
most nuanced and the most complex in its painterly disturbance of verisimilitude, and the third version is the

least, then the second, with its abbreviating *sfumato* making a halo around the child's haunted, saucer eyes and clutched hands is the one in which Richter's paternal apprehension most obviously matches that of his offspring.

The countenance Richter offers the world in his 1996 *Self-Portrait* (page 259) also has a somewhat haunted aspect, although without the heightened emphasis on the eyes found in the paintings of Moritz. Indeed, Richter's glance off to the left side of the picture breaks with the tradition of self-portraiture in that he does not stare straight ahead, as into a mirror, and by thus breaking anticipated eye contact with himself and with the viewer, he creates distance, interrupts reflex empathy, and underscores the photographic dimension of the image. As in his portraits of Genzken, Richter positions himself in front of a wall vertically divided into tonal zones that is bisected horizontally by his blue shirt, lending the symmetrical composition a spare formality reminiscent of the Spanish baroque realists Diego Velázquez and Francisco Zurbarán. The painting reminds one as well of the artist's early comments on the genre. "A portrait must not express anything of the sitter's 'soul,' essence, or character," Richter said. "Nor must a painter 'see' a sitter in any specific, personal way; because a portrait can never come closer to the sitter than when it is a very good likeness. For this reason, among others, it is far better to paint a portrait from a photograph, because no one can ever paint a specific person.... I never paint to create a likeness of a person or of an event. Even though I paint credibly and correctly, as if the likeness were important, I am really using it only as a pretext for a picture." [2] There is no melodrama in this self-portrait, but in the tension between his deadpan pose and the self-examination to which he submits himself much of the artist's character and something of his anxiety come through. In the tug-of-war in his own mind between the hidden motive for making a particular picture and its visible pretext, Richter's motionless but not quite emotionless face becomes the scene of the contest.

Similarly, *Court Chapel, Dresden* of 2000 (page 281), a double portrait of Richter and Buchloh, slowly reveals as much as it seems to conceal initially. Based on a snapshot, it shows the slight artist smiling tentatively in front of the larger, almost hulking form of the critic who also seems to be smiling but is looking away from the camera and from his companion. As to the significance of the historic site used as background we can gather little other than what the title tells us, that it is a church and it is in Dresden. By all appearances, then, a commonplace travel picture, the painting is, in fact, a portrait of the friendship between two men whose views of the world are almost diametrically opposed, except for their shared resistance to social conformity and their distaste for complacent art. For every one of Richter's doubts, Buchloh has a carefully worked out position. To Richter's hostility toward ideology in all its forms, Buchloh has responded by trying to adapt his own ideological assumptions to the demands of Richter's art, only to reassert them in the end. To Richter's devotion to painting, Buchloh counters with a deep hostility toward aesthetic conservatism of which painting is, for him, exemplary. The list goes on, although the bond between them has endured all manner of disagreement. But note where Richter has staged this encounter between the radical scourge of bourgeois false consciousness and the painter who has tested his faith in art and his own skeptical humanism against every possible challenge: in the portal of a church—as in a Gothic niche—in his native city, symbolizing a double homecoming in an age when we can never go home again, but must always remain the outsiders we have become.

In the meantime, Richter's increasingly numerous abstractions have ranged greatly in scale, material presence, and mood. In many the thick alternately buttery or pasty layers of pigment have accumulated to the point where the slippages caused by Richter's scraping techniques result in rich marblings, like those on the endpapers of antique books, although the tactile quality is more like moving lava with trace elements of different minerals providing the attenuated elastic patterns. In other instances, Richter has taken to flaying the painted skin of his canvases with a spatula in broad strokes or long, wavering stripes leaving behind abraded, shimmering surfaces that at their sheerest and most luminous look like the Aurora Borealis suspended above variously red, orange, yellow, green, blue, or violet planets. Inevitably, the vertical, lateral, and sometimes crisscross striations of his hard-edge tool recall—and undoubtedly are meant to recall—the classic modernist grid of Piet Mondrian and his heirs. But in the unstable painterly terrain saturated hues run together and smear in aggressively impure, sometimes lurid, sometimes garish combinations while the grid itself wobbles and shudders in the ebb and flow of viscous pigment. And between the chromatically rich paintings, such as *Wall* of 1994 (page 245), with its scorching reds, and *Abstract Picture* of 1992 (page 235), with its charcoal latticework, spreads a spectrum wider, more nuanced, and more disconcerting than that of any other contemporary artist. Seldom have colors so

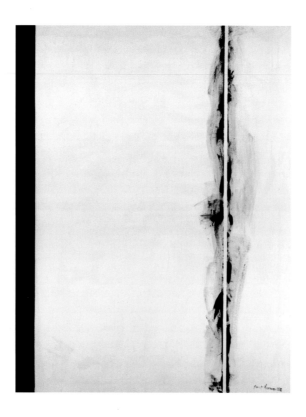

Barnett Newman. **The Stations of the Cross: Lema Sabachthani. First Station.** 1958. Magna on canvas, 6'5⅞" × 60½" (197.8 × 153.7 cm). National Gallery of Art, Washington, D.C. Robert and Jane Meyerhoff Collection

luxurious and so punishing appeared in the same painting, and seldom has the medium's hedonistic potential been so closely tied to its capacity for creating discomfort. For much of his career, Richter fended off or argued with abstraction; now it seems he has surrendered to it but never with abandon and always with a determination to paint past the anticipated gratification of a method fully under his control for the sake of haptic or purely optical sensations that veer toward the unpleasant as often as they coalesce into works of stunning beauty. In these paintings, the awkward materialism of his earlier experiments in building up the surfaces of his Art Informel paintings with torn or rumpled fabric and heavy pigments achieves a long sought-after fluency.

To attribute natural qualities to painting is not in any way to suggest that the geological, astronomical, or organic correlations alluded to are on the artist's mind while he works, much less the actual subject of the work. The procedural strictures Richter has laid down for himself are designed to avert painting by analogy in the romantic manner. Nevertheless, drawing correspondences between Richter's work and its formal precedents is unavoidable, and in some cases clearly intended by the artist. Among his abstractions, the outstanding example is the cycle of six canvases that he completed in 1998, all titled *Abstract Picture (Rhombus)* (pages 266–271). The project was initiated by representatives of the Catholic Church, who approached him with the idea of painting the stigmatization of Saint Francis for a modern church designed by the architect Renzo Piano. It would not have been the first time that a secular artist had undertaken such a commission; Henri Matisse created the windows and murals for the Chapel of the Rosary of the Dominican Nuns of Vence, France, without being much of a believer, and Communist artists such as Giacomo Manzú and David Alfaro Siqueiros had at different times made works at the behest of the Pope. Then, of course, there were the myth-obsessed but agnostic Jackson Pollock who planned to make paintings on canvas and on glass for a Catholic church conceived by the architect, painter, and sculptor Tony Smith, who was a religious man; and there are Barnett Newman's *The Stations of the Cross: Lema Sabachthani* (1958–66), a series of fourteen abstract canvases with a Christian theme by a Jewish anarchist with Cabalistic leanings, whom Richter greatly admired.

Richter's first response was to decline the offer, largely because he did not want to commit himself to illustrating a story with a figurative picture in his "style." He was sufficiently interested in the suggestion, however, to propose making a series of abstract pictures instead. The solution to the problem of giving a nonobjective pictorial space the iconographic content of traditional religious art involved rotating and squeezing the rectangle of the stretcher and executing a suite of virtually monochrome paintings on the diamond-shaped canvas ground. Following the example of Mondrian, whose rhomboid paintings were made early in the twentieth century, Richter thus created an anthropomorphic format in which the vertical and horizontal coordinates of the body—the trunk and arms—are implied in the axial orientation of the picture plane. Working off this implicit axis, Mondrian had reapportioned space with linear elements and blocks of color or tone; Richter dispensed with the depicted grid in favor of the variegations of surface achieved by his customary layering of pigments—in this case, a glaring orange flecked with blue, yellow, green, and white. The technique employed tends to "underline" the actual edge of the canvas with abrasions and sequential "skips"—distant cousins of Newman's "zips"—that follow the pressure of his scraper along the hard stretcher bar and reinforce the outer contours of the forms and with that its presence as the template of a human being standing straight with arms extended. Under other circumstances, one might have presumed this to be a variation of Vitruvius's proportional diagram, best known from Leonardo da Vinci's drawing of a man inside a square tracing a circle with his arms and legs, but given the nature of the commission it can only be one thing, an abstract crucifix. That interpretation has been confirmed by the artist and is further justified by the existence of a multiple of a Christian cross that Richter cast in silver and gold two years before the church commission became an issue, as well as by the cross that appears in *Funeral* (1988), the last painting in the Baader-Meinhof cycle completed ten years earlier.

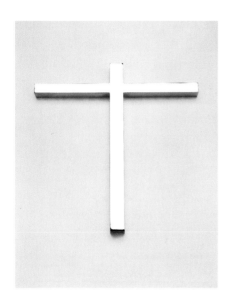

Gerhard Richter. **Cross [Kreuz].** 1996. Gold, 7⅝ × 7⅝ × ⅝" (19.5 × 19.5 × 1.5 cm). Private collection. Courtesy Anthony d'Offay Gallery, London

When asked by the author about his own relation to the Church, Richter noted that his parents were Protestant, rather than Catholic, and that he had renounced religion in his mid-teens, but then he added: "I was very moved when our two children were baptized.... That is my culture, my history, the last 2000 years were Catholic and it was not so bad."[3] Asked about the unorthodox configuration of the sculptural crucifix, with its elongated horizontal element and the high intersection point of the two cross bars Richter explained: "Any person proportioned according to the traditional cross would be deformed. They would have a very long head and really short arms, that is not a human proportion. I wanted to spare myself the figure of Christ and then came up with this idea. I stood against the wall and measured myself and that's how I did it. I put the man and the cross in one shape," adding with laughter, "I tried to make it my shape. It's not everybody's shape."[4] Simultaneously whimsical, hubristic, and serious, Richter's crucifix is, to this extent, yet another discreet self-portrait. Pressed to spell out his level of religious commitment, Richter finally declared: "I am a sympathizer."[5] When it was pointed out that the term had been applied to people who tacitly supported the revolutionary Marxist Red Army Faction, Richter made it plain that he had chosen it with care, was well aware of the ironic and ideologically problematic connotations he was invoking, and said: "The term 'sympathizer' is very much rooted in that history."[6]

Richter's words have the ring of a confession, but also of a characteristic inconclusiveness. Over the years Richter has been famously noncommittal on many topics, and has even seemed to encourage contradictory readings of his paintings, especially insofar as his Fluxus-inspired anti-art leanings in the 1960s and 1970s were concerned. However, Richter never considered himself part of this or any other avant-garde, nor was neo-Dada's tongue-in-cheek subversion of aesthetic values a primary means or an end of his own work. "I never think that way," he told an interviewer in 1990, "If I ever did admit to any irony, I did so for the sake of a quiet life."[7] Rather, he elaborated: "My own statements about my lack of style and lack of opinion were largely polemical gestures against contemporary trends that I disliked—or else they were self-protective statements, designed to create a climate in which I could paint as I wanted."[8] From the beginning, then, Richter's strategy has been one of what he calls "evasive action."[9] Using ready-made imagery to avoid ready-made artistic identities, he has invited association with movements and tendencies while at the same time distanced himself from them by rephrasing the tropes he has appropriated and insisting on the plurality of his affinities. Some observers have viewed this activity as an across-the-board travesty of styles and an articulation of a thoroughgoing aesthetic nihilism. During the 1960s and 1970s in an art-world context where Duchampian ideas prevailed, buttressed by a political critique of Richter's chosen medium, which left little room for a painter to explore his own intuitions, Richter took refuge in such interpretations because they shielded him from alignment with traditionalist exponents of the conventions with which he experimented. By the end of the 1980s, though, the ready-made identity that most threatened to distort the understanding of his art was the one that had provided him cover. By the 1990s he began to disengage himself from it, challenging postmodernist critics hostile to much that interested him to play catch-up as he headed in directions they shunned. Indeed, the critical injunctions taken for granted by his supporters in this camp seemed to have spurred Richter into going the other way.

Thus, a year after Richter exhibited *Abstract Picture* of 1992 (page 235), and *Gray Mirror* of the same year (page 237) in a pavilion at Documenta 9, along with thirteen other abstractions and a small image of a bouquet, *Flowers* of 1992 (page 236), Buchloh wrote: "Not even the category of the portrait seems ever to have attained the profound level of painterly decrepitude that still life would attain in the sinister harmlessness in the work of Matisse or Maurice de Vlaminck in the twentieth century."[10] Then he cut Richter enough slack to paint his own still lifes with the crabbed excuse that: "Richter's decision to search out the most obsolete of all still-life types might originate in an inverted gesture of opposition to the universal spectacularization to which all avant-garde models are now incessantly subjected."[11] Rebuttal of such arguments would be rated as little more than intramural squabbling among writers were it not for the fact that Richter criticism has been dominated by just this kind of tortured logic, and it has confused and alienated many who are nonetheless drawn to the work and prepared to deal with it in a more straightforward and complex way. Compare Richter's current account of his motives to those that presume such convoluted aims: "That was an attempt at self-protection—saying that I was indifferent, that I didn't care, and so on. I was afraid my pictures might seem too sentimental. I don't mind admitting now that it was no coincidence that I painted things that mattered to me personally—the tragic types, the murderers and suicides, the failures, and so on." [12] To the list of things that mattered to him one must now add flowers, his wife and children, and perhaps the cross.

Borrowing the tactics of their adversaries, reactionary artists have often tried to shock the avant-garde for their own amusement and that of others, but Richter is no more ironic in this regard than any other, nor is he in any way a reactionary. Yet, having upset philistines and conservatives for decades, Richter has now turned his attention to the progressives who have championed him, and to the dated ideas of modernism they apply with increasing scholasticism. Kitsch is the enemy of true feeling, and in the first phase of his career Richter employed every painterly method at his disposal to strip images of clichéd associations and emotions. Now he is doubling back to see if those same images can be painted in earnest and to see if sentiment can fill the space that sentimentality once occupied, and from which it had been expelled by his efforts. What *sentiment* connotes here is more than just the way Richter feels about the people, places, or things he chooses to paint, but how he feels about painting itself and how he responds to the unstoppable need to paint that he shared with Palermo and Polke but found wanting in the more worldly Lueg. In that connection, one is reminded of a remark reportedly made by Franz Kline to the effect that artists distinguish themselves from nonartists by their high threshold for embarrassment. Richter's increasing candor about his reasons for doing what he does raises that threshold in a period when the critical discussion of art is more skittish than ever when ordinary human desires, longings, or states of fulfillment are alluded to without disclaimer.

That said, the word *sentimental* is used advisedly, inasmuch as it has special significance in German aesthetic discourse as a result of the distinction made by the poet, playwright, and essayist Friedrich von Schiller in his seminal essay "On Naive and Sentimental Poetry." In Schiller's construct, which discriminates between the two types of poetry only in terms of their qualities, without questioning their respective artistic or philosophical validity, the naive artist is at one with nature or, in the sense that Jackson Pollock meant it, *is* nature. By contrast, the sentimental poet regards nature and the incarnations of the ideal engendered in his own mind at equal remove, and critically assesses the disparity between them. While forthright expression is available to the naive poets, sentimental poets are necessarily self-conscious when they speak. "Since the naive poet only follows simple nature and feeling, and limits himself solely to imitation of actuality, he can have only a single relationship to his subject, and in this respect there is for him no choice in his treatment." [13] At the other extreme, "The sentimental poet is…always involved with two conflicting representations and perceptions—with actuality as a limit and with his idea as infinite; and the mixed feelings he excites will always testify to this dual source."[14]

Within this framework, Richter would be classified as a sentimental poet increasingly drawn to the prospect of being a naive one, that is, one capable of the direct representation of images, thoughts, and emotions but aware of the impossibility of ever losing his self-consciousness. The two artistic modes in which the sentimental poet excels, according to Schiller, are satire and elegy, both of which focus on the gap between the world as it is and the world as it can be imagined, the first by using the ideal to criticize the real, the second by celebrating the ideal through mourning for its loss. To fit Richter into Schiller's schema without adjusting it would require viewing his works as ironic or melancholy displays of disillusionment, but this skews perceptions considerably. However, if one factors in the contributions of two other German thinkers, both of whom Richter read attentively in his youth, the formula becomes more accommodating, though less comfortable, and Richter's place in it easier to define. On the one hand, there is Arthur Schopenhauer's reasoned and relentless pessimism, his preoccupation with suffering and his striving to subjugate egotistical will and, thereby, limit its power to distort perception. On the other hand, there is Nietzsche's refutation of the Enlightenment's claims for the existence of unitary Truth in favor of the proposition that what we call truths are human constructs that have been ratified by custom and are not genuine representations of reality, which is always hypothetical and ultimately unknowable. While Schopenhauer believed that with art "we keep the sabbath of the penal servitude of willing," [15] Nietzsche wrote: "What then is truth? A mobile army of metaphors, metonymies, anthropomorphisms, a sum, in short, of human relationships which, rhetorically and poetically intensified, ornamented, and transformed, come to be thought of, after long usage by a people, as fixed, binding, and canonical. Truths are illusions which we have forgotten are illusions, worn out metaphors now important to stir the senses, coins which lost their faces and are considered now as metal rather than as currency." [16] Art, it follows, consists of illusions that declare themselves as such but in so doing sharpen understanding of our uncertain relation to truth, even as it offers glimpses of Apollonian (rational and orderly) or Dionysian (instinctual and cathartic) transcendence. And so, the philosopher Arthur Danto wrote of Nietzsche's relativist doctrine of Perspectivism: "We score the blank surface of reality with the longitudes and parallels of concepts, but the concepts and ideas are ours, and they have not the slightest basis in fact." [17]

In much the same way, Richter's statements and paintings assert the arbitrariness of pictures as representations of their ostensible subjects as well as our capacity for using images to conjure things that transcend our quotidian experience. Pure seeing is therefore an unreliable index of things as they are, although heightened scrutiny can, on occasion, partially reveal obscured dimensions of reality. But, at the same time, the same compulsion to render reality out of the materials at hand may offer insights about realms that escape our ordinary understanding. Sense data are, by this measure, always illusory; but the senses, in their speculative production of images, do allow us to project intuitions onto reality. We cannot be sure of anything we look at with the naked eye any more than we can be sure that the edited version of a thing reconstituted by art captures its essence; but we can learn about the limitations of our knowledge by repeated attempts at grasping the ungraspable. This holds true equally for commonplace objects within our reach as for remote phenomena—for the faces of those closest to us and the facts of history or the stars.

In this connection, Richter's recent multiples accent the poignant elusiveness and metamorphic flux of vision. Over the past several years he has made numerous photographic editions of his earlier photo-based paintings. Skeptics have suggested that the artist was simply taking advantage of popular demand for these images by disseminating copies of them. This, of course, is hardly an aesthetic crime if you consider that the history of printmaking in Germany began with Albrecht Dürer and his contemporaries making affordable woodcuts and engravings for the sake of people who could not afford paintings. But Richter seems, instead, to have been prompted by the desire to "repair" or somehow repossess key works that had left his hands: for example, *48 Portraits* and *Ema (Nude on a Staircase)*, which had been damaged; and others, such as *Betty* (1988) and *Small Bather*, which he no longer had about him. What is striking about these copies, however, is how different they are from the originals, not in their obvious details but in their overall presence. Just as the camera delivers a likeness of the object of its attention by impartially screening the information before it, it also reduces the quantity and quality of that information to what can be photographed, thereby distorting the image while seeming to reproduce it. Rather than try to restore the missing information by painting it back in from the model, Richter made those distortions more explicit by a variety of painterly manipulations. The effect of rephotographing the painting is to smooth out those manipulations and, where they remain, ascribe them to photographic causes. Thus, *Ema (Nude on a Staircase)*, *Betty*, or *Small Bather* assume an atmospheric naturalness that is, in truth, the height of unnaturalness insofar as it is the compound result of un-painting with a brush and un-painting (removing texture and other signs of painterly materiality) with a lens. The end product, beautiful as it is, is a telescoped sequence of simulacra, an inviting reality triply removed.

The two recent print multiples bracket this same issue with pointedly different subject matter. The first is an aerial shot of a bend in a river that embraces terrain dotted by houses and crisscrossed by roads, highways, and an elegantly winding clover-leaf interchange. Between our overhead vantage point and the ground below are clouds; it is a bird's-eye view of a landscape in which the modern infrastructure and the pastoral seem to coexist in harmony. However, careful inspection exposes a telltale pattern of circles scattered in all directions: bomb craters. Returning to the theme of mechanized warfare three decades after he painted B-52s, Mustangs, and Stukas, Richter chose a reconnaissance photograph taken by an Allied plane flying over the Rhine near Cologne in 1945, erased the cracks in the original print, deleted the caption identifying the source and date of the image, and subtly evened out the panorama so that only hard looking would seize upon the evidence of the destruction being represented. The second print is a facsimile of an item torn out of the newspaper in which light and dark blobs resembling an Art Informel painting cluster in an out-of-focus haze; the text headline explains that they are magnifications of an atom. Macrocosm and microcosm. Origin and end. Ready-made Alpha, ready-made Omega. Figuratively speaking, all the rest of the images in Richter's *Atlas*, and all the mundane things, places, and people in his paintings lie between these two subjects.

The poignancy inherent in this juxtaposition is fundamental to Richter's entire enterprise. In it one finds curiosity and moral gravity, fatalism and amazement. Above all, one feels along with the artist the tensions of a fragmented existence, of a richly, frighteningly various life lived in the absence of wholeness or a unifying principal or system of thought that promises its eventual achievement—but a life for which the idea of wholeness (a beautiful "uninjured" reality) remains, despite all doubt, the necessary compensatory counter-term. Modern or postmodern theories of art that promise utopian resolutions to this conflict between what is and what might be, based on the systematic negation of all illusions, are alien to Richter, inasmuch as the Schopenhauerian artist sees horror and vanity all around him, and the Nietzschean in him has renounced the quest for absolute truth as the last and most treacherous of illusions. What then of the man who, standing next to his primary postmodernist interlocutor at the door of the church he turned his back on after reading Nietzsche's devastating refutation of Christianity, declares himself Catholic "sympathizer," a man so moved by the secular passion of the Baader-Meinhof group that he devotes fifteen works to the violent advocates of ideas he categorically rejects because their belief in a false hope of resolving social injustice and ending human suffering is so compelling?

Reconciling Richter's preoccupation with belief—and religious belief in particular—and his stated loss of faith is not a new problem, and neither is it merely a personal one. While the majority of commentators have skirted the issue, it has, to their consternation, been central to his thinking from the very outset; repeated references to religion and God in his writings and interviews make this inescapably plain. Consider two examples, one from 1962, the other from 1988. Newly arrived from the East, where he had painted for the state, and arguing against the lack of purpose in Western-style art-for-art's-sake, Richter entered the following into his notes: "Picturing things, taking a view, is what makes us human; art is making sense and giving a shape to that sense. It is like the religious search for God. We are well aware that making sense and picturing are artificial, like illusion; but we can never give them up. For belief (thinking out and interpreting the present and the future) is our most important characteristic." [18] Twenty-six years later, having just completed work on *October 18, 1977*, he said: "Art is the pure realization of religious feeling, capacity for faith, longing for God." [19]

Such declarations—and there are many—cannot be glossed over. However, the fundamental question is not Richter's private, presumably constantly changing, relationship to Christianity or the Church, but the parallels with painting it suggests and the metaphorical richness of such correspondence. Working in a context where critics and colleagues had proclaimed painting dead with the same liberating but disorienting effect that followed Nietzsche's pronouncing the same sentence on God, Richter could only continue working as if no further harm would be done to the medium he had chosen since, in any event, there was nothing else for him to do. "Strange though this may sound," he wrote in 1962, "not knowing where one is going—being lost, being a loser—reveals the greatest possible faith and optimism, as against collective security and collective significance. To believe, one must have lost God: to paint one must have lost art." [20] Moreover, he wrote some four years later, even as he struck alternately indifferent, defiant, or irreverent poses in public: "Art is not a substitute religion: it is a religion (in the true sense of the word: 'binding back,' 'binding' to the unknowable, transcending reason, transcending being). This does not mean that art has turned into something like the Church

Gerhard Richter. **Bridge: February 14, 1945 [Brücke: 14. Februar 1945].** 2000–2001. Photolithograph, 18¹⁄₁₆ × 13⁹⁄₁₆" (45.9 x 34.5 cm). Private collection

and taken over its functions (education, instruction, interpretation, provision of meaning). But the Church is no longer adequate as a means of affording experience of the transcendental, and of making religion real—and so art has been transformed from a means into the sole provider of religion: which means religion itself."[21]

Call this affirmation Richter's wager. In the face of modern nihilism, whose pull he responds to instinctively as well as intellectually, Richter has persisted in the conviction that art *has* an ethical and transcendental function, much as Blaise Pascal's exemplary believer retains a faith in God in spite of God's refusal to answer human entreaties, in spite of the superior arguments of convinced rationalists who argue for or against his existence, and in spite of the rhetorical brilliance of skeptics who discount him altogether. In this regard, he shares much with Samuel Beckett whose protagonists incarnate blind faith and tragicomic futility. They are perhaps best exemplified by the first-person narrator of *The Unnamable* (1958), who ends his novel-length soliloquy with the words: "I'll never know, in the silence you don't know, you must go on, I can't go on, I'll go on." [22] In the same vein, the existential dimension of Richter's work mirrors that of Alberto Giacometti—another master of shivering but inertial grayness, another dedicated, sometimes desperate taxonomist of the erosion of impressions—whose paintings and sculptures are condensed dramas of contingent appearances. However, Giacometti's tunnel-vision art is narrow in its formal parameters if broad in its implications, whereas Richter's, equally broad in the latter regard, is encyclopedic in scope as well as formally disparate in its always ambiguous effect. Furthermore, while Giacometti is implicitly present in all his work—perspectival armatures that track his glance locate him behind the easel, and the marks he makes bridge the distance between him and the canvas, drawing board, or modeling stand—Richter's is for the most part only a specter in his work.

This last point bears reiteration and amplification in the light of the role assigned to the artist in this narrative of his art. In choosing to integrate Richter into the analysis of his work's unfolding, it is not my intention to reduce his paintings to biography in the manner all too frequently applied to interpretations of Vincent van Gogh, Pablo

Picasso, Jackson Pollock, Eva Hesse, and other modern innovators of form and metaphor, nor is it to suggest that the ultimate key to even the most personal pictures in his supposedly impersonal oeuvre lies in his direct relation to the subjects he selected. To do so would violate his own well-founded reservations about the intrusiveness of ego—and its Trojan horse, signature style—on vision and the experience of things that in their own domains ignore the artist's existence. If much of his work consists of a duel between classicism and romanticism, with photography aligned to the former and painterliness to the latter, then Nietzsche and Schopenhauer are the seconds, and neither promoted an aesthetic of the anecdotal self. This said, however, it is impossible to account for Richter's achievement if we take the critical conceit of "the death of the author" literally. Richter is the author of his images, and those images are informed by the time and circumstances in which they were made. They are not integers in a conceptual equation but pictures of objective and subjective worlds that defy definitive depiction.

Richter is acutely aware of the insurmountable discrepancy between what can be seen and what can be shown, what can be imagined and what can be represented: "Of course I constantly despair at my own incapacity, at the impossibility of ever accomplishing anything, of painting a valid, true picture or of even of knowing what such a thing ought to look like. But then I always have the hope that, if I persevere, it might one day happen. And this hope is nurtured every time something appears, a scattered, partial, initial hint of something which reminds me of what I long for, or which conveys a hint of it—although often enough I have been fooled by a momentary glimpse that then vanishes, leaving behind only the usual thing. I have no motif, only motivation."[23] This holds as true of abstraction (which is intuitional) as of figuration (which is empirical); rather than replicating fixed, verifiable phenomena, both constitute visual hypotheses about the world. Richter has written: "Every time we describe an event, add up a column of figures, or take a photograph of a tree, we create a model: without models we would know nothing about reality, and would be like animals. Abstract paintings are like fictitious models because they visualize a reality which we can neither see nor describe but which we nevertheless conclude exists. We attract negative names to this reality: the un-known, the un-graspable, the infinite, and for thousands of years we have depicted it in terms of absolute images like heaven and hell. With abstract painting we create a better means of approaching what can neither be seen nor understood because abstract painting illustrates with the greatest clarity . . . with all the means at the disposal of art, 'nothing.' . . . This is not an artful game, it is a necessity; since everything unknown frightens us and fills us with hope at the same time, we make these images as a possible explanation of the inexplicable or, at least, as a way of dealing with it. Of course, even representational paintings have this transcendental aspect: since every object, being part of the world whose last and first causes are finally unfathomable, embodies that world, the image of such an object in a painting evokes the general mystery more compellingly the less 'function' the representation has."[24]

Thus, Richter's identity is manifest throughout his work, not so much as a character in his own story (though there is a story worth telling) or as an individual seeking self-expression (though he conveys and elicits complex emotions) but as a force field whose powerful, shifting, and precariously balanced centrifugal and centripetal forces have proven capable of holding together the dispersing but not yet entropic fragments of modern experience and consciousness. The psychology of his art in all its extremes and contradictions is "impersonal" only in the sense that it is not limited to his private preoccupations but expands to encompass those of anyone who accepts that his or her reality—if he or she pays attention to all that it contains—is as plural, as unsettling, and as wondrous as Richter's.

In order for the public, for which he intended his work, to understand that it is looking at facets of its own manifold situation, Richter began his career by stepping aside. In recent years, he has edged closer to his paintings and to their audience, but he still refrains from placing himself between them, even when he has transformed himself and those dear to him into pictures. Nor does his work encourage viewers to impose their own unselfconscious sympathies onto the people, places, things, or states of being his paintings portray or evoke. In the 1960s and early 1970s, the austerity of his means blocked entry; in the late 1970s and 1980s, it was their explosive energy matched by a cool deliberateness. Although, in recent years, Richter's subject matter and gestural manner have seemed to beckon with a previously uncharacteristic intimacy, the painterly veil he drops over his photographic models and the slippages that obscure his abstractions continue to fend off would-be trespassers. The result is a privileged glimpse—a "slipping glimpse" to borrow Willem de Kooning's phrase—of

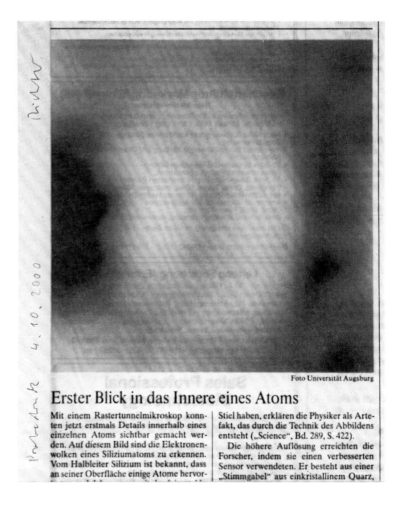

4. 10. 2000

Foto Universität Augsburg

Erster Blick in das Innere eines Atoms

Mit einem Rastertunnelmikroskop konn-
ten jetzt erstmals Details innerhalb eines
einzelnen Atoms sichtbar gemacht werden. Auf diesem Bild sind die Elektronen-
wolken eines Siliziumatoms zu erkennen.
Vom Halbleiter Silizium ist bekannt, dass
an seiner Oberfläche einige Atome hervor-

Stiel haben, erklären die Physiker als Arte-
fakt, das durch die Technik des Abbildens
entsteht („Science", Bd. 289, S. 422).
  Die höhere Auflösung erreichten die
Forscher, indem sie einen verbesserten
Sensor verwendeten. Er besteht aus einer
„Stimmgabel" aus einkristallinem Quarz,

Gerhard Richter. **First Look at the
Inside of an Atom** [Erster Blick in
das Innere eines Atoms]. 2000.
Photolithograph, $7\frac{1}{8} \times 5\frac{15}{16}$" (18.2 ×
13.2 cm). Private collection

a situation that may exclude even the artist himself, leaving behind the exquisitely isolated receptacle of painting partially filled by an evanescent image. Thus, whether laid down in opaque grays, flat colors, exuberant strokes, or diaphanous tints, Richter's canvases typically stop the eye at the surface of the paint and push viewers in the habit of projecting themselves into pictures back onto their feet and back into their actual surroundings.

A master at keeping his distance, Richter has created a vast and diverse body of work haunted by a funda-mental alienation, of which art can be a finely calibrated gauge, and for which it is a consolation but not a rem-edy. Eschewing the histrionics and solipsisms that vulgarized the worst postwar era existentialist art, though plainly cognizant of the positive examples set by the best, he makes us aware at every turn of the gaps between viewers and his pictures, and between the pictures and the world, with wit, sensitivity, and uncompromising pre-cision, and he offers that awareness and the intensified but never fully satisfied desire to overcome it as a token of shared knowledge. Indeed, the basic loss of bearings toward which all his paintings point may barely show itself at all, except as a constant subliminal tremor that subtly warps vision and casts an estranging light on the mundane and the marvelous. Once accustomed to this effect, and to the filter it places between perceptual objectivity and critical subjectivity, one may find the distance created has opened up vertigo-inducing vistas that routine inattention or fear normally hide from sight. Rather than lament reality's refusal to explain itself or struggle to force meanings upon it, we become aware that a kind of detached clarity of the mind and of the senses takes over. Keeping our own counsel in the fashion epitomized by the artist, it becomes possible to observe and record the distortions and ambiguities that dogmatic thought censures and from which consensus experience distracts us. A broadly philosophical painter, more than a strictly conceptual one, a radical thinker and often traditional maker, among the great artists of the second half of the twentieth century, and a frontline explorer of the twenty-first, Richter is an image-struck poet of alertness and restraint, of doubt and daring.

NOTES TO THE TEXT

Introduction

1. Friedrich Nietzsche, "Beyond Good and Evil," *The Philosophy of Nietzsche* (New York: Modern Library, 1937): 83.

2. Roberta Smith, "Flirting with All Styles but Embracing None," *The New York Times*, August 23, 1987.

3. Both Kiefer and Immendorff were born in 1945, both grew up in West Germany, and both were students of Beuys, with Immendorff being a special favorite. With these circumstances in common their divergent trajectories from Beuysian actions to painting represent two extremes of German neo-Expressionism. Kiefer synthesized Jean Fautrier, Jean Dubuffet, and Jackson Pollock and applied this fusion to mythic subject matter with heavy Wagnerian overtones, while Immendorff allied Max Beckmann, Renato Guttuso, a cartoony Socialist Realism, and eighteenth- and nineteenth-century caricature and put that lively admixture at the service of a scene-stealing Brechtian humor.

4. The anomaly of Richter's place in the lineup of German painting in the 1980s was apparent in *Refigured Painting: The German Image, 1960–1988*, organized by Thomas Krens at the Guggenheim museum. There, a cross section of Richter's Photo-Realist paintings shared space with examples of his abstract work, but the surrounding company they kept was overwhelmingly Expressionist.

5. Willem de Kooning, speaking to Rudolph Burckhardt, as quoted in Harry F. Gaugh, "De Kooning in Retrospect," *Artnews* 83, no. 3 (March 1984): 94. Pollock, who was convinced at times that Picasso was waiting for him around every artistic corner, shared de Kooning's sentiments.

6. Pat Gilmour, "Gerhard Richter and Hamish Fulton," *Arts Review*, April 13, 1979: 186.

7. Even those who accepted his implicit critique of style have come to this conclusion: "I like looking at these paintings, which is a lot as far as I am concerned, but I've never bought the theoretical groundwork that goes along with them. . . . I saw in [their] versatility a flexibility of thinking and guts to paint whatever [Richter] wanted. But today the variations look like empty moves, skittishness, a lure more than a trick on the market." Barbara Flynn, [Review] *Artforum* 16, no. 8 (April 8, 1978): 62.

8. Diedrich Diederichson, Isabelle Graw, Tom Holert, Jutta Koether, and Felix Reidenbach, "Richterrunde," *Texte zur Kunst* 4, no. 13 (March 1994): 124.

9. Like a number of other exhibitions in this country, the Onnasch show was initiated by the gallery without the artist's knowledge or approval, but when it became apparent that the dealer's ownership of or independent access to the paintings he was presenting would make it impossible for Richter to stop the project, Richter then added works in his control to round out the selection in accordance with his own ideas about the work.

10. Peter Frank, "Gerhard Richter (Onnasch)," *Artnews* 72, no. 9 (November 1973): 100.

11. Ibid.

12. Roald Nasgaard, "Gerhard Richter," in Terry A. Neff, ed., *Gerhard Richter: Paintings* (London: Thames & Hudson, 1988): 33.

13. The critic Douglas Crimp represents such attitudes, and while *Pictures*, an exhibition he organized at Artists Space in 1977, was a prescient and eye-opening presentation of emerging appropriation art of the period, his equally influential criticism at the time was polemical in tone and dogmatic in substance. Crimp's article, "The End of Painting," published in *October* magazine in spring 1981, is typical of the style of argument in which he and his postmodernist cohorts, specialized. In it, Crimp cites qualified exceptions to his anti-painting doctrine in the work of Robert Ryman and Frank Stella. He also quotes Richter selectively: for example, he cites Richter's statement that painting is "pure idiocy" entirely out of the context in which it was written in 1973. The full Richter quote, which attempts to defend painting, is the following: "One has to believe in what one is doing, one has to commit oneself inwardly, in order to do painting. Once obsessed, one ultimately carries it to the point of believing that one might change human beings through painting. But if one lacks this passionate commitment, there is nothing left to do. Then it is best to leave it alone. For basically painting is [pure] idiocy." Gerhard Richter, "Notes, 1973," in Hans-Ulrich Obrist, ed., *Gerhard Richter: The Daily Practice of Painting. Writings and Interviews, 1962–1993* (Cambridge, Mass.: MIT Press; London: Anthony d'Offay Gallery, 1995): 78.

14. Benjamin H. D. Buchloh, "Interview with Gerhard Richter," in Neff, *Richter: Paintings*: 21.

15. Ibid.

I: Beginnings

1. Ad Reinhardt, "The Artist Is Responsible," in Barbara Rose, ed., *Art as Art: The Selected Writings of Ad Reinhardt* (New York: Viking Press, 1975): 136.

2. Gerhard Richter, interview with the author, conducted with the assistance of Catharina Manchanda, on April 21–23, 2001; trans. Philip Glahn. Some portions of the interview appear in this volume. Hereafter, the unpublished portions of the interview will be referred to as RSGR, 2001.

3. Ibid.

4. Ibid.

5. Ibid.

6. Ibid.

7. Ibid.

8. Ibid.

9. Ibid.

10. Richter, "Interview with Hans-Ulrich Obrist, 1993," *Daily Practice*: 251.

11. RSGR, 2001.

12. Ibid.

13. Ibid.

14. Gerhard Richter, unpublished interview with the author, conducted with the assistance of Isabelle Moffat, in 1996.

15. RSGR, 2001.

16. Ibid.

17. Gerhard Richter, "Auseinandersetzungen halfen mir weiter," *Sonntag: Wochenzeitung für Kultur, Politik und Unterhaltung* 16 (April 20, 1958): 12.

18. RSGR, 2001.

19. Ibid.

20. Ibid.

21. Ibid.

22. In contrast, one might consider the situation of Ralf Winkler, better known by his pseudonym, A. R. Penck. Born in Dresden in 1939, he was repeatedly rejected by the art academies of Dresden and East Berlin, and painted in obscurity while eking out a living working as a boilerman, night watchman, and postman, rarely showing his work until 1961, when an exhibition at the East Berlin academy and contacts with galleries in the West eased his situation somewhat. Having crossed back into the GDR in 1961, shortly before the Wall went up after a visit with his friend Georg Baselitz, Penck was unable to leave the GDR until 1980.

23. RSGR, 2001.

24. Richter, "Interview with Benjamin H. D. Buchloh, 1986," *Daily Practice:* 132. In a recent conversation (RSGR, 2001), the artist partially backed away from this much publicized "Road to Damascus" version of his visit to Kassel: "The story has gained so much substance and truth it becomes hard for me to depart from it. I have memories, of course. I see myself walking through Documenta and making slides and slides and slides of the whole Documenta. And I looked at these slides in the evening later in Dresden, and I don't know where they are now. It would help to know what we liked. We were not looking for artists as daring and as awful as Fontana and Pollock, but works where one could recognize something, where something was said and felt. But simply to go like that [a cutting, or brushstroke, gesture] we thought that was a little dumb. [But] it was unbelievable. To see something like that was an explosion in your brain. I wish I was more open, and that this legend did not exist. Then maybe I would be free enough to remember. But now this story is so dominant. It is like a photograph; you don't remember actually what happened, you remember the photo."

25. Stephen Ellis, "The Elusive Gerhard Richter," *Art in America* (November 1986): 132.

26. Richter, "Interview with Buchloh," *Daily Practice:* 136.

27. Ibid.

28. Elizabeth Armstrong, "Fluxus and the Museum," in idem and Joan Rothfuss, *In the Spirit of Fluxus* (Minneapolis: Walker Art Center, 1993): 34.

29. Ibid.: 16.

30. Pierre Restany, "Preface for the Exhibition *40 Degrees above Dada*," in *1960: Les Nouveaux Réalistes*, Intro. Bernadette Contensou (Paris: Musée d'Art Moderne de la Ville de Paris, 1986): 266–267.

31. Joseph Beuys, "A propos de Palermo: Entretien de László Glozer avec Joseph Beuys," in *Palermo: Oeuvres 1963–1977* (Paris: Musée National d'Art Moderne, Centre Georges Pompidou, Galeries Contemporaines, 1985): 77.

32. Richter, "Interview with Buchloh," *Daily Practice:* 133.

33. RSGR, 2001.

34. Ibid.

35. Richter, "Interview with Wolfgang Pehnt, 1984," *Daily Practice:* 114; idem, "Letter to Jean-Christophe Amman, February 1973," ibid.: 80; idem, "Interview with Obrist," ibid.: 259.

36. Idem, "Notes, 1964," ibid.: 22. Around this time, Richter also painted the image of a dead person photographed through glass, which he framed and glazed to create a partial illusion that one was seeing the image the same way. The experiment anticipated his work with framed panes of painted and unpainted glass as well as his framed mirrors.

37. Asked about how the catalogue began, Richter said: "I was always a little bit nervous or in despair about the fact that I was so unorganized. So I decided to photograph whatever I was working on. And suddenly I didn't find it to be chaotic anymore. Before, I had the feeling that everything was very chaotic and that I didn't know what I wanted." RSGR, 2001.

38. Ibid.

39. Ibid.

40. Ibid.

41. Ibid.

42. Ibid.

43. "Johns was holding on to a culture of painting that had to do with Cézanne, and I rejected that. That's why I painted from photographs, just in order to have nothing to do with the art of 'peinture,' which makes any kind of contemporary statement impossible." Richter, "Interview with Buchloh," *Daily Practice:* 139.

44. RSGR, 2001.

45. Richter, "Notes, 1986," *Daily Practice:* 124.

46. Idem, "Notes, 1964," ibid.: 24.

47. RSGR, 2001.

48. Coosje van Bruggen, "Gerhard Richter: Painting as a Moral Act," *Artforum* 9 (May 1985): 84.

49. Richter, "Text for Exhibition Catalogue, Galerie h, Hannover, 1966, written jointly with Sigmar Polke," *Daily Practice:* 45.

50. Idem, "Letter to a Newsreel Company, 29 April 1963," ibid.: 15–16.

51. Prior to planning their exhibition at Berges, Richter and Lueg had prepared a proposal to show work on the roof of the Galeries Lafayette department store in Paris, but nothing came of it. RSGR, 2001.

52. Less than a month after the exhibition, Kennedy was shot, and the Sunday following his assassination Kasper König—a close friend of Lueg and Richter at that time and later an important curator and museum director—borrowed the sculpture and in Dadaesque gesture drove from Düsseldorf to Münster with it tied to the top of his car. RSGR, 2001.

53. Richter, "Program and Report," *Daily Practice:* 20.

54. RSGR, 2001.

55. Richard Hamilton, "Letter to Peter and Alison Smith" (1957), in Kristine Stiles and Peter Selz, eds., *Contemporary Art: A Sourcebook of Artists' Writings* (Berkeley: University of California Press, 1996): 297.

56. In an interview with G. R. Swenson, Andy Warhol was asked what Pop art was all about, and he replied: "It's liking things." See John Russell and Suzi Gablik, *Pop Art Redefined* (New York and Washington, D.C.: Frederick A. Praeger, 1960): 116.

57. Richter, "Notes, 1962," *Daily Practice:* 13.

58. Interestingly, the most Richteresque of Artschwager's early paintings, *Portrait I* (1962), is in the collection of Kasper König.

59. Richter, "Notes, 1964," *Daily Practice:* 22.

60. Idem, "Notes, 1964–1965," ibid.: 35.

61. Ibid.: 31.

62. Idem, "Galerie h, Hannover," ibid.: 55.

63. Idem, "Notes, 1964–1965," ibid.: 35.

64. John Cage, "Lecture on Nothing," in *Silence: Lectures and Writings by John Cage* (Middletown, Conn.: Wesleyan University Press, 1939): 109.

65. Roland Barthes, *Camera Lucida: Reflections on Photography*, trans. Richard Howard (New York: Hill & Wang, 1981): 15.

66. Richter, "Interview with Rolf Schön, 1972," *Daily Practice:* 73.

67. Ibid.

68. *Roland Barthes by Roland Barthes*, trans. Richard Howard (New York: Hill & Wang, 1977): 43.

69. Richter, "Interview with Pehnt," *Daily Practice:* 117. In recent criticism, there has been a tendency to confuse the opportunity a work affords to open up legitimate questions about the social and political context surrounding that work with an unstated and undemonstrated intention to do so on the part of the artist. Thus, a writer might say that Andy Warhol's *Campbell's Soup Cans* critiques consumer society, or that his *Gold Marilyn* critiques the cult of celebrity, when there is, in fact, no evidence that Warhol thought in such terms. Moreover, such formulations beg the question of what ideological point of departure the artist might have had. Such assumptions implicitly co-opt the authority of the artist in support of interpretations that must stand or fall on the theoretical constructs of the writer or critic. Rigorous critiques—Freudian, Marxist, post-structuralist, postmodernist, or any other—must proceed by rigorous adherence to the basic rules of the argument. Broad cultural critique cannot be pursued, and it certainly cannot sustain its powers of persuasion, in ignorance or in defiance of verifiable facts. Moreover, the most complex aesthetic and sociopolitical analysis may be derailed by semantic neutralization of the contradictions that may exist between what an artist meant and what the observer sees. Warhol was very far from being an anticapitalist, but his art does provide material for thinking critically about capitalism. In writing about Richter we must be particularly sensitive to these issues, especially as he has, in most cases, clearly stated his intent with regard to a given body of work and clearly rejected ideologically inspired readings of it. The gap between what he says about his work and the things critical theory suggests might be said about it does not disallow exploration of the latter but such criticism cannot proceed on the assumption that Richter, an anti-Marxist, with little interest in Freud or post-structuralist thought, has wittingly or unwittingly

followed a program allied to such positions.

70. Idem, "Notes, 1964–1965," ibid.: 33.

71. Christiane Vielhaber, "Interview mit Gerhard Richter," *Das Kunstwerk* 2, no. 39 (April 1986): 41–43.

72. Ibid.

73. Richter, "Notes, 1964," *Daily Practice:* 24.

74. The sources for the first version of *Toilet Paper* can be found in panel 14 of *Atlas;* the source used for versions two and three is in panel 15. Richter's treatment of the second and third versions dramatically softens the illumination in the photographic source, suggesting that he intended, if not to make a poetically atmospheric painting out of this unlikely subject, then at least to lend it greater subtlety. It should also be noted that cropped images of version three have been incorrectly substituted for versions one and two in the *Catalogue Raisonné 1962–1993* (Paris: Musée d'Art Moderne de la Ville de Paris, 1993).

75. Richter, "Interview with Sabine Schütz," *Daily Practice:* 211–212.

76. Ibid.: 211.

77. The difference between the "cocky" Richter who made the papier-mâché JFK, and the reticent Richter who painted *Women with Umbrella,* can be heard in the artist's explanation of why he selected the image: "I was embarrassed to paint Jacqueline Kennedy. It was such a beautiful photo of a woman crying." Van Bruggen, "Painting as a Moral Act": 86.

78. *Eight Student Nurses* appears to have been partially influenced by Warhol's *Thirteen Most Wanted Men* (1964). Richter has said he prefers victims to killers as his subjects. Exceptions to this are his atypically Pop *Oswald* (1964), and *Mr. Heyde* (1965).

79. Van Bruggen, "Painting as a Moral Act": 86.

80. Bernard Blistène, "Mécanique et manuel dans l'art de Gerhard Richter," *Galeries Magazine* (April–May 1988): 90–95,132, 141.

81. Dieter Hülsmanns, "Das perfekteste Bild: Ateliergespräch mit dem Maler Gerd Richter," *Rheinische Post* 102 (May 3, 1966). Despite this disclaimer,

Richter not only painted numerous pictures of family and friends at the beginning of his career, but also several commissioned portraits. Among these were paintings of the art historian Arnold Bode, the art dealer Alfred Schmela, a professor Zander, and the artist Paul Wunderlich.

82. Richter, "Notes, 1964–1965," *Daily Practice:* 31.

83. Idem, "Interview with Buchloh," ibid.: 138.

84. Chuck Close's portraits of 1967–68 come the nearest, in that they were based on photographs of family and friends, but Close's process-based formalism gives these images a very different cast.

85. RSGR, 2001.

86. Ibid. Richter's other maternal uncle was also killed early in the war.

87. Between June 9 and 10, 1942, the male population of Lidice (some 200 men) was killed, its women sent to concentration camps, and its children to German institutions, and all its buildings burned. This was done in reprisal for the assassination in nearby Prague of Reinhard Heydrich, German Deputy Reich Protector for the region, second in command to the SS chief Heinrich Himmler, and a principal planner of the Holocaust.

88. RSGR, 2001.

89. *The Murderers Are Among Us* (1946), directed by Wolfgang Staudte. The film tells the story of a concentration camp survivor who returns home to find that the Nazi commander of his camp is living nearby in relative prosperity.

90. Richter, "Interview with Schütz," *Daily Practice:* 212.

91. Idem, "Notes, 1964," ibid.: 23.

92. Idem, "Notes, 1966," ibid.: 58.

93. Idem, "Notes, 1964," Ibid.: 23. Mangel-wurzel is a kind of root vegetable.

94. Idem, "Notes, 1964–1965," ibid.: 33–34.

95. Charles Baudelaire, "The Painter of Modern Life," in *Baudelaire: Selected Writings on Art and Artists,* trans. P. E. Charvet (Cambridge: Cambridge University Press, 1972): 402–403.

96. Van Bruggen, "Painting as a Moral Act": 86. At the end of these remarks Richter says of his associating his paintings of reconstructed Germany to the bombing that preceded it: "But I never said I meant anything with them." I think he did, but wanted at all costs to avoid the appearance of making pictorial speeches.

97. Richter, "Notes, 1964–1965," *Daily Practice:* 35.

98. Ibid.: 37.

99. Idem, "Letter to Edy de Wilde, 25 February 1975," ibid.: 82–83.

100. Ibid.

101. Idem, "Notes, 1964–1965," ibid.: 35.

II: Openings and Culs de Sac

1. Theodor Adorno, "Lyric Poetry and Society," in Martin Jay, *Adorno* (Cambridge, Mass.: Harvard University Press, 1984): 155.

2. RSGR, 2001.

3. Georg Baselitz and Eugen Schönebeck, "First Pandemonium Manifesto" (1961), in Klaus Schrenk, ed., *Upheavals, Manifestoes, Manifestations: Conceptions in the Arts at the Beginning of the Sixties, Berlin, Düsseldorf, Munich* (Cologne: DuMont, 1984): 171.

4. RSGR, 2001.

5. Richter, "Interview with John Anthony Thwaites and Sigmar Polke," *Daily Practice:* 26–27. John Anthony Thwaites, the improbable pseudonym that Sigmar Polke chose for his mock interview with Gerhard Richter, was, in fact, the name of the English cultural affairs officer at the British Embassy in Munich. Thwaites was also an art critic who wrote a short monograph on the sculptor Norbert Kricke that was published by Harry N. Abrams in New York. A relatively conservative constructivist sculptor and the first German artist of the postwar generation to be given a one-person show at The Museum of Modern Art, New York, in 1961, Kricke was a member of the faculty of the art academy in Düsseldorf. In that capacity, he was the relentless enemy of his colleague Joseph Beuys, whom he attacked for indulging in what Kricke called, "Jesus kitsch."

Making Thwaites a figure of fun would thus seem, in the context of the mock interview, to have been a polemical gesture aimed at the modernist art establishment of the Rhineland by two young artists eager to dissociate themselves from it.

6. Ibid. This is not the only instance of such gallows humor on Richter's part. In the photo album he compiled before leaving for the West there are two pictures of the artist with Ema and a friend under what appears to be a metal tube in the disjointed pose of people hanging. Whatever prompted this particular jest, one cannot help but think of the lynchings that occurred during the war and the trauma they must have caused anyone who saw them or saw pictures of them.

7. Jürgen Harten, "The Romantic Intent for Abstraction," in idem, *Gerhard Richter Bilder, 1962–1985* (Cologne: DuMont, 1986): 28.

8. Richard Cork, "Gerhard Richter: A Divided German," *Apollo* (London) (January 1992): 49.

9. Richter, "Notes, 1992," *Daily Practice:* 245–246.

10. Harten, *Richter Bilder:* 32.

11. Richter, "Notes, 1981," *Daily Practice:* 99.

12. Idem, "Notes, 1971," ibid.: 64.

13. Idem, "Interview with Schön," ibid.: 73.

14. Idem, "Interview with Jonas Storsve," ibid.: 225.

15. Idem, "Interview with Buchloh," ibid.: 137.

16. Bruce Glaser, "Questions to Stella and Judd," in Lucy Lippard and Gregory Battcock, eds., *Minimal Art: A Critical Anthology* (New York: E. P. Dutton, 1968): 158.

17. Sol LeWitt, "Sentences on Conceptual Art," in Alicia Legg, ed., *Sol LeWitt* (New York: The Museum of Modern Art, 1978): 168.

18. Ibid.

19. Richter, "Text for Catalogue of Group Exhibition Palais des Beaux-Arts, Brussels, 1974," *Daily Practice:* 82.

20. Idem, "Interview with Peter Sager," ibid.: 69.

21. "In 1962 I found my first escape

hatch: by painting from photographs, I was relieved of the need to choose or construct a subject. . . . My appropriation of photographs, my policy of copying them without alteration and without translating them into a modern form (as Warhol and others do), represented a principled avoidance of the subject. This principle has been maintained, with few exceptions (doors, windows, shadows, all of which I dislike) to this day." Idem, "Notes, 1986," ibid.: 130.

22. Cork, "Divided German": 49.

23. Richter, "Interview with Storsve," *Daily Practice:* 223.

24. Idem, "Notes, 1964–1965," ibid.: 37.

25. Louis Aragon, *La Peinture au defi* [The Challenge to Painting] (Paris: Librairie Jose Corti, 1930): 15–16; trans. by the author.

26. Reinhardt, in Glaser, [Interview] *Art International* (December 1966): 18–21.

27. Richter, "Interview with Storsve," *Daily Practice:* 223.

28. Van Bruggen, "Painting as a Moral Act": 88.

29. Beuys, "A propos de Palermo": 77.

30. Gerhard Richter, "About Watercolors and Related Things: Gerhard Richter in Conversation with Dieter Schwarz. Cologne, June 26, 1999," in Dieter Schwarz, ed., *Gerhard Richter: Aquarelle/Watercolors, 1964–1999* (Winterthur: Kunstmuseum; Düsseldorf: Richter Verlag, 1999): 21.

31. Mark Rosenthal, "Interview with Gerhard Richter," in idem, ed., *Mark Rothko* (Washington, D.C.: National Gallery of Art, 1998): 363–366.

32. RSGR, 2001.

33. "Notes, 1984," *Daily Practice:* 108–109.

34. RSGR, 2001.

35. Ibid.

36. After Palermo's death, a modified version of the room originally created for the Heiner Friedrich gallery in Cologne was permanently installed at the Städtische Galerie im Lenbachhaus, Munich.

37. Michael Compton, "In Praise of the Subject," in *Marcel Broodthaers* (Minneapolis: Walker Art Center, 1989): 24.

38. Ibid.: 55.

39. Neither, for that matter, was Broodthaers interested in explicitly political counter-discourses. "The way I see it," he wrote, "there can be no direct communication between art and message, especially if the message is political, without running the risk of being burned by the artifice. Foundering. I prefer signing my name to these booby traps without taking advantage of this caution." Ibid.: 44.

40. Richter, "Interview with Doris von Drathen," *Daily Practice:* 239.

41. An analogous situation arose when Robert Rauschenberg requested a drawing from Willem de Kooning so that he could erase it in a gesture intended to symbolize his independence from the Abstract Expressionist aesthetic. De Kooning obliged, even though he was the Oedipal father being ritually dispatched, but reportedly he gave Rauschenberg a really good drawing and also one that had been heavily worked into the paper to make it harder for the younger artist to sacrifice the image and harder for him physically to unmake it.

42. RSGR, 2001.

43. Ibid.

44. Van Bruggen, "Painting as a Moral Act": 91. See also Susanne Ehrenfried, "Gespräch mit dem Maler Gerhard Richter am 8. August 1995" (in idem, "'Ohne Eigenschaften': Das Portrait bei Gerhard Richter." Diss., Munich: Ludwig-Maximillian-Universität München, c. 1995: 180), in which Richter answers a question about Buchloh having chided him for excluding women from *48 Portraits:* "Buchloh's remark is a reproach absolutely in keeping with the times. It couldn't have been made when I painted '48 Portraits.' At that time one did not think in this way. . . . The fact that only men were included reflects this notion of homogeneity. If women had been included the formal principles would no longer have been matched. In addition, it certainly had to do with a search for a father figure. After all I'm not in search of an image of a mother."

45. Benjamin H. D. Buchloh, "Divided Memory and Post-Traditional Identity: Gerhard Richter's Work of Mourning," *October* 75 (winter 1996): 73.

46. Ibid.: 75.

47. RSGR, 2001.

48. Ibid.

49. Ibid.

50. In the late 1970s Anselm Kiefer made several works that would seem to have been prompted by the example of *48 Portraits*. They are the painting *Ways of Worldly Wisdom* (1976–77) and a woodcut and multimedium work *Ways of Worldly Wisdom—Arminius's Battle* (1978–80). Kiefer assembled a portrait gallery of writers and philosophers, that included Enlightenment figures such as Emmanuel Kant but also romantics such as Heinrich von Kleist and the existentialist thinker and Nazi academic Martin Heidegger. Kiefer thus attempted a symbolic recovery of the past that was buried or contaminated by the Nazis. By contrast with Richter's work, which is internationalist, all of Kiefer's culture heroes are German. Moreover, rather than present them in a reportorial fashion as Richter does, he sets the stage for them with the maximum of painterly *Sturm und Drang*. Although not without its complexity, this amounts to affirmative cultural restoration as distinct from Richter's probing of cultural doubt. Also, in the late 1970s the American painter Leon Golub made a large number of portraits of political leaders of the Left and Right—Generalissimo Francisco Franco, Mao Tse-tung, Fidel Castro, John Foster Dulles, and Richard Nixon, among them. Although painted in a graphic expressionist manner, these pictures are close to Richter's work in their lack of painterly editorializing, leaving the viewer unsure of what to think but more acutely aware than before of what power looks like.

51. Richter, "Interview with Storsve," *Daily Practice:* 226.

52. Ibid.

53. Idem, "Notes, 1964–1965," ibid.: 39.

54. In 1975 Richter painted six portraits of Gilbert & George on a commission arranged through Konrad Fischer.

55. Harten, *Richter Bilder:* 47.

56. Richter, "Interview with Rolf Gunther Dienst, 1970," *Daily Practice*: 64.

57. Idem, "Interview with Schön," ibid.: 75.

58. Idem, "Letter to Ammann," ibid.: 81.

59. Van Bruggen, "Painting as a Moral Act": 83.

60. Richter, "Interview with Obrist," *Daily Practice:* 268. (Photographs from Richter's trip to Greenland were later used as the basis for a 1981 artist's book, *EIS*, published in Rome by Edizioni Galeria Peroni.) Friedrich's painting, *The Sea of Ice*, is also known as *The Wreck of the "Hope."*

61. Idem, "Notes, 1986," ibid.: 124.

62. Irmeline Lebeer, "Gerhard Richter ou la Réalité de l'Image," *Chronique de l'Art Vivant* 36 (February 1973): 16; trans. by the author.

63. Richter, "Notes, 1983," *Daily Practice:* 101.

64. Willem de Kooning, "A Desperate View, " in *Willem de Kooning: The Northern Light, 1960–1983* (Amsterdam: Stedelijk Museum, 1983): 67.

65. Gérard Audinet, "L'age d'oeuvre: Early and Late," *Kanaleurope* 3 (1992): 45.

66. Richter, "Interview with Storsve," *Daily Practice:* 227.

67. Dorothea Dietrich, "Gerhard Richter: An Interview," *Print Collectors' Newsletter* 16 (September–October 1985): 128.

68. Richter, "Interview with Buchloh," *Daily Practice:* 141.

69. Ibid.

70. Rosenthal, "Interview with Richter": n.p.

71. Ibid.

72. Richter, "Interview with Obrist," *Daily Practice:* 262.

73. Ellis, "Elusive Richter": 186.

74. Richter responded to Mark Rosenthal's questions about his relationship to Rothko and Romanticism saying: "For me romanticism is the likes of Philipp Otto Runge, that is, an artist who presents a tortured view of himself. Maybe in the widest sense of the word Rothko might be a romantic, as Robert Rosenblum suggested in his book, *Modern Painting and the Northern Romantic Tradition: From Friedrich to Rothko*." Rosenthal, "Interview with Richter": n.p.

75. Ellis, "Elusive Richter": 186.

76. Richter, "Notes, 1985," *Daily Practice:* 122.

77. RSGR, 2001.

78. Ibid.

79. Ibid.

80. Buchloh, "Interview with Richter," in Neff, *Richter: Paintings:* 18. (I have cited this version of Buchloh's interview, rather than the one published in *Daily Practice,* because of differences between the two translations that affect nuances of meaning.)

81. In 1995 Richter agreed to allow one of his candle paintings to be blown up and reproduced on a fabric sign that covered the entire side of a large building in Dresden near the edge of the Danube River: "I don't know any longer who in Dresden thought of the idea of having a picture by me covering this large facade. I think it was Dr. Schmidt from the museum and it was also he who suggested the candle motif. Then I collaged different candle pictures onto a photo of the facade, and that's how the two candles came about, that appeared to be the one that worked best. At the beginning it was supposed to be a pretty sight, but later one discovered that the candle picture also served as a useful political expression. That was due to the celebrations that took place in front of it on February 13, fifty years after Dresden was destroyed. Candles were always an important symbol of the GDR as a silent protest against the regime, and that was already very impressive. It naturally remains an unusual feeling to see that something quite different can come from such a small candle painting, something that I never intended." Hans-Ulrich Obrist, "Interview with Gerhard Richter" (1995), unpublished.

82. For an indication of how far the ramifications of what might seem to be the incomprehensible extremism of a tiny minority reach, how complex the dynamics of that period were, and how closely linked it is to the present, consider the aftermath for several individuals involved: Horst Mahler, a lawyer and Baader's early rival for leadership of the budding RAF is now legal counsel and ideological apologist for the far Right, arguably pro-Nazi, German Democratic Party; Otto Schilly, who helped shape the defense of the Baader-Meinhof group in the 1970s is now Minister of Justice in the government of the Social Democratic Chancellor Helmut Schröder; Joschka Fischer, the current Foreign Minister and Vice Chancellor was a radical activist in the same circles as Baader and Meinhof, although he publicly advocated setting bombs aside for paving stones; and Bettina Röhl, Meinhof's daughter and a journalist, is responsible for recently publishing images that exposed Fischer's attack on a policeman during a street-fighting incident in the 1970s.

83. Richter, "Notes for a Press Conference, November, December, 1989," *Daily Practice:* 173.

84. Ibid.

85. Ibid.: 174.

86. Idem, "Notes, 1983," ibid.: 102.

III: Permission Granted

1. Richter, "Notes, 1962," *Daily Practice:* 15.

2. Idem, "Interview with Dieter Hülsmanns and Fridolin Reske," ibid.: 57–58.

3. RSGR, 2001. (Moritz's sister Ella Maria was born in 1996.)

4. Ibid.

5. Ibid. The ideological nuances of the word *sympathizer* were noticed by Catharina Manchanda, who was present as a translator throughout the conversations between Richter and the author; it was she who fastened on the implications of the term and prompted these clarifications on the subject from him.

6. Ibid.

7. Richter, "Interview with Schütz," *Daily Practice:* 211.

8. RSGR, 2001.

9. Benjamin H. D. Buchloh, "Allegories of Painting," in *Gerhard Richter: Documenta IX, 1992* (New York: Marian Goodman Gallery, 1993): 13.

10. Ibid.

11. Ibid.

12. Richter, "Interview with von Drathen," *Daily Practice:* 233.

13. Friedrich von Schiller, "On Naive and Sentimental Poetry," in H. D. Nisbet, ed., *German Aesthetics and Literary Criticism: Winckelmann, Lessing, Hammna, Herder, Schiller and Goethe* (Cambridge: Cambridge University Press, 1985): 195.

14. Ibid.: 196.

15. Arthur Schopenhauer, cited in Paul Edwards, ed., *Encyclopedia of Philosophy*, vol. 7 (New York: Macmillan and The Free Press, 1967): 329.

16. Friedrich Nietzsche, as quoted in Arthur C. Danto, *Nietzsche as Philosopher: An Original Study* (New York: Columbia University Press, 1965): 38–39.

17. Ibid.: 67. I am much indebted to Professor Danto for his critical account of Nietzsche's thought.

18. Richter, "Notes, 1962," *Daily Practice*: 11–12.

19. Idem, "Notes, 1988," ibid.: 170.

20. Idem, "Notes, 1962," ibid.: 15.

21. Idem, "Notes, 1964–1965," ibid.: 38.

22. Samuel Beckett, *The Unnamable,* (New York: Grove Press, 1958): 179.

23. Richter, "Notes, 1985," *Daily Practice*: 118.

24. Gerhard Richter, [Catalogue text] in *Documenta 7,* vol. 1 (Kassel: Paul Dierichs, 1982).

PLATES

All the images on the following pages represent paintings and other works by Gerhard Richter. In the caption for each work, the title is given first in English and then in German within brackets. The date of the work, the medium, and the dimensions follow. Measurements are given in feet and inches, and in centimeters, height preceding width. The numeral after the letters GR indicates the catalogue raisonné number assigned to the work by the artist. A credit line, identifying the present owner of the work, is the final element in each caption.

Atlas: Panel 1. 1962–66. Black-and-white photographs, 20⅜ × 26¼" (51.7 × 66.7 cm). Städtische Galerie im Lenbachhaus, Munich

Atlas: Panel 2. 1962–66. Black-and-white photographs, 20⅜ × 26¼" (51.7 × 66.7 cm). Städtische Galerie im Lenbachhaus, Munich

Atlas: Panel 3. 1962–66. Black-and-white photographs, 20⅜ × 26¼" (51.7 × 66.7 cm). Städtische Galerie im Lenbachhaus, Munich

Atlas: Panel 4. 1962–66. Black-and-white photographs, 20⅜ × 26¼" (51.7 × 66.7 cm). Städtische Galerie im Lenbachhaus, Munich

Atlas: Panel 5. 1962–66. Black-and-white and color clippings and photographs, 20⅜ × 26¼" (51.7 × 66.7 cm). Städtische Galerie im Lenbachhaus, Munich

Atlas: Panel 6. 1962–66. Black-and-white and color photographs, 20⅜ × 26¼" (51.7 × 66.7 cm). Städtische Galerie im Lenbachhaus, Munich

Atlas: Panel 7. 1962–66. Black-and-white and color clippings, 20⅜ × 26¼" (51.7 × 66.7 cm). Städtische Galerie im Lenbachhaus, Munich

Atlas: Panel 8. 1962–66. Black-and-white clippings, 20⅜ × 26¼" (51.7 × 66.7 cm). Städtische Galerie im Lenbachhaus, Munich

Atlas: Panel 9. 1962–68. Black-and-white clippings and photograph, 20⅜ × 26¼" (51.7 × 66.7 cm). Städtische Galerie im Lenbachhaus, Munich

Atlas: Panel 10. 1962–68. Black-and-white clippings, 20⅜ × 26¼" (51.7 × 66.7 cm). Städtische Galerie im Lenbachhaus, Munich

Atlas: Panel 11. 1963–66. Black-and-white clippings and photographs, 20⅜ × 26¼" (51.7 × 66.7 cm). Städtische Galerie im Lenbachhaus, Munich

Atlas: Panel 12. 1963–66. Black-and-white clippings, 20⅜ × 26¼" (51.7 × 66.7 cm). Städtische Galerie im Lenbachhaus, Munich

Atlas: Panel 13. 1964–67. Black-and-white clippings and photograph, 26¼ × 20⅜"
(66.7 × 51.7 cm). Städtische Galerie im Lenbachhaus, Munich

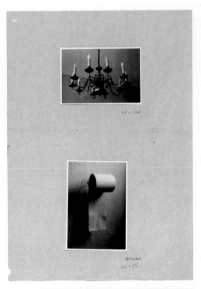

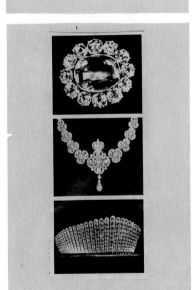

Atlas: Panel 14. 1964–67. Black-and-white clippings and photographs, 26¼ × 20⅜" (66.7 × 51.7 cm). Städtische Galerie im Lenbachhaus, Munich

Atlas: Panel 15. 1964–67. Black-and-white clippings and photographs, 26¼ × 20⅜" (66.7 × 51.7 cm). Städtische Galerie im Lenbachhaus, Munich

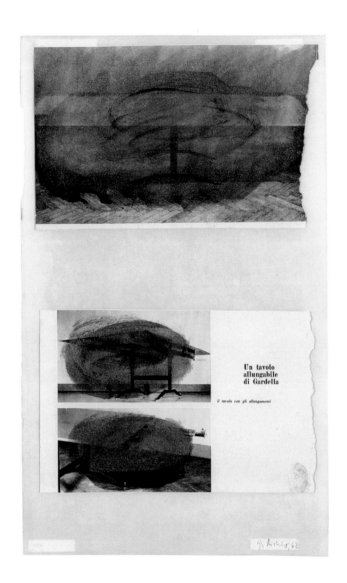

Maquette for Table [Entwurf für Tisch]. 1959. Magazine clippings with annotations
by the artist, approx. 18 × 12" (48 x 30 cm). Private collection, Frankfurt

106

Table [Tisch]. 1962. Oil on canvas, 35½ × 44½" (90.2 × 113 cm). GR 1.
San Francisco Museum of Modern Art. Extended loan from a private collection

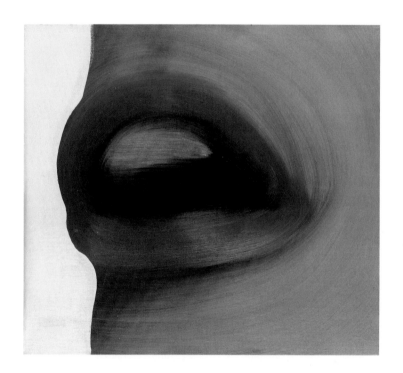

Mouth [Mund]. 1963. Oil on canvas, 26½ × 29¼" (67.3 × 74.3 cm). GR 11-1. The Art Institute of Chicago. Acquired through a prior gift of Mrs. Henry C. Woods and gift of Lannan Foundation, 1997

Coffin Bearers [Sargträger]. 1962. Oil on canvas, 53 ³⁄₁₆ × 70 ⁷⁄₈" (135 × 180 cm).
GR 5. Bayerische Staatsgemäldesammlungen, Munich. Acquired from the Galerie-Verein.

Stag [Hirsch]. 1963. Oil on canvas, 59" × 6' 6¾" (150 × 200 cm). GR 7.
Private collection

110

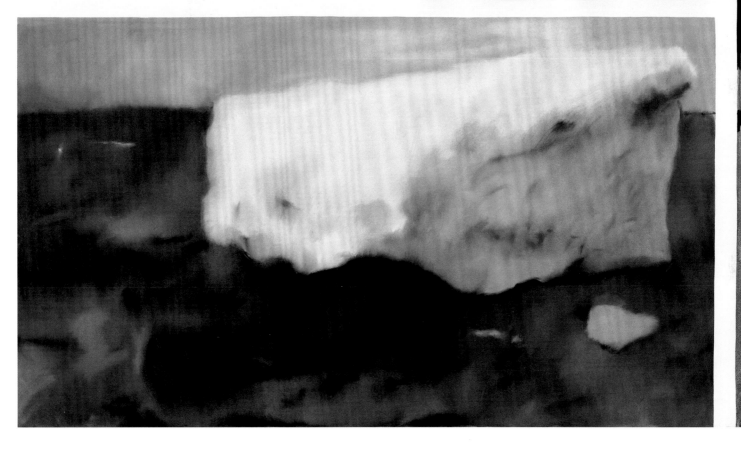

Dead [Tote]. 1963. Oil on canvas, 39¾ × 59¹⁄₁₆" (100 × 150 cm). GR 9.
Private collection, Frankfurt

Toilet Paper [Klorolle]. 1965. Oil on canvas, 21 $^{11}/_{16}$ × 15 ¾" (55 × 40 cm). GR 75-1.
Collection Joshua Mack and Ron Warren

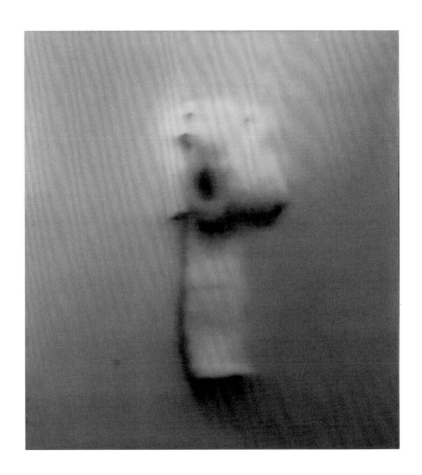

Toilet Paper [Klorolle]. 1965. Oil on canvas, 27⁹⁄₁₆ × 25⅝" (70 × 65 cm). GR 75-3.
Courtesy Massimo Martino Fine Arts and Projects, Mendrisio, Switzerland

Kitchen Chair [Küchenstuhl]. 1965. Oil on canvas, 39⅜ × 31½" (100 × 80 cm).
GR 97. Kunsthalle, Recklinghausen, Germany

Administrative Building [Verwaltungsgebäude]. 1964. Oil on canvas, 38¼ × 59"
(97.2 × 149.9 cm). GR 39. Private collection, San Francisco

Mustang Squadron [Mustang-Staffel]. 1964. Oil on canvas, 34½ × 59⅛"
(87.6 × 150.2 cm). GR 19. Collection Robert Lehrman, Washington, D.C.

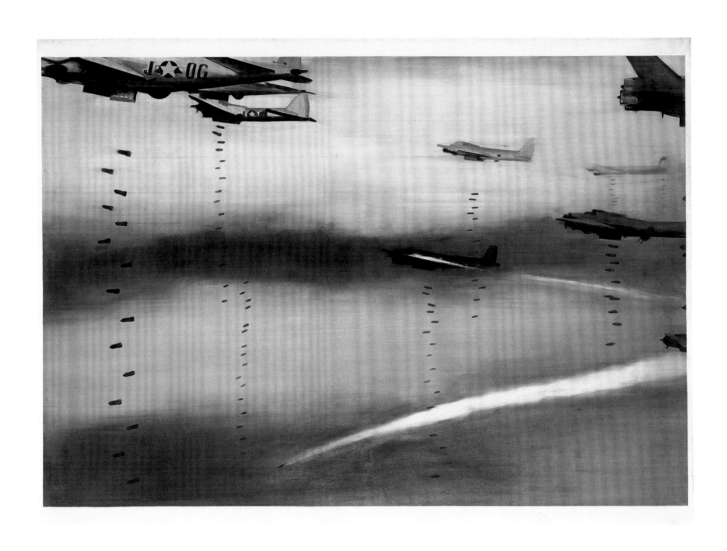

Bombers [Bomber]. 1963. Oil on canvas, 51 3/16 × 70 7/8" (130 × 180 cm). GR 13.
Städtische Galerie, Wolfsburg

Phantom Interceptors [Phantom Abfangjäger]. 1964. Oil on canvas, 55 ⅛" × 6' 2 ¾" (140 × 190 cm). GR 50. Froehlich Collection, Stuttgart

Uncle Rudi [Onkel Rudi]. 1965. Oil on canvas, 34¼ × 19¹¹⁄₁₆" (87 × 50 cm). GR 85.
The Czech Museum of Fine Arts, Prague. Lidice Collection

Horst and His Dog [Horst mit Hund]. 1965. Oil on canvas, 31 ½ × 23 ⅝"
(80 × 60 cm). GR 94. Private collection, New York

Cow [Kuh]. 1964. Oil on canvas, 51³⁄₁₆ × 59¹⁄₁₆" (130 × 150 cm). GR 15.
Kunstmuseum, Bonn. Hans Grothe Permanent Collection

Ägyptische Wüste bei Edfu

Felsenkarst bei Theben

Tempelweg bei Gizeh

Ramsestempel in Theben

rungen vorzunehmen, die eine Umgestaltum der Produktionsmittel erforderlich machen! würden.

Unter dem Druck einiger im Werk beschäftigter sportbegesteirter Ingenieure (wie Zoraf Arkus-Duntov, der mehrmals in Le Mans,- auch am Lenkrad eines Porsche, zu sehen war) wird aber schon seit Jahren hinter den Kulissen dern

gelegt, daß beim Bremsen Kräfte ausgelöst, werden, die es verhindern, daß sich der Wagen hinten zu stark hebt und vorn in die Knie geht. Die Lenkhebel haben an ihrem äußeren Ende zwei Löcher, in welche die Gelenke der Spurstangen beliebig eingeschraubt werden können, so daß dem Fahrer eine ziemliche direkte oder weniger direkte Lenkung zur

mit Rennreifen, die einen geringeren Rollwiderstand aufweisen, zweifellos eine um einiges höhere Geschwindigkeit hätte erreicht werden können. Für den Straßengebrauch ist, jedoch die Untersetzung 3,36 außerordentlich angenehm, zumal der Motor bis zur Höchstdrehzahl vibrationsfrei und verhältnismäßic ruhig dreht, wozu sich eine unbedenklich

Egyptian Landscape [Ägyptische Landschaft]. 1964. Oil on canvas, 59 1/16 × 65" (150 × 165 cm). GR 53. Courtesy Zwirner and Wirth, New York

Ferrari. 1964. Oil on canvas, 57" × 6'6½" (144.8 × 199.4 cm). GR 22. Modern Art Museum, Fort Worth. Purchase, Sid W. Richardson Foundation Endowment Fund

Spru
fach
Ingri
ihr E
zu e
Rost
ihre
Zehe

126

High Diver I [Turmspringerin I]. 1965. Oil on canvas, 6' 2 ¹³⁄₁₆" × 43 ⁵⁄₁₆" (190 × 110 cm). GR 43. Courtesy Massimo Martino Fine Arts and Projects, Mendrisio, Switzerland

Mrs. Marlow [Frau Marlow]. 1964. Oil on canvas, 30 ⁵⁄₁₆ × 37 ¹³⁄₁₆" (77 × 96 cm). GR 28. Private collection, Switzerland

Flemish Crown [Flämische Krone]. 1965. Oil on canvas, 35 7/16 × 43 5/16" (90 × 110 cm). GR 77. Private collection

Woman Descending the Staircase [Frau, die Treppe herabgehend]. 1965. Oil on canvas, 6'7" × 51" (200.7 × 129.5 cm). GR 92. The Art Institute of Chicago. Roy J. and Frances R. Friedman Endowment and gift of Lannan Foundation, 1997

Woman with Umbrella [Frau mit Schirm]. 1964. Oil on canvas, 63 × 37⅜" (160 × 95 cm). GR 29. Daros Collection, Switzerland

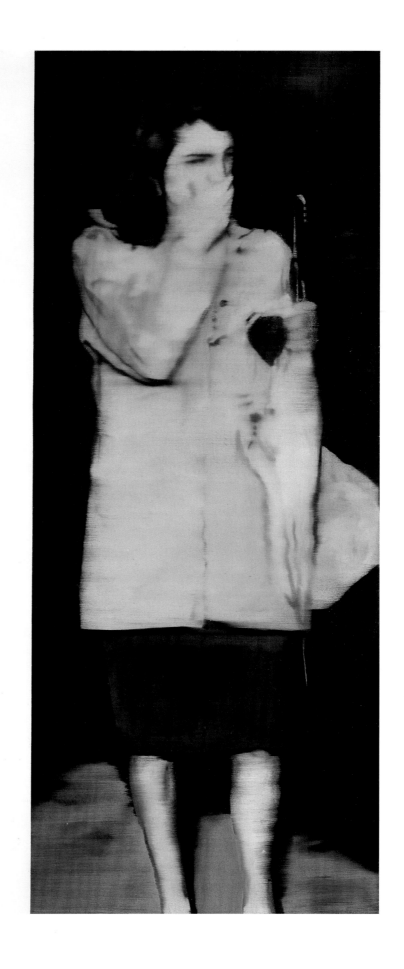

Helga Matura with Her Fiancé [Helga
Matura mit Verlobtem]. 1966. Oil on
canvas, 6′6⁹⁄₁₆″ × 39″ (199.5 × 99 cm).
GR 125. museum kunst palast,
Düsseldorf

Helga Matura. 1966. Oil on canvas,
70⁵⁄₁₆ × 43³⁄₁₆″ (178.5 × 109.7 cm).
GR 124. Art Gallery of Ontario,
Toronto. Gift of the Volunteer
Committee Fund, 1986

Helga Matura

Eight Student Nurses [Acht Lernschwestern]. 1966. Oil on canvas; 8 paintings, each,
36⅜ × 27⁹⁄₁₆" (95 × 70 cm). GR 130. Kunstmuseum, Winterthur. Permanent loan

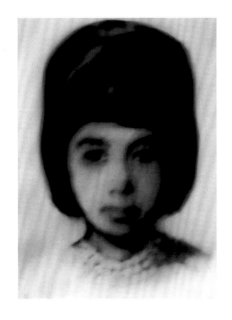   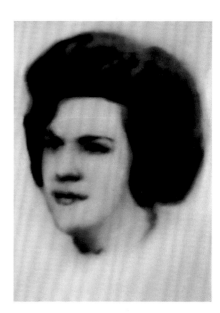

Ema (Nude on a Staircase) [Ema (Akt auf einer Treppe)]. 1966. Oil on canvas, 6'6¾" × 51³⁄₁₆" (200 × 130 cm). GR 134. Museum Ludwig, Cologne

Six Colors [Sechs Farben]. 1966. Synthetic polymer paint on canvas, 6′ 6¾″ × 66¹⁵⁄₁₆″ (200 × 170 cm). GR 142. Private collection, Berlin

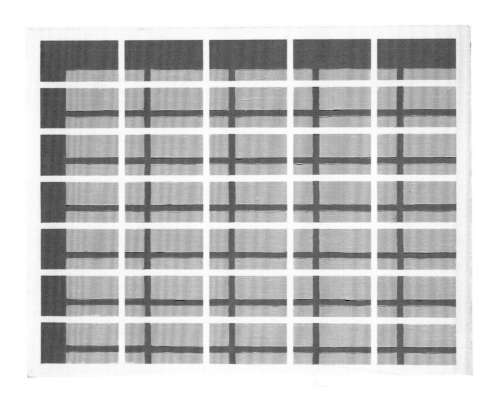

Shadow Painting [Schattenbild]. 1968. Oil on canvas, 26⅜ × 34¼" (67 × 87 cm).
GR 209-8. Museum of Contemporary Art, Pôrto, Portugal. Serralves Foundation
Collection

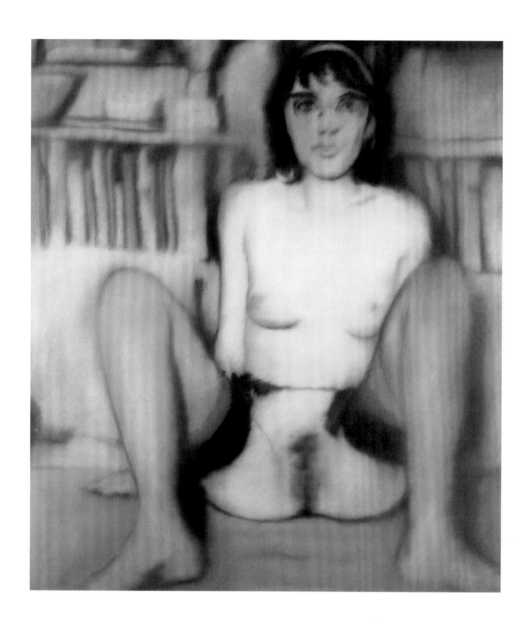

Student [Studentin]. 1967. Oil on canvas, 41 3/8 × 37 7/16" (105 × 95 cm). GR 149. Private collection

Motor Boat (first version) [Motorboot (erste Fassung)]. 1965. Oil on canvas, 66 15/16 × 66 15/16" (170 × 170 cm). GR 79-a. Private collection

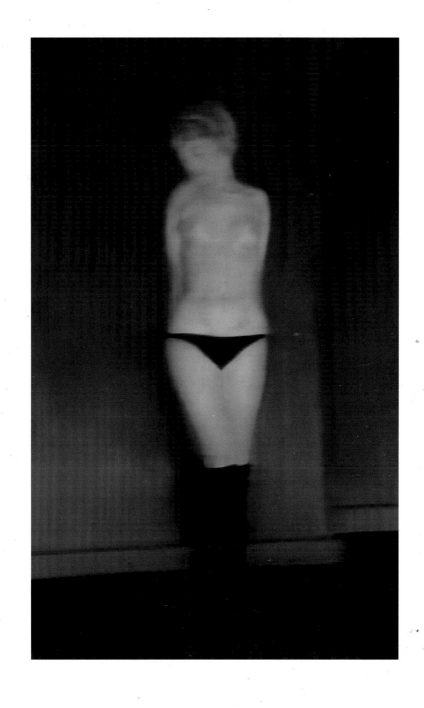

Olympia. 1967. Oil on canvas, 6'6¾" × 51³⁄₁₆" (200 × 130 cm). GR 157.
Private collection, Berlin

Small Nude [Kleiner Akt]. 1967. Oil on canvas, 50¼ × 31½" (127.6 × 80.1 cm).
GR 165. Collection Frances and John Bowes

Cathedral Square, Milan [Domplatz, Mailand]. 1968. Oil on canvas, 9'¼" × 9'6³⁄₁₆"
(275 × 290 cm). GR 169. Park Hyatt Collection, Chicago

146

Townscape Madrid [Stadtbild Madrid]. 1968. Oil on canvas, 9' 1 1/16" × 9' 6 15/16" (277 × 292 cm). GR 171. Kunstmuseum, Bonn. Hans Grothe Permanent Collection

Townscape SL [Stadtbild SL]. 1969. Oil on canvas, 48 7/16 × 48 13/16" (123 × 124 cm). GR 218-1. Courtesy Massimo Martino Fine Arts and Projects, Mendrisio, Switzerland

Townscape PL [Stadtbild PL]. 1970. Oil on canvas, 6'6½" × 6'6½" (199.6 × 199.6 cm). GR 249. The Museum of Modern Art, New York. Fractional and promised gift of Jo Carole and Ronald S. Lauder

Himalaya [Himalaja]. 1968. Oil on canvas, 6'6¾" × 63" (200 × 160 cm). GR 181. Collection Gilberto Sandretto

Untitled (Line) [Ohne Titel (Strich)]. 1968. Oil on canvas, 31½ × 15¾" (80 × 40 cm).
GR 194-9. Hamburger Kunsthalle, Hamburg. Elisabeth and Gerhard Sohst Collection

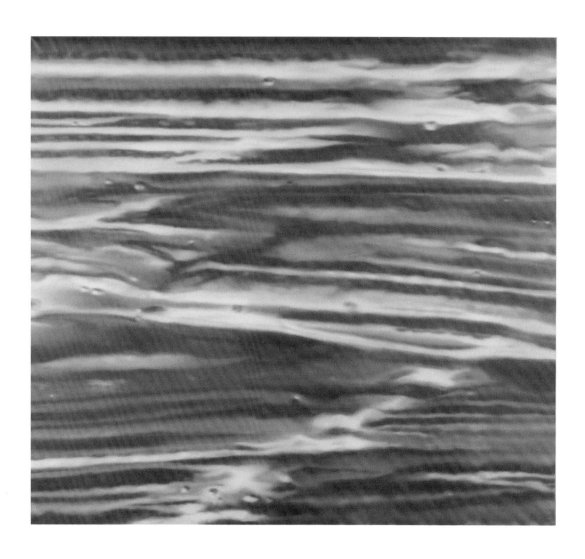

Detail (Brown) [Ausschnitt (braun)]. 1970. Oil on canvas, 53 3/16 × 59 1/16" (135 × 150 cm).
GR 271. Museum Folkwang, Essen

Bridge (by the Sea) [Brücke (am Meer)]. 1969. Oil on canvas, 36⅝ × 38⅝"
(93 × 98 cm). GR 202. Private collection, Berlin

Cloud [Wolke]. 1970. Oil on canvas, 6'6¾" × 9'10⁷⁄₁₆" (200 × 300.7 cm). GR 270-3.
National Gallery of Canada, Ottawa

Seascape (Sea–Sea) [Seestück (See–See)]. 1970. Oil on canvas, 6'6¾" × 6'6¾" (200 × 200 cm).
GR 244. Staatliche Museen zu Berlin, Preußischer Kulturbesitz, Nationalgalerie, Berlin

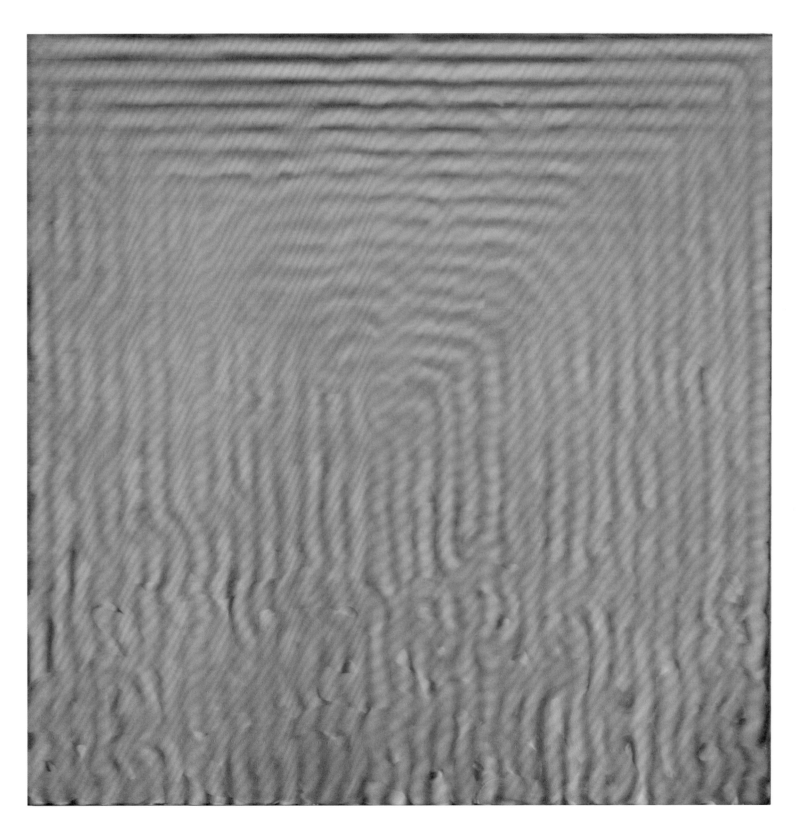

Gray Streaks [Grauschlieren]. 1968. Oil on canvas, 6' 6¾" × 6' 6¾" (200 × 200 cm). GR 192-1. Private collection

Seascape (Cloudy) [Seestück (bewölkt)]. 1969. Oil on canvas, 6'6¾" × 6'6¾" (200 × 200 cm).
GR 239-1. Private collection, Berlin

Eagle [Adler]. 1972. Oil on canvas, 27 9/16 × 19 11/16" (70 × 50 cm). GR 322-1. Private collection

Two Sculptures for a Room by Palermo [Zwei Skulpturen für einen Raum von Palermo]. 1971. Cast bronze, gray paint, and marble; two parts, each, 68 1/4 × 8 1/8 × 10 1/4" (173.4 × 20.6 × 26 cm). GR 297-3. Private collection

48 Portraits. 1971–72. Oil on canvas; 48 paintings, each, 27⁹⁄₁₆ × 21¹¹⁄₁₆" (70 × 55 cm).
GR 324-1 through 324-48. Museum Ludwig, Cologne

1. Mihail Sadoveanu, 1880–1961
2. José Ortega y Gasset, 1883–1955
3. Otto Schmeil, 1860–1943
4. Gustav Mahler, 1860–1911
5. William James, 1842–1910
6. Arrigo Boito, 1842–1918
7. Jean Sibelius, 1865–1957
8. Igor Stravinsky, 1882–1971
9. Hans Pfitzner, 1969–1949
10. Pyotr Ilich Tchaikovsky, 1840–1893
11. Frédéric Joliot, 1900–1958
12. Herbert George Wells, 1866–1946
13. James Chadwick, 1891–1974
14. Alfredo Casella, 1883–1947
15. Max Planck, 1858–1947
16. Paul Adrien Maurice Dirac, 1902–1984

17. James Franck, 1882–1964
18. Paul Claudel, 1868–1955
19. Manuel de Falla, 1976–1946
20. Nicolai Hartmann, 1882–1950
21. Paul Valéry, 1871–1945
22. Thomas Mann, 1875–1955
23. Enrico Fermi, 1901–1954
24. John Dos Passos, 1896–1970
25. Alfred Mombert, 1872–1942
26. Patrick Maynard Stuart Blackett, 1897–1974
27. Bjørnstjerne Bjørnson, 1832–1910
28. Franz Kafka, 1883–1924
29. Giacomo Puccini, 1858–1924
30. Louis Victor de Broglie, 1892–1987
31. Saint-John Perse, 1887–1975
32. Graham Greene, 1904–1991

33. Paul Hindemith, 1895–1963
34. Alfred Adler, 1870–1937
35. Albert Einstein, 1879–1955
36. Hugo von Hofmannsthal, 1874–1929
37. Wilhelm Dilthey, 1833–1911
38. Émile Verhaeren, 1855–1916
39. Isidor Isaac Rabi, 1898–1988
40. Oscar Wilde, 1854–1900
41. François Mauriac, 1885–1970
42. Anton Bruckner, 1824–1896
43. Rainer Maria Rilke, 1875–1926
44. William Somerset Maugham, 1874–1965
45. Karl Manne Siegbahn, 1886–1978
46. André Gide, 1869–1951
47. Anton Webern, 1883–1945
48. Rudolf Borchardt, 1877–1945

48 Portraits (detail): Paul Valéry

1.   2.   3.   4.   5.   6.

48 Portraits (details)

162

7.   8.   9.   10.   11.   12.

13.   14.   15.   16.   17.   18.

48 Portraits (details)

19.   20.   21.   22.   23.   24.

25.   26.   27.   28.   29.   30.

48 Portraits (details)

31.   32.   33.   34.   35.   36.

37.   38.   39.   40.   41.   42.

48 Portraits (details)

   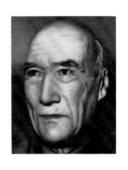  

43.   44.   45.   46.   47.   48.

48 Portraits (detail): Paul Hindemith

48 Portraits (detail): Patrick Maynard Stuart Blackett

Un-Painting (Gray) [Vermalung (grau)]. 1972. Oil on canvas, 6' 6¾" × 6' 6¾"
(200 × 200 cm). GR 326-4. Jung Collection

Gray [Grau]. 1973. Oil on canvas, 35 7/16 × 25 5/8" (90 × 65 cm). GR 348-7.
Private collection

Gray [Grau]. 1973. Oil on canvas, 8' 2 7/16" × 6' 6 3/4" (250 × 200 cm). GR 348-1.
Private collection, Cologne

175

Brigid Polk. 1971. Oil on canvas, 40 × 50" (101.6 × 127 cm). GR 309.
Private collection, San Francisco

Tourist (with 1 Lion) [Tourist (mit 1 Löwen)]. 1975. Oil on canvas, 66 ¹⁵⁄₁₆" × 6' 6 ¼"
(170 × 200 cm) GR 370-1. Flick Collection

Red–Blue–Yellow [Rot–Blau–Gelb]. 1972. Oil on canvas, 59 1/16 × 59 1/16" (150 × 150 cm).
GR 330. Di Bennardo Collection

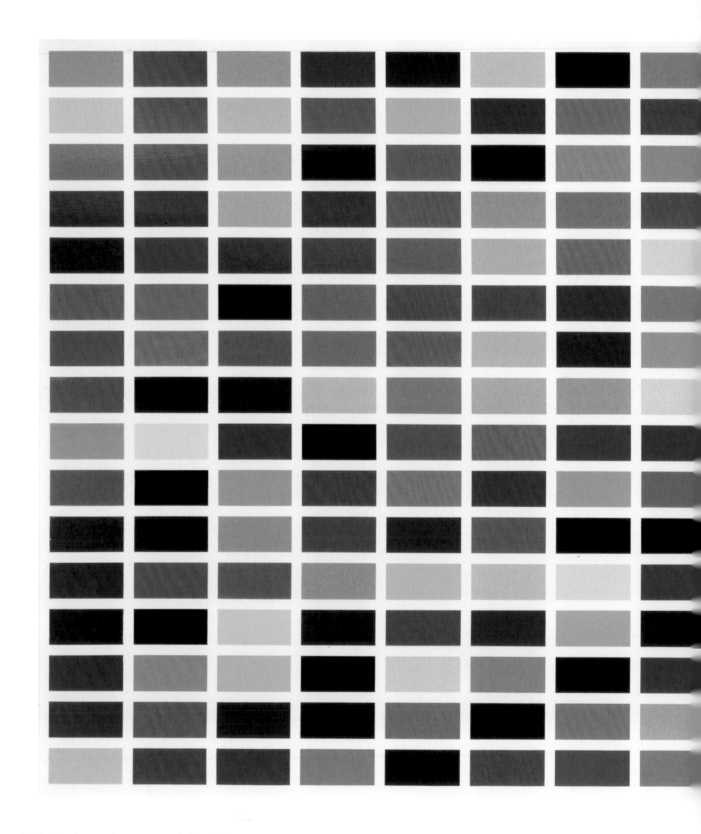

256 Colors [256 Farben]. 1974. Synthetic polymer paint on canvas, 7′ 3″ × 14′ 5″
(221 × 439.5 cm). GR 352-2. Private collection, San Francisco

180

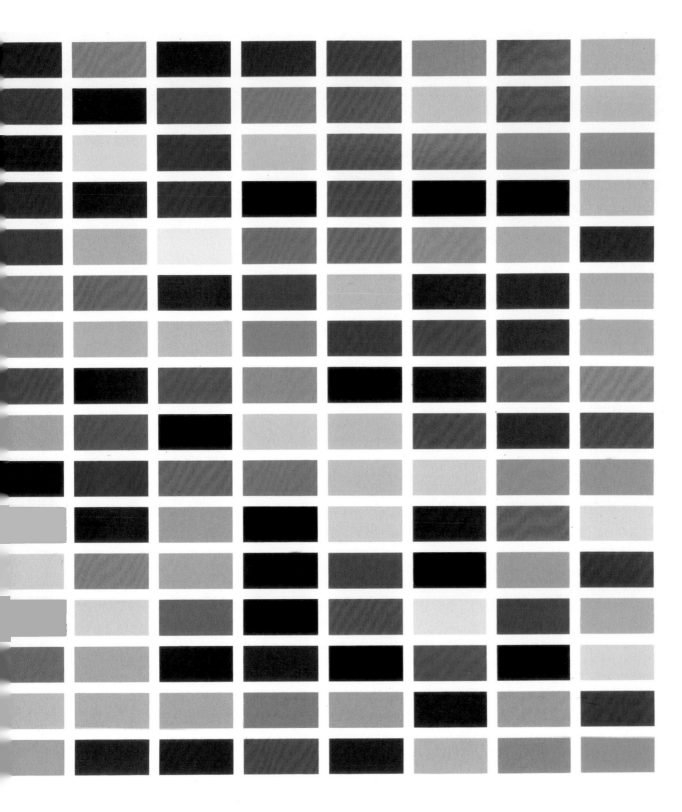

181

Annunciation after Titian [Verkündigung nach Tizian]. 1973. Oil on linen,
49⅜" × 6'6⅞" (125.4 × 200.3 cm). GR 343-1. Hirshhorn Museum and Sculpture
Garden, Smithsonian Institution, Washington, D.C. Joseph H. Hirshhorn Purchase
Fund, 1994

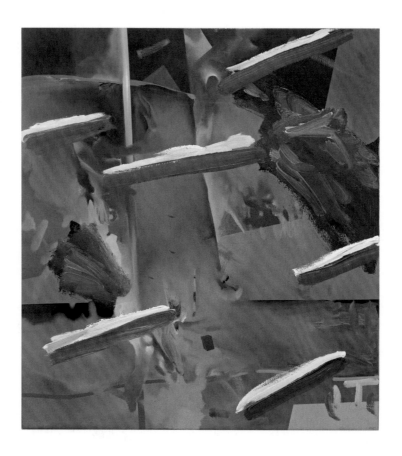

Abstract Picture [Abstraktes Bild]. 1976. Oil on canvas, 25⅞ × 23¾" (65 × 60.5 cm). GR 398-1. Courtesy Barbara Mathes Gallery, New York

Abstract Picture [Abstraktes Bild]. 1977. Oil on canvas, 9' 10⅛" × 6' 6¾" (300 × 200 cm). GR 422. Collection Gabriele Henkel

Abstract Picture [Abstraktes Bild]. 1977. Oil on canvas, 7'4⅝" × 6'6¼"
(225.1 × 200.5 cm). GR 417. Art Gallery of Ontario, Toronto. Purchase, 1980

Betty. 1977. Oil on canvas, 11¹³⁄₁₆ × 15¾" (30 × 40 cm). GR 425-4.
Private collection

Davos S. 1981. Oil on linen, 27⅝ × 39⁷⁄₁₆" (70.2 × 100.2 cm). GR 468-3.
Collection Ron and Ann Pizzuti, Columbus, Ohio

Iceberg in Fog [Eisberg im Nebel]. 1982. Oil on canvas, 27½ × 39⅜" (70 × 100 cm).
GR 496-1. Private collection, San Francisco

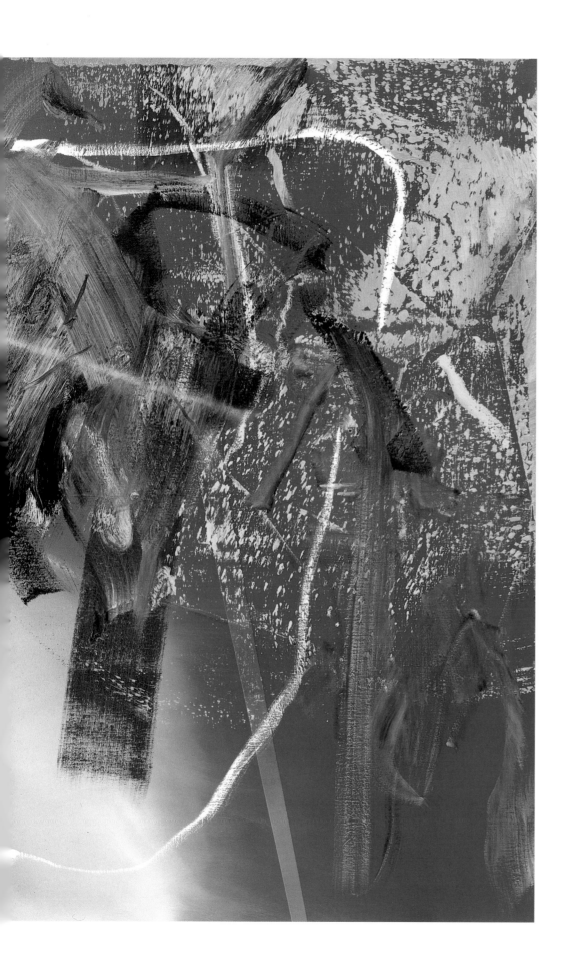

Clouds [Wolken]. 1982. Oil on canvas;
two parts, overall, 6′7″ × 8′6⅝″
(200.7 × 260.7 cm). GR 514-1. The
Museum of Modern Art, New York.
Acquired through the James Thrall
Soby Bequest and purchase

Abstract Picture [Abstraktes Bild]. 1984. Oil on canvas, 6'6 ¼" × 63" (200 × 160 cm).
GR 554-2. Private collection, Germany. Courtesy Galerie Neher, Essen

Skull [Schädel]. 1983. Oil on canvas, 21 ¹¹⁄₁₆ × 19 ¹¹⁄₁₆" (55 × 50 cm). GR 548-1.
Private collection

Two Candles [Zwei Kerzen]. 1982. Oil on canvas, 55⅛ × 55⅛" (140 × 140 cm).
GR 512-2. Collection Lise Spiegel Wilks

Abstract Picture [Abstraktes Bild]. 1984. Oil on canvas, 19 11/16 × 27 9/16" (50 × 70 cm).
GR 551-6. Courtesy Galerie Bernd Lutze, Friedrichshafen, Germany

Bush [Busch]. 1985. Oil on canvas, 25 ⅝ × 31 ½" (65 × 80 cm). GR 572-7.
Collection Howard and Linda Karshan

Pavilion [Pavillon]. 1982. Oil on canvas, 39⅜ × 27⁹⁄₁₆" (100 × 70 cm). GR 489-1.
Private collection, Berlin

Marian. 1983. Oil on canvas, 6' 6¾" × 6' 6¾" (200 × 200 cm). GR 544-2.
Collection Maria Rosa Sandretto

Barn [Scheune]. 1984. Oil on canvas, 37⁷⁄₁₆ × 39⅜" (95 × 100 cm). GR 550-1.
Courtesy Massimo Martino Fine Arts and Projects, Mendrisio, Switzerland

Meadowland [Wiesental]. 1985. Oil on canvas, 35 ⅝ × 37 ½" (90.5 × 94.9 cm).
GR 572-4. The Museum of Modern Art, New York. Blanchette Rockefeller,
Betsy Babcock, and Mrs. Elizabeth Bliss Parkinson Funds, 1985

Venice (Staircase) [Venedig (Treppe)]. 1985. Oil on canvas, 20 × 28" (50.8 × 70.1 cm).
GR 586-3. Stefan T. Edlis Collection

Cathedral Corner [Domecke]. 1987. Oil on canvas, 48 1/16 × 34 1/4" (122 × 87 cm).
GR 629-1. Collection Samuel and Ronnie Heyman, New York

AB, St. Bridget. 1988. Oil on canvas, 6' 6¾" × 8' 6⅜" (200 × 260 cm). GR 653-3.
Fundació "la CAIXA," Barcelona. Collection of Contemporary Art

October 18, 1977 [18. Oktober 1977]. 1988. Fifteen paintings, oil on canvas, installation variable. The Museum of Modern Art, New York. The Sidney and Harriet Janis Collection, gift of Philip Johnson, and acquired through the Lillie P. Bliss Bequest (all by exchange); Enid A. Haupt Fund; Nina and Gordon Bunshaft Bequest Fund; and gift of Emily Rauh Pulitzer

Youth Portrait [Jugendbildnis]. 1988. Oil on canvas, 28½ × 24½" (72.4 × 62 cm).
GR 672-1

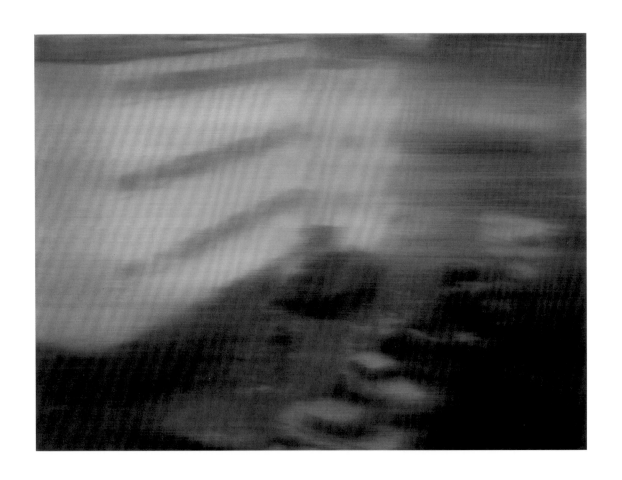

Arrest 1 [Festnahme 1]. 1988. Oil on canvas, 36½ × 49¾" (92 × 126.5 cm). GR 674-1

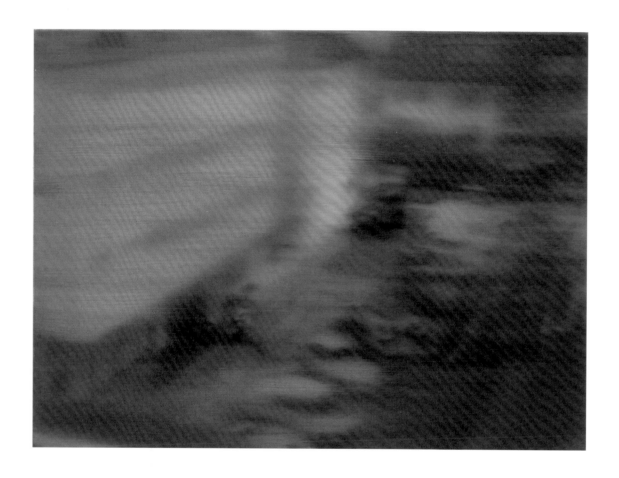

Arrest 2 [Festnahme 2]. 1988. Oil on canvas, 36½ × 49¾" (92 × 126.5 cm). GR 674-2

Confrontation 1 [Gegenüberstellung 1]. 1988. Oil on canvas, 44 × 40¼"
(112 × 102 cm). GR 671-1

Hanged [Erhängte]. 1988. Oil on canvas, 6' 7⅛" × 55⅛" (201 × 140 cm). GR 668

Confrontation 2 [Gegenüberstellung 2]. 1988. Oil on canvas, 44 × 40¼"
(112 × 102 cm). GR 671-2

Confrontation 3 [Gegenüberstellung 3]. 1988. Oil on canvas, 44 × 40 ¼"
(112 × 102 cm). GR 671-3

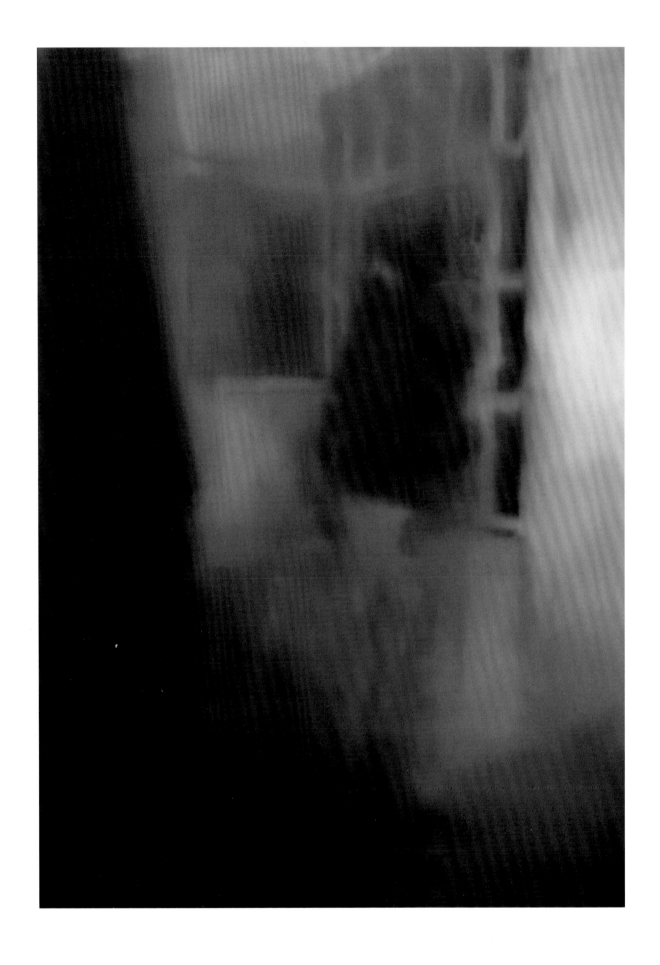

Record Player [Plattenspieler]. 1988. Oil on canvas, 24⅝ × 32¾" (62 × 83 cm). GR 672-2

Cell [Zelle]. 1988. Oil on canvas, 6' 7⅛" × 55⅛" (201 × 140 cm). GR 670

214

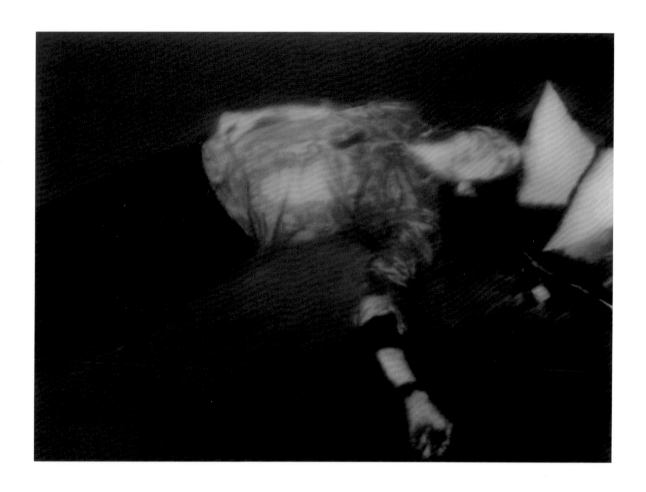

Man Shot Down 1 [Erschossener 1]. 1988. Oil on canvas, 39½ × 55¼"
(100.5 × 140.5 cm). GR 669-1

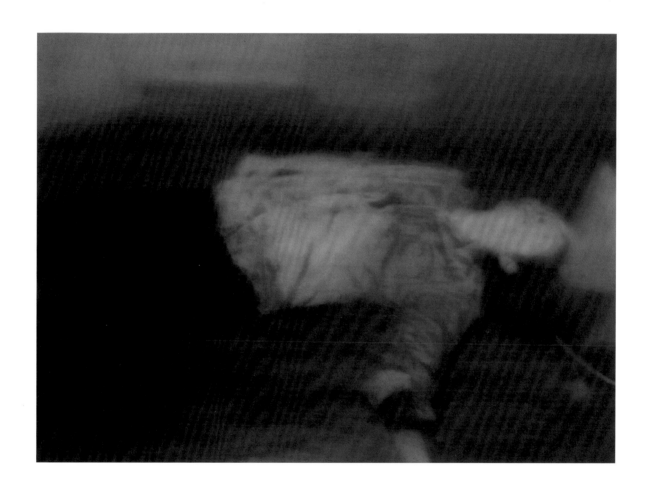

Man Shot Down 2 [Erschossener 2]. 1988. Oil on canvas, 39 ½ × 55 ¼"
(100.5 × 140.5 cm). GR 669-2

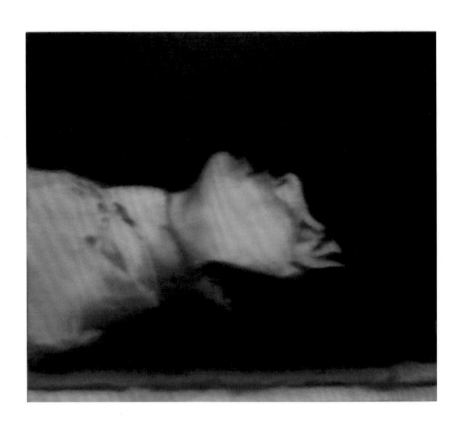

Dead [Tote]. 1988. Oil on canvas, 24½ × 28¾" (62 × 73 cm). GR 667-1

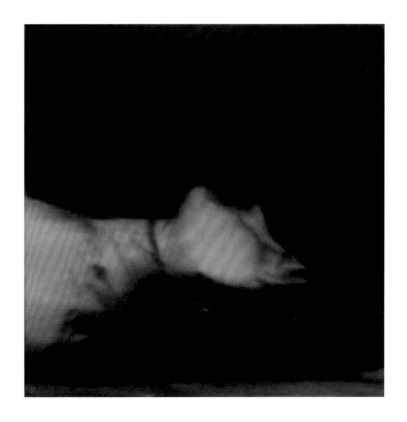

Dead [Tote]. 1988. Oil on canvas, 24½ × 24½" (62 × 62 cm). GR 667-2

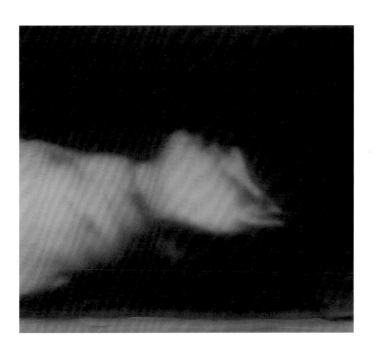

Dead [Tote]. 1988. Oil on canvas, 13 ¾ × 15 ½" (35 × 40 cm). GR 667-3

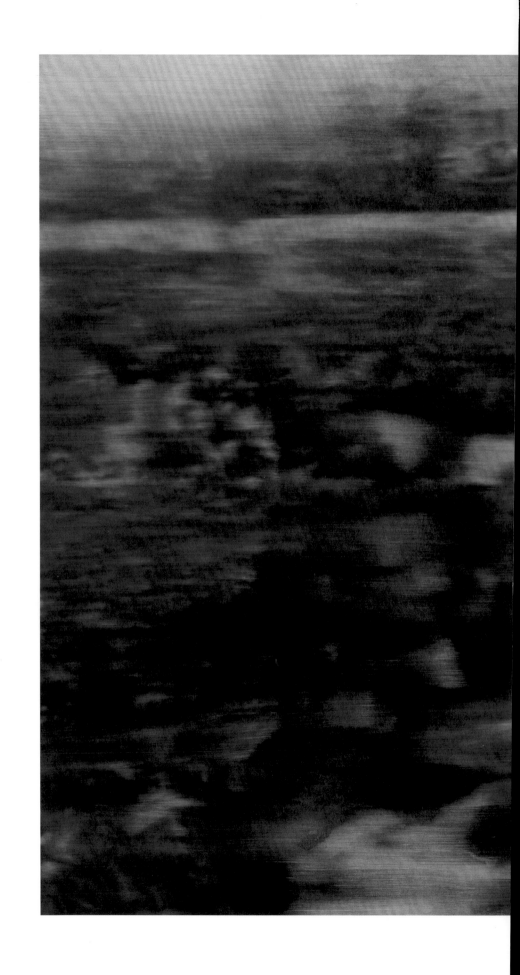

Funeral [Beerdigung]. 1988. Oil on canvas, 6'6¾" × 10'6"
(200 × 320 cm). GR 673

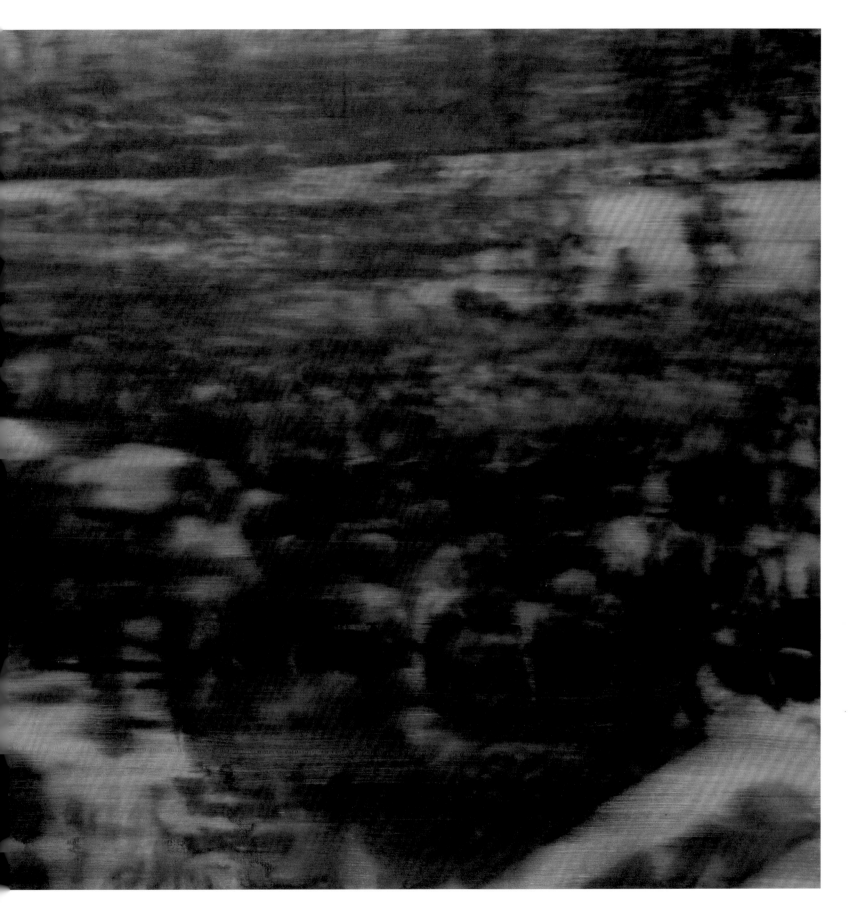

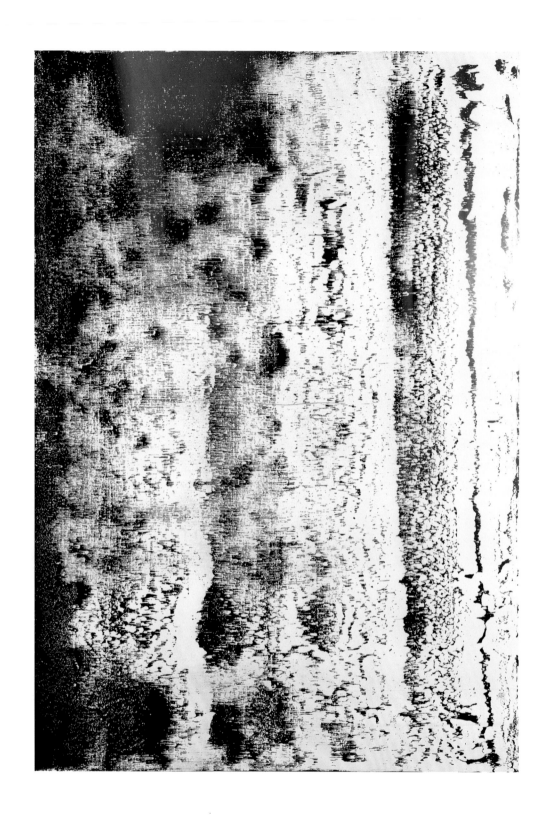

Blanket [Decke]. 1988. Oil on canvas, 6'6¾" × 55" (200 × 140 cm). GR 680-3.
Private collection, Berlin

Betty. 1988. Oil on canvas, 40⅛ × 23⅞" (101.9 × 59.4 cm). GR 663-5. The Saint Louis Art Museum. Funds given by Mr. and Mrs. R. Crosby Kemper, Jr., through the Crosby Kemper Foundation, Arthur and Helen Baer Charitable Foundation, Mr. and Mrs. Van-Lear Black III, Mr. John Weil, Mr. and Mrs. Gary Wolff, Senator and Mrs. Thomas F. Eagleton; Museum Purchase, Dr. and Mrs. Harold Joseph, and Mrs. Edward Mallinckrodt, by exchange

January [Januar]. 1989. Oil on canvas, two parts, overall, 10'6" × 13'1½" (320 × 400 cm). GR 699. The Saint Louis Art Museum. Funds given by Mr. and Mrs. James E. Schneithorst, Mrs. Henry L. Freund and the Henry L. and Natalie Edison Freund Charitable Trust; and Alice P. Francis, by exchange

227

December [Dezember]. 1989. Oil on
canvas; two parts, overall, 10'6" ×
13'1 ½" (320 × 400 cm). GR 700. The
Saint Louis Art Museum. Funds given
by Mr. and Mrs. Donald L. Bryant, Jr.,
Mrs. Francis A. Mesker, George and
Aurelia Schlapp, Mr. and Mrs. John E.
Simon, and the Estate of Mrs. Edith
Rabushka in memory of Hyman and
Edith Rabushka, by exchange

November. 1989. Oil on canvas; two parts, overall, 10'6" × 13'1½" (320 × 400 cm). GR 701. The Saint Louis Art Museum. Funds given by Dr. and Mrs. Alvin R. Frank and the Pulitzer Publishing Foundation

230

231

Ice (2) [Eis (2)]. 1989. Oil on canvas, 6'8" × 63⅞" (203.2 × 162.6 cm). GR 706-2.
The Art Institute of Chicago. Acquired through a prior gift of Joseph
Winterbotham and gift of Lannan Foundation, 1997

Abstract Picture [Abstraktes Bild]. 1990. Oil on canvas, 36 × 50" (92 × 126 cm).
GR 724-4. Collection Peter Gidal and Thérèse Oulton

Mirror, Blood-Red [Spiegel, blutrot]. 1991. Oil under glass, 35 1/16 × 36 1/4"
(89 × 92 cm). GR 736-4. Private collection

Abstract Picture [Abstraktes Bild]. 1992. Oil on canvas, 69" × 8' 2 ½" (175 × 250 cm).
GR 757. Joseph Hackmey Collection

Flowers [Blumen]. 1992. Oil on canvas, 49¾ × 36¼" (41 × 51 cm). GR 764-2. Private collection

Gray Mirror [Grauer Spiegel]. 1992. Oil under glass; two parts, each, 7' 2¾" × 31½" (220 × 80 cm). GR 765. Statens Museum for Kunst, Copenhagen

Chicago. 1992. Oil on canvas, 48 × 32¼" (122 × 82 cm). GR 778-1.
Collection Martha and Bruce Atwater

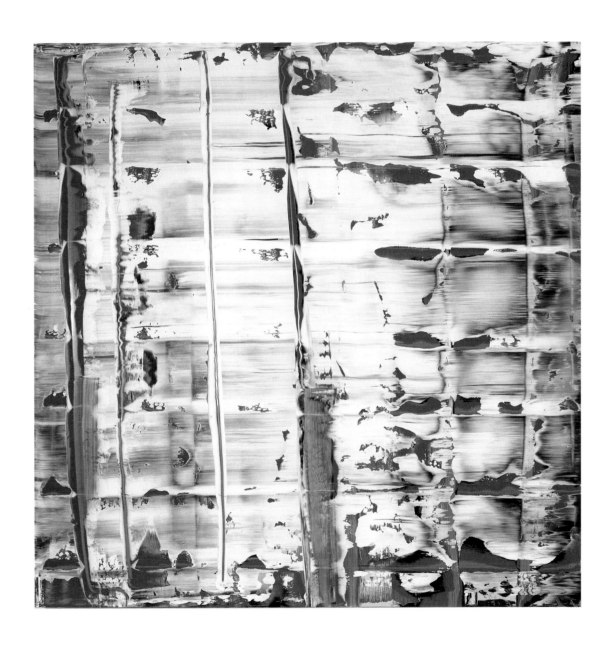

Abstract Picture [Abstraktes Bild]. 1992. Oil on aluminum panel, 39½ × 39½"
(100 × 100 cm). GR 778-4. Private collection

March [März]. 1994. Oil on canvas, 8' 2 $\frac{7}{16}$" × 6' 6 $\frac{3}{4}$" (250 × 200 cm). GR 807.
Private collection

I.G. 1993. Oil on canvas, 28⅜ × 32¼" (72 × 82 cm). GR 790-5. Private collection

242

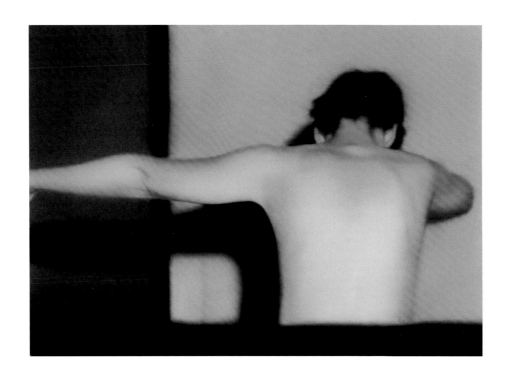

I.G. 1993. Oil on canvas, 28⅜ × 40⅛" (72 × 102 cm). GR 790-4. Private collection

Wall [Wand]. 1994. Oil on canvas, 7'10½" × 7'10½" (240 × 240 cm). GR 806. Private collection

245

S. with Child [S. mit Kind]. 1995. Oil on canvas, 14 ³⁄₁₆ × 16 ⅛" (36 × 41 cm).
GR 827-1. Eigentum der Stiftung zur Förderung der Hamburgischen
Kunstsammlungen, Hamburg

S. with Child [S. mit Kind]. 1995. Oil on canvas, 16⅛ × 14³⁄₁₆" (41 × 36 cm).
GR 827-2. Hamburger Kunsthalle, Hamburg

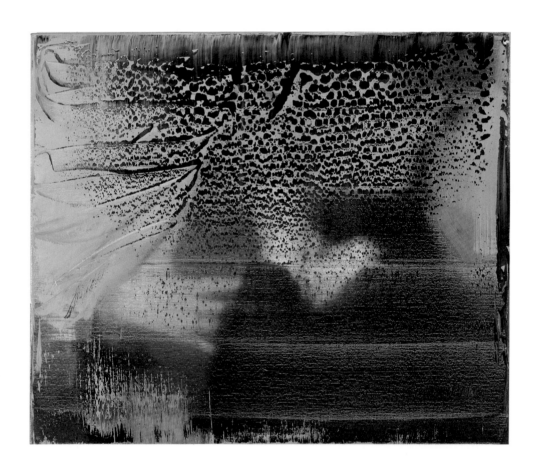

S. with Child [S. mit Kind]. 1995. Oil on canvas, 20½ × 24⁷⁄₁₆" (52 × 62 cm).
GR 827-3. Hamburger Kunsthalle, Hamburg

S. with Child [S. mit Kind]. 1995. Oil on canvas, 20 1/16 × 22 1/16" (51 × 56 cm).
GR 827-4. Hamburger Kunsthalle, Hamburg

S. with Child [S. mit Kind]. 1995. Oil on canvas, 24 × 20 1/16" (61 × 51 cm).
GR 827-5. Eigentum der Stiftung zur Förderung der Hamburgischen
Kunstsammlungen, Hamburg

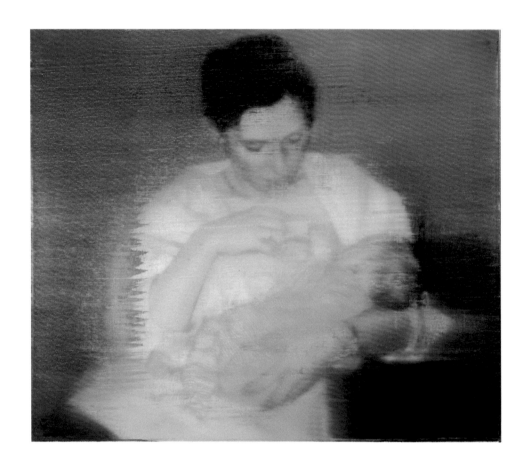

S. with Child [S. mit Kind]. 1995. Oil on canvas, 24⁷⁄₁₆ × 28³⁄₈" (62 × 72 cm).
GR 827-6. Eigentum der Stiftung zur Förderung der Hamburgischen
Kunstsammlungen, Hamburg

S. with Child [S. mit Kind]. 1995. Oil on canvas, 14 3/16 × 20 1/16" (36 × 51 cm).
GR 827-7. Hamburger Kunsthalle, Hamburg

S. with Child [S. mit Kind]. 1995. Oil on canvas, 18⅛ × 16⅛" (46 × 41 cm).
GR 827-8. Hamburger Kunsthalle, Hamburg

Small Bather [Kleine Badende]. 1994. Oil on canvas, 20 1/16 × 14 3/16" (51 × 36 cm).
GR 815-1. Private collection

Reading [Lesende]. 1994. Oil on linen, 28½ × 40¼" (72.4 × 102.2 cm). GR 804. San Francisco Museum of Modern Art. Purchased through the gifts of Mimi and Peter Haas and Helen and Charles Schwab, and the Accessions Committee Fund

Abstract Picture, Kine [Abstraktes Bild, Kine]. 1995. Oil on linen, 48¹³⁄₁₆ × 35⁷⁄₁₆"
(124 × 90 cm). GR 832-3. Collection Isabel and David Breskin

Jerusalem. 1995. Oil on canvas, 49⅝ × 36⅜" (126 × 92.3 cm). GR 835-2.
Collection Frieder Burda

Self-Portrait [Selbstportrait]. 1996. Oil on linen. 20⅛ × 18¼" (51.1 × 46.4 cm).
GR 836-1. The Museum of Modern Art, New York. Fractional and promised gift
of Jo Carole and Ronald S. Lauder and Committee on Painting and Sculpture
Funds, 1996

Abstract Picture [Abstraktes Bild]. 1997. Oil on aluminum panel, 18⅞ × 21⅝"
(48 × 55 cm). GR 842-4. Private collection

Abstract Picture [Abstraktes Bild]. 1997. Oil on aluminum panel, 18⅞ × 21⅝"
(48 × 55 cm). GR 842-5. Collection C. and J. Plum

Abstract Picture [Abstraktes Bild]. 1997. Oil on aluminum panel, 18⅞ × 21⅝"
(48 × 55 cm). GR 842-7. Collection Isabel and David Breskin

Abstract Picture [Abstraktes Bild]. 1997. Oil on aluminum panel, 18⅞ × 21⅝"
(48 × 55 cm). GR 842-9. Private collection, Germany

Waterfall [Wasserfall]. 1997. Oil on linen, 64⅞ × 43⅜" (164.8 × 110.2 cm). GR 847-2. Hirshhorn Museum and Sculpture Garden, Smithsonian Institution, Washington, D.C. Joseph H. Hirshhorn Purchase Fund, 1998

Abstract Picture [Abstraktes Bild]. 1999. Oil on aluminum panel, 21 11/16 × 18 15/16"
(55 × 48 cm). GR 857-4. Private collection

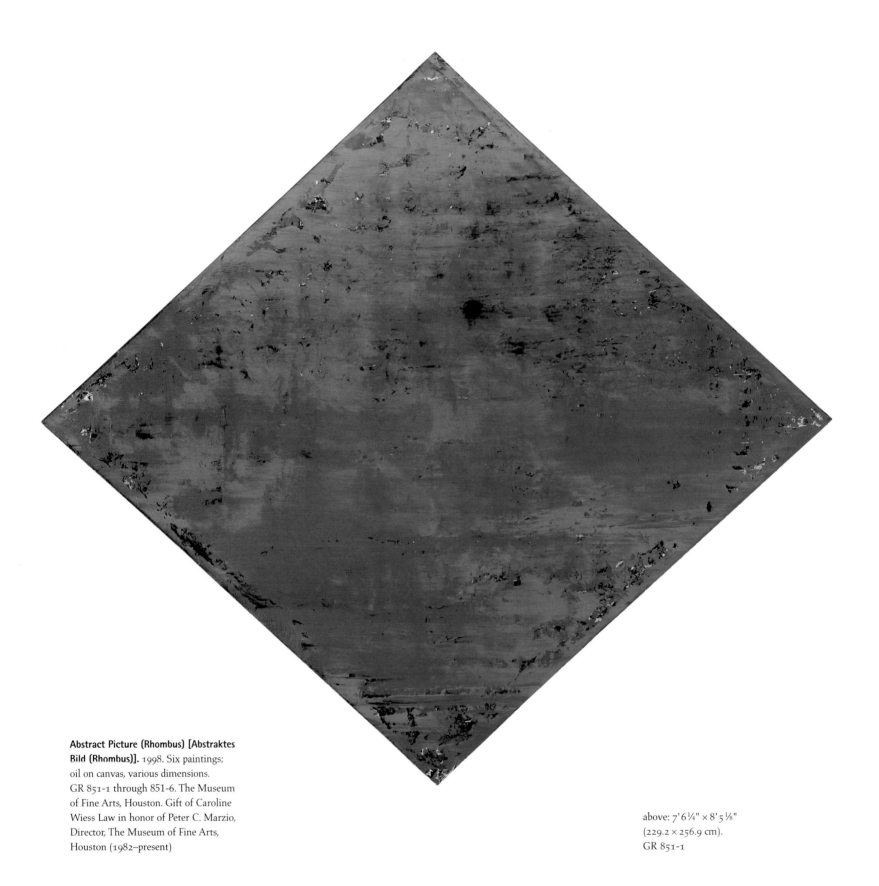

Abstract Picture (Rhombus) [Abstraktes Bild (Rhombus)]. 1998. Six paintings; oil on canvas, various dimensions. GR 851-1 through 851-6. The Museum of Fine Arts, Houston. Gift of Caroline Wiess Law in honor of Peter C. Marzio, Director, The Museum of Fine Arts, Houston (1982–present)

above: 7' 6¼" × 8' 5⅛" (229.2 × 256.9 cm). GR 851-1

Abstract Picture (Rhombus). 1998.
Oil on canvas, 6' 1 ⅛" × 6' 10 ⅛"
(185.7 × 208.6 cm). GR 851-2

Abstract Picture (Rhombus). 1998.
Oil on canvas, 6' 1 " × 6' 11¾"
(185.4 × 211.8 cm). GR 851-3

Abstract Picture (Rhombus). 1998.
Oil on canvas, 6' 1 ⅛" × 6' 10 ⅛"
(185.7 × 208.6 cm). GR 851-4

Abstract Picture (Rhombus). 1998.
Oil on canvas, 6' 1⅛" × 6' 10"
(185.7 × 208.3 cm). GR 851-5

Abstract Picture (Rhombus). 1998.
Oil on canvas, 6' 1 ¼" × 6' 10"
(186.1 × 208.3 cm). GR 851-6

Abstract Picture [Abstraktes Bild]. 1998. Oil on canvas, 14 3/16 × 16 1/8" (36 × 41 cm).
GR 854-2. Private collection

Abstract Picture. [Abstraktes Bild]. 1999. Oil on aluminum panel, 18 15/16 × 21 11/16"
(48 × 55 cm). GR 857-3. Private collection

Snow [Schnee]. 1999. Oil on canvas, 22 ¹⁄₁₆ × 20 ¹⁄₁₆" (56 × 51 cm). GR 861-2.
Collection Frieder Burda

Farm [Gehöft]. 1999. Oil on canvas, 18⅛ × 20¹⁄₁₆" (46 × 51 cm). GR 861-1.
Private collection

Moritz. 2000. Oil on canvas, 20 1/16 × 18 1/8" (51 × 46 cm). GR 863-1.
Courtesy Marian Goodman Gallery, New York

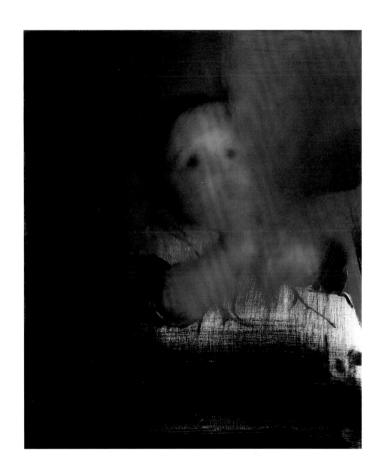

Moritz. 2000. Oil on canvas, 24⁷⁄₁₆ × 20½" (62 × 52 cm). GR 863-2.
Courtesy Marian Goodman Gallery, New York

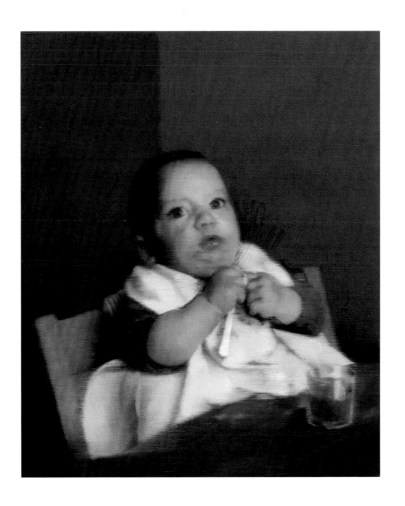

Moritz. 2000–2001 (work in progress). Oil on canvas, 24⁷⁄₁₆ × 20½" (62 × 52 cm).
GR 863-3. Private collection

Demo. 1997. Oil on canvas, 24⁷/₁₆ × 24⁷/₁₆" (62 × 62 cm). GR 848-3.
The Rachofsky Collection

Court Chapel, Dresden [Hofkirche Dresden]. 2000. Oil on canvas, 31 ½ × 36 ⅝"
(80 × 93 cm). GR 865-3. The Museum of Modern Art, New York. Promised and
fractional gift of Donald L. Bryant, Jr.

Seascape [Seestück]. 1998. Oil on canvas, 9'6⅛" × 9'6⅛" (289.9 × 289.9 cm). GR 852-1. San Francisco Museum of Modern Art. Fractional gift of an anonymous donor

Abstract Picture (Abstraktes Bild). 2000. Oil on canvas, 68 15/16" × 8'2 7/16" (175 × 250 cm). GR 867-3. Courtesy Marian Goodman Gallery, New York

INTERVIEW WITH GERHARD RICHTER

BY ROBERT STORR

This interview was conducted in German and English over several days in April 2001. Catharina Manchanda both participated in the discussions and assisted with translation when necessary. The tapes were transcribed and translated by Philip Glahn.

ROBERT STORR: In the United States in the 1980s there was a burst of gallery activity, and a lot of attention was given to art coming from Europe, and from Germany, in particular. Many Americans first discovered your work all at once and, for the most part, they saw your gestural abstractions from the 1970s and 1980s next to the paintings inspired by Pop art from the 1960s without knowing much about how these different bodies of work from a single artist were related. The assumption was that you were taking painting apart, style by style, by doing different things at the same time. So I wonder just how you understood the reception that you got back then; how comfortable or uncomfortable did you feel with this view of you as a kind of destructive painter?

GERHARD RICHTER: I didn't notice that view. Perhaps I was glad to receive any attention at all. Some people would even claim that it was pretty smart. There was a demand for paintings that I satisfied, and at the same time there was this conceptual notion against painting—and so I served both sides. That was rather smart, a legitimation to enjoy them.

Yes, pleasure without remorse. Because with this intellectual, conceptual background, you would always have an excuse. They are colorful and painterly but they are also very intellectual. Be careful! [*Laughter*]

RS: You laugh now, but in America at that time, these battles were fought very seriously. There was no laughter at all. Under the name of *politics* there was a puritanical belief that pleasure was bad, that the aesthetic was suspect, and that only by making anti-aesthetic, unpleasurable things could there be a justification for making paintings at all.

GR: I remember an opening party at Marian Goodman's [in the 1990s] when Lawrence Weiner gave a speech that said: "Painting is not possible anymore, but Gerhard shows us that it is possible.... We all knew it was over, that one could not paint abstract paintings anymore. But here it is!" He got a lot of applause.

RS: But that, in a sense, is the easy answer. The harder problem is that this rhetoric was used to say that the only way for painting to be serious was for the painter to think of it as a time-bomb that the painter had planted—you had planted—to explode the reasons for painting, one by one, until at the end of this process painting would be finished. So people said: "It's great that he's doing this, and for now it's okay to like painting like that; but when he's done, there will be no more painting."

GR: Nice. [*Laughter*] I didn't know that.

RS: There is a precedent in American painting—Ad Reinhardt said: "You must understand that I am making the last paintings possible." As a logical gambit that's very elegant. But there is a difference between taking such a position for the challenge that it provides and actually believing it to be true.

GR: People often declare the end of painting.

RS: Yes, but is there a difference between how an artist says something like this—uses it as a point of departure—and how a critic arrives at and argues such a conclusion?

GR: I don't know because I always have thought, "This is my end." During every crisis I have thought, "This is it for me, but everything else will go on." I never generalized this to be the end of painting, even though I realized that it [painting] didn't do so well at certain points. But I conceived those times as breaks.

RS: Back in the 1980s, Douglas Crimp wrote a famous article called "The End of Painting" in which (in addition to misrepresenting your statement "painting is pure idiocy") he proposed that what a painter—such as you or Daniel Buren—does under the circumstances is simply to go through the motions and critically "enact" painting in order to prove its futility.

GR: That is presumptuous and arrogant—or useless—because then you have to take a look at all of life. When somebody goes shopping that's an idiotic act. Even feeding the kids is an idiotic act. From that perspective, everything is meaningless. You have to believe in the idea that it does make sense. It doesn't matter whether it is painting or working in your backyard, most of these things are so meaningless, you can't even watch them.

Gerhard Richter in his studio, c. 1967

RS: Well that was one interpretation, but there was also the strong view that you were a very important painter because what you were up to was undoing painting in the most masterful way. Is that true?

GR: Yes.

RS: Another thing I have heard sometimes in conversation is: "Richter is no good because he always avoids taking a position. He says Yes and No, and No and Yes, in a way that suggests he is an aesthetic cynic."

GR: I believe that it would be a misunderstanding to call what I do cynical. I'd rather call it sentimental. I wouldn't call it professional because being cynical is not professional. Rather, what I do is naive.

Also, my work has been accused of being cold and distant. In retrospect I think, "How could they say that about me, about somebody who exposes himself much more than others? More than Ellsworth Kelly." Nobody ever accuses them of being distant. I open myself up, shame-

lessly sometimes, and then I am told that I am cynical and that nothing means anything to me. That's why, for me, the word *cynical* is absolutely out of place.

RS: Why do you think people have such reactions?

GR: One reason is that people sometimes talk about my work in terms of virtuosity. That is an absolute exaggeration. Unfortunately I am not a virtuoso at all. I have some taste. I have an eye for bad things. But in terms of making things I am not a virtuoso, and that has always been my flaw. Today, there is almost nobody (or only a few bad examples) who has the virtuosity to draw something. I depend on the photograph and mindlessly copy what I see. I am clumsy in that regard, even though I seem very skillful. But I do have the ability to judge whether something is good or bad.

The second reason could be that I made a few remarks that have circulated, things like: "I don't believe in anything"; "I don't care about anything"; and "the motifs in my paintings have no meaning whatsoever, I might have just as well painted cabbage." These remarks gave people a certain impression of me. That's how they saw me. People still claim that only painting has an important story, never the subject.

RS: Why did you say those things? What was the context?

GR: I made those statements in order to provoke and in order not to have to say what I might have been thinking at that point, not to pour my heart out. That would have been embarrassing. I didn't know why I painted *Uncle Rudi* or *Aunt Marianne*. I refused to admit any kind of meaning that these paintings could have had for me. Therefore, it was much easier to say what I said.

RS: There are personal stories attached to these images, then, but there are also historical issues too. If you look at the date of these paintings—1965—you see that it was very early for a German artist to be making pictures about World War II that were not simply rhetorical. There were political artists making antifascist paintings, but to make a personal image of something connected to the war was almost unheard of. And there you were making pictures that bring that past into the open and very close to home. Did you feel as if you were in a no-man's-land when you made those paintings?

GR: Maybe that is the main reason why the audience, as well as myself, had to fall back on a strategy of laughter. That's how it worked; people thought it was mischievous and prankish and not too serious and, therefore, it was so much easier to deal with it.

RS: It is striking, though, that almost nobody has written about your pictures of 1962 to 1965, for example, when you made eight paintings of military aircraft—Allied bombers, fighters from the 1940s, and new German jets—with regard to the specific situation in postwar Germany.

These paintings were an incredibly strong statement at that time. Yet, because you worked in a manner that looked neutral, it seems as if people just ignored what was in front of their eyes. But, in fact, the images were much more pointed—and in some cases more poignant—than what anybody thought then, or even now.

GR: We [artists influenced by Pop art] refused to take anything seriously. That was important for survival. We were unable to see the statement in the work, neither the audience nor me. We rejected it; it didn't exist. Part of the reason was that there existed a different kind of painting, and [Georg] Baselitz was the right man for that German tradition. People thought my painting was somehow modern, but they couldn't admit that it had any kind of quality. Instead, it was somehow funny but copied from the Americans. So people thought that we were traitors. Baselitz said to me: "You have betrayed your fatherland."

RS: What did he mean by that?

GR: That I was giving in to the international style, but he remained a German. That's how it was. That was also [Sigmar] Polke's fate because he was painting raster dots like [Roy] Lichtenstein. People said that it was lousy plagiarism.

RS: But let's shift from style to subject matter. If Lichtenstein made pictures from World War II comic books with G.I. Joe fighter planes going "Bang" that's one thing. It is very different if you are a German artist and make a picture of American planes over Germany. And it is very different to make a painting of a German soldier, such as *Uncle Rudi*, which is neither a Hero picture like Baselitz's nor a cartoon of a soldier like Lichtenstein's, but, rather, the image of a real soldier who is also your uncle.

GR: But this painting *Bomber*—American bomb—was forbidden. You were not allowed to take it seriously. You could only take it as a joke.

RS: You didn't paint it as a joke.

GR: No, but I was satisfied that it was taken as such. I would have been embarrassed if it were too serious. It was not an accusation; I wasn't accusing the Americans. I never wanted to accuse anything, except life maybe and how shitty it is. But never…after all, they were right. Everything was fine. [*Laughter*] I would have been attacked as a prosecutor.

RS: You've explained your position to avoid declarations, to avoid rhetoric, but even without commentary, painting American B-52s and Mustangs or a postwar German fighter squadron against a social background where memories of the Allied bombings were vivid and debate over German remilitarization was in progress must have stirred many emotions and raised a lot of questions.

GR: But there is only one painting of a German plane—the Schärzler.

RS: Yes, but here we have a picture of American bombers, and a picture of fighter planes, one of the Luftwaffe Stukas, and then the Schärzler. Altogether, there are eight pictures of military aircraft.

GR: I am a specialist in airplanes. [*Laughter*]

RS: What I am trying to say is that I understand and accept the idea that you did not make them for polemical reasons, but the choice of subject cannot have been arbitrary. The planes are specific—none, for example, is a commercial passenger plane—and the paintings have their moment in the 1960s when Germany was beginning to look at the recent past, but also when Germany was at the center of the Cold War and starting to rearm.

GR: What am I supposed to say to that?

RS: Well, you must have been aware that while you were making neither political art nor mythological art about the ravages of war, like Baselitz, you were touching a nerve. After all, you have said: "The *Mona Lisa* is not a turnip." There are hierarchies of subject matter; a cow, which you have also painted, is not a 1940s fighter plane or a 1960s fighter plane.

GR: I never knew what I was doing. What am I supposed to say now? Now I could lie here, like I am on an analyst's couch, and try to figure out my actual motives with the help of others and make sense of them. Is that what we want to do now?

RS: I don't want to put you on the couch, but there must have been some level on which these images had meaning attached to the actual situation around you or to the past that you and others had experienced. What might have been historical denial in 1960 or 1965 is connected in an odd way with the postmodernist notion that images are just signs, arbitrary fragments of language, in a no longer functioning system of signs. In that manner, one kind of denial, which was historically motivated, connects with another kind of denial, which is ideologically or aesthetically driven; and yet there you were making pictures that were very, very strong about things that were very, very real. When people in 1988 were surprised that you painted the October paintings and said, "Wait, this is different, this is a Richter unlike the one we know because he has never painted paintings with so much emotion and so much historical specificity before," I think, "Now wait a minute, that's not true."

GR: Yes, you are right. The October paintings came after a period when I had done very different things and people like [art dealer] René Block accused me of giving in to the fine arts and losing my political edge. He said that I had been political during the 1960s and then turned to the fine arts, beaux-arts. After he said that I was really "established" and colorful and aesthetic, so the Baader-Meinhof paintings came as a surprise.

RS: Actually, my position is not at all to be a psychoanalyst but, rather, to be a close reader of pictorial texts. And there is a sense now that texts are completely open, that anything can be read in any way the reader chooses. I'm supposing that perhaps this is not the right way to go about things—or at any rate not the most productive or interesting way to read images—and that there may be intentions expressed in bodies of work of which the artist is only partially conscious or aware, which nevertheless emerge very powerfully through reiteration, and that such latent intentions have to be closely examined and seriously considered. So my question is more about now than the past, how you think about them now, how you relate these images to each other. Does such a relation stand out?

GR: All right, I understand. That makes the questions very interesting. Sometimes I am surprised that I have never asked myself something, and sometimes one can discover something.

RS: For example, take the painting *Mr. Heyde*. The man in the wide-brim hat whose face is turned away from the viewer was, in actuality, Dr. Werner Heyde, who was responsible for killing mentally retarded, mentally ill, and chronically sick hospital patients as a part of a euthanasia program that pioneered the techniques of the "Final Solution." In 1959, the date included in the picture, he was exposed after having lived and worked for years in Germany under an assumed name. When you painted this picture, six years after his arrest, virtually no one had dealt in this direct way with the issue of hidden war criminals. Weren't you aware of the significance of his arrest, and wasn't it also significant that your aunt Marianne, who was a schizophrenic, was a victim of the system of medical murder he set up?

GR: Out of my mind, of my consciousness. I was surprised myself when many years later—I believe it was on the occasion of the exhibition *Deutschlandbilder*—somebody told me that he was a war criminal.

RS: So you didn't know who Heyde was?

GR: I am sure I knew it. But I repressed it right away, and it became a picture like every other. I tried to show that this was a guy like every other guy that gets arrested. You can see those two policemen. I did not want to be part of the faction that accuses. I do not belong to those who present themselves as antifascists, because I am not. I am also not a fascist. I was disinclined to be conscious of too many things; I just wanted to let myself go. And it is still the same today.

At the time I do something, I really don't know what I am doing. Afterwards I think, "Oh that's why you did that, now I understand." It's the same with the paintings. But I was much more introverted back then, and I would have refused any connection between Heyde

and myself. I would have said, well, it's a nice picture; it doesn't mean anything.

RS: So was there no conscious connection between Heyde's program during the Third Reich and your aunt's death?

GR: Absolutely never, not even once. It did not exist. There are no conscious connections within me at all. [*Laughter*] But I am certain that I knew of it because I read it somewhere.

RS: This raises the issue of what can be painted and what can't be painted. In *Atlas*, there are images of the concentration camp—of prisoners and bodies—and at one point you thought about making an exhibition with the pictures of the camp next to the porno pictures. Finally, you decided that it was not possible to juxtapose such things nor even to make paintings from the documentary photos of the Holocaust. Why wasn't it possible?

GR: I'd say that it would have been impossible for *me*. I saw no possible moral or formal solution for how to exhibit the camp and the porno pictures as Konrad [Lueg] and I had planned. We had this plan in a Düsseldorf gallery, and we each collected photos; then we gave it up. It didn't work. We didn't find a way. We would have gotten a lot of attention, but it would have been unproductive and inadequate—at least inadequate.

RS: What is the difference between an image that you can look at, incorporate into your visual memory, and one that you can paint? The camp pictures appear in *Atlas*, and one sees them as part of a much wider array of pictures, yet they are not paintable. What determines that something is unpaintable?

GR: I believe that there is no picture that can't be painted. But there are personal limits and limits of the time, situations where the reception would go so predictably wrong that it doesn't work. It is also the personal inadequacy to not be able to give something the right form. Three years ago, I tried to use the camp pictures again, and again it didn't work. But that was my fault.

RS: In other words, there is no such thing as an image that is absolutely taboo, there are only images that an individual cannot paint at a particular time?

GR: Yes. I still have some photographs in the studio that I am thinking about. Who knows? There are only unfinished themes. There are some that have simply become uninteresting. A painting that is unpaintable is a painting I know would go wrong—something I can't do—one that would cause people to say: "He meant well, but maybe, he's getting old." [*Laughter*] That is the only criterion. Other than that nothing is unpaintable.

RS: What qualities make an image that already exists in a photograph fascinating or substantial for you once it becomes a painting?

GR: That is impossible to answer. I don't know why I like things. [*Looking at a book of images*] I like this or this. This has too much to do with Courbet, but nevertheless I like it.

RS: I am not so much asking why a photograph makes you want to paint it, but what happens in the process of painting an image that makes the result interesting or acceptable, so that you don't destroy it or paint over it?

GR: That is also an impossible question. [*Laughter*]

RS: That won't stop me from asking.

GR: Why doesn't it work like that? Why can't I let this go? Why can't I do this better? Why don't I know that? Like this one. [*Pointing to a canvas on the studio wall*] I don't like this one. But I don't know why. One can't answer that, at least I can't.

RS: Speaking from the outside, I would think maybe it's the point at which there is a specific quality or experience that was not in the photograph that suddenly appears in the picture.

GR: Yes, sounds pretty good.

RS: And is there any way of describing or saying how this happens or even what happens?

GR: No. But it also works the other way around. Sometimes I make a print from a painting, a multiple, using photography, and that takes a lot of time. First I have a reproduction and it looks horrible. Then I begin to change it, make it out of focus or something, or put it under plexiglass, so that it somehow becomes an independent object.

RS: I don't think anybody anticipated this doubling back to photography as a medium. In the past there had been a one-way street from the photograph to the painting, where you added and subtracted qualities from the source image. When you photograph a painting such as *Uncle Rudi* or *Cathedral Corner,* what kind of transformations are you looking for?

GR: In the photograph, I take even more focus out of the painted image, which is already a bit out of focus, and make the picture even smoother. I also subtract the materiality, the surface of the painting, and it becomes something different.

RS: The effect of removing the materiality from the image is very interesting, but how is that important or significant?

GR: I wouldn't know how to say that—to say how the new quality of the photographic work is different from a reproduction.

RS: That wasn't what I was asking, but it is an interesting question because I think some people see these works as "just" a multiple.

GR: The painting is better. [*Laughter*]

RS: Yes, but what matters is that the visual experience is different. From your point of view what are the significant differences?

From my perspective, each stage of this process seems to have a different relation to light, to the form that light assumes. In a sense, a photograph is the direct record of light, whereas a painting represents light. The second-generation photograph that comes after the painting and is the third generation of an image holds or emits light in a very different way, both from the painting and the original photograph. The visual phenomenon it captures is, in a way, further refined, not better or worse but perceptually different.

GR: I am sure that's right. But I have a problem with the term *light*. I never in my life knew what to do with that. I know that people have

Gerhard Richter, mid-1970s

Konrad Lueg and Gerhard Richter,
c. 1966–67

mentioned on some occasions that, "Richter is all about light," and that, "The paintings have a special light"; and I never knew what they were talking about. I was never interested in light. Light is there and you turn it on or you turn it off, with sun or without sun. I don't know what the "problematic of light" is. I take it as a metaphor for a different quality, which is similarly difficult to describe. Good.

RS: This astonishes me because it not only seems so central to what you do but to what was done by the painters that you like: Velázquez, Manet, and Vermeer.

GR: That I don't understand either. Velázquez and light. Of course, we have light, here. Without light we couldn't see each other. There is something lacking in me.

RS: I don't mean light as a kind of metaphysical thing, I mean light as a phenomenon.

GR: Yes, we have beautiful light, cold light, warm light, southern light; people in Italy have a different light. I do see all that. I once got into trouble with [Norbert] Kricke when he told me that I had to understand his sculptures in spatial terms, that they dealt with space. And I replied that there's space even in the smallest house. And he was very mad at me for being so dismissive about space, the elementary

medium of sculpture. That always comes to mind when I hear the word *light* in conjunction with painting. *Appearance,* that to me is a phenomenon.

RS: Let me give you an example.

GR: Now I am curious.

RS: Okay, these are the first and the last versions of *Toilet Paper*. The first one has a strong shadow, which makes the image very volumetric, and that is reinforced by the direct way it is painted. In the third version the shadows and the overall touch are softened, and the form has a kind of glow to it. In the first version, the treatment is very objective, but in the third it is atmospheric.

GR: Right.

RS: These paintings have the same subject, same tonality, same technique, but the difference is the difference of light. Much later the candles and the skulls are painted in more or less the same manner as the third version of *Toilet Paper*. Now, that shift in emphasis must mean something. I am not saying that it means the same thing for you as it means for me, but these two examples represent different realities or different attitudes toward reality.

GR: Yes, I like that because you look at the light from a practical, pragmatic perspective. Yes, I can see that. That's true. I agree. Then the light in the photograph is different. Sometimes the light is harder as, for example, in *Small Bather*. In that case, the painting is much softer and more atmospheric, while the photograph has more contrast, has a harder light, is crisper. That was the only solution. I couldn't do it softer, maybe. If I made it any softer, it would have disappeared. And I needed to spice it up. It was also good for the viewers. If it is too soft you have to be so sensitive in order to appreciate it. That would not have been possible in a photograph.

RS: It means that you are thinking about the viewer.

GR: The audience, yes.

RS: When you say only the most lyrically inclined people can handle this, it is as if you are saying, "I can see trouble coming if I make things too lyrical," as if there were a group of people who could take this lyricism, while the rest all want something more cut-and-dried.

GR: This edition is for a hundred people who want to have something solid. Painting is looking for just that one person. But one hundred people get that which is a bit more ephemeral and a little crisper.

RS: It is as if you are projecting onto your audience a preference for something tough. It this true?

GR: Yes.

RS: You happen to be the owner of this painting, and you like something soft.

GR: In this case.

RS: There is an interesting discrepancy between your acceptance, if you will, of the gentler image, and your view that in the public discourse the images have to be tougher.

GR: Yes, stable; and I have to maintain that. The multiple has not turned into a hard picture; it has merely become a little more lively.

RS: That's the practical answer. The buyers of this work are somewhat different.

GR: It became a completely different object with a frame, with a sheet of plastic over the image which hangs so freely; you see the fragility. It was a substitute for the fragility of the painting. It showed all these interesting qualities that the painting does not have. I had to explain all of these relations to Dieter Schwarz who once wanted to produce them just as they were. But I said that he needed to include the frame and the distance produced by the glass and so on. That's all part of it. It has become an object, not just a picture. That's why we can't reduce it to the perkiness; it became a whole other thing.

RS: In the beginning, you talked a lot about how important it is that the pictures you worked from are givens, ready-mades, pictures from an album, or from a magazine. What you do is to alter that given by painting it.

GR: Why am I changing the qualities of the photograph? Because it is too small. [*Laughter*] I am a painter, I love to paint. Using photographs was the only possible way to continue to paint. I couldn't just have used a model. That was impossible and an untimely endeavor that would have cut everything short. I can't do that. Not even Mr. [Lucian] Freud could to do that. I had to use photographs. They provided new contents that were relevant to me and to others. That was my conviction.

RS: What contents were those?

GR: What touches us.

RS: But the range of subjects goes from things that are totally banal, like *Toilet Paper,* to images that are not so banal, like *Mr. Heyde*.

GR: To make a photo from a painting that you can put up on the wall again is comparable to making a painting from a photo. But these are the old questions where one only has excuses. Take music as an example, how some simply hear when it's right. In painting, think of the Bob Ryman exhibition in Bonn, where you suddenly find a painting that has something, that looks "right" and nobody knows why.

RS: No, but could you describe certain qualities that give you this feeling of rightness?

GR: I don't know how to describe that. Whether or not it has been fulfilled or how wrong it went is a different question, but the demand was, and remains, to address the things that are most important, that concern us all. And so in relation to the history of art, where nobody had ever painted toilet paper, it was time to paint toilet paper, which is not really banal.

RS: Why?

GR: It's important; it cannot be banal. Then there's the "banality of evil." It's a beautiful term—what Hannah Arendt said about [Adolf] Eichmann. And the same for *Mr. Heyde*. This is important.

RS: Now I am confused. In a sense, *Mr. Heyde* and the toilet paper are both banal and, in another sense, evil is also banal.

Sigmar Polke and Gerhard Richter, c. 1996.

GR: And both are important. I just want to get away from the label: "He paints the banalities of life and that's all," or "He is one of those people who are not interested in anything." For a while that was just fine with me. At least I was being left alone.

RS: But now you want to get rid of that characterization?

GR: Yes. I want to at least correct it. *Banality* means a little bit more than *unimportant*.

RS: What does it mean?

GR: Just more. I mentioned "the banality of evil" in order to show that banality has at some point been described as something horrific. It can be a concern to describe the banal as something terrifying. The chandelier [*Flemish Crown*] is a monster. I don't need to paint a monster; it is enough to paint this thing, this shitty, small, banal chandelier. That thing is terrifying. I've already said some time ago that in order to dissociate myself from Francis Bacon, I didn't have to distort faces. It is much scarier to paint people's faces as banal as I find them in photographs. That is what makes the banal more than just banal.

RS: How do you mean something monstrous?

GR: It is more terrifying to me.

RS: I'm interested by what you said in a couple of ways. First of all, in American Pop art, the emphasis was on ordinary commercial goods, things you buy in a store, images in magazines, and so on. More recently, Jeff Koons made a whole show dedicated to banality. But it was banality in a grotesque way, an exaggerated banality. And you are also talking about the grotesque or the monstrous, in a form that is very detached, subdued, not exaggerated. It is not a rhetorical statement that you make the image in a certain way that is very . . .

GR: Well, modest. Very small and quiet. Yes, I'd say that it is small, modest, quiet. I hope that it functions like that. That something is heard although it approaches quietly. That was my hope. That was the trick.

RS: Are the paintings supposed to have a certain uncanny quality?

GR: No, but you are reminded of something. In the ideal case, somebody looks at the work and asks what this is supposed to be and why anybody would paint such a banal object. And then the person comes to think that maybe there is something more to it, that maybe the object is not that banal after all, that maybe it is horrible. It stands for something . . . maybe for a terrible living room.

RS: But not as a symbol?

GR: No, not as a symbol. But the longer you see it, the more it becomes frightening.

RS: For example, the *Flemish Crown* is a piece of a larger reality that is frightening, not a symbol of something but part of the thing itself.

GR: It is an image of this horror, a detail of it.

RS: Of ugliness?

GR: Of the misery of this world. [*Laughter*] Perhaps this special culture.

RS: Which special culture?

GR: A petit bourgeois culture. But I refuse to discuss it in those terms because now it turns into social criticism where I attack a certain class, the petit bourgeois, those who had this thing in the middle of their living room, the Flemish crown. That was part of our culture, and I don't want to attack that even though I myself might have suffered under it. And although it was terrible, it was never meant to be an accusation. Now those people are all gone. There was nothing but crime and misery in those living rooms. There is only crime and misery in general. [*Laughter*]

RS: So you didn't want to make a critique?

294

GR: No, it's a report. Remember people; don't forget, please. [*Laughter*]

RS: In general, American Pop art concentrated on public imagery and commercial culture. But previously you told me that as German Pop artists Polke, Lueg, and you wanted to represent a broader experience, a wider view of reality. I wondered if you could say something more about this larger vision in relation to the focus of American Pop art.

GR: Maybe we didn't even have a chance. The message of American Pop art was so powerful and so optimistic. But it was also very limited, and that led us to believe that we could somehow distance ourselves from it and communicate a different intention.

RS: So, where does that difference lie?

GR: It was not possible for us to produce the same optimism and the same kind of humor or irony. Actually, it was not irony. Lichtenstein is not ironic but he does have a special kind of humor. That's how I could describe it: humor and optimism. For Polke and me, everything was more fragmented. But how it was broken up is hard to describe.

RS: Are you talking about a historical experience or a personal experience of fragmentation?

GR: They come together, right? I don't know why. Otherwise, we would have had to play a role. Some people did that; they really participated. They imitated the Americans: optimistic, big, colorful, strong.

RS: Lueg is more like the American Pop and you are much more . . .

GR: Broken? Yes, maybe.

RS: One American Pop artist who is definitely broken is [Andy] Warhol.

GR: Yes, that's true.

RS: Do you feel a particular affinity to Warhol?

GR: I always liked him the most. But there is a huge difference between us, and that was the freedom that he had. People here in Germany are all very uptight. But he was not. His life story, his homosexuality—that was not possible here. Polke took some liberties, but those were very different from the freedom that Warhol had. You have to have a basis for being received like he was. That did not exist for us.

RS: One aspect of Warhol that is very strong is his morbidity. Do you identify with that quality?

GR: Those are paintings by Warhol I like the most, the Disaster paintings. And also some of the films. But everything else, like

his huge production of commissioned portraits, was not my cup of tea.

RS: I am less interested in Warhol than I am in you, but I think there are some telling parallels to be pointed out, and some telling contrasts. For example, when Warhol selected and transposed an image, he took things away from it, he removed information. Now you have said yourself that you have many tools at your disposal, but elimination is perhaps the most important one. Could you talk about what it means to eliminate or reduce elements of an image?

GR: I believe that the quintessential task of every painter in any time has been to concentrate on the essential. The hyperrealists didn't do that; they painted everything, every detail. That's why they were such a surprise. But for me it was obvious that I had to wipe out the details. I was happy to have a method that was rather mechanical. In that regard I owe something to Warhol. He legitimized the mechanical. He showed me how it is done. It is a normal state of working, to eliminate things. But Warhol showed me this modern way of letting details disappear, or at least he validated its possibilities. He did it with silkscreening and photography, and I did it through mechanical wiping. It was a very liberating act.

RS: Is the process of elimination an arbitrary one, where the results are a surprise, or did you anticipate what would be removed before actually doing it?

GR: Well, it's in between. You can imagine what has to be wiped out, smeared away. And then there were also accidents. In any case, it was a wonderful utopian way to do this mechanically and not to consciously decide what has to go and what can stay. It fit the climate of the time to make everything easy and simple and happy—the utopian climate of the 1960s. It was part of the *Zeitgeist* to say: "I want to be like a machine." I don't even remember who said that. Polke said something like that, and Warhol did too. Today that's unthinkable. Now all of these paintings seem handmade, painterly, imperfect. It was different then. People only saw the similarity to the photograph, the technical perfection, which by now is outdated. Because of their age, the paintings have become so painterly and now look like old handmade paintings. Back then, they were provocative, as if produced by a machine: "Richter paints with such perfection that the surface is like that of a photograph."

RS: So there's a difference in reception?

GR: Yes.

RS: But are you talking mostly about the critical response?

GR: No, overall. I remember those paintings as being much more perfect. The ability to do that so perfectly was my trademark. But when you look at them today, they are far from perfect. It is rather the earlier ones that are more perfect, and maybe the later landscapes. Do you agree with this?

RS: No.

GR: Maybe in the 1960s one didn't see this mechanical quality, one wasn't able to see this. In terms of reception, they were said to be "as perfect as the Americans." And then after a while it became obvious that compared to the Americans they were not perfect but had a very European hand-made quality to them.

RS: That's true. But I also think that either there is an evolution in the work or a paradox that was always there, which is the fact that, on the one hand, technically they belong to the tradition of fine studio painting and, on the other hand, that something apparently arbitrary or mechanical has been done to pictures made in that tradition. After all, you are a master of the disruptive technique as well. The thing that makes it blur is not a machine but a bigger brush or squeegee. It was never so mechanical; it was never so arbitrary, correct?

GR: Yes.

RS: And then again, you said earlier that what separated you from other artists was not simply that you have this technical command but that you have the ability to recognize when a work has achieved a certain rightness.

GR: Yes.

RS: So the defining quality of what you do is both a matter of the mastery of materials and a question of recognition and decision. It was never about violence done to the picture in the same way that some people have seen this kind of disruptive physicality as aggression, pure and simple.

GR: Yes, that's true.

RS: In some ways, what you're up to is closer to what [Alberto] Giacometti did than to the kind of painting that is usually described as wild or violent. It is about working away at the image and at the paint until you can see something.

GR: Yes.

RS: So, in that respect, your approach is similar to Giacometti's but involves a different formal language with a different set of conventions, and is being pursued at a different time.

GR: Yes, that sounds good.

RS: The other day, you said that when you were in East Germany you and your friends wanted to find a "third way" between the Russian and the American models. Together, you identified your efforts with certain artists, and Giacometti was one you mentioned. Now Giacometti comes out of [Paul] Cézanne and a tradition you have avoided, yet, at the same time, you seem to have strived for a certain quality that was in those paintings. Is it fair to say, then, that you invented a different way of painting in order to arrive at the same place?

GR: And this commitment to quality still clings to me like a clubfoot and makes me unfree, unproductive, and impotent.

RS: If you are impotent, the rest of us are really in trouble. [Laughter] But I didn't mean quality with a capital Q, as in a hierarchy of values but, rather, a certain feeling, a certain type of visual and emotional experience. Let's go back to basics: you paint ordinary life in a revealing but undramatic light, you use painterly languages that belie style. In a way, Giacometti attempted to do something quite similar— to capture the appearance of things that kept retreating or disappearing and then partially clicked and snapped into focus. The other day when I watched you working, the same kind of thing seemed to be happening. You have a process in which you rough in, or state, the image, then blur, or unstate, it. And after this has gone on for a while, an image becomes visible that is fundamentally different from what you started with. I don't want to force the comparison with Giacometti, but the existential aspect of his work wasn't a matter of expressive style so much as it was this pursuit of an elusive reality, a pursuit carried on without melodrama.

GR: Yes. I would be very embarrassed if I were staging some sentimental drama here.

RS: It is existential and it is humanist but it is not sentimental and it is not melodramatic.

GR: Yes. Only a bit. [Laughter]

RS: You admit it! [Laughter] That is interesting because it is as if, by way of Pop art and mechanical reproduction that was very much of that moment, you were able to come all the way back around and answer some of the questions that confronted artists of your generation in the 1950s, except that the answers you provided don't look like anything that would have issued from the tradition in which those questions were posed.

GR: Good.

RS: There are three basic critical explanations for deliberate elimination or erasure in modern painting. The first one is destruction. Do you see what you do as a destructive act?

GR: Yes, very often I have the feeling that what I do is very destructive, born out of the need and inability to construct. It is my wish to create a well-built, beautiful, constructive painting. And there are many moments when I plan to do just that, and then I realize that it looks terrible. Then I start to destroy it, piece by piece, and I arrive at something that I didn't want but that looks pretty good. Therefore I understand if somebody calls it destructive. I find that congenial but maybe it is just... I don't know.

RS: That makes me think, for example, of [Lucio] Fontana. It was said of him that in cutting and puncturing the canvas, he was attacking it, but, the result is very beautiful. Does this paradox in Fontana's work relate in any way to what you do?

GR: Maybe. I find him to be much more productive. Because even though at the beginning he and Polke and others destroyed their work out of rage and anger, later on they were able to direct those actions. I was never able to do that. I can't plan to make something look out of focus in a certain way. That doesn't work. For example, this painting [*Snow*] was created out of a different initial impulse; and this gray painting was intended to be very different from what it eventually turned into. That's why it is impossible for me to re-create them. But that's another topic. However, I already have to revise that statement I just made: there are many abstract paintings that I did plan and execute. They are mostly small and part of some sort of multiple work. For instance, I once made one hundred small paintings for Munich. They simply flowed one after the other and all of them perfect. Fontana would have been amazed.

RS: For *October 18, 1977* you did several versions of some images.

GR: Yes, those were planned like that and made according to the plan.

RS: A second explanation for erasure or elimination is that the image is not about the act of the destruction that left it in its ultimate state, but about loss. What you see in such paintings is an absence.

GR: I believe that Dieter Schwarz once mentioned something like that. I feel very close to this idea of seeing the pain and the loss in the work. I can't paint as well as Vermeer—we have lost this beautiful culture, all the utopias are shattered, everything goes down the drain, the wonderful time of painting is over. It is an inclination of mine to see it that way. I don't know anybody else who is so attached to the history of art and loves the old masters as much or wants as much to paint like them. There are examples where I have tried to reincarnate Titian and others, but of course it didn't work out. I wanted to paint the Annunciation for myself. That is an example of how it is impossible to paint like that today. I understand why people see it that way.

RS: So, the subject of these works is a reality that has not yet entirely disappeared but which is retreating?

GR: It is a reality that is unreachable. It is a dream. It's over. But I am old-fashioned enough or stupid enough to hang on. I still want to paint something like Vermeer. But it is the wrong time and I cannot do it. I am too dumb. Well, I am not able to.

RS: But I think more about visual phenomena that can be captured than the historical precedents for capturing it. What happens when the subject is not Titian but a toilet paper roll? Does that mean that reality itself, everyday reality, is something we've lost the ability to hold onto in a picture?

GR: No, that's never the problem. I never wanted to capture and hold reality in a painting. Maybe at a weak moment I did, but I don't remember. However, that was never my intention. But I wanted to paint the appearance of reality. That is my theme or my job.

RS: The third explanation for erasing or paring down an image is that what you are left with in the end is something irreducible and basic. Rather than performing a symbolic act of destruction or painting loss, you arrive at a distillation of the image's essential qualities.

Joseph Beuys and Gerhard Richter, c. early 1980s

297

GR: I hope that's the case. You can say that, I can't.

RS: But if that's the purpose of working in this way then what you finally have is neither the depicted object in itself nor a clear mirror image of the subject struggling to perceive that object, but a strange in-between entity representing the exchange of appearance between the object painted and the subject looking at it, the thing and the viewer.

GR: That is something for intellectuals. [*Laughter*]

RS: I am actually trying to describe an experience and not just a logical abstraction. The book in front of me has its own reality, and I have mine. They are separate. But when I pick it up and look at it and I try to grasp an image on the page with my eyes, those realities overlap and are confounded. Visually, I step part way out of myself and part way into this other world, but I can also lose my bearings and be stranded between self-awareness and awareness of the things represented in the picture.

GR: Yes.

RS: And that's where painting happens, at any rate, one kind of painting. If I want to make paintings about what is going on inside me then I become a surrealist or an expressionist. But I am talking about a kind of painting that is neither totally reflexive nor totally objective.

GR: That's probably right, but you overestimate me.

RS: You have talked about how working with photographs freed you from certain expectations. You didn't have to have style; you didn't have to have a theme in the traditional sense of the term; you could paint all kinds of disparate things. But in these early statements, you also made an issue of photography's apparent neutrality. Could you say a little bit about why seeming to be detached in this manner was so crucial for you then?

GR: Yes, it was my wish to be neutral. I saw it as an opportunity. It was the opposite of ideology. And to be as objective as possible offered a legitimization for painting since you were being objective and doing what was necessary, enlightening, and so on.

RS: In the 1930s, the English novelist Christopher Isherwood cast the narrator of his "Berlin Stories" in a similar role by having him say, "I am a camera," by which he meant that he was not taking positions but merely recording what was going on around him. When you first appropriated photographs to make paintings were you also assuming such a cameralike objectivity?

GR: The paintings have the advantage that I can still add a little something—because the notion of neutrality and objectivity is an illusion,

of course. That is somehow impossible. Every painting automatically includes my inability, my powerlessness, my relation to reality, things that are subjective. Therefore, it was legitimate to be painted. It was not about absolute purity but about the greatest possible purity.

RS: In many respects, Isherwood's stance was the literary equivalent of *Neue Sachlichkeit* in painting during the same period, but in fact *Neue Sachlichkeit* pictures could be extremely editorial.

GR: That was very often the case.

RS: And you were looking for something that was more neutral, more . . .

GR: Complex.

RS: *Neue Sachlichkeit* art was in part a reaction to earlier forms of modernism, in particular, Expressionism, Cubism, and Dada, and their fracturing and reconfiguration of traditional picture-making. A lot of Pop art in America used modernist methods for breaking up images and recombining the pieces. For example, this happens in Warhol and [Robert] Rauschenberg. By contrast, your paintings are almost always whole.

GR: Yes, that is true.

RS: So even though you cut or crop images and reframe them inside the rectangle you paint on, you treat those edited details as complete pictorial units and, with only a couple of exceptions, you've never collaged or juxtaposed images from different sources in the same work.

GR: I can't explain why I have such an aversion to collages. To me it always seemed cheap, and it was too sloppy, too loose. I always wanted to make a painting.

RS: What is the appeal of making a painting, in this sense?

GR: Well, it is somehow my duty and my task to fill the space of painting, to make a whole out of it, and everything else seems inappropriate.

RS: Of course, Polke is a maker of collages, and your sensibility is very close to Polke's in some respects, but on this issue you are very different.

GR: Yes, I am also the more classical one. Somebody once said that I am Goethe and Polke is Schiller; or I am Thomas Mann and he is Heinrich Mann.

RS: Could you explain to an American audience what this distinction means?

GR: The classical is what holds me together. It is that which gives me form. It is the order that I do not have to attack. It is something that tames my chaos or holds it together so that I can continue to exist. That was never a question for me. That is essential for life.

RS: In terms of the situation here in the Rhineland in the 1960s, with the impact of Fluxus and Joseph Beuys, almost everybody else in your circle found themselves on the other side.

GR: Yes, it seems as if Beuys was on the other side, and also [Nam June] Paik and [John] Cage. But Cage is really a classical man—so scrupulous in the way he holds his things together, does so little, and makes that beautiful. He never even thinks about being sloppy. Sometimes he pretends to be but he never is. He is probably even more uptight than I am and maybe more scrupulous.

RS: You've said that in the 1960s you were very impressed by Cage's "Lecture on Nothing," in which he at one point said: "I have nothing to say and I am saying it." How did you understand that paradox then, and how did you relate it to your own desire to avoid making big declarative statements in your own work?

GR: I thought that this was born out of the same motivation that makes him use the notion of chance, which is that we can't know or say very

much at all, in a very classical philosophical sense: "I know that I don't know anything."

RS: Back then, when you talked about your use of photographs as the source for paintings, the range of choices you had, and the disparateness of your selection, were you thinking of the apparent arbitrariness of Cage's procedures as a model?

GR: Cage is much more disciplined. He made chance a method and used it in constructive ways; I never did that. Everything here is a little more chaotic.

RS: Chaotic in a sense of more arbitrary or more chaotic in a sense of more intuitive?

GR: Maybe more intuitive. I believe that he knew more what he was doing. I might be absolutely wrong about this, but that was my impression.

RS: You mean a more rigorous aesthetic philosophy?

GR: Yes, the fact that he had a theory that he could name and describe. He could talk or write about what he was doing.

RS: And you proceeded by . . .

GR: From accident to accident. [*Laughter*]

RS: But let's suppose that it was not a question of going from accident to accident but from intuition to intuition. That means that you have a hunch, you don't know the answer, and you don't know exactly why you chose certain images, and yet in some way they were connected in your mind, in some way that suggested each other or created associations as you considered them. Certainly by the time of the *48 Portraits* there was deliberateness in your choices. What kind of instinct or motivation did you have in order to move from making images of contemporary reality to making images of historical figures?

GR: I can only say that that's the way it was. Polke drifted away into the psychedelic direction and I into the classical. I found support in Gilbert & George where I discovered the same tendencies. And then in [Blinky] Palermo who was also retrieving the classical.

RS: And [Marcel] Broodthaers, too?

GR: Yes, but I couldn't understand him—ever.

RS: But virtually all the things he refers to all belong to the nineteenth century.

GR: But that was nineteenth century, and I wanted something more classical.

RS: In America, Pop addressed the present. Even though Lichtenstein painted Mickey Mouse as he had looked forty years before, still he was painting Mickey Mouse. However, in Europe, artists used a pictorial language that developed out of Pop to look at historical things. For example, Broodthaers catalogued cows in a manner that simultaneously derived from Warhol's enumeration of Coca-Cola bottles, soup cans, movie-star smiles, and old-fashioned diagrams. And when Polke painted a row of books labeled *Polke's Collected Works,* he made them look like they came off the shelf of an old library. When you went from making pictures of speed boats, cars, planes, and Jackie Kennedy, to making the *48 Portraits* something of the same anachronism entered into the equation. You say that what you are striving for is a kind of classicism, but it has more dimensions than that.

GR: *48 Portraits* was supposed to be many things. Those were the typical neutral pictures that one finds in an encyclopedia. The issue of neutrality was my wish and main concern. And that's what they were. That made them modern and absolutely contemporary.

RS: That's true. But who are the people in this index? They are all scientists, philosophers, writers, musicians.

GR: Yes, clever people.

RS: There is no painter, no artist.

GR: That would be too close to me. People would have tried to figure out why I included that painter but not the other one. I chose figures that I had the least to do with. Of course I also had some connection to musicians and writers but there are a lot missing who I like much more than those portrayed—[Sigmund] Freud and Nietzsche, for example. But I didn't want to portray my favorites but the typical, the leveling; that's the reason all that was contemporary, the neutrality of the encyclopedia, which neutralizes everything and all ideology. That's why I chose many that I didn't know and took out many that I did know. It was the opposite of truth. [Theodor] Adorno said: "Every art work is the arch-enemy of another." They can't exist next to one another. The encyclopedia makes that possible. We can do it in the world. That is the present situation.

RS: So were you arguing against exalting cultural figures as heroes?

GR: Not really. No, it was not my ambition to be against heroes. I love them too much. I am happy that those people exist.

RS: Were you arguing in favor of a plural culture?

GR: Yes, that's what it is, without endorsing it. It is a fact: we make everything the same. But it is not an attack. It is ambiguous because I hung them in a wonderfully classical way, like a shrine. This is its classical aspect, and that had to do with Gilbert & George.

RS: In this sense, the casts that you made of Palermo and yourself [*Two Sculptures for a Room by Palermo*] almost seem to belong to the row of heads in *48 Portraits*?

GR: Yes, at least they have the same formal style. But we never wanted to join that lineup or saw ourselves like that. It was a formal matter. Maybe it was a polemic against the *Zeitgeist* of egalitarianism, pluralism, and this whole anti-aesthetic debate. Maybe because art was irrelevant. Maybe we made those heads and lauded the classical in order to be polemical, against the time.

I remember seeing those pieces in Munich, where I also visited an exhibition called *Italian Art Today*, with people like [Giulio] Paolini who made similar classical stuff. And suddenly I realized how substantial my two heads were compared to what Paolini had produced, this decorative game. I suddenly understood how dead serious mine was. That it was somehow inconsistent with the humor of Pop art. If it was humorous, it was that way in a tragic manner.

RS: Of course every work of art of any value has multiple levels of meaning; one can be funny and one can be serious at various levels.

Paolini is funny and serious in his love affair with classical art, but the intensity of the ambivalence is lower.

GR: Yes.

RS: But your situation was different. Your evocation of the classical was basically a response to the whole mood of the late 1960s, early 1970s, where the general rules were: Away with the old; Everything must be relevant; and Everything must be a cultural critique.

GR: Yes, exactly.

RS: But that interpretation differs from what many people seem to think this work is about.

GR: Oh, really!

RS: Some critics seem to regard the *48 Portraits* as an empty, almost postage-stamp-like array of cultural icons. Why do you think it has had such a strong response?

GR: If it was only postage stamps it wouldn't be as elaborate and there wouldn't be as much trouble. It is too big and there is too much presence, and always people wonder what it is about. Women are angry because there are no women. It keeps upsetting people again and again. People are always upset when confronted with something traditional and conservative, and therefore they don't want it. You're not allowed to do that; it is not considered to be part of our time. It's over, reactionary.

RS: Some critics explain it to themselves—make it okay to like—by arguing that it's an exercise in rhetoric, the rhetoric of a certain kind of representation of culture that questions or nullifies that culture's authority.

GR: And as I mentioned, you also have the psychological or subjective timeliness of the father problem. This affects all of society. I am not talking about myself because that would be rather uninteresting, but the absence of the father is a typical German problem. That is the reason for such agitation; that is why this work has such a disquieting effect.

RS: So it is about restoring a sense of history that has been broken or truncated.

GR: It's not a restoration. It is a reference to this loss. It takes account of the fact that we have lost something. It asks the question of whether or not we need to do something. It is not about the establishment of something.

Bruce Nauman and Gerhard Richter, c. late 1970s

RS: A question of whether what has been lost can be brought back or not?

GR: Yes, but I don't believe that it comes back.

RS: Was making the paintings a way of putting those images out to see whether they still exerted power on their own?

GR: That was not my intention. My intention was to get attention. [*Laughter*] I wanted to be seen.

RS: Bruce Nauman once made a neon with the text, "The true artist helps the world by revealing mystic truths," which he put in the window of his studio like a beer sign. That piece was addressed both to himself and to the public.

GR: That's good!

RS: And what appeared to be a declaration was really a question: "Do you believe this? Do I believe this?" Is there any parallel between what he was doing and what you're after?

GR: Yes, I believe that there is something like that. That's possible. But I have too much respect for Bruce Nauman to simply claim that we share the same concern, that we are thinking about the same things. It doesn't work like that.

RS: Another way of approaching the problem might be to talk a little bit about your decision to copy Titian's *Annunciation* or your interest in landscape.

GR: It is all the same motivation.

RS: In other interviews, you've suggested that using nostalgia or using an anachronism was a way of being subversive. But painting in traditional modes can also involve an assimilation of traditions. Were you employing these images as a tool for upsetting the fixed ideas of the avant-garde, or were you reaffirming the basic paradigms to which you resorted? Were they primarily a tool, or a goal?

GR: That is too difficult.

RS: Alright, but take the landscapes and the Titian copy: not only was the style in which they were painted a departure from modernism, but so were the images. The idea of someone in your position painting a Titian or painting a beautiful landscape in a somewhat romantic way was bound to get a reaction, was bound to make people say, "What is he doing?"

GR: On the one hand, it was a polemic against this annoying modernist development that I hated. And, of course, the assertion of my freedom: "Why shouldn't I paint like this and who could tell me not to?" And then the affirmation was naturally there, the wish to paint paintings as beautiful as those by Caspar David Friedrich, to claim that this time is not lost but possible, that we need it, and that it is good. And it was a polemic against modern art, against tin art, against "wild art"—and for freedom, that I could do whatever I wanted to.

RS: Tin art?

GR: Much modern stuff looked like aluminum. Modern, pure. Minimalism was going on at that time. I remember just a little story that took place when I was first in New York with Palermo. We had some photographs of our work—just in case. And we showed them to someone—I think it was Bob Ryman—and I thought that he would, of course, prefer the abstract paintings, but he was only interested in my first landscape, which was *Corsica (Fire)*.

And I was so surprised that he liked this painting. I thought, he is a modern artist, a real artist, not like me. But he liked it.

RS: Well, he is a modern artist and he is a real artist, which is precisely why he would have liked it. But in that period from the late 1960s to the middle 1970s, one gets the impression that things were very hard for you.

GR: Yes, it was at that time I lost the ground under my feet.

RS: How so? Because the world changed on you or because you began to doubt what you were doing?

GR: I didn't know what to do but to paint. I was "out."

RS: But if I understand the situation correctly to be out and to choose an entirely unexplored direction can also be a kind of freedom?

GR: Well, the freedom and the comfort gained from being out were not very substantial. Being out didn't have such a positive effect. After all, I wanted to be on the inside. I don't know where I was.

RS: But, in fact, being in that position opened up a whole different way of thinking about the work, didn't it?

GR: I don't remember it being so different. Anyway, only much later did I realize that these crises were not something to get agitated about but that they were the normal way of working. Everybody has them. Well, maybe it is not as simple as that. There are people who work with more confidence and others who stumble from crisis to crisis. It was somewhere in between. But I don't know if it was a special crisis, maybe it was.

RS: I am not so much asking how you felt about it or about the immediate circumstances. I am only thinking that if you step back and look at the larger picture, here was someone associated with the avant-garde who suddenly was making pictures of traditional subject matter and making them in a classical style. That went against the grain of just about everything that was going on then, and it also went against what was expected of you in particular. And it went against what many of your supporters valued. Somehow, given these factors, you must have had some understanding of the necessity for doing all of that.

GR: Alright. But that's what I don't know. I wouldn't know how to reply to that. Certainly the situation animated me to try different directions so that I would find something of more substance and importance. I was very sure that the big "Detail" paintings I had been making were not the direction.

RS: Okay, let's talk about the shift toward more abstract pictures. In one statement, you have said: "If abstract paintings show my reality, then the landscapes and still lifes show my yearning." In what sense do you mean that the abstract paintings show your reality?

GR: That was later, and the reality of abstraction was what could I make directly—mentally, physically, psychologically. This was my daily challenge and those were normal difficulties; it has no relation to any kind of yearning or dream. And if it did, it would be hard to recognize it as such and I wouldn't call it a yearning. But the figurative ones were some sort of a break and recovery from everyday work. That's why I called it a yearning because there I could afford to do something romantic or nostalgic. That was a polemical remark; it has never been just like that. But in order to de-emphasize them I said they were nostalgic—a luxury.

RS: In what sense, that the making of the abstract pictures was less about an illusion and more about a physical process?

GR: Yes, exactly. Like a musician who has to know his stuff and has to work and to make the music, to build it.

RS: Robert Ryman has also talked about abstract painting as being the most realist kind of painting, because everything that counts is right there in front of you—the materials, the surface. The experience doesn't depend on anything outside or beyond the painting but only on what can be directly perceived, what is "real." Do you mean something similar when you talk about the reality of abstract pictures?

GR: Yes, but his reality, the one he is talking about, is different. To him it is a physically present reality, and he would probably deny any imaginary relations. At some point I said polemically that Ryman reminds us of something, tells us something. There is always some sort of narrative or reference, though I believe that he would deny that and say that to him it's all about structure or whatever.

RS: What kind of narrative quality was in your abstract painting in the mid- to late 1970s, for example? How do you mean the narrative when you look at pictures like this?

GR: This reminds me of a time when Buchloh asked me the same thing, and I said that I saw red rain falling here [pointing to an abstract work of the early 1970s] and a lake behind it, and there are broken cliffs and poles running around and one floats through spaces. He was appalled and said, "You can't be serious! That's not true!" And I replied, "No, it's true!" As if a child said, "Look mom, that's red rain, those drips right there."

RS: Well, first of all, I think that you can be serious about this. However, I am surprised that you see qualities so directly associated with nature. When you are making those paintings, are you actually thinking in metaphors all the time?

GR: No, never. And I also try to avoid that something in the painting resembles a table or other things. It's terrible if it does because then all you can see is that object.

RS: So you allow for aspects or suggestions of images in the abstract work but not actual pictures?

GR: Not actual pictures. I just wanted to reemphasize my claim that we are not able to see in any other way. We only find paintings interesting because we always search for something that looks familiar to us. I see something and in my head I compare it and try to find out what it relates to. And usually we do find those similarities and name them: table, blanket, and so on. When we don't find anything, we are frustrated and that keeps us excited and interested until we have to turn away because we are bored. That's how abstract painting works. That was my argument with Buchloh because I said that's how Malevich and Ryman work as well. And only like that. You can interpret the *Black Square* of Malevich as much as you like, but it remains a provocation; you are compelled to look for an object and to come up with one.

RS: It is important whether an artist actually gives you an indication that there is such an object or teases you with the possibility that there might be one or whether the artist, in effect, lets you know that there isn't actually an image of that sort; there is something there but it is not a representation.

GR: I just wanted to insist on the way we function. Basically we always try to identify a relation of a picture to some sort of appearance. It's not about the recognition of a particular subject matter.

RS: Of course Leonardo da Vinci talked about looking at patterns on the ceiling and finding faces, and maybe there is a basic human tendency to do this, but whether the artist encourages or discourages this tendency is a huge issue for abstract painting.

GR: Most artists have tried to avoid that. And still they cannot escape this mechanism. Even those paintings that are supposed to be nothing but a monochrome surface are looked at in that searching manner. The effect of these paintings depends on that mechanism. I don't even know how it could work otherwise.

RS: In a way it does relate your abstract pictures to your figurative ones because in the figurative paintings people are reassured when they see a certain kind of image. They crave the verification of the object and long to see what they know about or bring to the object, and yet you create a distance in which that object becomes ambiguous. People want a picture that adds up to their expectations, and you do things that remove qualities from the image or cancel it out. You make paintings at the expense of pictures, or at least at the expense of the depicted object.

GR: I don't know if you are right about that or whether I could agree. But I also don't know if I understood you correctly.

RS: I am just saying that you use painting as a way of making it difficult for people to just read the image.

GR: Yes, that's right.

RS: Many of the gray abstract pictures that preceded the color abstractions had quite painterly surfaces. By comparison, the first full-color abstractions were anti-painterly, but the combination of hues was often very strident. In these ways the contrast between the two groups of work in touch, texture, and achromatic versus chromatic effects was very dramatic. How did you first arrive at this use of color; how was it supposed to operate in contrast to the monochrome gray paintings?

GR: It was very sudden because I thought that it couldn't go on like that. The gray didn't work any more. That was the end. And then I started with a weird color abstract painting that was very big and not very good and then I did the small ones. The transition was easy to make because I was working off a photo that I could enlarge.

RS: What was the impulse behind this jump into very dramatic color?

GR: To do the opposite, to free myself of any constraints. I asked myself, "Why not?" Do we want some psychoanalysis? [*Laughter*]

RS: No. If you want to offer some psychoanalysis, I'll take it, but that is not what I am asking. I was wondering about formal impulse.

GR: Well, I never dared to show these paintings anywhere. I thought they were crazy. The early ones that is, which, after all, I made as copies from parts of other paintings. I found that by copying those paintings I was able to construct them in an acceptable manner. You can't just show this wild stuff, those helpless smears that are absolutely random and senseless, against all rationality and taste, against everything. But then, after I had painted copies of the originals I felt comfortable enough to show them—in Halifax, Nova Scotia. It was a test and I realized that people took them seriously, and then I continued to make them.

RS: That was also the time when you made your artist's book, *128 Details from a Picture*, which is basically a catalogue of black-and-white photographs of the surface of an abstract painterly painting.

GR: Yes.

RS. Among the last of the photo-based color abstractions you made before you started to make direct, gestural abstraction, was a picture called *Faust*. Did you think at that time that assuming the role of gestural painter in some way involved a Faustian bargain?

GR: That was pure smugness. It was a very big and boisterous picture, and I don't remember if anything reminded me of Faust. It was a conscious decision to never declare it as being either one thing or another. Of course, in the back of my head I thought that hopefully people would understand it as Walpurgis Night in Goethe's *Faust*.

RS: I am wondering how many different levels we are dealing with here. After all, Faust makes a deal with the devil. Who is the devil in this case?

GR: Part of it was the fear of my own courage. It was very important for me to create a painting like this. That's why I gave it such a title. But at the same time I knew it was pretentious, that it was not quite right.

RS: But also that it was going the right direction.

GR: But it was the last of the translations or copies. After that, all the other abstractions were painted directly.

RS: This jump from indirect to direct painting coincides with a general turn toward painterly painting in the late 1970s and early 1980s, and to the advent of the neo-Expressionist work that came out of Europe and America.

GR: To the *Zeitgeist*.

RS: Were you conscious of this general shift? Did you feel you were a part of it or independent from it? Does the term neo-Expressionist have any positive value with regard to what you were doing?

GR: No, I was absolutely sure that I had nothing to do with that. They were mute and I was not. Silent and bad and terrible, but not me.

RS: How do you mean silent?

GR: Mute, dumb, dull; they had all the bad qualities. But, yes, I was certainly a child of the *Zeitgeist*. There's absolutely no doubt about it. One is affected by what is going on at the time. But I have always been a little different from the others and somehow always stood apart from the center.

RS: I am using the word with a little "e" not a big "E"; but did you intend your paintings to be read as expressive or expressionist in a particular way?

GR: Not expressionist, no. Expressive, yes. But more in the sense of "artificial" or something like that. That was the first time that I had the feeling that those types of paintings were cold and distant and clear— that they were not sentimental.

RS: And the color, the stridency of the color was chosen to create that effect?

GR: I believe so. It is part of a general feeling or attitude toward life, a desire to conquer such an artificial space for oneself.

RS: Now *I* am confused.

GR: I had the hope, carried by a fresh wind, to make something free, clear, open, crystal, visible, transparent, a utopia.

RS: Talk a minute about the Candle paintings, which could hardly have been more different from your abstractions of the early 1980s. If I am not mistaken, they were not very well received when you first exhibited them.

GR: Of the six I showed, none sold. They later became so expensive. [*Laughter*]

RS: Meanwhile, the critical response to the work was mixed, as it had been with the abstractions. At the time, it was assumed that either you were engaged in a direct satire of specific historical styles of painting or, as we discussed before, that you were engaged in a more general postmodern demolition of painting's conventions in which every style you touched on was exposed as empty.

GR: Buchloh said *rhetorical*. Well, there is nothing I can say to that. But I have to take back what I said about the abstractions being free from all meaning and opinion, that they are merely a crystal-clear dynamic world. That is not quite right. That would be reductive because it has to do with atmospheres and contents. They are narrative and sentimental. There are certain principal intentions that are part of all the paintings. It is not that big a difference. Yet they have the character of something more clear, free, dynamic, and so on.

RS: You seem to be saying, on the one hand, that these paintings are not to be read as traditional, serious, melodramatic gestural painting, but, on the other hand, that they still contain some ambitions for painting within the tradition to which they refer. They are neither "retro," nor "neo," nor part of a Duchampian game.

GR: No.

RS: In the final analysis, they are meant to be looked at as abstract painting.

GR: Yes. I am reminded of when I showed my paintings in the Netherlands and I talked to a critic and she said: "It is not possible that these are real paintings; they just pretend that they are." She liked them very much but she said that the real quality of these paintings was that they pretended to be paintings. I believe that somehow that was her question; she did not know how to handle the paintings. That's why she said something similar to what Buchloh was talking about when he talked about "rhetoric," that these are not really paintings.

RS: And what did you think of that?

GR: I am struck by the fact that these paintings are viewed according to three different standpoints: you say that the paintings are neither this nor that, Buchloh says, the paintings are not paintings but rhetoric, and the woman said that they are not paintings but play at being paintings. Therefore, there has to be some truth to it.

RS: But I am not agreeing with either of the two.

GR: But there is something right about the woman's question, something about these paintings that sometimes look like great gestural painting but it also suggests that there is a lack of conviction that it is possible to paint like that. Unlike people like [Franz] Kline and others who could paint an expressionist painting with conviction—the same kind of conviction in every stroke that he paints. They had the conviction that what they were doing was good and right. And that's it. I lack that in every stroke.

RS: In a way, though, these paintings are much more like those of [Jackson] Pollock than Kline or [Willem] de Kooning because Pollock's big allover paintings are no longer symbolist or narrative, and the energy in them is no longer that of muscular struggle. In the great allover works, the painting becomes, in a sense, independent. The distance that opens up between the painter and the painting is a space the viewer also can share, but the painting itself has become both intensely stimulating and formally self-sustaining, so that its persuasiveness no longer depends on the conviction or latent presence of its creator.

GR: You are absolutely right, and now we are on a different level because I don't believe that the paintings merely pretend to be paintings. But at the time it was not possible to accept them as paintings, at least not in Europe.

RS: But there is a big difference between a painting that is made in order to deal with convention, either satirically, critically, or analytically and a painting that accepts that conventions exist but tries to create a physical and visual reality that is as free of those conventions as possible. Does that make sense?

GR: Yes, absolutely! The paintings have nothing to do with the articulation of theoretical conventions, of painting itself, but they have a different intention. That is absolutely right. That's why I refused to accept when anyone tried to attribute such intentions and motives to my work.

RS: True classical art—as distinct from conservative classical or neoclassical style—may be defined as an art that accepts its own conventions, but

does not simply repeat them formulaically. Rather, it uses them to transform itself and extend its range. A crucial dimension of such classical art, though, is that it is deeply impersonal. Pollock, when he painted the big allover abstractions of the late 1940s and early 1950s, was, for perhaps the only time of his life, free of himself as a painter and thoroughly involved with the paint and the space and the process. In that sense, his was a classical art. [John] Cage and Merce Cunningham are classical artists in the same way. In your case, there is an irony in the fact that the painterly abstractions you started in the 1970s and continue to make have been referred to as either being expressionist or polemically anti-expressionist, but the term *expressionist* doesn't fit either usage.

GR: The only thing that is polemical is that I took the liberty and made the paintings the way they are, without regard to whether they were reminiscent of something explosive or expressionist.

RS: From my perspective, though, the irony is that you have approached a style—expressionism—which for many people cannot, by definition, be classic, and you have demonstrated the contrary, that it is possible to make a visually exciting, physically expansive, even aggressive picture that is classical in that it is not about the painter in any obvious way, and not emotional in the most banal sense.

GR: Yes, that sounds very good.

RS: The other model we inherit from the early modernists is that of Kandinsky, the idea of abstraction as a metaphysical or transcendentalist art. Now at one point you said: "Abstract paintings are fictive models that make visible a reality we can neither see nor describe but whose existence we can postulate." Do you in fact view your abstract paintings—either the gray paintings, the color paintings, or both—as being as much about the yearning for transcendent states of being as the landscapes are about a yearning for the beauty found in nature?

GR: If I understood you correctly, I would say that the landscapes are closer to such an intention than the abstract paintings. They are further removed from a stated intention to be models of a reality. You mentioned Kandinsky—I can't stand any of his paintings or the work of most artists similar to him who have said: "I am like a child," as if they could invent the world from the very beginning. I don't relate to any of that stuff. I was not interested in anything of the kind. I thought they were all stupid.

RS: But I wasn't talking specifically about Kandinsky's words or his style but of the kind of aspiration for modern abstract art with which he was associated. It's a tendency with which Mondrian, Rothko, and Newman were also connected, a drive to find a pictorial means for referring to philosophical or spiritual ideas, for representing things that, in essence, cannot be represented. Does that make sense to you at all?

GR: Yes, but you put it somehow in a naive way. It's not that simple. But every art, whether it is philosophy, literature, music, or painting, can touch something; it can't depict, never depicts. And I believe the painters you mentioned were talking about depiction, and that's impossible.

There is some truth to the idea of the paintings being models of a world, but the word *model* seems to be the wrong term. Because one might really take it for a model in the sense that "this is what it looks like in a different world" and that is not how it is meant. I have to distance myself from the concept of the *model*.

RS: But apart from your own painting, do you think that this is something art can do?

GR: Yes. A painting can help us to think something that goes beyond this senseless existence. That's something art can do.

RS: And you think it can still do that despite everything you've said?

GR: Yes, absolutely.

RS: And do you think it does happen?

GR: Yes, from time to time. And I am certain that we will find different forms and maybe then painting becomes obsolete, but we will always need something, right?

RS: But many people seem to think that the possibility of making art that is significant in that way has simply been used up. They believe too much of history and too much experience argues against such idealism.

GR: Our time looks as if we finally got over all of the nonsense, got rid of our need for a larger scheme, forgot history, rejected art, and rejected our fathers so that everything will be free and animalistic, techno-animalistic. I don't believe in any of that. That's just a movement. It is probably unavoidable. We now have the techno-animalistic age. It begins. But what will we do when everything is needless and meaningless?

RS: Do you think that there is actually such a dramatic change going on right now, a change more dramatic than what went on in the 1960s?

GR: Maybe, yes. Today there are more *facts* that are changing. All the great things such as the computer world, the Internet, and genetic engineering are very real and very important. Compared to that, the 1960s were just a dream. The 1960s were nothing real, only dreams—strawberry fields. [*Laughter*]

RS: Maybe that is the occasion to talk a little bit about the October paintings. After all, the idealism of the Baader-Meinhof group and how it went wrong are the subjects of the work, and the act of completing the works was implicitly idealistic as well insofar as it set a high stan-

Sabine Moritz and Gerhard Richter, c. 1998

dard for what painting could do, how much it could communicate. You seem to believe that idealism in an aesthetic context is possible but that in a practical, political context it is dangerous. Is that a fair summation?

GR: It is impossible to exist without idealism. I always imagined that I was one of the few who could live without idealism in order to discover later that all that time I was full of illusions. Even when I was against it, I *believed* in my opposition to it. It's a difficult subject.

RS: When did you think of yourself in these terms, of having no illusions?

GR: Maybe during the time I made the October paintings when I dealt with the subject matter and took notes and cursed the ideologues. When I realized that I myself *believed*, that I was euphoric, that I was carried by belief, I realized, this is wrong—it is merely a belief itself.

RS: To whom did you find yourself opposed in this situation?

GR: The opposition were primarily the terrorists, but it was also the faction of the art world that was possessed by big beliefs. I remember the kind of worship around Malevich and others. I could never participate in that. I was never interested in that. I never shared any of those beliefs. For me the government was the smaller evil because it believed the least. They were merely gangsters, of the sort that are always around in any period. But those who were full of beliefs, they were dangerous. I was convinced that the government had no ideology what-soever, whether it was [Helmut] Schmidt or [Helmut] Kohl. I was against believing, as such, against the fact that one could poison so many brains and have such power. I thought I was free from belief.

RS: But in a way your resistance converted you to a kind of belief even though you didn't accept the opinions of the members of the Baader-Meinhof group whom you were painting. You were forced to acknowl-edge that belief of an intensity such as theirs has value.

GR: In the end I was just as unfree. I was carried by some sort of belief.

RS: In many ways *October 18, 1977* marks a turning point in your work. The landscape paintings, the Titian paintings, even the *48 Portraits* are still engaged in a game of hide-and-seek with tradition, but after the October paintings you seem to paint your subjects with less distance. Take the flower paintings, for example. They are less shy about being beautiful paintings than the early landscapes. Likewise, the portraits that you have done of Sabine are very different from previous portraits you've painted of people close to you. There's an intimacy to these images that is different in quality from earlier works.

GR: What about Ema? The staircase?

RS: Yes and no. It is a very beautiful picture, but . . .

GR: But it is also a demonstration.

RS: Yes, there's something between you and the picture. An idea.

GR: Yes, it is staged. And the little nude of Sabine [*Small Bather*] is not staged.

RS: I am not thinking of the nude so much as the pictures of her reading. Those are really in a realm with Vermeer, not in style, not historical refer-ence, but because it allows the viewer to look into a private situation—with great reserve, but one can look. Do you think such a change has occurred?

GR: If I could take an impartial look at myself I would say: "That guy has matured a little, he has gained some sovereignty, he is older." That sometimes happens in painting. If I would not be sitting here, that's what I would say. Same with Velázquez: when he became older his paintings became better. Nice. Thank you for this. [*Laughter*]

RS: As you get older, you paint better, but you paint better not for tech-nical reasons, not for formal reasons, but because you have a different understanding.

GR: With a little more ease.

RS: Or, to choose a different word, with greater permission. When you are young, people around you say, No, you can't do this or that, and then also a voice inside says No to the things that matter most. But it is as if, after the Baader-Meinhof paintings, you gave yourself permission to make pictures with a different quality. Is that true?

GR: Yes, even though there were a lot of backlashes, and I produced a lot of garbage in between. For example, the difficulties I am having now. I can see this beautiful quality that you just described in a few paintings, once in a while, and then suddenly it disappears and then it resurfaces again. It is not as if this quality has become the rule now. That would be wonderful.

RS: I guess I am not talking about beauty alone, but also about the over-all resistance to change abating in some degree.

GR: Yes, but that's not true either. If I could count on that being a con-stant feature now, then all paintings would be much more relaxed—but they are not. There are always exceptions. But you are right; something has changed, but not enough.

RS: So what is it? What is the obstacle?

GR: The constraints persist. You said that when one is young that there are a lot of restrictions, and I still am subject to those restrictions. Only sometimes am I free of them, maybe more often than before, I don't know. I wish that I could give myself those permissions and that free-dom on a more regular basis, but I can't. Otherwise there wouldn't be as many forced paintings.

RS: These pressures are?

GR: I don't know where they come from. They exist. Yesterday we saw the catalogue of Goya drawings, and I realized that when Goya was very old he made much more relaxed drawings. He was allowed to make things that way. Or there is somebody like Matisse. And I was a little bit jealous because I have not yet achieved this permission. But now we have talked much too long about this, and this is not even our topic. I am sorry.

RS: Along with granting oneself permission to do certain things, there can also be an element almost of defiance. For example, in the last five years you've made a number of images that raised the hackles of the avant-garde.

GR: I don't know.

RS: You made a series of pictures of Sabine with your son—almost as if she were a Madonna and Child. And you made a multiple of the cross.

GR: Oh yes. [*Laughter*]

RS: Did you anticipate the negative reactions that those works received in some quarters?

GR: Well, I don't know much about that. People don't tell me these things. Sometimes I simply hear something through others. I only came across it once myself in a critical review of the *Small Bather*. That's where I finally read it. The review was titled "Holy, Holy, Holy," and then it went off. I understand why they get upset, but when they tell me that this is reactionary, I don't understand it.

RS: I don't agree with it, but I think I understand it. This is a period when there is almost no room for the kinds of words that you have used recently to discuss the October paintings, like *faith* or *belief*, or as far back as the early 1960s when you talked about art as being a substitute *religion*. Using such vocabulary or making allusions to such traditional symbols or iconography is extremely provocative, given its misuse by fundamentalists or people in positions of power. You can be misunderstood in many, many ways. And perhaps the question is not how many ways you can be misunderstood but how would you like to be understood?

GR: I don't know how I would like to be understood. Maybe as the keeper of tradition. [*Laughter*] Rather that than any other misunderstandings.

RS: As a guardian of an aesthetic tradition or as a guardian of a philosophical and moral tradition?

GR: Whatever you can get. [*Laughter*]

CHRONOLOGY

COMPILED BY CATHARINA MANCHANDA

This listing is organized within each year by up to three sections. Key events in Gerhard Richter's life are given in sans serif type; this is followed by notable cultural events in roman type; and by pertinent world events in italics.

1932
Born in Dresden, Gerhard Richter grows up in Reichenau and Waltersdorf, Oberlausitz/Saxony. His mother, Hildegard Richter, née Schönfelder, is the daughter of a gifted pianist and encourages her son's artistic interests. His father, Horst Richter, is a local school teacher.

1933
January 30: Adolf Hitler becomes Reich Chancellor. The Third Reich succeeds the Weimar government in Germany.

1937
July–November: The exhibition *Degenerate "Art"* is presented in Munich, and then tours to other cities. The exhibition shows works of art by German and other modernists of whom the fascist regime does not approve and seeks to denigrate.

1939
September 1: Germany invades Poland.
September 3: Britain, France, and other countries declare war on Germany.

1939–45
During the war years, Richter's father and two uncles are called up to serve in the German army. Both uncles die in action; his father survives. His mentally disabled aunt Marianne is killed as part of the Nazi euthanasia program. The family moves from Dresden to the countryside, deemed safer than the city in wartime.

1941
June 22: Germany invades the Soviet Union.
December 7: Japan bombs American ships at Pearl Harbor. United States enters the war on the side of Britain.

1945
February: Dresden is heavily bombed by the Allies; the Richters are living in a nearby town, within earshot of the bombardment.

May 7: Unconditional surrender of all German forces.
September 2: Japan surrenders.

1948
Richter leaves school after tenth grade with a certificate of graduation. He apprentices himself as an advertising and stage-set painter in the town of Zittau.

August: Under the auspices of American, British, French, and Soviet occupying forces, a survey of nearly six hundred works of art by German artists is shown in Dresden. Many of the artists had been featured in the *Degenerate "Art"* exhibition of 1937.

June 23: Berlin Blockade: USSR closes all land routes from the Western Zones to Berlin and stops supplies to sectors in West Berlin. Allied powers create Berlin Air Lift to fly in goods until May 12, 1949.

1949
April 4: North Atlantic Treaty Organization (NATO) formed for defense of Europe and North America from Soviet Union.
May 23: Federal Republic of Germany (FRG), known as West Germany, founded. A new constitution, called Basic Law, emphasizes its provisional character until Germany can be reunited.
October 7: Soviet Occupied Zone declared a separate state: the German Democratic Republic (GDR), known as East Germany.

1950
Richter applies to the Dresden Art Academy, but is rejected.

April: Exhibition, *Zen 49*, at Gallery of the Central Art Collecting Point, Munich, dedicated to abstraction, inaugurates a group that includes artists Willi Baumeister, Rupprecht Geiger, and Fritz Winter.

1951
Richter begins job painting political banners for a state-owned business.

July: Exhibition, *Subjective Photography*, at Staatliche Schule für Kunst und Handwerk, Saarbrücken, organized by Otto Steinert.

1952
Richter reapplies to Dresden Art Academy and is accepted to the "free painting" class. Studies there for four years; during final year, works in the mural painting class.

December: Exhibition of neo-Expressionist art by Quadriga, a new artists' group in Frankfurt. One of the members is Karl Otto Götz, Richter's future teacher.

July: Socialist Party (SED) convention decides to model East German society on Soviet-style socialism; immediate effects on economy and educational facilities.

1953
Gruppe 53 founded in Düsseldorf, a *tachiste* group that includes artists Gerhard Hoehme, Winfried Gaul, and Peter Brüning.

March 5: Joseph Stalin dies in Moscow.
June 17: Demonstrations by some 50,000 workers escalate following East German government announcement of increases in production quotas for construction workers. Martial law is declared. Days later, rebellion crushed by Soviet Army.

1955
Richter tours West Germany and travels for a week to Paris.

July–September: Exhibition, Documenta, at Kassel. First in a series, organized by Arnold Bode and Werner Haftmann, the show surveys prewar art developments, with particular emphasis on German Expressionism and abstraction. Introduces contemporary artists who continue prewar, abstract artistic traditions.

May 5: FRG joins NATO.

1956
Richter paints mural at the German Hygiene Museum, Dresden, as graduation project. Becomes a Master Student and is given a studio at the academy for three years.

February–March: Exhibition, *Kurt Schwitters*, at Kestner-Gesellschaft, Hannover, organized by Werner Schmalenbach; first postwar show of Schwitters's work.
February–March: Exhibition, *Yves Klein: Propositions monochromes*, at Galerie Colette Allendy, Paris. Yves Klein's first exhibition of monochromes. British Pop artist Richard Hamilton creates influential collage: *Just What Is It that Makes Today's Homes so Different, so Appealing?*

November: Revolt in Hungary crushed by Soviet troops.

1957
Richter marries Marianne [Ema] Eufinger; they travel to West Germany on their honeymoon.

May 2: Jean-Pierre Wilhelm opens Galerie 22, Düsseldorf, with survey of German *tachistes*. Wilhelm, well-connected to the art and literary scene in Paris, promotes local and French *tachistes*: Jean Fautrier, Antoni Tàpies, Emil Schumacher, and others. Wilhelm also has ties to experimental musicians; Galerie 22 later becomes the site of the first Happenings in Germany.
May 31: Alfred Schmela opens Düsseldorf gallery with exhibition, *Yves Klein: Propositions monochromes*.

Willy Brandt elected mayor of West Berlin.

1958
April–May: Exhibition, *Yves Klein: The Refinement of Sensibility in a Primary State of Stabilized Pictorial Sensibility (the Void)*, Galerie Iris Clert, Paris.
September–October: Exhibition, *Dada: Documents of a Movement*, organized by Karl-Heinz Herring and Ewald Rathke, with Richard Huelsenbeck, at Kunstverein für die Rheinlande und Westfalen and Städtische Kunsthalle, Düsseldorf, is first comprehensive Dada exhibition.
Robert Rauschenberg creates first solvent transfers of photographic reproductions.

1959
Richter obtains permission to visit West Germany to see Documenta 2 exhibition at Kassel; sees Abstract Expressionism and Art Informel for the first time.

July–October: Exhibition, Documenta 2, Kassel. Will Grohmann joins Bode and Haftmann on Documenta committee. American Abstract Expressionism, Art Informel, and geometric abstraction featured. Porter A. McCray, Director of the International Program at The Museum of Modern Art, New York, selects works by American artists, including Jackson Pollock, Willem de Kooning, Sam Francis, Franz Kline, and Helen Frankenthaler. Among the German artists are Ernst Wilhelm Nay, Karl Otto Götz, and Winfried Gaul.
November 13: Exhibition, *Nam June Paik: Homage to John Cage*, at Galerie 22, Wuppertal.
Exhibition, *Eight German Tachists*, Institute of Contemporary Arts, London,

includes work by Karl Otto Götz.

1960
June: Last exhibition at Galerie 22, Düsseldorf: work by Americans Robert Rauschenberg and Cy Twombly.
Andy Warhol creates Dick Tracy, Superman, and Popeye canvases.

1961
Richter travels to Moscow. On return trip the train stops unexpectedly in West Berlin, where he deposits his luggage before returning to East Germany. In Dresden, he asks a friend to drive him and his wife to East Berlin; from there, they travel via subway to West Berlin. A friend suggests they move to Düsseldorf. Applies to Düsseldorf Art Academy, and is accepted into the class of Ferdinand Macketanz; subsequently he studies for two years with Karl Otto Götz. At the academy, meets Konrad Lueg (later Konrad Fischer), Sigmar Polke, and Blinky Palermo. Influenced by Jean Dubuffet, Alberto Giacometti, and Jean Fautrier, Richter creates paintings with titles such as *Wound* and *Scar*: begins photo album of his early work.

January–February: Yves Klein's *Monochromes and Fire* shown at Museum Haus Lange, Krefeld.
March–April: First German artist to be exhibited after the war at The Museum of Modern Art, New York, is Norbert Kricke.
Joseph Beuys appointed professor of monumental sculpture at Düsseldorf Art Academy.
July: Heinz Mack and Otto Piene publish the magazine *Zero III* in conjunction with exhibition at Galerie Schmela, Düsseldorf, and organize a Zero party in historic district along the Rhine.
October–November: Exhibition, *The Art of Assemblage*, organized by William C. Seitz at The Museum of Modern Art, New York, includes such artists as Arman, Alberto Burri, César, Joseph Cornell, Raymond Hains, Kurt Schwitters, and Jean Tinguely.
November: On the occasion of their exhibition, *Pandämonium I*, at Hochschule der bildenden Künste, Berlin, Eugen Schönebeck and Georg Baselitz issue "The First Pandemonium Manifesto."
Roy Lichtenstein paints *Look Mickey*, one of his first paintings with screen-print dots.

January 20: John F. Kennedy inaugurated thirty-fifth U.S. President.
August 13: Berlin Wall erected.

1962
September: Richter's first exhibition in West Germany, *Manfred Kuttner/Gerd Richter: Düsseldorf*, is held at Galerie Junge Kunst, Fulda. Thirty-seven Richter paintings dated 1962 are listed in catalogue; most appear to have been destroyed by the artist later that year. Richter also showed forty-nine drawings.
Later that year he abandons Art Informel and paints his first photo-based paintings, using a projector.

June 6: Yves Klein dies at age thirty-four.
June 9: Event, *Small Summer Festival: after John Cage,* at Galerie Parnass, Wuppertal.
June 16: Fluxus event, *Neo-Dada in Music,* with Nam June Paik, Wolf Vostell, Dick Higgins, George Maciunas, and others at Kammerspiele, Düsseldorf.
June: Venice Biennale marks end of dominance of Abstract Expressionism, Art Informel, and *tachisme*.
September: *Fluxus-Festival of Recent Music* at Städtisches Museum, Wiesbaden, with John Cage, Tom Riley, George Brecht, Nam June Paik, and others.

October–December: Reprise of the exhibition, *Degenerate "Art,"* at Haus der Kunst, Munich; criticized for presenting incomplete picture of the 1937 show. Richard Artschwager paints his first realist paintings.

October 22–November 11: Cuban Missile Crisis.

1963
Spring: Richter and Lueg travel to Paris, where they see Yves Klein's work at Galerie Iris Clert and introduce themselves to art dealer Ileana Sonnabend as German Pop artists.
May: Exhibition, *Kuttner, Lueg, Polke, Richter*, in a temporary space scheduled for demolition, on Düsseldorf's Kaiserstrasse. The invitation invokes an extensive list of existing and imaginative art movements, each with a question mark: among them are Imperialist Realism? Pop Art? Pop Around? Neo Dada? Junk Culture?
October 11: Exhibition, *Gerhard Richter/Konrad Lueg: Life with Pop: A Demonstration for Capitalist Realism [Gerhard Richter/Konrad Lueg: Leben mit Pop, eine Demonstration fur den Kapitalistischen Realismus]*, held at Berges furniture store, Düsseldorf.
Richter starts inventory of his works, and numbers them sequentially; begins with *Table* (1962). This becomes his catalogue raisonné.
Signs a two-year contract with the art dealer Heiner Friedrich, who represents Galerie Friedrich and Dahlem, Munich.

February 2–3: Event, *Festum Fluxorum Fluxus: Music and Antimusic, the Political Theater, [Festum Fluxorum Fluxus: Musik und Antimusik, das politische Theater]*, at Düsseldorf Art Academy, with Beuys among others.
February 8: Exhibition, *New Realists [Nouveaux Réalistes]*, organized by Pierre Restany, at Neue Galerie im Künstlerhaus, Munich.
March–April: Exhibition and Zero group's manifesto at Galerie Diogenes, Berlin. Zero, founded by Günther Uecker and Heinz Mack, maintains close ties to a number of European artists; exhibition also includes works by Yves Klein, Piero Manzoni, Jean Tinguely, and Arnulf Rainer.
Spring: Exhibition, *American Pop Art*, Galerie Ileana Sonnabend, Paris, shows work by Lee Bontecou, Claes Oldenburg, Andy Warhol, James Rosenquist, John Chamberlain, and Tom Wesselmann. Sonnabend shows Roy Lichtenstein in the summer. and in the fall the exhibition, *Pop Drawing [Dessins Pop]*, featuring work by Jasper Johns, Roy Lichtenstein, Claes Oldenburg, Robert Rauschenberg, Andy Warhol, and others.
June–August: Exhibition, *Text and Image II*, at Staatliche Kunsthalle Baden-Baden, shows contemporary artists Jasper Johns, Mark Tobey, Robert Rauschenberg, Hans Hartung, and Dieter Roth among others.

June 26: Kennedy visits West Berlin.
November 22: Kennedy assassinated in Dallas; Lyndon B. Johnson sworn in as thirty-sixth U.S. President.

1964
September: Richter has first one-person exhibition, *Gerhard Richter*, at Galerie Schmela, Düsseldorf.
September–November: Richter included in inaugural exhibition at Galerie René Block, Berlin, *Neodada, Pop, Décollage, Capitalist Realism [Neodada, Pop, Décollage, Kapitalistischer Realismus]*; works by K. P. Brehmer, K. H. Hödicke, Konrad Lueg, Sigmar Polke, Gerhard Richter, Wolf Vostell, and others.
November 1964–January 1965: Second one-person exhibition, *Gerd Richter: Pictures of Capitalist Realism [Gerd Richter: Bilder des Kapitalistischen Realismus]*, at Galerie René Block, Berlin.

June–October: At Venice Biennale, Robert Rauschenberg is awarded International Grand Prize in Painting; only the third American artist to receive it.

June–October: Exhibition, Documenta 3, Kassel, shows Joseph Beuys's *The Silence of Marcel Duchamp Is Overrated*. In November, the same Action is performed live on a television broadcast, with assistance of Bazon Brock, Tomas Schmit, and Wolf Vostell.
July 20: Fluxus event, *Festival of New Art*, with, among others, Joseph Beuys, Wolf Vostell, and Bazon Brock. During the performance Beuys is hit by a student, and the event is closed down.
Vija Celmins paints her first Photo-Realist paintings.

August 7: Tonkin Gulf Resolution passed in the U.S. Congress, signaling the beginning of the Vietnam War.

1965
Richter creates his first multiple, *Dog [Hund]*, in an edition of eight.

February–March 1: Exhibition, *Pop Art, Nouveau Réalisme, etc.*, at Palais des Beaux-Arts, Brussels; catalogue essay by Pierre Restany.
April–May: Exhibition, *Marcel Duchamp: Ready Mades*, Museum Haus Lange, Krefeld. Richter visits this exhibition.
June 5: Event, *Happening 24 Hours*, at Galerie Parnass, Wuppertal. Happening, lasting twenty-four hours, beginning at midnight. Participants: Joseph Beuys, Bazon Brock, Charlotte Moorman with Nam June Paik, Wolfgang Rahn, Tomas Schmit, and Wolf Vostell.
November–December: At the opening of the exhibition *Joseph Beuys…any Old Noose…*, at Galerie Schmela, Düsseldorf, Beuys performs *How to Explain Paintings to a Dead Hare*.

February–March: Escalation of bombing in Vietnam.

1966
Richter begins to work on Color Charts, exhibited the same year at Galerie Friedrich and Dahlem, Munich.
Birth of daughter Babette (Betty).
March: Exhibition, *Polke/Richter*, Galerie h, Hannover. Catalogue features text-collage by the artists, and is illustrated with "performative" photographs of Polke and Richter.
December: Event, *Homage to Schmela*. Series of art activities in honor of Alfred Schmela at his Düsseldorf gallery before its temporary closing. Participating artists are Joseph Beuys, John Latham, Konrad Lueg, Heinz Mack, Otto Piene, Sigmar Polke, and Gerhard Richter. (From January 1967 to spring 1971, the gallery operates from Schmela's Düsseldorf apartment before it reopens in a new location near the Düsseldorf Art Academy.) On December 11 Lueg contributes *Coffee and Cake*, transforming the gallery space into a café where artists and friends gather. For the occasion, Richter paints a portrait, *Alfred Schmela*, which is placed on the wall at the head of the table. On December 13, Richter contributes *Volker Bradke*, an exhibition of paintings, photographs, and a film about Bradke, a denizen of the art scene, who is present at the Schmela event.

Founding of an association of progressive art dealers, which initiates the Cologne Art Fair, the first commercial art fair in postwar Germany; the art dealer Hein Stünke is president of the association.

Coalition government is elected in the FRG; Willy Brandt becomes Foreign Minister and Vice Chancellor.

1967
Richter becomes visiting professor at the Hochschule für bildende Künste, Hamburg, and is awarded the art prize "Junger Westen" by the German city of Recklinghausen.

Creates *4 Panes of Glass*; paints first Gray paintings.
October–November: Richter participates in exhibition, *Homage to Lidice*, at Galerie René Block, Berlin. The exhibition is held in memory of a Czech mining village that had been destroyed, and its inhabitants massacred, by the German SS on June 10, 1942, as a reprisal for the May 27 assassination of SS leader and Deputy Reich Protector of Bohemia, Reinhard Heydrich. Richter shows his painting *Uncle Rudi* in this exhibition.

Guy Debord publishes *Society of the Spectacle* [*La Société du Spectacle*]. Werner Haftmann becomes director of the Nationalgalerie, West Berlin.
Summer: Opening of the Städtische Kunsthalle, Düsseldorf, under director Karl Ruhrberg.
September: First Cologne Art Fair opens; many galleries show early modernist works. Among the galleries are René Block, Berlin; Schmela, Düsseldorf; and Zwirner, Cologne. Despite critics, the fair is a financial success.
October 21: Konrad Fischer opens his first gallery, with works by Carl Andre, in Düsseldorf. The gallery is located around the corner from the Düsseldorf Art Academy. The show marks the beginning of a gallery practice promoting Conceptual and Minimal work, with an emphasis on American artists. (Richter will have six shows at gallery: in 1970, 1972, 1975, 1977, 1979, 1983.)

June 2: During a demonstration against the Shah of Iran in West Berlin, the student Benno Ohnesorg is shot and killed by police. This event sets off mass demonstrations in many German cities.
June 22: As a reaction to the student demonstrations following Ohnesorg's death, Beuys founds the German Student Party in Düsseldorf.

1968
Beginning in 1968, Richter paints townscapes, landscapes, and Shadow paintings.

The Darmstadt collector Karl Ströher acquires the largest existing American Pop art collection from Leon Kraushar; the collection tours to a number of German cities.
Heinz Ohff publishes *Pop and Its Effects or The Art of Finding Art on the Street* [*Pop und die Folgen oder Die Kunst, Kunst auf der Strasse zu finden*]. The book includes a hypothetical conversation with Richter that centers on issues of reality, and naturalism.
June–October: Thirty-fourth Venice Biennale.
June–October: Documenta 4, organized by Jan Leering, prominently features Pop art. The press conference and opening speeches are cut short by demonstrators, including a Happening: Wolf Vostell and Jörg Immendorff are among the participants who protest the omission of Fluxus and Happenings.
September: Art fair, *Prospect 68*, created by Konrad Fischer and Hans Strelow, as an international avant-garde fair, in opposition to the First Cologne Art Fair, where only German art galleries are represented. By comparison, *Prospect 68* includes only one German gallery (Thelen, Essen) along with Iris Clert, Yvon Lambert, Ileana Sonnabend, Paris; Dwan, New York; Swart, Amsterdam, among others
September 1968–September 1969: Marcel Broodthaers opens the first manifestation of his *Museum of Modern Art, Eagle Department, 19th Century Section* [*Museé d'Art Moderne, Département des Aigles, Section XIXème Siècle*] at his home in Brussels.
October: Second Cologne Art Fair.
November 24: Nine professors at the Düsseldorf Art Academy circulate a letter criticizing Beuys and his activities.
December 9: Immendorff proclaims the LIDL-Academy. A "LIDL" class is established as an anti-art school in the halls of the Düsseldorf Art Academy. Fifty-five members enlist.

January 31: Vietcong guerrillas, aided by North Vietnamese Army troops, launch the Tet Offensive, attacking cities and towns throughout South Vietnam.
March 16: My Lai massacre. During an assault against suspected Vietcong encampments, Vietnamese civilians are killed by members of a U.S. Army unit.
April 11: Assassination attempt on the student party leader Rudi Dutschke in West Berlin. Violent mass demonstrations follow in Berlin and many West German cities.
August: Soviet troops, supported by army contingents from the GDR, Poland, Hungary, and Bulgaria invade Prague and stop the Czechoslovakian Communist Party's reform efforts, known as "Prague Spring."
Mass demonstrations about the Vietnam War and other grievances are staged by students and workers in the U.S., France, Italy, Spain, and Mexico.

1969
Richter reviews materials collected throughout the 1960s and starts to assemble pieces for *Atlas*, an ongoing compilation of photographs, clippings, and sketches.
Publishes the multiple *Picture Index* [*Bilderverzeichnis*], a single sheet indexing his paintings, starting with *Table* (1962), as number 1, and ending with *Evening Atmosphere* (1969), as number 243. The multiple is issued in an edition of 100 plus 20 artist's proofs.
May–June: Richter's first New York appearance in exhibition, *Nine Young Artists: Theodoron Awards*, at Solomon R. Guggenheim Museum, New York; he is the only German artist in the show.

January–February: Exhibition, *Minimal Art*, organized by Karl Ruhrberg, at Städtische Kunsthalle, Düsseldorf, includes works by Carl Andre, Dan Flavin, Donald Judd, Sol LeWitt, Robert Smithson, and others.
March–April: Exhibition, *Square Pegs in Round Holes* [*Op Losse Schroeven: Situaties en Cryptostructuren*], organized by Wim Beeren, at Stedelijk Museum, Amsterdam, includes work by European and American Minimal, Process, Land, and Conceptual art and Italian Arte Povera artists.
March–April: Exhibition, *When Attitudes Become Form: Works—Concepts—Processes—Situations—Information: Live in Your Head*, organized by Harald Szeemann, at Kunsthalle, Bern, offers a cross section of recent developments in the arts. Travels to Museum Folkwang, Essen, and a revised version tours to Museum Haus Lange, Krefeld, and Institute of Contemporary Arts, London.
May: Düsseldorf Art Academy is closed by the Ministry of Culture following an unauthorized "international meeting" of the LIDL-Academy.
September–October: Marcel Broodthaers opens his *Museum of Modern Art, Eagle Department, 17th Century Section* [*Musée d'Art Moderne, Département des Aigles, Section XVIIème Siècle*] in Antwerp on the same day the nineteenth-century section closes in Brussels.
September–October: *Prospect 69*, at Städtische Kunsthalle, Düsseldorf.
October: Cologne Art Fair, Kunsthalle Köln. In opposition to the commercialism of this art fair, an anti-art fair is initiated by Michael Siebrasse, promoting multiples.
October–November: Exhibition, *Konzeption—Conception: Documentation of an Art Style*, at Schloss Morsbroich, Leverkusen, organized by Konrad Fischer and Rolf Wedewer.
Galerie Reinhard Onnasch is founded in Berlin, Cologne, and New York.
Wieland Schmied publishes *New Objectivity and Magic Realism in Germany 1918–1933* [*Neue Sachlichkeit und Magischer Realismus in Deutschland 1918–1933*]. It represents the first in-depth investigation of the German *Neue Sachlichkeit* movement in forty years, at a time when painterly abstraction has dominated debates on contemporary art and twentieth-century art in postwar Germany.

January 20: Richard M. Nixon is inaugurated thirty-seventh U.S. President.
October: Willy Brandt becomes Chancellor of the Federal Republic of

Germany in a coalition government. Brandt is the first social-democratic chancellor since the republic's founding in 1945.

1970

Richter and Palermo travel to New York.
Paints Seascapes, Clouds, Gray paintings.
February–May: Richter is represented, along with nearly seventy artists, in exhibition *Now: Today's Arts in Germany* [*Jetzt: Künste in Deutschland heute*], at Kunsthalle Köln. Features contemporary German art since 1965; includes Beuys, Polke, Immendorff and the LIDL-group, as well as Zero artists, Happenings, performance, and film.

February: Marcel Broodthaers, *Museum of Modern Art, Eagle Department, 19th Century Section (encore)* [*Musée d'Art Moderne, Département des Aigles, Section XIXème Siècle (Bis)*], at Städtische Kunsthalle, Düsseldorf.
Summer: Marcel Broodthaers, *Museum of Modern Art, Eagle Department, Documentary Section* [*Musée d'Art Moderne, Département des Aigles, Section Documentaire*], on beach at Le Coq, Belgium.
July–September: Exhibition, *Information*, at The Museum of Modern Art, New York, organized by Kynaston McShine. Introduces recent artistic developments ("dematerialization of the work of art") to an American audience.
October 30: Daniel Spoerri opens his Eat-Art gallery in Düsseldorf.
November 1970–January 1971: Exhibition, *History of the Happening*, organized by Harald Szeemann, at Kölnischer Kunstverein; includes a Happening festival featuring Beuys, George Brecht, Jim Dine, Robert Filliou, Dick Higgins, Allan Kaprow, Otto Muehl, Wolf Vostell, Ben Vautier, and others.
Joseph Beuys forms "Organization for Direct Democracy by Referendum," which operates from a storefront office near the Art Academy in Düsseldorf.

Chancellor Willy Brandt seeks to improve relations with East Germany and other countries in the Eastern Bloc; a treaty with the Soviet Union accepts then current European borders, and a non-aggression treaty with Poland reaffirms the inviolability of existing border between the GDR and Poland (Oder-Neisse Line).

1971

Richter becomes tenured professor at Düsseldorf Art Academy.
Paints landscapes, Brigid Polk series, and *48 Portraits*.
October: Richter included in exhibition, *Prospect 71*, at Städtische Kunsthalle, Düsseldorf; focuses entirely on film and photography and includes Richter's film *Volker Bradke*, and works by Bernd and Hilla Becher, Joseph Beuys, Wolf Vostell, and Franz Erhard Walther.

February 10: Beuys, Klaus Staeck, and Erwin Heerich publish a text critiquing the "monopolizing efforts" of the Cologne and Berlin art fairs.
September 9: Alfred Schmela opens his new Düsseldorf gallery with a Joseph Beuys exhibition.
October: *Museum of Modern Art, Eagle Department, Financial Section* [*Musée d'Art Moderne, Département des Aigles, Section Financière*], is put up for sale by Marcel Broodthaers at the Cologne Art Fair, "due to bankruptcy."
Winter 1971–fall 1972: Marcel Broodthaers, *Museum of Modern Art, Eagle Department, Movie Section* [*Musée d'Art Moderne, Département des Aigles, Section Cinéma*], at Burgplatz 12, Düsseldorf.
Joseph Beuys begins preliminary plans for a "Free International School for Creativity and Interdisciplinary Research"; the following year the writer Heinrich Böll and Beuys publish a manifesto.

September 3: Four-Power Agreement signed in Berlin. Britain, France, the Soviet Union, and the United States pledge to resolve disagreements concern-

ing the city of Berlin in a peaceful manner.
December 10: Willy Brandt is awarded the Nobel Peace Prize.

1972

Richter paints his first Un-Paintings; also Gray paintings and Red-Blue-Yellow paintings.
June–October: Richter's *48 Portraits* shown in the German Pavilion at thirty-sixth Venice Biennale.
June–October: Richter's *Eight Student Nurses* shown in Jean-Christophe Ammann's much-disputed "Realism" section *Questioning Reality—Image Worlds Today* [*Befragung der Realität—Bildwelten heute*], at Documenta 5, Kassel, organized by Harald Szeemann.
December: Richter's *Atlas* is shown for first time at Museum voor Hedendaagse Kunst, Utrecht, and the following year at Kunsthalle Bremerhaven.

May–July: Marcel Broodthaers, *Museum of Modern Art, Eagle Department, Figurative Section (The Eagle from the Oligocene to Today)* [*Musée d'Art Moderne, Département des Aigles, Section des Figures (Der Adler vom Oligozän bis heute)*], shown at Städtische Kunsthalle, Düsseldorf.
July–September: Exhibition, *Rhine-Ruhr Scene '72* [*Szene Rhein-Ruhr '72*], at Museum Folkwang, Essen.
October 10: Joseph Beuys is dismissed from the Düsseldorf Art Academy following the occupation of the administrative offices to protest against policy of limiting the number of new students.
English edition of Udo Kultermann's *Radikaler Realismus* is published as *New Realism*.

January 28: During search for members of German terrorist organization Red Army Faction (RAF), the heads of the German states, chaired by Chancellor Willy Brandt, pass the so-called "Extremistenbeschluss": all applicants for state posts are to be screened for their constitutional convictions, and must pledge to actively support the free and democratic ideals outlined in the German "Basic Law." Decree is widely criticized as a ban directed against anyone with Leftist views.
February: President Nixon travels to China.
May 26: SALT I Treaty signed by President Nixon and General Secretary Brezhnev at a summit meeting in Moscow; an Anti-Ballistic Missile Treaty and the interim agreement on strategic offensive arms.

1973

Richter paints large Color Charts and pictures after Titian's *Annunciation*.
April 4: Exhibition, *Gerhard Richter: Atlas, Designs, Photographs, Sketches, 295 Sheets from 1962–1973* [*Gerhard Richter: Atlas, Entwürfe, Fotografien, Skizzen, 295 Blätter von 1962–1973*], at Galerie Heiner Friedrich, Munich; includes 295 panels from *Atlas*.
September–October: Richter included in *Prospect '73: Maler, Painters, Peintres*, at Städtische Kunsthalle, Düsseldorf, along with Palermo and Polke, among other German painters.
September–November: Richter has first one-person exhibition in New York, *Gerhard Richter*, at Reinhard Onnasch Gallery.

February: Beuys establishes first branch of the Free University in Düsseldorf.
September–October: Cologne Art Fair, Kunsthalle Köln.

January 15: U.S. signs treaty with Vietnam.
January 18: German Chancellor Willy Brandt speaks out for the independence of art at the national assembly; states that government can create a climate where openness toward art can grow and proposes a National Art Foundation.

September 18: East and West Germany join the United Nations.

1974
Richter paints large Color Charts and Gray pictures.

April–May: Exhibition, *Art on Art* [*Kunst-über-Kunst*], Kölnischer Kunstverein, focuses on Minimal and Conceptual art. In conjunction with the exhibition, Gerd de Vries publishes *On Art* [*Über Kunst*], which includes texts by the twelve artists in the show, among them Carl Andre, Daniel Buren, Douglas Huebler, Donald Judd, Sol LeWitt, and Lawrence Weiner.
May–June: Exhibition, *First Berlin Biennial*, an artists' initiative that includes ten artists, among them Markus Lüpertz and Eugen Schönebeck.
October–November: Exhibition, *Art into Society—Society into Art*, at Institute of Contemporary Arts, London, shows eight German artists: Albrecht D, K. P. Brehmer, Joseph Beuys, Hans Haacke, Dieter Hacker, Gustav Metzger, Michael Ruetz, and Klaus Staeck.

May 6: German Chancellor Willy Brandt resigns when it is discovered that one of his personal assistants is a GDR spy. Helmut Schmidt succeeds Brandt.
August 8: Richard Nixon resigns from presidency when Watergate scandal implicates him in cover-up of illegal activity.

1975
Richter paints *Tourist (with 1 Lion)*, seascapes, and portraits of Gilbert & George.
April–June: Richter's Gray paintings shown in exhibition, *Fundamental Painting* [*Fundamentale Schilderkunst*], organized by Edy de Wilde, Rini Dippel, Geert van Beijeren, Piet van der Have, and Dorine Mignot at Stedelijk Museum, Amsterdam. Includes American and European painters.

Benjamin Buchloh begins two years of teaching the history of contemporary art at Düsseldorf Art Academy.
November: Exhibition, International Art Fair, Cologne; a fusion of the Cologne Art Fair and the International Fair for Current Art, Düsseldorf.

1976
Richter paints Gray pictures and begins to work on Abstract Pictures.
Blinky Palermo moves into Richter's former Düsseldorf studio.
February–March: Richter's *Atlas* shown at Museum Haus Lange, Krefeld.

February–March: Exhibition, *Body Language*, Frankfurter Kunstverein, Frankfurt.
October: Exhibition, *Prospect/Retrospect*, organized by Benjamin Buchloh, Konrad Fischer, Rudi Fuchs, John Matheson, and Hans Strelow, at Städtische Kunsthalle, Düsseldorf; presents a history of the avant-garde since 1945. The idiosyncratic selections draw criticism from a number of art critics and curators, including Jürgen Harten and Georg Jappe.
Marcel Broodthaers dies in Cologne at age fifty-two.

December 15: German Chancellor Helmut Schmidt is reelected.

1977
Richter begins to paint watercolors; these are related to his Abstract Pictures.
Meets the sculptor Isa Genzken through Benjamin Buchloh.
February–March: Exhibition, *Gerhard Richter*, organized by Pontus Hulten and Benjamin Buchloh, at Centre national d'art et de culture, Georges Pompidou, Paris.
April: Richter is one of the artists in exhibition, *21 German Artists*, organized by Klaus Gallwitz, at Louisiana Museum, Humlebaeck, Denmark.
June–November: Richter withdraws his paintings (Abstract Pictures) on the day of the opening of exhibition, Documenta 6, at Kassel, organized by artistic director

Manfred Schneckenburger, and Klaus Honnef and Evelyn Weiss (painting section), following last-minute rearrangements of the painting section.
October–November: Richter included (*256 Colors*; Gray painting) in exhibition, *Europe in the Seventies: Aspects of Recent Art*, organized by Anne Rorimer and A. James Speyer, at The Art Institute of Chicago; also works by Anselmo, Bernd and Hilla Becher, Marcel Broodthaers, Daniel Buren, Jan Dibbets, Hanne Darboven, Richard Long, Panamarenko, and Rinke; show travels to several other U.S. venues.

January 20: Jimmy Carter inaugurated thirty-ninth U.S. President.
September–October: Members of RAF try to free imprisoned RAF leaders by kidnapping the President of the Federal Association of German Employers, Hans-Martin Schleyer.
October 18, 1977: Following the hijacking of a Lufthansa airplane, and an unsuccessful attempt to negotiate the release of several RAF members, the three leading RAF figures, Andreas Baader, Gudrun Ensslin, and Ulrike Meinhof, are found dead at Stammheim, the high-security prison near Stuttgart. A fourth RAF member, Irmgard Möller, is found with severe stab wounds.

1978
At the invitation of Benjamin Buchloh, who had begun teaching contemporary art history at the Nova Scotia College of Art and Design, Halifax, in 1977, Richter travels to the college as a visiting professor, where he teaches for one semester. During his time in Halifax, Richter creates and publishes *128 Details from a Painting*.
January–February: Exhibition, *Gerhard Richter: New Paintings*, at Sperone Westwater Fischer, New York.
October–November: An exhibition of Richter's abstract paintings, *Paintings* [*Bilder/Schilderijen*], at Stedelijk Van Abbemuseum, Eindhoven; travels as *Abstract Paintings* to the Whitechapel Art Gallery, London, in spring 1979.

November–December: Exhibition, *13° E—Eleven Artists Working in Berlin*, at Whitechapel Art Gallery, London; show includes K. P. Brehmer, Günter Brus, Markus Lüpertz, and Wolf Vostell.

1979
Richter paints Abstract Pictures and yellow brushstrokes for installation at the Kreisberufsschule in Soest.

September–November: Exhibition, *Highlights: An Inventory of Current Art in the Rhineland 1979* [*Schlaglichter: Eine Bestandsaufnahme aktueller Kunst im Rheinland 1979*], organized by Klaus Honnef, at Rheinisches Landesmuseum, Bonn; some fifty-five artists selected by a jury.
November 1979–January 1980: Exhibition, *Joseph Beuys*, organized by Caroline Tisdall, at Solomon R. Guggenheim Museum, New York; the artist's first retrospective in the United States.

1980
Richter paints Abstract Pictures.

January–March: Exhibition, *The New Wild Ones* [*Les nouveaux Fauves—Die neuen Wilden*], at Neue Galerie-Sammlung Ludwig, Aachen; catalogue text by Wolfgang Becker.
May–July: Exhibition, *Turning Point—Art in Europe c. 1960* [*Wendepunkt—Kunst in Europa um 1960*], at Museum Haus Lange, Krefeld; includes Joseph Beuys, Yves Klein, Jannis Kounellis, Piero Manzoni, Cy Twombly, and others.

May: Joseph Beuys runs as Green Party candidate in the state elections of North Rhine-Westphalia.

1981

Richter is awarded the Arnold Bode Prize at Kassel.

Edition Pieroni publishes *EIS [Ice]*, a book of photographs by Richter, taken during a trip to Greenland.

January–March: Richter included in exhibition, *A New Spirit in Painting*, organized by Christos M. Joachimides, Mark Rosenthal, and Nicholas Serota, at Royal Academy of Arts, London; also features Francis Bacon, Georg Baselitz, Graubner, Philip Guston, Anselm Kiefer, Willem de Kooning, Markus Lüpertz, A. R. Penck, Robert Ryman, Sigmar Polke, Cy Twombly, and Andy Warhol among others.

January–March: Richter included in exhibition, *German Art Today [Art Allemagne Aujourd'hui]*, at Musée d'Art Moderne de la Ville de Paris, with Georg Baselitz, Joseph Beuys, Hanne Darboven, Hans Haacke, Anselm Kiefer, Blinky Palermo, Sigmar Polke, Dieter Roth, and others.

May–August: Richter is represented with a few works from the 1960s in exhibition, *Westkunst: West German Art since 1939*, organized by László Glozer, Kasper König, Karl Ruhrberg, and Hugo Borger, at Rheinhallen, Cologne.

January 20: Ronald Reagan is inaugurated fortieth U.S. President.
September 14: U.S. Secretary of State Alexander Haig visits Germany, provoking riots in Bonn and Berlin.
October: Mass demonstrations against NATO resolution to post mid-range missiles in Germany.

1982

Richter works on a series of Candle paintings.
Marries Isa Genzken.

June–September: Richter shows an Abstract Picture at exhibition, *Documenta 7*, Kassel, organized by Rudi Fuchs. A statement by the artist is published in the catalogue, in which he speaks of abstract pictures as fictive models.

October 1982–January 1983: Exhibition, *Zeitgeist: International Art Exhibition Berlin 1982*, organized by Christos M. Joachimides and Mark Rosenthal, at Martin-Gropius-Bau, Berlin; exhibits forty-five contemporary painters and sculptors with recent work. Among them are Georg Baselitz, Joseph Beuys, Francesco Clemente, Gilbert & George, Jörg Immendorff, Anselm Kiefer, Malcolm Morley, Mario Merz, A. R. Penck, Sigmar Polke, and Frank Stella.

October 1: Helmut Kohl becomes German Chancellor.

1983

Richter moves from Düsseldorf to Cologne.

May–July: Exhibition, *An Inclination toward the Total Work of Art [Der Hang zum Gesamtkunstwerk]*, organized by Harald Szeemann, at Kunstverein und Kunsthalle, Düsseldorf; explores interdisciplinary artistic approaches by nineteenth- and twentieth-century artists, with Joseph Beuys, John Cage, Marcel Duchamp, Philipp Otto Runge, Kurt Schwitters, and Richard Wagner featured.

June–August: *Expressions: New Art from Germany*, organized by Jack Cowart, at The Saint Louis Art Museum; works by Georg Baselitz, Jörg Immendorff, Anselm Kiefer, Markus Lüpertz, and A. R. Penck shown. Tours in U.S., closing in September 1984 at Corcoran Gallery of Art, Washington, D.C.

March 23: President Reagan announces Star Wars program.

1984

Richter begins to work again in watercolors, having stopped in 1978.

January–March: Richter's first exhibition of watercolors, *Gerhard Richter: Watercolors and Drawings [Gerhard Richter: Aquarelle und Zeichnungen]*, at Galerie Thomas Borgmann, Cologne.

September–December: Richter is represented with three barn paintings and thirteen abstractions from the early 1980s in exhibition featuring new German art, *From Here: 2 Months of New German Art in Düsseldorf [Von hier aus, 2 Monate neue deutsche Kunst in Düsseldorf]*, at Messegelände, Düsseldorf. Artistic director Kasper König.

October–November: Richter represented in exhibition, *Upheavals, Manifestoes, Manifestations: Conceptions in the Arts at the Beginning of the Sixties in Berlin, Düsseldorf, Munich*, organized by Klaus Schrenk at Städtische Kunsthalle, Düsseldorf. Berlin artists: Georg Baselitz, K. H. Hödicke, Markus Lüpertz, A. R. Penck, and others; Düsseldorf artists: Joseph Beuys, Konrad Lueg, Sigmar Polke, and Zero artists; Munich artists: members of SPUR group.

September–November: Exhibition, *When Art Was Set in Motion [Als Bewegung in die Kunst kam]*, at Museum Haus Lange, Krefeld; kinetic works, including those by Josef Albers, Marcel Duchamp, Hans Haacke, Yves Klein, Otto Piene, Man Ray, Dieter Roth, Günther Uecker, Jean Tinguely, and others.

December 1984–April 1985: Exhibition, *La Grande Parade*, organized by Edy de Wilde, at Stedelijk Museum, Amsterdam; a review of painting since 1940. Max Beckmann, Anselm Kiefer, and Sigmar Polke are among German artists in show.

1985

Richter paints Candles, Skulls, and landscapes.
Receives the Oskar Kokoschka Prize in Vienna.

February–April: Richter shows four abstractions in exhibition, *The European Iceberg: Creativity in Germany and Italy Today*, organized by Germano Celant, at Art Gallery of Ontario.

March: Exhibition, *Gerhard Richter*, jointly organized by Marian Goodman and Sperone Westwater in New York. Richter's first painting show at Marian Goodman gallery.

October–December: Exhibition, *German Art in the Twentieth Century: Painting and Sculpture 1905–1985*; survey organized by Christos M. Joachimides, Mark Rosenthal, and Wieland Schmied, at Royal Academy of Arts, London. Richter represented with several works from the 1960s. The show travels to the Staatsgalerie Stuttgart the following year.

March 12: Mikhail S. Gorbachev becomes Secretary General of the Communist Party, USSR.

1986

Richter paints Abstract Pictures.

January–March: Richter's first retrospective exhibition, *Gerhard Richter: Bilder, 1962–1985*, organized by Jürgen Harten, at Städtische Kunsthalle Düsseldorf. Travels to Berlin, Bern, and Vienna.

December 1986–January 1987: Richter shows work dating back to 1964 at Barbara Gladstone Gallery, New York.

January 23: Joseph Beuys dies at age sixty-three.
August–November: Exhibition, *The '60s: Cologne's Journey to an Art Center. From Happening to Art Fair [Die 60er Jahre: Kölns Weg zur Kunstmetropole. Vom Happening zum Kunstmarkt]*, organized by Wulf Herzogenrath, at Kölnischer Kunstverein; celebrates Cologne as a postwar artistic center.

1987

Richter paints *Cathedral Corner*, landscapes, Abstract Pictures.

February–April: A selection of Richter's notes published for the first time on the occasion of exhibition, *Gerhard Richter: Werken op papier 1983–1986, notities 1982–1986*, organized by Christiaan Braun, at Museum Overholland, Amsterdam.

May–September: Richter included in exhibition, *Focal Point Düsseldorf [Brennpunkt*

Düsseldorf], organized by Stephan von Wiese, at Kunstmuseum Düsseldorf; traces Fluxus movement and highlights the artistic contributions made to the Düsseldorf art scene, including those of Joseph Beuys, Marcel Broodthaers, Eva Hesse, Nam June Paik, Blinky Palermo, Sigmar Polke, and others.
July–September: Exhibition, *Gerhard Richter/Matrix 95*, organized by John Paoletti, at Wadsworth Atheneum, Hartford.

June–September: Exhibition, Documenta 8, Kassel, organized by Manfred Schneckenburger.
June–September: Exhibition, *BERLINART*, organized by Kynaston McShine, at The Museum of Modern Art, New York; features German artists and others who worked in a divided Berlin, including Georg Baselitz, Joseph Beuys, Günter Brus, Christo, Martin Kippenberger, Helmut Middendorf, Tomas Schmit, Daniel Spoerri, Ben Vautier, and many others.
December 1987–January 1988: Exhibition, *Anselm Kiefer*, The Art Institute of Chicago. Organized by Mark Rosenthal, Philadelphia Museum of Art, and Neal Benezra, The Art Institute of Chicago, the show travels to several U.S. venues and closes at The Museum of Modern Art, New York, in 1989.

1988
Richter paints fifteen-canvas cycle *October 18, 1977* and *Betty*.
Becomes guest professor at the Städelschule in Frankfurt.
Awarded the Kaiserring der Stadt Goslar.
March–April: Exhibition, *Gerhard Richter: The London Paintings*, Anthony d'Offay Gallery, London.
April–July: Retrospective exhibition, *Gerhard Richter: Paintings*, Art Gallery of Ontario, Toronto. Organized by Michael Danoff, Museum of Contemporary Art, Chicago, and Roald Nasgaard, Art Gallery of Ontario, the show travels from Toronto to Chicago, Washington, D.C., and San Francisco.

1989
Richter paints Abstract Pictures, landscapes.
October 18, 1977 is shown in Krefeld and Frankfurt and prompts an overwhelming response by the press. The series tours to England, the Netherlands, and the United States.

April–June: Exhibition, *Marcel Broodthaers*, organized by Marge Goldwater, at Walker Art Center, Minneapolis.

January 20: George Bush inaugurated forty-first U.S. President.
September: "Velvet Revolution" in Czechoslovakia; mass demonstrations in the GDR; migration of thousands of East Germans to Hungary and West Germany following opening of the Austro-Hungarian border.
October 18: GDR State Secretary Erich Honnecker resigns..
Late October: Continued pressure from mass demonstrations results in the resignation of the Council of Ministers and the East German SED Politbüro.
November 9: Berlin Wall opened between East and West.
November 28: German Chancellor Helmut Kohl publishes a ten-point program envisioning the reunification of Germany.

1990
Richter paints Abstract Pictures.
Shows simultaneously in New York at the Marian Goodman and Sperone Westwater galleries.

November 1990–January 1991: Exhibition, *Sigmar Polke*, organized by John Caldwell, at San Francisco Museum of Modern Art; travels to a number of U.S. venues, including The Brooklyn Museum, New York.

March 18: Lothar de Mazière is elected Prime Minister of the GDR, heading a coalition government.
June 21: Checkpoint Charlie closes in Berlin.
July: West German currency is introduced to the GDR.
August 31: GDR State Secretary Günter Krause and Federal Minister of the Interior Wolfgang Schäuble sign Unification Treaty.
Mikhail S. Gorbachev is awarded the Nobel Peace Prize.

1991
Richter paints Abstract Pictures, Mirror installation for Hypo-Bank, Düsseldorf.
October 1991–January 1992: Retrospective exhibition, *Gerhard Richter*, organized by Sean Rainbird at Tate Gallery, London.
April–June: *Mirrors*, an exhibition of Richter's mirrors at Anthony d'Offay Gallery, London.

1992
Paints Abstract Pictures, Gray Mirrors.
June–September: Richter creates a room of Abstract Pictures and Gray Mirrors in a pavilion in the Rheinaue for exhibition, Documenta 9, Kassel, organized by Jan Hoet. In addition, the painting *Flowers* is shown.

1993
Richter's writings are published in German as *Gerhard Richter: Texte*, edited by Hans-Ulrich Obrist.
Paints I.G. series, Abstract Pictures.
March: *Parkett* 35 dedicated to Gerhard Richter. For this issue the artist produces a special edition of paintings.
September–November: Exhibition, *Gerhard Richter: Retrospective*, organized by Kasper König and Benjamin Buchloh. The show tours from Paris to Bonn, Stockholm, and Madrid. In conjunction with the exhibition, a fully illustrated catalogue raisonné of the artist's paintings and sculptures is published.
October–November: *Gerhard Richter: Multiples 1965–1993*, organized by Siegfried Salzmann and Andreas Kreul, at Kunsthalle Bremen. Accompanied by a catalogue raisonné of Richter's multiples compiled by Hubertus Butin.
Exhibition at Marian Goodman gallery.

January 20: William J. Clinton is inaugurated forty-second U.S. President.

1995
Receives the Wolf Prize in Arts, Jerusalem.
Richter's writings are published in English as *Gerhard Richter: The Daily Practice of Painting: Writings and Interviews, 1962–1993*.
Paints series S. with Child, Still Lifes, Abstract Pictures.
April 1995–February 1996: Richter's *Atlas: 1964–1995* exhibited at Dia Center for the Arts, New York.
The Museum of Modern Art, New York, acquires *October 18, 1977*.
Richter marries Sabine Moritz.
Birth of son Moritz.

May–September: Exhibition, *Georg Baselitz*, at Solomon R. Guggenheim Museum, New York.

1996
Richter moves to a new home and studio.
Paints *Self-Portrait*.
Birth of daughter Ella Maria.

1997
June–November: Forty-seventh Venice Biennale; Richter is awarded the Golden Lion.

Receives the Praemium Imperiale Prize, Tokyo.
June–September: Richter exhibits Abstract Pictures from 1997 at exhibition Documenta 10, Kassel; organized by Catherine David.
September 1997–January 1998: Exhibition, *German Pictures: Art from a Divided Country [Deutschlandbilder: Kunst aus einem geteilten Land]*, features German art of the formerly divided country from 1945 to 1998, with a review of the prewar German avant-garde. Significant attention is given to Richter's *October 18, 1977.*

1998

Richter receives the Wexner Prize.
Paints Rhombus series, Abstract Pictures, seascapes.

October 27: Helmut Schröder inaugurated German Chancellor, heading a SPD/Green Party coalition government.

1999

Richter paints *Snow, Farm,* and Abstract Pictures.

September–November: Exhibition, *Gerhard Richter: Drawings 1964–1999,* at Kunstmuseum Winterthur, organized by Dieter Schwarz. This show of drawings and watercolors is accompanied by a catalogue raisonné.

2000

Richter paints first two Moritz paintings, double-portrait with Benjamin Buchloh, Abstract Pictures.

September 2000–January 2001: As part of exhibition, *Open Ends,* at The Museum of Modern Art, New York, Richter's *October 18, 1977* is exhibited.

2001

Richter paints Abstract Pictures, the third Moritz painting, and works on an installation of Gray mirrors.
December: Richter is honored by the city of Cologne. He is asked to enter his name in Cologne's Golden Book.

June–November: At forty-ninth Venice Biennale, Richter's series *Untitled (Rhombus)* is shown as part of Harald Szeemann's *Plateau of Humankind.*

SELECTED BIBLIOGRAPHY

COMPILED BY ELIZABETH GRADY AND CATHARINA MANCHANDA

This selected listing of published material on Gerhard Richter is organized in the following sections: I. Gerhard Richter: Writings and Interviews; II. Monographs; III. Exhibition Catalogues; IV. Essays and Articles; V. Exhibition Reviews; and VI. Radio, Television, and Film. Additional materials on exhibition reviews and unpublished theses and dissertations are accessible in the Museum Archives. An anthology of Richter's writings published in 1993 is given in full in the first section and subsequently abbreviated as *Daily Practice*. Detailed documentation of writings on the *October 18, 1977* cycle can be found in an extensive bibliography in Robert Storr's *Gerhard Richter: October 18, 1977*, listed under Exhibition Catalogues. Additional texts on the October paintings may also be found in Ulrich Wilmes's *Presseberichte zu Gerhard Richter 18. Oktober 1977*, given as *Presseberichte*. References to radio and television broadcasts use the following abbreviations: ORF=Österreichischer Rundfunk; WDR=Westdeutscher Rundfunk; SDR= Süddeutscher Rundfunk; HR=Hessischer Rundfunk; DRK=Deutschlandradio Köln; SFB=Sender Freies Berlin; SWR=Südwestdeutscher Rundfunk; NDR=Norddeutscher Rundfunk.

I. Gerhard Richter: Writings and Interviews

WRITINGS BY THE ARTIST

Obrist, Hans-Ulrich, ed. *Gerhard Richter: The Daily Practice of Painting: Writings and Interviews, 1962–1993*. Cambridge, Mass.: MIT Press; London: Anthony d'Offay Gallery, 1995. German ed.: *Gerhard Richter: Texte*. Leipzig and Frankfurt: Insel Verlag, 1993.

Richter, Ger[har]d. "Auseinandersetzungen halfen mir weiter." *Sonntag: Wochenzeitung für Kultur, Politik und Unterhaltung* 16 (April 20, 1958): 12.

_____. "Arbeitsübersicht." In *14 x 14: Junge deutsche Künstler*. Baden-Baden: Staatliche Kunsthalle, 1968: n.p.

_____. [Statement] *Art International* 12, no. 3 (March 20, 1968): 54–55.

_____. "About eight years ago…" In *Fundamentale Schilderkunst [Fundamental Painting]*. Amsterdam: Stedelijk Museum, 1975: 57.

_____. [Untitled] In *Documenta 7*, vol.1. Kassel: D+V, Paul Dierichs, 1982: 443. Repr. in *Daily Practice*: 100.

_____. "Notes." In *Gerhard Richter: Werken op papier 1983–1986, notities 1982–1986*. Amsterdam: Museum Overholland; Munich: Verlag Fred Jahn, 1987: 4–16.

_____. "Ein Kratzer ohne Folgen? Diskussionsbeiträge von Künstlern, Sammlern, Kunstvermittlern." *Kölner Stadt-Anzeiger* 125 (June 1, 1989).

_____. "Der rote Faden Hoffnung: Aus Gerhard Richters Notizen 1962–1993." *Neue bildende Kunst. Zeitschrift für Kunst und Kritik* (June 1993): 8–9.

_____. *Gerhard Richter: 128 Fotos von einem Bild (WVZ 432-5)/128 Details from a Picture, Halifax 1978*. Cologne: Walther König, 1998.

_____. "Über meine Arbeit im Deutschen Hygienemuseum Dresden." *Farbe und Raum* 18 (September 9, 1956): 7–11.

_____. "Wunden kann ich nicht malen." *Der Spiegel* 16 (April 14, 2001): 165.

_____, and Isa Genzken. "Beschreibung der Konzeption für die Gestaltung des U-Bahnhofes 'König-Heinrich-Platz.'" In *U-Bahn-Kunst in Duisburg*. Duisburg: Wilhelm Lehmbruck Museum, 1992: n.p.

_____, Manfred Kuttner, Konrad Lueg, and Sigmar Polke. [Letter] "An die Neue Deutsche Wochenschau." Düsseldorf (April 29, 1963); trans. "Letter to a Newsreel Company, 29 April 1963"; repr. in *Daily Practice*: 15–16.

_____, and Konrad Lueg. "Bericht über 'Eine Demonstration für den kapitalistischen Realismus' von Konrad Lueg und Richter, am Freitag, den 11. Oktober 1963, in Düsseldorf, Flingerstrasse 11 (Bergeshaus)." In *Graphik des Kapitalistischen Realismus*. Berlin: Galerie René Block, 1964: 31–35; trans. "Programme and report: The Exhibition Leben mit Pop—Eine Demonstration für den kapitalistischen Realismus"; repr. in *Daily Practice*: 18–21.

_____, and Sigmar Polke. [Untitled] In *Polke/Richter*. Hannover: Galerie h, 1966, n.p.; repr. in *Gerhard Richter*. Essen: Museum Folkwang, 1972: 27–33; trans. repr. in *Daily Practice*: 39–56.

INTERVIEWS WITH THE ARTIST

Buchloh, Benjamin H. D. "Interview with Gerhard Richter." In Terry A. Neff, ed., *Gerhard Richter: Paintings*. New York and London: Thames & Hudson, 1988: 15–29; repr. in *Daily Practice*: 132–166.

Butin, Hubertus. "Mit der RAF ins Museum of Modern Art: Gerhard Richter im Gespräch." *Neue Zürcher Zeitung*, int. ed. (Oct 23, 1995); repr. "Richters RAF-Zyklus nach New York verkauft: Kultureller Gewinn oder Verlust?" In *Kunstforum International* 132 (November 1995–January 1996): 432–435.

Cork, Richard. "Gerhard Richter: A Divided German." *Apollo* (London) (January 1992): 48–49.

Dienst, Rolf-Günter. "Interview mit Gerhard Richter." In *Noch Kunst*. Düsseldorf: Droste Verlag, 1970: 192–199; repr. in *Gerhard Richter*. Essen: Museum Folkwang, 1972: 19–21; repr. in *Daily Practice*: 60–64.

Dietrich, Dorothea. "Gerhard Richter: An Interview." *Print Collectors' Newsletter* 16 (September–October 1985): 128–132.

von Drathen, Doris. "Entretien avec Gerhard Richter." *Les Cahiers du Musée National d'Art Moderne* 40 (summer 1992): 86–89.

_____. "'Malen ist etwas ganz und gar Lebensnotwendiges': Gerhard Richter im Gespräch mit Doris von Drathen." *Kunstforum International* 131 (August–October 1995): 265–267.

Ehrenfried, Susanne. "Gespräch mit dem Maler Gerhard Richter am 8. August 1995." In Susanne Ehrenfried, "'Ohne Eigenshaften': Das Portrait bei Gerhard Richter." Diss., Munich: Ludwig-Maximilians-Universität München, c. 1995: 180–182.

Ferguson, Bruce, and Jeffrey Spalding. "Gerhard Richter." *Parachute* 13 (winter 1978): 31–33.

Griffin, Tim. "The Richter Scale: An Ever-Ambiguous Gerhard Richter Continues to Shake Up the Art World." *Time Out New York* 314 (October 4–11, 2001).

Grüterich, Marlis. "Interview mit Gerhard Richter." In *Poetische Aufklärung.* Zürich: InK, Halle für internationale neue Kunst, 1978: 86–94.

Haase, Amine. "Malerei als Schein." *Rheinische Post* (Düsseldorf) (September 16, 1977); repr. in Amine Haase, *Gespräche mit Künstlern.* Cologne: Wienand, 1981.

———. "Kunst ist die höchste Form der Hoffnung: Interview mit Preisträger Gerhard Richter." *Kölner Stadt-Anzeiger* (September 15, 1982); French trans. in *Artistes* (December 1983): 36–42.

———. "'Wie ein Schreiner': Gespräch mit Gerhard Richter in Bonn." *Kölner Stadt-Anzeiger* 288 (December 11–12, 1993).

Hülsmanns, Dieter. "Das perfekteste Bild: Ateliergespräch mit dem Maler Gerd Richter." *Rheinische Post* 102 (May 3, 1966).

Koldehoff, Stefan. "Stammheim in New York: Das ist nichts speziell Deutsches: Gerhard Richter über den Verkauf seines Gemäldezyklus '18. Oktober 1977.'" *Die Tageszeitung* (Berlin) (October 28/29, 1995).

———. "Gerhard Richter: Die Macht der Malerei." *Art* (December 1999): 12–20.

Lebeer, Irmeline. "Gerhard Richter ou la réalité de l'image." *Chronique de l'Art Vivant* 36 (February 1973): 13–16.

Magnani, Gregorio. "Gerhard Richter: For Me It Is Absolutely Necessary that the Baader-Meinhof Is a Subject for Art." *Flash Art* 146 (May/June 1989): 94–97; repr. in *Presseberichte*: 67–69.

Nabakowski, Gislind. "Zur 'Verkündigung nach Tizian': Interview mit Gerhard Richter." *Heute Kunst* 7 (July–August 1974): 3–5.

Obrist, Hans-Ulrich. "Reflections on Painting (Reflections of a Painter): Gerhard Richter interviewed by

Hans-Ulrich Obrist." *Frieze* 13 (November–December 1993): 33–37.

———. "Gerhard Richter: La construzione dell' Immagine come uno specchio frantumato." *Flash Art* 192 (June/July 1995): 73–79.

Raussmüller, Urs. [Interview] In *Poetische Aufklärung in der europäischen Kunst der Gegenwart bei Joseph Beuys, Marcel Broodthaers, Daniel Buren, Jannis Kounellis, Mario Merz, Gerhard Richter—Geschichte von heute und morgen.* Zurich: InK, Halle für internationale neue Kunst, 1978: 87–88.

Rosenthal, Mark. "Interview with Gerhard Richter" In *Mark Rothko.* Washington, D.C.: National Gallery of Art, 1998: 363–366.

Sager, Peter. "Gespräch mit Gerhard Richter." *Das Kunstwerk* 25 (July 1972): 16–27; repr. in Peter Sager, *Neue Formen des Realismus. Kunst zwischen Illusion und Wirklichkeit.* Cologne: DuMont, 1973: 244–245.

Schön, Rolf. "Unser Mann in Venedig: Fragen an Gerhard Richter." *Deutsche Zeitung* (April 14, 1972); trans. in *Gerhard Richter.* Essen: Folkwang Museum, 1972: 23–25; repr. in *Daily Practice*: 71–75.

Schreiber, Matthias. "Ein gutes Foto von mir gibt es nicht: Gespräch mit dem Maler Gerhard Richter." *Kölner Stadt-Anzeiger* (June 14, 1972).

Schütz, Sabine. "Gerhard Richter (an interview)." *Journal of Contemporary Art* 3 (fall/winter 1990): 34–46; repr. in *Daily Practice*: 207–218.

Schwarz, Dieter, ed. "About Watercolors and Related Things: Gerhard Richter in Conversation with Dieter Schwarz. Cologne, June 26, 1999." In idem, *Gerhard Richter: Aquarelle/Watercolors 1964–1997.* Winterthur: Kunstmuseum; Düsseldorf: Richter Verlag, 1999: 17–27.

Storsve, Jonas. "Gerhard Richter: La Peinture à venir." *Art Press* 161 (September 1991): 12–20; repr. in *Daily Practice*: 223–231.

Tilroe, Anna. "Sensaties voor het

oog. Museum Overholland heeft een Primeur: Werken op papier van Gerhard Richter" *De Volkskrant* (February 20, 1987): 19–21.

Vielhaber, Christiane. "Interview mit Gerhard Richter." *Das Kunstwerk* 2 no. 39 (April 1986): 41–43.

Weirich, Stefan. "Wieder mal malen." *Bonner Rundschau* (November 26, 1993).

II. Monographs
Arranged alphabetically by author.

Buchloh, Benjamin H. D. "Gerhard Richter: Painting after the Subject of History." Ph.D. Diss., City College of New York, 1994.

———, Jean-François Chevrier, Armin Zweite, and Rainer Rochlitz. *Photography and Painting in the Work of Gerhard Richter: Four Essays on Atlas.* Barcelona: Consorci del Museu d'Art Contemporani de Barcelona, 2000.

Butin, Hubertus. *Zu Richters Oktober-Bildern.* Cologne: Walther König, 1991.

Dienst, Rolf-Günter. *Noch Kunst: Neuestes aus deutschen Ateliers.* Düsseldorf: Droste Verlag, 1970.

Ehrenfried, Susanne. *'Ohne Eigenschaften': Das Portrait bei Gerhard Richter.* Vienna: Springer Verlag, 1997.

Eis (1973/1981). Rome: Edizione Galleria Pieroni, 1981.

Elger, Dietmar. *Gerhard Richter: Florence.* Ostfildern-Ruit: Cantz, 2001.

Gerhard Richter. Paris: Éditions voir, 1985. Texts by Gertrud Koch, Luc Lang, and Jean-Philippe Antoine.

Gerhard Richter: Stammheim. London: Anthony d'Offay Gallery, 1995.

Hemken, Kai-Uwe. *Gerhard Richter, 18. Oktober 1977.* Frankfurt: Insel, 1998.

Henatsch, Martin. *Gerhard Richter, 18. Oktober 1977: Das verwischte Bild der Geschichte.* Frankfurt: Fischer, 1998.

Hofmann, Andrea, ed. *Gerhard Richter: Malerei aus drei Jahrzehnten.* Friedrichshafen: Kunstverein, 2001. Texts by Andrea Hofmann and Dietmar Elger.

Honisch, Dieter. *Gerhard Richter. Laudatio zur Verleihung des Kaiserrings in der Kaiserpfalz Goslar.* Goslar: Verein zur Förderung moderner Kunst, 1988.

Katz, Benjamin. *Atelier Gerhard Richter: Photos.* Ostfildern-Ruit: Cantz, 1993.

Loock, Ulrich, and Denys Zacharopoulos. *Gerhard Richter.* Munich: Verlag Silke Schreiber, 1985.

Misterek-Plagge, Ingrid. *Kunst mit Fotografie und die frühen Fotogemälde Gerhard Richters.* Münster: Lit, 1992.

Obrist, Hans-Ulrich, ed. *Gerhard Richter: Sils.* Munich: Oktagon, 1992. Text by Peter André Bloch.

Pelzer, Birgit. *Le désir tragique: Gerhard Richter.* Paris: Les presses du réel, 1993.

Schneede, Uwe M. *Gerhard Richter in der Hamburger Kunsthalle.* Hamburg: Hamburger Kunsthalle, 1997.

Schwarz, Dieter. *Gerhard Richter: Zeichnungen 1964–1999, Werkverzeichnis.* Winterthur: Kunstmuseum Winterthur, 1999. Text by Birgit Pelzer.

———. *Gerhard Richter: Übersicht.* Stuttgart: Institut für Auslandsbeziehungen; Cologne: Walther König, 2001.

Shapiro, Michael Edward. *Gerhard Richter: Paintings, Prints and Photographs in the Collection of the Saint Louis Art Museum.* St. Louis, Mo.: Saint Louis Art Museum, 1992. Orig. pub. in *Saint Louis Art Museum Bulletin* n.s. 20, no. 2 (summer 1992).

Shimizu, Minoru. *Geruharuto Rihita shashinron kaigaron [Theory on Richter's Photographic Painting].* Kyoto: Tankosha, 1996.

66 Zeichnungen: Halifax 1978. Cologne: Walther König, 1997.

Thomas-Netik, Anja. *Gerhard Richter: mögliche Aspekte eines postmodernen Bewusstseins.* Essen: Blaue Eule, 1986.

Oswald Mathias Ungers, Gerhard Richter, Sol LeWitt. Düsseldorf: Hypo-Bank, 1991.

Wilmes, Ulrich, ed. *Presseberichte zu Gerhard Richter 18. Oktober 1977.* Frankfurt: Museum für Moderne Kunst; Cologne: Walther König, 1989.

III. Exhibition Catalogues
Arranged chronologically.

1962
Manfred Kuttner/Gerd Richter, Düsseldorf. Eine Ausstellung in der Galerie Junge Kunst in Fulda, vom 8.–30. Sept. 1962. Fulda: Galerie Junge Kunst, 1962.

1964
de la Motte, Manfred. *Gerd Richter: Bilder des Kapitalistischen Realismus.* Berlin: Galerie René Block, 1964.

1966
Richter. Venice: Galleria del Leone, 1966.

1969
Honnef, Klaus. *Gerhard Richter.* Aachen: Gegenverkehr, Zentrum für aktuelle Kunst, 1969.

1970
Gerhard Richter: Graphik 1965–1970. Essen: Museum Folkwang, 1970. Text by Dieter Honisch.

1971
Block, René. *Grafik des Kapitalistischen Realismus: K.P. Brehmer, Hödicke, Lueg, Polke, Richter, Vostell, Werkverzeichnisse bis 1971.* Berlin: Galerie René Block, 1971.

Gerhard Richter: Arbeiten 1962 bis 1971. Düsseldorf: Kunstverein für die Rheinlande und Westfalen, 1971. Text by Dietrich Helms.

1972
Gerhard Richter. Essen: Museum Folkwang, 1972. Texts by Dietrich Helms, Dieter Honisch, Klaus Honnef, Heinz Ohff, Rolf-Günter Dienst, Rolf Schön, and Sigmar Polke and Gerhard Richter.

Gerhard Richter, atlas van de fotos en schetsen. Utrecht: Museum voor Hedendaagse Kunst, 1972.

Realismus und Realität: 18. Internationales Kunstgespräch. Vienna: Galerie nächst St. Stephan, 1972.

1973
Gerhard Richter: Verkündigung, nach Tizian. Milan: Galleria la Bertesca, 1973. Texts by Jean-Christophe Ammann and Peter Sager.

Informationen 5. Bremerhaven: Kunstverein Bremerhaven, 1973. Text by Helmut Heissenbüttel.

23. Mai–1. Juli 1973: Gerhard Richter. Munich: Städtische Galerie im Lenbachhaus, 1973. Texts by Michael Petzet, Jean-Christophe Ammann, and Armin Zweite.

1974
Gerhard Richter. Mönchengladbach: Städtisches Museum Mönchengladbach, 1974. Text by Johannes Cladders.

Gerhard Richter. Leverkusen: Städtisches Museum Leverkusen Schloss Morsbroich, 1974. Text by Walter Ehrmann.

1975
Fundamentale Schilderkunst [Fundamental Painting]. Amsterdam: Stedelijk Museum, 1975. Text by Rini Dippel.

Gerhard Richter: Bilder aus den Ausstellung Jahren 1962–1974. Bremen: Kunsthalle Bremen, 1975. Texts by Manfred Schneckenburger and Marlis Grüterich.

Gerhard Richter: Graue Bilder. Braunschweig: Kunstverein Braunschweig, 1975. Text by Heinz Holtmann.

1976
Gerhard Richter. Florence: Edizioni Masnata-Spagnoli, 1976. Text by Giorgio Cortenova.

Gerhard Richter: Atlas der Fotos, Collagen und Skizzen. Krefeld: Museum Haus Lange, 1976.

Honnef, Klaus. *Gerhard Richter.* Recklinghausen: Verlag Aurel Bongers, 1976.

1977
Gerhard Richter. Paris: Centre national d'art et de culture Georges Pompidou, 1977. Text by Benjamin H. D. Buchloh.

Europe in the Seventies: Aspects of Recent Art. Chicago: The Art Institute of Chicago, 1977: 6–14. Texts by Jean-Christophe Ammann and Benjamin H. D. Buchloh.

1978
Gerhard Richter: Abstract Paintings. Eindhoven: Stedelijk Van Abbemuseum, 1978; London: Whitechapel Art Gallery, 1979.

1980
Gerhard Richter. Rome: Galleria Pieroni, 1980. Text by Bruno Corà.

Gerhard Richter: Zwei gelbe Striche. Essen: Museum Folkwang, 1980.

Text by Zdenek Felix.

1981
Baselitz–Richter. Düsseldorf: Städtische Kunsthalle, 1981. Text by Jürgen Harten.

Gerhard Richter: Abstrakte Bilder 1976 bis 1981. Munich: Verlag Fred Jahn, 1981.

1982
Matino, Lucia, ed. *Gerhard Richter.* Milan: PAC (Padiglione d'Arte Contemporaneo di Milano), 1982.

1983
Fuchs, Rudi H. *Isa Genzken/Gerhard Richter.* Rome: Galleria Mario Pieroni, 1983.

1984
Gerhard Richter. St. Etienne: Musée d'Art et d'Industrie, 1984. Text by Bernard Blistène.

1985
Gerhard Richter: Aquarelle. Munich: Galerie Fred Jahn, 1985. Texts by Ulrike Gauss and Ulrich Loock.

Gerhard Richter: March 1985. New York: Marian Goodman/Sperone Westwater, 1985. Text by Benjamin H. D. Buchloh.

Herzogenrath, Wulf, and Stephan von Wiese, eds. *Rheingold: 40 Künstler aus Köln und Düsseldorf.* Cologne: Wienand Verlag, 1985. Text on Richter by Ulrich Loock.

Modus Vivendi: Elf Deutsche Maler 1960–1985. Wiesbaden: Museum Wiesbaden, 1985. Text by Jürgen Harten.

1986
Dickhoff, Wilfried, ed. *Gerhard Richter: Paintings 1964–1974.* New York: Barbara Gladstone Gallery; Cologne: Rudolf Zwirner Gallery, 1986.

Harten, Jürgen, ed. *Gerhard Richter: Bilder/Paintings 1962–1985.* Cologne: DuMont, 1986.

Gerhard Richter: Bilder 1963–1986. Bern: Kunsthalle, 1986. Texts by Ulrich Loock and Benjamin H. D. Buchloh.

Positionen: Malerei aus der Bundesrepublik Deutschland. Stuttgart-Bad Cannstatt: Cantz, 1986. Text by Klaus Honnef.

1987
Gerhard Richter: 20 Bilder. Cologne: Galerie Rudolf Zwirner, 1987.

Gerhard Richter: Paintings, March 1987. New York: Marian Goodman Gallery and Sperone Westwater Gallery, 1987. Text by Denys Zacharopoulos.

Gerhard Richter: Werken op papier 1983–1986, notities 1982–1986. Amsterdam: Museum Overholland; Munich: Verlag Fred Jahn, 1987.

1988
Gerhard Richter: The London Paintings. London: Anthony d'Offay Gallery, 1988. Text by Jill Lloyd.

Gerhard Richter, 19 mars–23 avril 1988: Liliane et Michel Durand-Dessert. Paris: Durand-Dessert, 1988. Text by Denys Zacharopoulos.

Neff, Terry A., ed. *Gerhard Richter: Paintings.* New York and London: Thames & Hudson, 1988. Texts by Benjamin H. D. Buchloh, Roald Nasgaard, and I. Michael Danoff.

Gerhard Richter: Neun Bilder, 1982–1987. Munich: Galerie Fred Jahn, 1988.

1989
Jahn, Fred, ed. *Gerhard Richter Atlas.* Munich: Verlag Fred Jahn, 1989. Text by Armin Zweite.

Gerhard Richter: 18. Oktober 1977. Krefeld: Museum Haus Esters; Frankfurt: Portikus; Cologne: Walther König, 1989. Texts by Benjamin H. D. Buchloh, Gerhard Storck, and Stefan Germer. Trans. London: Institute of Contemporary Arts in association with Anthony d'Offay Gallery, 1989.

Gerhard Richter, 1988–89. Rotterdam: Museum Boijmans Van Beuningen, 1989. Foreword by Karel Schampers, texts by Anna Tilroe and Benjamin H. D. Buchloh.

Scott, Deborah Emont. *Gerhard Richter.* Kansas City: Nelson-Atkins Museum of Art, 1989.

1990
Schmidt, Werner, ed. *Ausgebürgert: Künstler aus der DDR und aus dem sowjetischen Sektor Berlins 1949–1989.* Berlin: Argon Verlag, 1990.

1991
Gerhard Richter: Mirrors. London: Anthony d'Offay Gallery, 1991.

Gerhard Richter. London: Tate Gallery, 1991. Texts by Sean Rainbird, Stefan Germer, and Neal Ascherson.

Gerhard Richter. Paris: Durand-Dessert, 1991.

1992

Butin, Hubertus, ed. *Grafik des Kapitalistischen Realismus*. Frankfurt: Galerie Bernd Slutzky, 1992.

Garrels, Gary, ed. *Photography in Contemporary German Art: 1960 to the Present*. Minneapolis: Walker Art Center, 1992. Text by Gary Garrels.

Gerhard Richter: Frühe Druckgrafik. Frankfurt: Galerie Bernd Slutzky, 1992. Text by Hubertus Butin.

1993

Gerhard Richter. 3 vols. Bonn: Kunst- und Ausstellungshalle der Bundesrepublik Deutschland GmbH, 1993. Vol. 1: illus. works in exhibition; vol. 2: texts by Benjamin H. D. Buchloh, Peter Gidal, and Birgit Pelzer; vol. 3: catalogue raisonné of Richter's paintings and sculptures from 1962 to 1993.

Gerhard Richter: Arbeiten auf Papier. Quakenbrück: Städtische Galerie, 1993. Text by Lothar Romain.

Gerhard Richter, Ausschnitt: 20 Bilder von 1965–1991. Berlin: Neuer Berliner Kunstverein, 1993.

Gerhard Richter: Editionen 1965–1993. Munich: Verlag Fred Jahn, 1993. Texts by Hubertus Butin, Siegfried Salzmann, and Andreas Kreul.

Gerhard Richter: Documenta IX, 1992. New York: Marian Goodman Gallery, 1993. Text by Benjamin H. D. Buchloh.

1994

Gerhard Richter. Madrid: Museo Nacional Centro de Arte Reina Sofia, 1994. Texts by Maria de Corral, José Lebrero Stals; interview with Benjamin H. D. Buchloh (1988).

Gerhard Richter und die Romantik. Essen: Kunstverein Ruhr, 1994. Texts by Hubertus Butin and Peter Friese.

1995

Bilder/Paintings, 1964–1994. Stuttgart: Oktagon, 1995. Text by Roman Kurzmeyer (German and English).

Gerhard Richter. Jerusalem: Israel Museum, 1995. Text by Susanne Landau.

Gerhard Richter: Painting in the Nineties. London: Anthony d'Offay, 1995. Text by Peter Gidal.

Martino, Massimo, ed. *Gerhard Richter: Selected Works 1963–1987*. New York: Luhring Augustine, 1995. Text by James Lewis.

1996

Ichihara, Kentaro. *Gerhard Richter: The Painting of Schein*. Tokyo: Wako Works of Art, 1996.

Pelzer, Birgit, and Guy Tosatto. *Gerhard Richter: 100 Paintings*. Ostfildern-Ruit: Cantz, 1996; pub. in German. French ed., Nîmes: Carré d'Art, Musée d'Art Contemporain de la Ville de Nîmes, 1996.

Gerhard Richter: Paintings/Malerei. Bolzano: Museion, 1996; Vienna: Folio Verlag, 1997. Texts by Peter Weiermair and Pier Luigi Siena.

Abstract Painting 825–II: 69 Details. Zürich: Scalo Books, 1996. Trans. Catherine Schelbert; French ed.: Paris: L'Arche, 1996; German ed.: Frankfurt: Insel, 1996. Text by Hans-Ulrich Obrist.

1997

Finckh, Gerhard, ed. *Die Maler und ihre Skulpturen: Von Edgar Degas bis Gerhard Richter*. Cologne: DuMont, 1997. Text by Hubertus Butin.

Friedel, Helmut, and Ulrich Wilmes, eds. *Gerhard Richter: Atlas der Fotos, Collagen und Skizzen*. Cologne: Oktagon, 1997. Text by Helmut Friedel.

Gillen, Eckhart, ed. *German Art from Beckmann to Richter: Images of a Divided Country*. Cologne: DuMont, 1997. Texts on Richter by Ulf Erdmann Ziegler, Kai-Uwe Hemken, and Susanne Küper.

Shimizu, Minoru. *Gerhard Richter: Öl auf Photographie, ein Grundmodell*. Tokyo: Wako Works of Art, 1997. Japanese and German.

1998

DeLong, Lea Rosson. *Shifting Visions: O'Keeffe, Guston, Richter*. Des Moines, Iowa: Des Moines Art Center, 1998.

Elger, Dietmar, ed. *Gerhard Richter: Landscapes*. Ostfildern-Ruit: Cantz, 1998. Texts by Dietmar Elger and Oskar Bätschmann.

Gerhard Richter: Det umuliges kunst—Malerier 1964–1998/ Gerhard Richter: The Art of the Impossible—Paintings 1964–1998. Oslo: Astrup Fearnley Museum of Modern Art, 1998. Text by Jutta Nestegard.

Hentschel, Martin, and Helmut Friedel. *Gerhard Richter*. London: Anthony d'Offay, 1998.

1999

Gerhard Richter: A cura di Bruno Corà. Prato: Gli Ori, 1999. Texts by Italo Moscati, Bruno Corà, Benjamin H. D. Buchloh, and Jean-François Chevrier.

Gerhard Richter: Werke aus Aachener Sammlungen, 14. November 1999–9. Januar 2000. Ausstellung in der ehemaligen Reichsabtei Aachen-Kornelimünster. Aachen: 1999.

Schwarz, Dieter, ed. *Gerhard Richter Aquarelle/Watercolors 1964–1997*. Düsseldorf: Richter Verlag, 1999.

2000

Heynan, Julian, ed. *Gerhard Richter: Bilder 1999*. Cologne: Walther König, 2000.

Merkert, Jörn, Dieter Ronte, and Walter Smerling, eds. *Gesammelte Räume, gesammelte Träume: Kunst aus Deutschland von 1960 bis 2000*. Cologne: DuMont, 2000. Text by Hubertus Butin.

Schwarz, Dieter, ed. *Von Edgar Degas bis Gerhard Richter: Arbeiten auf Papier aus der Graphischen Sammlung des Kunstmuseums Winterthur*. Winterthur: Kunstmuseum Winterthur; Düsseldorf: Richter Verlag, 2000.

Storr, Robert. *Gerhard Richter: October 18, 1977*. New York: The Museum of Modern Art, 2000.

2001

Slippage. Victoria, B.C.: Art Gallery of Greater Victoria, 2001. Texts by Lisa Baldissera and Mark Cheetham.

Gerhard Richter. New York: Marian Goodman Gallery, 2001. Text by Benjamin H. D. Buchloh.

Gerhard Richter: Gemälde. Friedrichshafen: Kunstverein Friedrichshafen, 2001.

Onkel Rudi, Onkel Rudi…in One Painting, Two Glasses, One Edition, One Show. [Internet only: www.massimomartino.com]. Text by Bruno Corà.

Das XX. Jahrhundert: ein Jahrhundert Kunst in Deutschland. Berlin: Nicolai, c. 1999. Texts by Almut Otto, Lars Blunck, Anke Pötzscher.

IV. Essays and Articles

Essays appearing in monographs and exhibition catalogues are listed below with articles in periodicals, and arranged alphabetically by author.

Ammann, Jean-Christophe. "Gerhard Richter." In *Gerhard Richter: Verkündigung, nach Tizian*. Milan: Galleria la Bertesca, 1973: n.p.

_____. "Zu Gerhard Richter." In *23. Mai–1. Juli 1973: Gerhard Richter*. Munich: Städtische Galerie im Lenbachhaus, 1973: n.p.; repr. in "Gerhard Richter." *Art International* 17 (September 1973): 25–28, 50.

_____. "18. Oktober 1977/October 18th, 1977." In *Gerhard Richter*. Frankfurt: Museum für Moderne Kunst, 1991. [Brochure]

Antoine, Jean-Philippe. "Photography, Painting, and the Real: The Question of Landscape in the Painting of Gerhard Richter." In *Gerhard Richter*. Paris: Éditions dis voir, 1985: 53–89.

_____. "Ne pas voir la peinture en peinture: Les images de Gerhard Richter." In Jean-Louis Froment, ed. *Peinture: Emblèmes et références*. Bordeaux: CAPC Musée d'art contemporain, 1994: 165–174.

Ascherson, Neal. "Revolution and Restoration: Conflicts in the Making of Modern Germany." In *Gerhard Richter*. London: Tate Gallery, 1991: 33–39.

Bätschmann, Oskar. "Landscapes at One Remove." In Dietmar Elger, ed. *Gerhard Richter: Landscapes*. Ostfildern-Ruit: Cantz, 1998: 24–38.

Becker, Wolfgang. "Gerhard Richter in der Sammlung Ludwig." In *Gerhard Richter: Werke aus Aachener Sammlungen, 14. November 1999–9. Januar 2000*.

Ausstellung in der ehemaligen Reichsabtei Aachen-Kornelimünster. Aachen: 1999: 79–81.

Blistène, Bernard. "Gerhard Richter, réflexion sur l'échec de la peinture." *Art Press* (February 1983): 23–26.

_____. "Gerhard Richter ou l'exercice du soupçon." In *Gerhard Richter.* St. Etienne: Musée d'Art et d'Industrie, 1984: 5–8.

_____. "Mécanique et manuel dans l'art de Gerhard Richter." *Galeries Magazine* (April–May 1988): 90–95, 137, 141.

Bloch, Peter André. "Rings nur Welle und Spiel."/ "Partout, rien que les vagues et leur jeu."/ "Around Nothing but Waves and Play." In Hans-Ulrich Obrist, ed. *Gerhard Richter: Sils.* Munich: Oktagon, 1992: 69–86.

Block, René. "Mein letztes Wort (ich will hier nicht erklären warum)." In René Block, *Grafik des Kapitalistischen Realismus: K.P. Brehmer, Hödicke, Lueg, Polke, Richter, Vostell.* Berlin: Galerie René Block, 1971: 15, 30.

Bode, Peter M. "Immer anders, immer er selbst." *Art* (Hamburg) (May 1983): 46–61.

Brehm, Margit. "Über das Konstituieren visueller Wahrheit beim Malen."/ "The Constitution of Visual Truth During Painting." In Jochen Poetter, ed. *Sammlung Frieder Burda: Gerhard Richter, Sigmar Polke, Arnulf Rainer.* Ostfildern-Ruit: Cantz, 1996: 33–42/43–52.

Buchloh, Benjamin H. D. "Formalism and Historicity–Changing Concepts in American and European Art Since 1945." In *Europe in the Seventies: Aspects of Recent Art.* Chicago: The Art Institute of Chicago, 1977: 107–111.

_____. "Readymade, Photography, and Painting in the Painting of Gerhard Richter." In *Gerhard Richter: Abstract Paintings.* London: Whitechapel Art Gallery, 1979: 5–20; Orig. pub. in French in *Gerhard Richter.* Paris: Centre national d'art et de culture Georges Pompidou, 1977: 11–58; repr. in *Neo-Avantgarde and the Culture Industry: Essays on European and American Art from 1955

to 1975.* Cambridge, Mass.: MIT Press, 2000: 365–403.

_____. "Parody and Appropriation in Francis Picabia, Pop, and Sigmar Polke." *Artforum* (March 1982): 28–34.

_____. "Gerhard Richter: 18. Oktober 1977." In *Gerhard Richter: 18. Oktober 1977.* Krefeld: Museum Haus Esters; Frankfurt: Portikus; Cologne: Walther König, 1989: 55–59.

_____. "Richter's Facture: Between the Synecdoche and the Spectacle." In Andreas Papadakis, Clare Farrow, and Nicola Hodges, eds. *New Art.* London: Academy Group Ltd., 1991: 190–196.

_____. "Gerhard Richter und die Allegorie des Abstrakten Kabinetts." *Texte zur Kunst* (Cologne) (December 1992): 35–41. Trans. "Allegories of Painting." In *Gerhard Richter: Documenta IX, 1992.* New York: Marian Goodman Gallery, 1993: 9–14.

_____. "Pandora's Painting: From Abstract Fallacies to Heroic Travesties." In *Gerhard Richter: Documenta IX, 1992.* New York: Marian Goodman Gallery, 1993: 44–50.

_____. "Divided Memory and Post-Traditional Identity: Gerhard Richter's Work of Mourning." *October* 75 (winter 1996): 60–82.

_____. "Gerhard Richter's *Atlas*: The Anomic Archive." *October* 88 (spring 1999): 117–144; repr. in Benjamin H. D. Buchloh, Jean-François Chevrier, Armin Zweite, and Rainer Rochlitz, *Photography and Painting in the Work of Gerhard Richter: Four Essays on Atlas.* Barcelona: Consorci del Museu d'Art Contemporani de Barcelona, 2000: 11–30.

_____. "Archaeology to Transcendence: A Random Dictionary for/on Gerhard Richter." In *Gerhard Richter.* New York: Marian Goodman Gallery, 2001: 7–21.

Butin, Hubertus. "The Un-Romantic Romanticism of Gerhard Richter." In Keith Hartley, Henry Meyric Hughes, Peter-Klaus Schuster, and William Vaughan, eds. *The Romantic Spirit in German Art 1790–1990.* London: Hayward

Gallery, South Bank Centre, 1994: 461–463.

_____. "Gerhard Richter—ein deutscher Romantiker?" In *Gerhard Richter und die Romantik.* Essen: Kunstverein Ruhr, 1994: 7–30.

_____. "Gerhard Richters frühe Druckgrafik 1965–1974." In *Gerhard Richter: Frühe Druckgrafik.* Frankfurt: Galerie Bernd Slutzky, 1992: 7–11.

_____. "René Block and the Graphics of Capitalist Realism of 1967/68." In Hubertus Butin, *Graphics of Capitalist Realism.* Frankfurt: Galerie Bernd Slutzky, 1992: 31–43. German and English.

_____. "Richters RAF-Zyklus nach New York verkauft: Kultureller Gewinn oder Verlust?" *Kunstforum International* 132 (November–January 1996): 432–435.

_____. "Gerhard Richter: Die List der Reflexion." In Gerhard Finkh, ed. *Die Maler und ihre Skulpturen: Von Edgar Degas bis Gerhard Richter.* Cologne: DuMont, 1997: 299–308.

_____. "Gerhard Richter: Paradigmen des Malerischen." In Jörn Merkert, Dieter Ronte, and Walter Smerling, eds. *Gesammelte Räume, gesammelte Träume: Kunst aus Deutschland von 1960 bis 2000.* Cologne: DuMont, 2000: 124–126.

Chevrier, Jean-François. "Zwischen den bildenden Künsten und den Medien: Das deutsche Beispiel." In *Texte: Photographie in der deutschen Gegenwartskunst.* 1993: 26–64.

_____. "Between Fine Arts and the Media (The German Example: Gerhard Richter)." In *Gerhard Richter: A cura di Bruno Corà.* Prato: Gli Ori, 1999: 173–182. Repr. in Benjamin H. D. Buchloh, Jean-François Chevrier, Armin Zweite, and Rainer Rochlitz, *Photography and Painting in the Work of Gerhard Richter: Four Essays on Atlas.* Barcelona: Consorci del Museu d'Art Contemporani de Barcelona, 2000: 31–92.

Cladders, Johannes. "Grau is doch auch eine Farbe, und manchmal ist sie mir die wichtigste." In *Gerhard Richter.* Mönchengladbach:

Städtisches Museum, 1974: n.p. (Brochure).

Corà, Bruno. "Intuizioni di una richiesta—l'occasione Richter." In *Gerhard Richter.* Rome: Galleria Pieroni, 1980: n.p.

_____. "Gerhard Richter: The Experience of Painting in the Knowledge of Reality." In *Gerhard Richter: A cura di Bruno Corà.* Prato: Gli Ori, 1999: 23–35.

Cortenova, Giorgio. "Gerhard Richter." In *Gerhard Richter.* Florence: Edizioni Masnata-Spagnoli, 1976: n.p.

Criqui, Jean-Pierre. "Three Impromptus on the Art of Gerhard Richter." *Parkett* 35 (1993): 38–42.

_____. "Heterogeneity: An Introduction to the Work of Gerhard Richter." In Terry A. Neff, ed. *Gerhard Richter: Paintings.* New York and London: Thames & Hudson, 1988: 9–14.

Dickel, Hans. "Wolke (1–3)." *Kunst und Antiquitäten* 4 (April 1991): 45–48.

Dickhoff, Wilfried. "Gerhard Richter: Malen ist eine moralische Handlung." *Wolkenkratzer Art Journal* (April–June 1985): 34–41.

Diederichsen, Diedrich, Isabelle Graw, Tom Holert, Jutta Koether, and Felix Reidenbach. "Richterrunde." *Texte zur Kunst* 4, no. 13 (March 1994): 120–141.

Dienst, Rolf-Günter. "Deutsche Kunst: Eine neue Generation." *Das Kunstwerk* 9–10 (June–July 1968): 3–49.

von Drathen, Doris. "Gerhard Richter: Les Pouvoirs de l'Abstraction." *Les Cahiers du Musée National d'Art Moderne* 40 (summer 1992): 67–85.

_____. "Gerhard Richter: An die Macht der Bilder glauben." *Kunstforum International* 31 (August–October 1995): 247–264.

Ehrmann, Walter. "Gerhard Richter: Landschaften." In *Gerhard Richter.* Leverkusen: Städtisches Museum Leverkusen Schloss Morsbroich, 1974: n.p.

Elger, Dietmar. "Gerhard Richter: Autonome Wirklichkeiten." In *Aquarelle: Kasseler Kunstverein.* Kassel: Kunstverein, 1985: n.p.

_____. "Landscape as a Model." In Dietmar Elgar, ed. *Gerhard Richter: Landscapes.* Ostfildern-Ruit: Cantz, 1998: 8–23.

_____. "Gerhard Richters Bilder über die Wahrheiten der Wirklichkeit." In *Gerhard Richter: Werke aus Aachener Sammlungen, 14. November 1999–9. Januar 2000. Ausstellung in der ehemaligen Reichsabtei Aachen-Kornelimünster.* Aachen: 1999: 83–86.

_____. "Gerhard Richter: Bilder sind fiktive Modelle." In Andrea Hofmann, ed. *Gerhard Richter: Malerei aus drei Jahrzehnten.* Friedrichshafen: Kunstverein, 2001: 5–11.

Ellis, Stephen. "The Elusive Gerhard Richter." *Art in America* (November 1986): 130–139.

Faust, Wolfgang Max., and Gerd de Vries. "Gerhard Richter." In *Hunger nach Bildern.* Cologne: DuMont, 1982: 42–48.

Felix, Zdenek. "Wirklichkeit und Illusion oder vom Realismus zum Hyperrealismus, (I. Folge)." *Kunstnachrichten* 9 (October 1972): n.p.

_____. "Wirklichkeit und Illusion oder vom Realismus zum Hyperrealismus, (II. Folge)." *Kunstnachrichten* 9 (November 1972): n.p.

_____. "Zwei gelbe Striche." In *Gerhard Richter: Zwei gelbe Striche.* Essen: Museum Folkwang, 1980: 3–6.

Fischer, Klaus-Jürgen. "Aspekte des Realismus in Deutschland." *Das Kunstwerk* 29 (1976): 3–58.

Flemming, Victoria von. "Enigma within an Enigma." *Contemporanea* (November 1989): 39–45.

François, Alain-Henri. "…La pure image." *Voir* 8 (1990): 18–19.

Friese, Peter. "Von der Kunst des Zuspätkommens (mit einem Exkurs von Hans Joachim Lenger)." In *Gerhard Richter und die Romantik.* Essen: Kunstverein Ruhr, 1994: 31–45.

Friedel, Helmut. "The Atlas 1962–1997." In *Gerhard Richter: Atlas of the Photographs Collages and Sketches.* Cologne: Oktagon, 1997: 5–7.

_____. "Gerhard Richter's Waterfall, 1997: A View of Landscape." In *Gerhard Richter.* London:

Anthony d'Offay Gallery, 1998: 23–25.

Fry, Edward F. "Gerhard Richter, German Illusionist." *Art in America* (November–December 1969): 126–127.

Fuchs, Rudi H. "Artificial Miracles." In *Gerhard Richter: Abstract Paintings.* Eindhoven: Stedelijk Van Abbemuseum; London: Whitechapel Art Gallery, 1978–1979: 3.

_____. "Zweierlei deutsche Kunst." *Frankfurter Allgemeine Zeitung* (August 2, 1990).

Garrels, Gary. "Gerhard Richter." In Gary Garrels, ed. *Photography in Contemporary German Art.* Minneapolis: Walker Art Center, 1992: 19–20.

Germer, Stefan. "Ungebetene Erinnerung." In *Gerhard Richter: 18. Oktober 1977.* Krefeld: Museum Haus Esters; Frankfurt: Portikus; Cologne: Walther König, 1989: 51–53.

_____. "Retrospective Ahead." In *Gerhard Richter.* London: Tate Gallery, 1991: 22–32.

_____. "Le Retour du Refoulé. Le traitement de l'histoire allemande chez Georg Baselitz, Anselm Kiefer, Jörg Immendorff et Gerhard Richter." *Les Cahiers du Musée National d'Art Moderne* 48 (summer 1994): 82–99.

_____. "Familienanschluss. Zur Thematisierung des Privaten in neueren Bildern Gerhard Richters." *Texte zur Kunst* 7 (June 1997): 109–116.

Gidal, Peter. "Endless Finalities." *Parkett* 35 (1993): 45–48.

Grasskamp, Walter. "Augenschein. Über die Lesbarkeit des Portraits und die Handschrift des Fotografen." *Kunstforum International* 52 (August 1982): 14–37.

_____. "Gerhard Richter: Verkündigung nach Tizian." In *Der vergessliche Engel: Künstlerportraits für Fortgeschrittene.* Munich: 1986: 44–61. Trans. "Gerhard Richter: An Angel Vanishes." *Flash Art* 128 (May/June 1986): 30–35.

Green, David. "From History Painting to the History of Painting and Back Again: Reflections on the Work of Gerhard Richter." In

David Green and Peter Seddon, eds. *History Painting Reassessed: The Representation of History in Contemporary Art.* Manchester, U.K.: Manchester University Press; New York: St. Martin's Press, 2000: 31–49.

Greene, Alison de Lima. "Gerhard Richter." In Harald Szeemann, ed. *La Biennale di Venezia: 49. Esposizione internazionale d'arte. Plateau of Humankind.* Vol. 1. Venice: Giardini di Castello, Arsenale, 2001: 30–31.

Grohmann, Will. "Gerd Richter." *Quadrum* 18 (1965): 150–151.

Gronert, Stefan. "Mit Gerhard Richter und Isa Genzken in den Untergrund." *Orte. Kunst für öffentliche Räume* 3 (October 1992): n.p.

Grout, Catherine. "Le paysage en question." *Artefactum* (June, July, August 1990): 11–14.

Grüterich, Marlis. "Gerhard Richters Phänomenologie der Illusion—eine gemalte Ästhetik gegen die reine Malerei." In *Gerhard Richter: Bilder aus den Jahren 1962–1974.* Bremen: Ausstellung Kunsthalle, 1975: 16–100.

Haase, Amine. "Die Farbe denkt." *Kunstforum International* 88 (1987): 84–88.

Harten, Jürgen. "Zum Vergleich." In *Baselitz–Richter.* Düsseldorf: Städtische Kunsthalle, 1981: n.p.

_____. "Gerhard Richter." In Kasper König, ed., *Von hier aus, 2 Monate neue deutsche Kunst.* Cologne: DuMont, 1984: 293–295.

_____. "Stil oder Methode." In *Modus Vivendi: Elf Deutsche Maler 1960–1985.* Wiesbaden: Museum Wiesbaden, 1985: 38–39.

_____. "Der romantische Wille zur Abstraktion." / "The Romantic Intent for Abstraction." In Jürgen Harten, ed. *Gerhard Richter: Bilder/Paintings 1962–1985.* Cologne: DuMont, 1986: 9–62.

Heere, Heribert. "Die Abstrakten Bilder: Zur Frage des Inhalts." In *Gerhard Richter: Abstrakte Bilder.* Bielefeld: Kunsthalle Bielefeld, 1982: 9–20.

Hegewisch, Katharina. "Dem Leben eine Bühne bauen." In *Oswald Mathias Ungers, Gerhard Richter,*

Sol LeWitt. Düsseldorf: Hypo-Bank, 1991: 7–13.

Heissenbüttel, Helmut. "Klappentext Nr. 24 für Gerhard Richter." In *Informationen 5.* Bremerhaven: Kunstverein Bremerhaven, 1973: n.p.

Helms, Dietrich. "Über Gerhard Richter." In *Gerhard Richter: Arbeiten 1962 bis 1971.* Düsseldorf: Kunstverein für die Rheinlande und Westfalen, 1971: n.p.; repr. in *Gerhard Richter.* Essen: Museum Folkwang, 1972: 7–12.

Hemken, Kai-Uwe. "Von 'Engeln der Geschichte' und ästhetischer Melancholie: Zur Geschichtserfahrung in der Gegenwartskunst." In Kai-Uwe Hemken, ed. *Gedächtnisbilder: Vergessen und Erinnern in der Gegenwartskunst.* Leipzig: Reclam, 1996: 9–15, 143–155.

_____. "Suffering from Germany—Gerhard Richter's Elegy of Modernism: Philosophy of History in the Cycle *October 18, 1977*." In Eckhart Gillen, ed., *German Art from Beckmann to Richter: Images of a Divided Country.* Cologne: DuMont, 1997: 381–403. German ed., *Deutschlandbilder. Kunst aus einem geteilten Land,* 1997.

Hentschel, Martin. "On Shifting Terrain: Looking at Richter's Abstract Paintings." In *Gerhard Richter.* London: Anthony d'Offay Gallery, 1998: 11–19; repr. in German as "Auf wechselndem Terrain: Richters abstrakte Bilder anschauen." *Noëma* 50 (January–March 1999): 39–51.

_____, and Ulrich Loock. "Gerhard Richter." *Artistes* (December 1983): 36–42.

_____, and Ulrich Loock. "Gerhard Richter." *Nike* 11 (December–February 1986): 10–15.

Hickey, Dave. "Richter in Tahiti." *Parkett* 35 (1993): 82–87.

Hofmann, Andrea. "Gerhard Richter in Friedrichshafen." In Andrea Hofmann, ed. *Gerhard Richter: Malerei aus drei Jahrzehnten.* Friedrichshafen: Kunstverein, 2001: 13–16.

Holtmann, Heinz. "Grau als Indifferenz." In *Gerhard Richter:*

Graue Bilder. Braunschweig: Kunstverein Braunschweig, 1975: n.p.

Honisch, Dieter. "Die 'Graphik' Gerhard Richters." In *Gerhard Richter: Graphik 1965–1970*. Essen: Museum Folkwang, 1970: n.p.

———. "Zu den Arbeiten Gerhard Richters." In *Gerhard Richter*. Essen: Museum Folkwang, 1972: 3–5.

———. "What Is Admired in Cologne Might Not Be Accepted in Munich." *Art News* (October 1978): 62–67.

Honnef, Klaus. "Schwierigkeiten beim Beschreiben der Realität—Richters Malerei zwischen Kunst und Wirklichkeit." In *Gerhard Richter*. Aachen: Gegenverkehr, Zentrum für aktuelle Kunst, 1969: n.p.; repr. in *Gerhard Richter*. Essen: Museum Folkwang, 1972: 13–16.

———. "Richter's New Realism." *Art and Artists* (September 1973): 34–37.

———. "Problem Realismus: Die Medien des Gerhard Richters." *Kunstforum International* 1 (April–May 1973): 68–91.

———. "Gerhard Richter." In *Positionen: Malerei aus der Bundesrepublik Deutschland*. Stuttgart-Bad Cannstatt: Cantz, 1986: 166–171.

———. "Die geplante und analytische, fundamentale und elementare Malerei–bevor sie radikal wurde: Die siebziger Jahre." *Kunstforum International* 88 (1987): 127–133.

Jollet, Etienne. "Gerhard Richter und die Technik des Malers." *Texte zur Kunst* 4 (March 1994): 166–170.

Joyce, Conor. "Gerhard Richter." *Art Monthly* 152 (December 1991–Janurary 1992): 3–5.

Koch, Gertrud. "The Open Secret." ["Le secret de Polichinelle"] In *Gerhard Richter*. Paris: Éditions Dis Voir: 1985, 9–28.

———. "The Richter-Scale of Blur." *October* 62 (Fall 1992): 103–113.

———. "Verlauf der Zeit."/ "Sequence of Time." *Parkett* 35 (1993): 73–75, 76–79.

Kozloff, Max. "Gerhard Richter: He Who Misleads." *Art in America* (September 1994): 98–105, 133.

Kramer, Hilton. "MoMA Helps Martyrdom of German Terrorists." *The New York Observer* (July 3–10, 1995): 1, 23.

Krüger, Klaus. "Der Blick ins Innere des Bildes: Ästhetische Illusion bei Gerhard Richter." *Pantheon* (1995): 149–166.

Küper, Susanne. "Gerhard Richter: Capitalist Realism and His Painting from Photographs, 1962–1968." In Eckhart Gillen, ed. *German Art from Beckmann to Richter: Images of a Divided Country*. Cologne: DuMont; [Berlin]: Berliner Festspiele GmbH and Museumspädagogischer Dienst Berlin, 1997: 233–236. German ed.: *Deutschlandbilder. Kunst aus einem geteilten Land*, 1997.

Kuspit, Donald B. "Gerhard Richter's Doubt and Hope." *C Magazine* 20 (winter 1989): 18–24.

———. "All Our Yesterdays." *Artforum* 8 (April 1990): 129–132.

Lang, Luc. "La Main du photographe (Gerhard Richter)." In Jean-Louis Froment, ed. *Peinture: Emblèmes et références*. Bordeaux: CAPC Musée d'art contemporain, 1994: 186–192. Trans., "The Photographer's Hand: Phenomenology in Politics." In *Gerhard Richter*. Paris: Éditions Dis Voir, 1985: 55–92.

Lewis, James. "Gerhard Richter: The Problem of Belief." *Art Issues* (summer 1990): 12–14.

———. "Gerhard Richter: Betty." *Artforum* (September 1993): 132–133, 196.

———. "A Two Part Invention." In Massimo Martino, ed. *Gerhard Richter: Selected Works 1963–1987*. New York: Luhring Augustine, 1995: 11–14.

Lloyd, Jill. "Gerhard Richter: The London Paintings." In *Gerhard Richter: The London Paintings*. London: Anthony d'Offay Gallery, 1988: n.p.

Loock, Ulrich. "Das Ereignis des Bildes." In Ulrich Loock and Denys Zacharopoulos. *Gerhard Richter*. Munich: Verlag Silke Schreiber, 1985: 81–125.

———. "Gerhard Richter: Das Ereignis des Bildes." In Wulf Herzogenrath and Stephan von Wiese, eds.

Rheingold: 40 Künstler aus Köln und Düsseldorf. Cologne: Wienand, 1985: 205–207.

———. "Zu Gerhard Richters Ausstellung in Bern." In *Gerhard Richter: Bilder 1963–1986*. Bern: Kunsthalle, 1986: 3–5. [Brochure]

———. "Gerhard Richter." *Parachute* (December, January, February 1988/89): 4–11.

Manchanda, Catharina. "De ontschilderde voorstelling: 18. Oktober 1977 van Gerhard Richter." *Obscuur* 7 (April 2001): 48–58.

Meinhardt, Johannes. "Gerhard Richter." In *Brennpunkt Düsseldorf: Joseph Beuys, Die Akademie: Der allgemeine Aufbruch, 1962–1987*. Düsseldorf: Kunstmuseum, 1987: 175–177.

———. "Unmögliche Malerei." *Kunstforum International* 131 (August–October 1995): 236–246.

Metzger, Rainer. "Flächenland: Anmerkungen zu Gerhard Richters Arbeit an der Evidenz." *Noëma* 50 (January–March 1999): 30–38.

Moscati, Italo. "The Veils of the Sphinx." In *Gerhard Richter: A cura di Bruno Corà*. Prato: Gli Ori, 1999: 7.

de la Motte, Manfred. "Gerd Richter oder der kapitale 'Kapitalistische Realismus.'" In *Gerd Richter: Bilder des Kapitalistischen Realismus*. Berlin: Galerie René Block, 1964: n.p.

Murken, Axel Hinrich. "'Dass ich erkenne, was die Welt im Innersten zusammenhält.'" In *Gerhard Richter: Werke aus Aachener Sammlungen, 14. November 1999–9. Januar 2000. Ausstellung in der ehemaligen Reichsabtei Aachen-Kornelimünster*. Aachen: 1999: 9–15.

———, and Christa Murken-Altrogge. "Künstler—die wichtigsten Leute der Welt: Betrachtungen zum Menschenbildnis Gerhard Richters." *Deutsches Ärzteblatt* 14 (April 7, 1977): 967–970. Cont.: 15 (April 14, 1977): 1039–1042; 16 (April 21, 1977): 1101–1105.

Nasgaard, Roald. "Art as the Highest Form of Hope: Paintings by Gerhard Richter." *AGO News* [Art Gallery of Ontario] 10 (April 1988): 1–2.

———. "Gerhard Richter." In Terry A. Neff, ed. *Gerhard Richter: Paintings*. New York and London: Thames & Hudson, 1988: 31–111.

Nestegard, Jutta. "Gerhard Richter— Mannen som vil hoppe over sin egen skygge."/ "Gerhard Richter— Trying to Jump over his Own Shadow." In *Gerhard Richter: Det umuliges kunst—Malerier 1964–1998/Gerhard Richter: The Art of the Impossible—Paintings 1964–1998*. Oslo: Astrup Fearnley Museum of Modern Art, 1998: 8–55.

Obrist, Hans-Ulrich. "Circulus Vitiosus Pictus." In *Gerhard Richter: Sils*. Munich: Oktagon, 1992: 7–20.

Oddy, Jason. "An Outsider Art." *Modern Painters* (summer 2000): 97–99.

Ohff, Heinz. *Pop und die Folgen, oder die Kunst, Kunst auf der Strasse zu finden*. Düsseldorf: Droste Verlag, 1968: 110–113. Repr. as, "Über Gerhard Richter." In *Gerhard Richter*. Essen: Museum Folkwang, 1972: 17–18.

———. "Das Neue Porträt oder: Was ist neu daran?" *Kunstforum International* 6/7 (1973): 94–123.

Paoletti, John T. "Gerhard Richter/MATRIX 95." In *Gerhard Richter/MATRIX 95. July 2–September 6, 1987*. Hartford, Conn.: Wadsworth Atheneum, 1987: 2–6. [Brochure]

———. "Gerhard Richter: Ambiguity as an Agent of Awareness." *The Print Collectors' Newsletter* 29 (March–April 1988): 1–6.

Pelzer, Birgit. "The Tragic Desire."/ "Das tragische Begehren." *Parkett* 35 (1993): 66–71/58–65.

Phillipi, Desa. "Moments of Interpretation." *October* 62 (Fall 1992): 115–122.

Polke, Sigmar. "Interview between John Anthony Thwaites and Gerhard Richter." (October 1964); repr. in *Daily Practice*: 26–28.

Rainbird, Sean. "Variations on a Theme: The Painting of Gerhard Richter." In *Gerhard Richter*. London: Tate Gallery, 1991: 11–21.

Restany, Pierre. "Mechanische Malerei." *Das Kunstwerk* 20 (February–March 1967): 3–19.

———. "Gerhard Richter." *Texte zur Kunst* 32 (December 1998): 94.

Ritchie, Christina. "Gerhard Richter. Helga Matura." *Art Gallery of Ontario: Collection in Focus* 7 (1992–93).

———. "Gerhard Richter: The Illusion and Reality of Painting." *Art Gallery of Ontario: Collection in Focus* 7 (1992–93).

Rochlitz, Rainer. "Where we have got to." In *Photography and Painting in the Work of Gerhard Richter: Four Essays on Atlas*. Barcelona: Consorci del Museu d'Art Contemporani de Barcelona, 2000: 103–125.

Romain, Lothar. "Gerhard Richter: 'Die Kunst ist die höchste Form von Hoffnung.'" In *Gerhard Richter: Arbeiten auf Papier*. Quakenbrück: Städtische Galerie, 1993: 5–8.

Rorimer, Anne. "Gerhard Richter: The Illusion and Reality of Painting." In *Gerhard Richter: Paintings*. New York: Marian Goodman Gallery/Sperone Westwater Gallery, 1987: n.p.

Sager, Peter. "Mit der Farbe denken." *Zeitmagazin* 49 (November 28, 1986): 24–30, 33–34, 37.

Scheer, Thorsten. "Gerhard Richter and Art & Language: Conceptual Aspects of Modernism."/ "Die Ausdauer der Postmoderne: Konzeptuelle Aspekte im Werk von Gerhard Richter und Art & Language." *Artefactum* 42 (1992): 52–53/6–9.

Schnackenburg, Bernhard. "Gerhard Richter." In *Kunst der sechziger Jahre in der Neuen Galerie Kassel*. Kassel: Staatliche Kunstsammlungen, 1982: 68–71.

Schneckenburger, Manfred. "Gerhard Richter oder ein Weg, weiterzumalen." In *Gerhard Richter: Bilder aus den Jahren 1962–1974*. Bremen: Ausstellung Kunsthalle Bremen, 1975: 10–15.

Schwarz, Dieter. "Leserbrief (an Stefan Germer)." *Texte zur Kunst* 7 (July 1997): 165–167.

Schmidt, Julia. "Buchbesprechung: Gerhard Richter, Atlas der Fotos, Collagen und Skizzen." *Zeitschrift für Kunstgeschichte* 62 (1999): 144–151.

Stals, José Lebrero. "Contrapintura." In *Gerhard Richter*. Madrid: Museo Nacional Centro de Arte Reina Sofia, 1993: 17–26.

Stemmler, Dierk. "Universale Malerei des unerklärlichen wegen: Gerhard Richter." In *Sammlung deutscher Kunst seit 1945*. Vol. 2. Bonn: Städtisches Kunstmuseum, 1984: 639–661.

Stobl, Andreas. "Bildbetrachtung. Gerhard Richter, Ohne Titel (Venedig)." *Neue bildende Kunst* (June 1993): 10–11.

Storck, Gerhard. "Beschäftigung mit Gerhard Richters Sammelwerk: Atlas der Fotos, Collagen und Skizzen." In *Gerhard Richter: Atlas der Fotos, Collagen und Skizzen*. Krefeld: Museum Haus Lange, 1976. n.p.

———. [Untitled]. In *Gerhard Richter: 18. Oktober 1977*. Krefeld: Museum Haus Esters; Frankfurt: Portikus; Cologne: Walther König, 1989: 11–18.

Thomas, Karin. "Vernetzte Zeiten." *Kunstforum International* (April–June 2000): 298–309.

Thorn-Prikker, Jan. "Malerei, Erlösung, Gewalt: Zu Gerhard Richters Zyklus "18. Oktober 1977." *Kunst und Kirche* (March 1989): 159–160.

———. "Der Schein bestimmt das Bewusstsein: Fragmentarische Gedanken zum Verhältnis von Kunst und Politik." *Neue bildende Kunst: Zeitschrift für Kunst und Kritik* 3 (1992): 15–18.

Thwaites, John Anthony. "Last Summer on the Rhine and Ruhr." *Studio International* 169 (January 1965): 16–21.

———. "German Prophets without Honor." *Art in America* (December 1965–January 1966): 110–111, 112, 114.

Tilroe, Anna. "Gerhard Richter." In *Gerhard Richter, 1988–89*. Rotterdam: Museum Boijmans Van Beuningen, 1989: 15–31.

Tosatto, Guy. "The Woman, the Child and the Painting." In Birgit Pelzer and Guy Tosatto. *Gerhard Richter. 100 Paintings*. Ostfildern-Ruit: Cantz, 1996: 9–16. French ed., Nîmes: Carré d'Art, Musée d'Art Contemporain de la Ville de Nîmes, 1996.

van Bruggen, Coosje. "Gerhard Richter: Painting as a Moral Act." *Artforum* 9 (May 1985): 82–91.

Wedewer, Rolf. "Über Gerhard Richter." In *Graphik der Gegenwart*. Leverkusen: Städtisches Museum Leverkusen Schloss Morsbroich, Westermann Galerie, c. 1971: 17–18.

———. "Zum Landschaftstypus Gerhard Richters." *Pantheon* 33 (January–March 1975): 41–49.

Weiermair, Peter. "The Painter as Sisyphus." *Gerhard Richter: Paintings*. Bolzano: Museion; Vienna: Folio, 1997: n.p.

Weiss, Evelyn. "Pop Art und Deutschland." In Marco Livingstone, ed. *Pop Art*. Munich: Prestel Verlag, 1992: 221–225.

Wilmes, Ulrich. "Gleichnisse einer unbegreiflichen Wirklichkeit. Zur Malerei von Gerhard Richter." In *Gerhard Richter: Eine Einführung in sein Werk und Schaffen*. Frankfurt: Deutsche Bank, 1989: 3–5. [Brochure]

Winter, Peter. "Bildräume mit Fragezeichen." *Das Kunstwerk* 28 (July 1975): 3–7.

Wood, Paul. "Truth and Beauty: The Ruined Abstraction of Gerhard Richter." In John Roberts, ed. *Art Has No History!* London: Verso, 1994: 180–199.

Wylie, Charles. "Gerhard Richter in Dallas Collections." Dallas: Dallas Museum of Art, 2000: n.p. [Brochure]

Zacharopoulos, Denys. "Die Figur des Werkes." In *Gerhard Richter*. Munich: Verlag Silke Schreiber, 1985: 7–80.

———. "Abstract Paintings." In *Gerhard Richter: Paintings*. New York: Marian Goodman Gallery/Sperone Westwater Gallery, 1987: n.p.

———. "L'atelier de Richter, la peinture." In *Gerhard Richter*. Paris: Liliane & Michel Durand-Dessert, 1988: 3–5.

Zevi, Adachiara. [Untitled] In *Montagne: Gerhard Richter*. Rome: Zerynthia, Associazione per l'Arte Contemporanea, 1992: 7–15.

Ziegler, Ulf Erdmann. "How the Soul Leaves the Body: Gerhard Richter's Cycle October 18, 1977, the Last Chapter in West German Postwar Painting." Eckhart Gillen, ed. *German Art from Beckmann to Richter: Images of a Divided Country*. Cologne: DuMont, 1997: 374–380. German ed., *Deutschlandbilder. Kunst aus einem geteilten Land*, 1997.

Zweite, Armin. "Gerhard Richters 'Atlas der Fotos, Collagen und Skizzen.'" In Fred Jahn, ed. *Gerhard Richter: Atlas*. Munich: 1989: 7–20. Trans., "Gerhard Richter's Album of Photographs, Collages, and Sketches." In *Photography and Painting in the Work of Gerhard Richter: Four Essays on Atlas*. Barcelona: Consorci del Museu d'Art Contemporani de Barcelona, 2000: 61–101.

V. Exhibition Reviews
Arranged chronologically.

1964
Strelow, Hans. "Die Kunst, die wir verdienen: Erste deutsche Pop-Art Ausstellung." *Stadt-Nachrichten* (Düsseldorf) (January 11, 1964).

1967
Sello, Gottfried. "Wer will zur documenta? Junge deutsche Kunst in Dortmund, Berlin und Recklinghausen." *Die Zeit* (February 17, 1967).

1969
Ammann, Jean-Christophe. "Schweizer Brief." *Art International* 13 (October 1969): 65–69, 79.

1970
Friedrichs, Yvonne. "Moralische Anti-Kunst im ehemaligen Friseursalon: Gerhard Richter stellt in Konrad Fischers neuer Galerie aus." *Rheinische Post* (April 4, 1970).

Meister, Helga. "Foto und Streifen: Gerhard Richters Arbeiten bei Konrad Fischer." *Düsseldorfer Nachrichten* (May 5, 1970).

1971
Honnef, Klaus. "Kunstbericht aus dem Rheinland: Gerhard Richter im Kunstverein Düsseldorf." *Magazin Kunst* 11 (1971): 2413–2414.

Jappe, Georg. "Zwar Talent–Aber Talent: Gerhard Richter im

Düsseldorfer Kunstverein." *Frankfurter Allgemeine Zeitung* (July 20, 1971).

Reuther, Hanno. "Fenster in die schöne Welt: Die Malerei Gerhard Richters im Düsseldorfer Kunstverein." *Frankfurter Rundschau* (July 3, 1971).

Ueberfeldt, Gottfried Peer. "So schön ist das alles: Maler Gerhard Richter im Kunstverein Düsseldorf." *Frankfurter Allgemeine Zeitung* (July 13, 1971).

1972

Abadie, Daniel. "Gerhard Richter ou le saississement du réel." *Lettres Françaises* (August 23, 1972).

Elderfield, John. "Grids." *Artforum* 10 (May 1972): 52–59.

Stachelhaus, Heiner. "Doubts in the Face of Reality: The Paintings of Gerhard Richter." *Studio International* 184 (September 7, 1972): 76–80.

1973

Frank, Peter. "Gerhard Richter (Onnasch)." *Artnews* 72, no. 9 (November 1973): 100.

Goedl-Roth, Monika. "Städtische Galerie im Lenbachhaus: Ausstellung, Gerhard Richter." *Pantheon* 31 (October–December 1973): 434.

Kneubühler, Theo. "'Stil ist Gewalttat': Zur Ausstellung von Gerhard Richter, Ernst Maass und Max von Moos im Kunstmuseum." *Vaterland* 18 (January 23, 1973).

Stitelman, Paul. "Gerhard Richter." *Arts Magazine* 48 (December 1973): 58–59.

1974

"Atlas: Gerhard Richter." *Domus* 537 (August 1974): 46, 59.

Collins, James. "Gerhard Richter, Onnasch Gallery." *Artforum* (January 1974): 72–73.

Glozer, László. "Die Vor-Bilder der Bilder: Gerhard Richter breitet sein Arbeitsmaterial aus." *Süddeutsche Zeitung* 97 (April 26, 1974).

1975

Kipphoff, Petra. "Kissenkunst, zerrissene Kunst." *Die Zeit* (December 19, 1975).

1976

Glozer, László. "Meister der Unschärfe: Gerhard Richter in der

Bremer Kunsthalle." *Süddeutsche Zeitung* 6 (January 9, 1976).

Ingenpahs, Heinz-J. "Vor-Bilder aus dem Chaos Welt: Gerd Richters, 'Atlas der Fotos, Collagen und Skizzen,' im Museum Haus Lange." *Rheinische Post* (Krefeld) (February 7, 1976).

Winter, Peter. "Gerhard Richter: Kunsthalle Bremen (30.11.75–18.1.76), Palais des Beaux-Arts, Brüssel (Februar 76)." *Das Kunstwerk* 29 (January 1976): 62–63.

———. "Bremen Kunsthalle Ausstellung: Gerhard Richter: Bilder aus den Jahren 1962–1974, 30. November 1975 bis 18. Januar 1976." *Pantheon* 34 (April, May, June 1976): 141–142.

1977

Murken, Axel Hinrich. "Auf der Suche nach der Wirklichkeit: Das Menschenbildnis im künstlerischen Werk von Gerhard Richter." *Die Kunst und das schöne Heim* 89 (1977): 29–32.

1978

Danoff, I. Michael. "Gerhard Richter: Multiple Styles." *Arts Magazine* 52 (June 1978): 150–151.

Welish, Marjorie. "Gerhard Richter at Sperone Westwater Fischer." *Art in America* 66 (May–June 1978): 116.

1979

Cooper, Emmanuel. "Hamish Fulton–Gerhard Richter." *Art and Artists* 14 (May 1979): 50.

Gilmour, Pat. "Gerhard Richter and Hamish Fulton." *Arts Review* (April 1979): 186.

Pohlen, Annelie. "Gerhard Richter." *Heute Kunst* 24 (January–February 1979): 6–7.

———. "Neues vom InK." *Heute Kunst* 24 (January–February 1979): 8.

1980

Lawson, Thomas. "Gerhard Richter: Sperone, Westwater, Fischer." *Flash Art* 96–97 (March–April 1980): 18.

Pohlen, Annelie. "Gerhard Richter: 'Zwei gelbe Striche,' Museum Folkwang, Essen, 8.6.–3.8." *Kunstforum International* 40 (1980): 161.

1981

Friedrichs, Yvonne. "Georg Baselitz/Gerhard Richter: Kunsthalle

Düsseldorf (3.5–5.7.81)." *Das Kunstwerk* 34 (1981): 80–81.

1982

Heybrock, Christel. "Farbe, ein Abenteuer als Selbstzweck? 'Abstrakte Bilder' 1976 bis 1981 von Gerhard Richter im Mannheimer Kunstverein." *Mannheimer Morgen* (April 22, 1982).

Winter, Peter. "Streicheleinheiten für die Leinwand. Bilder von Gerhard Richter." *Frankfurter Allgemeine Zeitung* 34 (February 10, 1982).

———. "Gerhard Richter: Abstrakte Bilder 1976–1981." *Das Kunstwerk* 35 (April 1982): 64–65.

1983

Linker, Kate. "Gerhard Richter: Sperone Westwater Fischer." *Artforum* (April 1983): 71–72.

Pickshaus, Peter Moritz. "Van Abbe en miniature, Kunst auf dem platten Land: Das Kabinett für aktuelle Kunst in Bremerhaven." *Kunstforum International* 58 (February 1983): 144–153.

1984

Zacharapoulos, Denys. "Gerhard Richter, Musée d'Art et d'Industrie." *Artforum* (Summer 1984): 101.

1985

Derfner, Phyllis. "Gerhard Richter at Marian Goodman and Sperone Westwater." *Art in America* (September 1985): 138.

Dienst, Rolf-Günter. "Der künstliche Dschungel: Die neuen Aquarelle von Gerhard Richter in der Staatsgalerie in Stuttgart." *Frankfurter Allgemeine Zeitung* (February 13, 1985).

Indiana, Gary. "Living with Contradictions." *Village Voice* (March 26, 1985).

Meinhardt, Johannes. "Gerhard Richter: 77 Aquarelle, Staatsgalerie Stuttgart Graphische Sammlung, 19.1.–17.2.1985." *Kunstforum International* 77–78 (January–February 1985): 351–352.

1986

Beaucamp, Eduard. "Der virtuose Zweifler: Gerhard Richters verschlungene Wege. Zur Düsseldorfer Ausstellung." *Frankfurter Allgemeine Zeitung* (January 23, 1986).

Glozer, László. "Doppelspiel der Bildwelt: Retrospektive in der Kunsthalle Düsseldorf." *Süddeutsche Zeitung* (February 8–9, 1986).

Haase, Amine. "Totenlieder auf die Malerei: Illusion als Wunsch und als Widerstand." *Kölner Stadt-Anzeiger* (January 22, 1986).

Hohmeyer, Jürgen. "Einfach ein Bild: Expedition an die Grenzen der Malerei: In Düsseldorf wird das Werk Gerhard Richters im Überblick gezeigt." *Der Spiegel* 4 (January 1986): 160–165.

Hollenstein, Roman. " 'Ich mag das Unbestimmbare': Gerhard Richter in der Kunsthalle Bern." *Neue Zürcher Zeitung* (June 28, 1986).

Honnef-Harling, Gabriele. "Gerhard Richter: Bilder 1962–1985, Städtische Kunsthalle Düsseldorf und Kunstverein für die Rheinlande und Westfalen, 18.1.–23.2.1986; Kunsthalle Bern, 13.6.–20.7.1986; Museum moderner Kunst/ Museum des 20. Jahrhunderts Wien, 1.8.–21.9.1986." *Kunstforum International* 83 (March, April, May 1986): 232–235.

Müller, Hans-Joachim. "Der Zweifler und der Malerfürst: Gerhard Richter in Düsseldorf, Markus Lüpertz in München." *Die Zeit* (February 14, 1986).

Ohff, Heinz. "Proteus als Maler: Retrospektive Gerhard Richter in der Nationalgalerie." *Der Tagesspiegel* (April 25, 1986).

Soutif, Daniel. "Cherchez le Richter." *Libération* (Paris) (March 22–23, 1986).

Zimmermann, Marie-Louise. "Kunst ist ein Vorwand für das, was man nicht sagen kann." *Berner Zeitung* (June 12, 1986).

1987

Smith, Roberta. "Flirting with All Styles but Embracing None." *The New York Times* (August 23, 1987).

1988

Allen, Jane Addams. "Enigmatic Gerhard Richter: Trapped in a prison of mirrors." *Washington Times* (December 19, 1988).

Artner, Alan G. "Richter's scale: Values may change, but his questions remain." *Chicago Tribune* (September 25, 1988).

Kimmelman, Michael. "Style as Contradiction of Style." *New York Times* (December 17, 1988).

Laing, Carol. "Gerhard Richter: Art Gallery of Ontario, Toronto, April 29–July 10." *Parachute* 53 (December, January, February 1988–89): 39–41.

1989

Dreher, Thomas. "Gerhard Richter: Atlas of the Photographs, Collages, Sketches." *Das Kunstwerk* (December 1989): 105–106.

Hegewisch, Katharina. "Im Dschungel der Bilder: Gerhard Richter im Münchener Lenbachhaus." *Frankfurter Allgemeine Zeitung* (September 7, 1989).

Hübl, Michael. "The 'Melancholist of Virtuosity.'" *Art News* (February 1989): 120–125.

Wilson, William. "Gerhard Richter's Hat Trick." *Los Angeles Times* (March 26, 1989).

1990

Decter, Joshua. "Gerhard Richter." *Contemporanea* (Summer 1990): 119.

Kuspit, Donald. "All Our Yesterdays." *Artforum* 8 (April 1990): 129–132.

Schjeldahl, Peter. "Gerhard Richter." *7 days* (New York) (April 4, 1990).

1991

Cork, Richard. "Mounting Tension in Blurred Visions." *The Times* (London) (November 1, 1991): 14.

Jennings, Rose. "The Godfather, Parts One and Two." *New Statesman and Society* (November 8, 1991): 29.

Joyce, Conor. "Gerhard Richter." *Art Monthly* (December 1991/January 1992): 3, 5.

Lamarre, André. "Gerhard Richter: Musée des beaux-arts de Montréal, 11 mai–1er juillet." *Parachute* 61 (January, February, March 1991): 52–53.

Lebovici, Elisabeth. "Gerhard Richter, une peinture pas très nette." *Libération* (Paris) (November 13, 1991): 43.

Schjeldahl, Peter. "Past Perfect." *The Village Voice* (January 16, 1991).

Williams, Joseph. "Radical Change in the Richter Scale." *The Sunday Times* (October 27, 1991).

Ziegler, Ulf Erdmann. "Meisterschaft und ihre Verhöhnung: Der Maler

Gerhard Richter in der Tate Gallery." *Die Tageszeitung* (December 16, 1991).

1992

Beaucamp, Eduard. "Maler des Zweifels." *Frankfurter Allgemeine Zeitung* (February 8–9, 1992).

1993

von Drathen, Doris. "Gerhard Richter: Retrospektive." *Kunstforum* 124 (November–December 1993): 425–427.

Feeser, Sigrid. "Der Maler als unsicherer Kantonist: Grosse Retrospektive auf das Werk von Gerhard Richter in der Bundeskunsthalle Bonn." *Rheinpfalz* (Ludwigshafen) (December 21, 1993).

von Flemming, Viktoria. "Was vermag die Malerei? Gerhard Richters Suche nach Möglichkeiten—jetzt in der Bonner Retrospektive." *Frankfurter Rundschau* (December 24, 1993).

Jager, Hans den Hartog. "Ingewortelde twijfel." *HP/De Tijd* (December 17, 1993).

Königer, Maribel. "'Stil ist Gewalttat': Gerhard Richter—Retrospektive in Paris und Bonn." *Neue bildende Kunst. Zeitschrift für Kunst und Kritik* (June 1993): 4–7.

Spies, Werner. "Emotional und eisig: In der Hölle der Berührungsängste: Gerhard Richter im Modernen Museum der Stadt Paris." *Frankfurter Allgemeine Zeitung* 244 (October 20, 1993).

Zevi, Adachiara. "Grandi Mostre Gerhard Richter al Musée d'art moderne de la Ville di Parigi: Il pittore ha perso l'etichetta, Figurativo, astratto, pop: Alla fine, quasi fotografico." *Corriere della Sera* (November 7, 1993): 25.

1994

Criqui, Jean-Pierre. "Blindness in Hindsight: Gerhard Richter at the Musée d'Art Moderne de la Ville de Paris." *Artforum* (January 1994): 98–99.

Kozloff, Max. "Gerhard Richter: He Who Misleads." *Art in America* 8 (September 1994): 98–104, 133.

Prange, Regine. "Das ironische Gesamtkunstwerk: Zur Richter-Retrospektive in der Kunst- und Ausstellungshalle der Bundesre-

publik Deutschland, Bonn, 10. Dezember 1993–13. Februar 1994." *Kunstchronik* 47 (September 1994): 563–579.

Rimanelli, David. "Pas de trois: Gerhard Richter at Marian Goodman Gallery, New York." *Artforum* (January 1994): 99–100.

Risaliti, Sergio. "Gerhard Richter." *Flash Art* (February 1, 1994): 50.

Schmitz, Rudolf. "Gerhard Richter." *Frankfurter Allgemeine Zeitung Magazin* (January 7, 1994).

1995

Butin, Hubertus. "Gerhard Richter: Zwei Kerzen für Dresden (Two Candles for Dresden)." *Camera Austria International* 50 (1995): 4–8.

Schjeldahl, Peter. "Images Count." *Village Voice* (May 23, 1995).

Smith, Roberta. "A German Master Takes an Epic Journey." *New York Times* (June 4, 1995).

Spies, Werner. "Lachende Leere: Volltreffer des Zeitgeists: Gerhard Richter in Jerusalem." *Frankfurter Allgemeine Zeitung* (October 9, 1995).

von Drathen, Doris. "Gerhard Richter—An die Macht der Bilder glauben." *Kunstforum International* 131 (August–October 1995): 247–264.

1996

Chervel, Thierry. "Wie die Schönheit möglich ist." *Basler Zeitung* (August 20, 1996).

Dietrich, Dorothea. "Gerhard Richter's 'Atlas': One-Man Show in a Shipping Crate." *Print Collectors' Newsletter* 26 (January–February 1996): 204–209.

Haxthausen, Charles W. "New York, Gerhard Richter." *Burlington Magazine* (January 1996): 56–57.

Reeve, Charles. "Gerhard Richter: Dia Center for the Arts, New York, April 27–February 15." *Parachute* 83 (July, August, September 1996): 57–58.

1998

Bätschmann, Oskar. "Gemalte Irritationen: Gerhard Richters Prinzip der Unschärfe." *Neue Zürcher Zeitung* 265 (November 14–15, 1998): 65.

Dittmar, Peter. "Die Angst vor dem Schönen: Was soll uns die Natur,

was soll sie der modernen Kunst? Gerhard Richters, 'Landschaften.'" *Die Welt* (October 6, 1998).

Gross, Roland. "Alles ist eins, zwischen Abstraktion und Romantik: Gerhard Richters 'Landschaften,' im Sprengel-Museum Hannover." *Berliner Morgenpost* (October 7, 1998).

Kipphoff, Petra. "Vom Nutzen der verlogenen Bilder: Das Sprengel Museum in Hannover zeigt Landschaften von Gerhard Richter." *Die Zeit* (October 22, 1998).

Wagner, Thomas. "Caspar David Friedrich in Hubbelrath: Gerhard Richter nimmt die Romantik auf, das Sprengel-Museum zeigt die, 'Landschaften.'" *Frankfurter Allgemeine Zeitung* (October 27, 1998).

Ziegler, Ulf Erdmann. "Mit dem Grusel der Ähnlichkeit." *Die Tageszeitung* (October 17–18, 1998).

1999

Andersen, Jeannette. "Atlas—ein personlig Historie." *Kunst* 2 (1999): 62–63.

Diehl, Ute. "Rette sich, wer malt: Nun staunen die Italiener: Gerhard Richter in Prato." *Frankfurter Allgemeine Zeitung* (November 11, 1999).

2000

Meister, Helga. "Gerhard Richter—Zeichnungen, Aquarelle, neue Bilder." *Kunstforum International* 151 (July–September 2000): 342–345.

2001

Koldehoff, Stefan. "Gerhard Richter: Bilder im Farbrausch." *Art* 7 (July 2001): 58–63.

VI. Radio, Television, and Film

RADIO BROADCASTS

Grüterich, Marlis. "Fünf Europäer. Geschichte von heute und morgen, Versuch einer Kunstgeschichte der Gegenwart." Stuttgart: SWR (March 5, 1979): 52 min.

Pehnt, Wolfgang. *Kunst und Künstler: Unterhaltungen mit documenta-Teilnehmern,* "Wolfgang

Pehnt im Gespräch mit dem Maler
Gerhard Richter." Cologne: DRK
(July 4, 1982): 27 min.

Vielhaber, Christiane. "Gespräch mit
dem Maler Gerhard Richter
anlässlich einer Richter Retrospektive in Düsseldorf." Cologne:
WDR (February 1, 1986): 11 min.

Ganz, Rudolph. "Gespräch mit dem
Düsseldorfer Maler Gerhard
Richter anlässlich der Retrospek-
tive seines Schaffens in der
Berliner Nationalgalerie." Berlin:
SFB (April 24, 1986): 13 min.

Wagener, Sybill. *Texte und Zeichen,*
"Kein Programm, kein Stil, kein
Anliegen." Hannover: NDR
(August 16, 1989): 9 min.

TELEVISION PROGRAMS AND
FILMS

Hügler, Elmar. "Kunst und Ketchup.
Ein Bericht über Pop-Art und
Happening." Stuttgart: SDR
(February 14, 1966): 45 min.

Richter, Gerhard. *Volker Bradke.*
1966. B/W 16mm film. 15 min.

Langer, Detlef. *"Hierzulande–
Heutzutage: Almanach der
Woche,* "Retrospektive des Malers
Gerhard Richter im Kunstzentrum,
'Gegenverkehr,' in Aachen."
Cologne: WDR (April 1, 1969):
4 min.

Karalus, Paul. *Spectrum: Ein Maga-*
zin aus Kunst und Wissenschaft,
"Porträt Gerhard Richter." Cologne:
WDR (October 18, 1969): 8 min.

Koch, Dieter. *Titel, Thesen, Tempera-*
mente, "Gerhard Richter." Frankfurt: HR (March 10, 1972): 7 min.

Neufert, Detlef F. *Hierzulande–
Heutzutage: Almanach der
Woche,* "Ausstellung Gerhard
Richter." Cologne: WDR (February
10, 1976): 5 hr. 33 min.

Hepper, Heiner. *Aktuelle Stunde:
Blickpunkt Düsseldorf,* "Ausstellung Kunsthalle Düsseldorf."
Cologne: WDR (January 17,
1986): 6 min.

Smerling, Walter. *Dreizehn mal
documenta,* "Tendenzen der
Malerei." Vienna: ORF (June 21,
1987): 11 min.

von Flemming, Viktoria. *Kultur
aktuell,* "Gerhard Richter: Todes-
Bilder über Stammheim." Hannover: NDR (April 12, 1989):
10 min.

————. "Meine Bilder sind klüger
als ich." [First version] Hannover:
NDR (June 9, 1987): 59 min. [Sec-
ond version, 1992.] Dist. as Vikto-
ria von Flemming, *Gerhard
Richter: meine Bilder sind klüger
als ich/ein Film von Viktoria von
Flemming.* Video, 55 min.
Cologne: DuMont creativ/
DuMont-Video/Editionen der
Avantgarde, 1993.

EXHIBITION HISTORY

COMPILED BY ELIZABETH GRADY

This listing of exhibitions is organized in two sections: I. One-Person Exhibitions and II. Group Exhibitions. Within each section, exhibitions are listed chronologically and then alphabetically by city. An asterisk at the end of an entry indicates that a catalogue accompanied the exhibition. The entries give city, institution or gallery, name of exhibition, and exhibition dates where available.

I. One-Person Exhibitions

1964

Berlin, Galerie René Block, *Gerd Richter: Bilder des Kapitalistischen Realismus*, November 17, 1964–January 5, 1965. *

Düsseldorf, Galerie Schmela, *Gerhard Richter*, September 9–30.

Munich, Galerie Friedrich und Dahlem, *Gerhard Richter: foto-bilder, Porträts und Familien*.

1966

Berlin, Galerie René Block, *Gerhard Richter*, December 9, 1966–January 21, 1967.

Düsseldorf, Galerie Schmela, *Hommage an Schmela*, series of seven events that took place December 9–15. Richter participated on December 11 and 13.

Munich, Galerie Friedrich und Dahlem, *Farbtafeln*, October 11–27.

Rome, Galleria la Tartaruga, *Gerd Richter*, January 20.

Venice, Galleria del Leone, *Richter*. *

Zürich, City-Galerie Bruno Bischofberger, *Gerhard Richter*, March 30–April 16.

1967

Antwerp, Wide White Space, *Gerhard Richter*, October 13–November 14.

Munich, Galerie Heiner Friedrich, *Neue Bilder*, May 23–June 24.

Recklinghausen, Kunsthalle Recklinghausen, *Kunstpreis Junger Westen 67*, January 28–March 12. *

1968

Cologne, Galerie Rudolf Zwirner, *Gerhard Richter*, opened July 11.

Kassel, Galerie Rolf Ricke, *Gerhard Richter*, March 2–March 30.

1969

Aachen, Gegenverkehr, Zentrum fur aktuelle Kunst, *Gerhard Richter*, March 27–April 22. *

Berlin, Galerie René Block, *Gerhard Richter: Städte*, January 17–February 5.

Milan, Galleria del Naviglio, *Gerhard Richter*, March.

1970

Düsseldorf, Galerie Konrad Fischer, *Gerhard Richter*, April 11–May 7.

Essen, Museum Folkwang, *Gerhard Richter: Graphik 1965–1970*, October 15–31. *

Munich, Galerie Heiner Friedrich, *Gerhard Richter*, May 15–30.

1971

Bremerhaven, Kabinett für aktuelle Kunst, *180 Farben*, October 9–November 7.

Cologne, Galerie Thomas Borgmann, *Grafik von 1965–71*, closed August 28.

Düsseldorf, Kunstverein für die Rheinlande und Westfalen, *Arbeiten 1962–1971*, June 22–August 22. *

Naples, Galleria Lucio Amelio.

1972

Amsterdam, Suermondt-Museum, *Gerhard Richter*, October–November 19.

Cologne, Galerie Rudolf Zwirner, *48 Portraits*, opened December 12.

Düsseldorf, Galerie Konrad Fischer, *Gerhard Richter*, December.

Munich, Galerie Heiner Friedrich, *Gerhard Richter: Bilder nach Polaroids von Brigid Polk*, April 20–May 6.

Utrecht, Museum voor Hedendaagse Kunst, *Gerhard Richter: Atlas van de foto's en schetsen*, December 1–30. *

1973

Amsterdam, Galerie Seriaal, *Rot-Blau-Gelb (GR 338)*, September 8–27.

Bremerhaven, Kunsthalle Bremerhaven, *Gerhard Richter: Atlas der Fotos und Skizzen*, June 24–July 22.

Bremerhaven, Kabinett für aktuelle Kunst, *Parkstück*, June 24–July 22.

Hannover, Galerie Ernst, *Gerhard Richter: Neue Bilder*, August 24 September 29.

Lucerne, Kunstmuseum Luzern, *Gerhard Richter*, January 21–February 25.

Milan, Galleria la Bertesca, *Gerhard Richter: Verkündigung, nach Tizian*, opened December 5. *

Milan, Galleria del Naviglio, *Richter*, March.

Munich, Galerie Heiner Friedrich, *Gerhard Richter: Atlas, Entwürfe, Fotografien, Skizzen, 295 Blätter von 1962–1973*, opened April 4.

Munich, Städtische Galerie im Lenbachhaus, *Gerhard Richter*, May 23–July 1. *

Naples, Modern Art Agency, *Stadtbilder 1968*, opened January 4.

New York, Reinhard Onnasch Gallery, *Gerhard Richter*, September 15–November 15.

1974

Berlin, Galerie René Block, *Vier Bilder von 1973*, February 9–March 15.

Cologne, Galerie Wilbrand, *Gerhard Richter*.

Cologne, Galerie Rudolf Zwirner, *Farbtafeln*, July 5–August 30.

Leverkusen, Studio Schloss Morsbroich, *Gerhard Richter*. April 1–28. *

Mönchengladbach, Städtisches Museum Abteiberg, *Gerhard Richter*, December 4, 1974–January 12, 1975. *

1975

Basel, Galerie Rolf Preisig, *4 graue Bilder von Gerhard Richter*, May 13–July 7.

Braunschweig, Kunstverein Braunschweig, *Gerhard Richter: Graue Bilder*, February–March. *

Bremen, Kunsthalle Bremen, *Gerhard Richter: Bilder aus den Jahren 1962–1974*, November 30, 1975–January 18, 1976. Traveled to Palais des Beaux-Arts, Brussels, as *Tableaux 1962–1975*, February. *

Bremerhaven, Kabinett für aktuelle Kunst, *Zwei Seestücke 1975*, November 29, 1975–January 4, 1976.

Düsseldorf, Galerie Konrad Fischer, *Gerhard Richter*, September 27–October 21.

Milan, Galleria la Bertesca, *Gerhard Richter*, opened December 9, 1975.

1976

Florence, Galleria Renzo Spagnoli, *Gerhard Richter*, January–February. Traveled to Galleria la Bertesca, Genoa, opened February 26. *

Krefeld, Museum Haus Lange, *Gerhard Richter: Atlas der Fotos, Collagen und Skizzen*, February 8–March 14. *

Munich, Galerie Heiner Friedrich, *Atlas: Entwürfe, Fotografien, Skizzen. 295 Blätter von 1962–1973*.

Naples, Galleria Lucio Amelio, *Il turista: 4 Quadri di Gerhard Richter*, May–June.

Paris, Liliane & Michel Durand-Dessert, *Gerhard Richter*, February 17–March 13.

1977

Düsseldorf, Galerie Konrad Fischer, October 22–November 22.

Paris, Galerie expérimentale, Centre national d'art et de culture Georges Pompidou, *Gerhard Richter*, February 1–March 21. *

1978

Eindhoven, Stedelijk Van Abbe-museum, *Bilder/Schilderijen*, October 8–November 5, 1978. Traveled as *Abstract Paintings* to Whitechapel Art Gallery, London, March 14–April 22, 1979. *

Halifax, Nova Scotia College of Art and Design, Gallery Anna Leonowens, *Gerhard Richter: 17 Pictures*, July 4–18.

Halifax, Nova Scotia College of Art and Design, *Gerhard Richter: 128 Photographs of a Painting (Halifax, August 1978)*, August 21–September 9.

Milan, Galleria Massimo Valsecchi, *Opere da 1966–1972.*

New York, Sperone Westwater Fischer, *New Paintings*, January 14–February 11.

Nottingham, Midland Group, *48 Portraits*, September 22–October 31. *

1979

Friedrichshafen, Galerie Bernd Lutze, *Gerhard Richter: Bilder und Druckgraphik, 1962–1978*, part 1, March 16–May 5; part 2, May 9–June 23.

Isernhagen, Galerie Isernhagen.

1980

Eindhoven, Stedelijk Van Abbe-museum, *Gerhard Richter: Zwei gelbe Striche*, September 12–October 5. Traveled to Museum Folkwang, Essen, June 8–August 3. *

New York, Sperone Westwater Fischer, *Gerhard Richter*, February 2–March 1.

Rome, Galleria Pieroni, *Gerhard Richter*, March 28–April 30. *

1981

Munich, Galerie Fred Jahn, *Aquarelle und Zeichnungen*, January 7–31.

1982

Bielefeld, Kunsthalle Bielefeld, *Gerhard Richter: Abstrakte Bilder 1976 bis 1981,"* January 10–February 21. Traveled to Mannheimer Kunstverein, Mannheim, April 18–May 16. *

Hamburg, Raum für Kunst, *Gerhard Richter*, February 15–April 2.

Krefeld, *Halifax: 128 Details of a Picture (Halifax 1978)*, August 24–September 9.

Milan, Padiglione d'Arte Contempor-aneo (PAC), *Gerhard Richter*, January 13–February 21. *

Munich, Galerie Fred Jahn, *Abstrakte Bilder 1976–1981*, June 3–26. *

Stuttgart, Max-Ulrich Hetzler GmbH, *Gerhard Richter: Neue Bilder*, November 5–December 12.

Zurich, Galerie Konrad Fischer, *Gerhard Richter*, October 9–November 6.

1983

Chicago, Marianne Deson Gallery, *Gerhard Richter*, May 18–June 18.

Düsseldorf, Galerie Konrad Fischer, *Gerhard Richter*, opened July 1.

Naples, Lucio Amelio Foundation for Contemporary Art, *Gerhard Richter*, opened March 12.

New York, Sperone Westwater, *Gerhard Richter*, January 8–29.

1984

Cologne, Galerie Thomas Borgmann, *Aquarelle und Zeichnungen*, January 14–March 2.

Cologne, Galerie Wilkens und Jacobs, *Gerhard Richter, Farbfelder*, October 26, 1984–January 1985.

Munich, Städtische Galerie im Lenbachhaus, *Gerhard Richter: Zwei Skulpturen für einen Raum von Palermo, 1971*, opened May 15.

Paris, Galerie Liliane & Michel Durand-Dessert, *Gerhard Richter*, February 25–March 31.

St. Etienne, Musée d'Art et d'Industrie. *

Stuttgart, Galerie Tilly Haderek, *Gerhard Richter: 40 Fingermalereien aus 1971*, October 24–November 30.

1985

Athens, Galerie Jean Bernier, *Gerhard Richter*, April 25–May 25.

Friedrichshafen, Galerie Bernd Lutze, *Gerhard Richter: Abstrakte Bilder 1978–1984*, December 7, 1985–January 4, 1986.

New York, Marian Goodman/Sperone Westwater, *Gerhard Richter*, March 5–26.

Stuttgart, Staatsgalerie Stuttgart, Graphische Sammlung, *Aquarelle*, January 19–February 17, 1985.

1986

Berlin, Galerie Michael Haas, *Gerhard Richter*, April 26–May 31.

Düsseldorf, Städtische Kunsthalle und Kunstverein für die Rheinlande und Westfalen, *Bilder 1962–1985*, January 18–March 23. Traveled to the Nationalgalerie, Berlin, April 25–June 1; Kunsthalle Bern, June 14–July 20; Museum moderner Kunst/Museum des 20. Jahrhunderts, Vienna, August 1–September 21. *

New York, Barbara Gladstone Gallery, *Selected Early Works*, December 13, 1986–January 17, 1987. *

1987

Amsterdam, Museum Overholland, *Gerhard Richter: Werken op papier 1983–1986*, February 20–April 20. *

Cologne, Galerie Rudolf Zwirner, *Gerhard Richter: 20 Bilder*, October 3–November 10. *

Hartford, Wadsworth Atheneum, *Gerhard Richter/Matrix 95*, July 2–September 6, 1987. *

London, Karsten Schubert Gallery, *Works on Paper*, July 11–August 30.

New York, Marian Goodman Gallery/Sperone Westwater Gallery, *Gerhard Richter: Paintings*, March 5–April 4. *

1988

Friedrichshafen, Galerie Bernd Lutze, *Gerhard Richter 1968–1988*, September 9–November 5.

Goslar, Mönchehaus-Museum für moderne Kunst, *Gerhard Richter: Goslarer Kaiserringträger 1988, Bilder aus zwei Jahrzehnten*, September 24–December 11.

London, Anthony d'Offay Gallery, *Gerhard Richter: The London Paintings*, March 11–April 16. *

Munich, Galerie Fred Jahn, *Gerhard Richter: Neun Bilder, 1982–1987*, January 7–January 30. *

New York, David Nolan Gallery, *Gerhard Richter: Multiples and Complete Prints*, June 2–30.

Paris, Durand-Dessert, *Gerhard Richter*, March 19–April 23. *

Toronto, Art Gallery of Ontario, *Gerhard Richter: Paintings*, April 29–July 10. Traveled to Museum of Contemporary Art, Chicago, September 17–November 27; Hirshhorn Museum and Sculpture Garden, Washington, D.C., December 14, 1988–February 12, 1989; San Francisco Museum of Modern Art, March 15–May 28, 1989. *

Toronto, Evelyn Aimis Fine Art, *Gerhard Richter*, May 14–31.

1989

Athens, Galerie Jean Bernier, *Gerhard Richter*, May 11–June 3.

Frankfurt, Portikus, *Drei Bilder*, December 12–19.

Kansas City, Nelson-Atkins Museum of Art, *Gerhard Richter*, September 1–October 22. *

Krefeld, Museum Haus Esters, *18. Oktober 1977*, February 12–April 9. Traveled to Portikus, Frankfurt, April 29–June 11. *

London, Institute of Contemporary Arts, *18. Oktober 1977*, August 23–October 1. *

Munich, Galerie Fred Jahn, *Gerhard Richter: Monotypien, Öl auf Papier*, September 1–12.

Munich, Städtische Galerie im Lenbachhaus, *Atlas der Fotos, Collagen und Skizzen*, August 2–October 22. Traveled to Museum Ludwig, Cologne, February 13–April 16. *

New York, David Nolan Gallery, *Gerhard Richter: Works on Paper*, November 29, 1989–January 13, 1990.

Rotterdam, Museum Boijmans Van Beuningen, *Gerhard Richter, 1988/89*, October 15–December 3. *

1990

St. Louis Art Museum, *Gerhard Richter: 18. Oktober 1977*, January 6–February 4. Traveled to Grey Art Gallery and Study Center, New York, March 5–April 21; Musée des Beaux-Arts de Montréal, May 11–June 24; Lannan Foundation, Los Angeles, July 1–August 12; Institute of Contemporary Art, Boston, January 18–March 18, 1991.

New York, Marian Goodman Gallery, *Paintings*, February 2–24.

New York, Sperone Westwater Gallery, February 3–24.

1991

Dublin, Douglas Hyde Gallery.

Frankfurt, Galerie Achenbach.

Friedrichshafen, Galerie Bernd Lutze, *Gerhard Richter: Arbeiten auf Papier*, November 15, 1991–January 18, 1992.

London, Anthony d'Offay Gallery, *Painting, Sculpture, and Mirrors*, April 23–June 17. *

London, Tate Gallery, *Gerhard Richter*, October 30, 1991–

January 12, 1992. *

Munich, Galerie Jahn und Fusban, *Gerhard Richter: Foto-Edition ("2.5.89–7.5.89"), Aquarelle und Bilder*, April 4–27. Concurrently at Galerie Fred Jahn, Stuttgart, April 6–27.

Paris, Durand-Dessert, *Gerhard Richter*, September 7–October 12. *

1992

Frankfurt, Galerie Bernd Slutzky, *Gerhard Richter: Frühe Druckgrafik*, January 16–April 10. *

London, Goethe Institut, *Gerhard Richter: Works on Paper*, January 10–February 8.

New York, Nolan/Eckman Gallery, *Gerhard Richter: Watercolors, Photographs and Drawings*, December 1, 1992–January 16, 1993.

Rome, Zerynthia: Associazione per l'Arte Contemporanea, *Montagne: Gerhard Richter*, October 3–December 6. *

Sils-Maria/Engadin, Nietzsche-Haus, *Sils*. *

Vienna, Galerie nächst St. Stephan, *Gerhard Richter*, June 3–August 28.

1993

Berlin, Neuer Berliner Kunstverein, *Gerhard Richter, Ausschnitt: 20 Bilder von 1965–1991*, February 27–April 10. *

Bremen, Kunsthalle Bremen, *Gerhard Richter: Editionen 1965–1993*, October 24–November 21.

Mönchengladbach, Galerie Löhrl, *Editionen*, December 11, 1993–January 29, 1994.

Munich, Galerie Fred Jahn, *Gerhard Richter: Bilder und Arbeiten auf Papier*, November 23–December 18.

New York, Marian Goodman Gallery, *Gerhard Richter*, September 10–October 23. *

Paris, Musée d'Art Moderne de la Ville de Paris, *Gerhard Richter: Retrospective*, September 23–November 21. Traveled to Kunst und Ausstellungshalle der BRD, Bonn, December 10, 1993–February 13, 1994; Moderna Museet, Stockholm, March 12–May 8, 1994; Museo Nacional Centro de Arte Reina Sofía, Madrid, June 7–August 22, 1994. *

Quakenbrück, Stadtmuseum Quakenbrück, *Arbeiten auf Papier*, November 5–December 3. *

Tokyo, Wako Works of Art, *Gerhard Richter*, January 20–February 20.

Toronto, Art Gallery of Ontario, *Gerhard Richter: Helga Matura*, April 24–June 20. Prior venues: Rodman Hall Arts Centre, St. Catharines, September 11–October 4, 1992; Art Gallery of Windsor, November 28, 1992–January 17, 1993; Art Gallery of Algoma, Sault Ste. Marie, February 4–March 14, 1993. *

1994

Essen, Kunstverein Ruhr, *Gerhard Richter und die Romantik*, May 8–June 12. *

Friedrichshafen, Galerie Bernd Lutze, *Gerhard Richter: Grafik und Auflagenbilder*, January 22–March 12.

New York, David Zwirner Gallery, *Gerhard Richter Prints: 1966–1993*, January 27–March 5.

1995

Berlin, Haus am Waldsee, *Gerhard Richter: Editionen 1965–1993*, December 9, 1995–January 14, 1996. Traveled as *Editionen 1965–1995*, to Neuer Sächsischer Kunstverein e.V. at Kunsthalle im Seidler Art'otel, Dresden, March 16–27, 1996. (*1993)

Dresden, Neuer Sächsischer Kunstverein, *Zwei Kerzen*, February 11.

Jerusalem, Israel Museum, *Gerhard Richter*, September 19–December 30. *

London, Anthony d'Offay Gallery, *Gerhard Richter: Painting in the Nineties*, June 1–August 4. *

London, Anthony d'Offay Gallery, *Sculpture*, December 7, 1995–January 26, 1996.

New York, Dia Center for the Arts, *Atlas: 1964–1995*, April 27, 1995–February 25, 1996.

Zürich, Sammlung Hauser & Wirth, *Gerhard Richter Bilder 1964–1994*, October 28–December 23. *

1996

Bozen (Bolzano), Museion, Museum für moderne Kunst, *Gerhard Richter: Paintings*, June 7–August 25. *

New York, Luhring Augustine, *Selected Works 1963–1987*, November 4, 1995–January 13, 1996. *

New York, Marian Goodman

Gallery, *Two Sculptures for a Room by Palermo*, October 18–November 30.

Nîmes, Carré d'Art, Musée d'Art Contemporain de la Ville de Nîmes, *Gerhard Richter: 100 Bilder*, June 15–September 15. *

Tokyo, Wako Works of Art, *Gerhard Richter*, Part 1: April 6–May 4; Part 2: May 8–31. *

1997

Edinburgh, The FruitMarket Gallery, *Gerhard Richter*, August 2– September 27.

Krefeld, Kaiser Wilhelm Museum, *66 Zeichnungen Halifax*, May 11–June 29. *

Munich, Städtische Galerie im Lenbachhaus, *Gerhard Richter: Fuji*, March 4–9.

Tokyo, Wako Works of Art, *Gerhard Richter*, October 24–November 28. *

1998

Aachen, Neuer Aachener Kunstverein, *Gerhard Richter: Printing*, June 21–August 9.

Columbus, Ohio, Wexner Center of the Arts, *Gerhard Richter*, January 31–April 12.

Dachau, Neue Galerie, *Druckgraphik*, March 27–May 24.

Friedrichshafen, Galerie Bernd Lutze, *Gerhard Richter: Bilder 1972–1996*, May 16–August 1.

Hannover, Sprengel Museum, *Gerhard Richter: Landschaften*, October 4, 1998–January 3, 1999. *

London, Anthony d'Offay Gallery, *New Paintings*, September 11–October 22. *

Munich, Städtische Galerie im Lenbachhaus, *Gerhard Richter: Atlas der Fotos, Collagen und Skizzen*, December 16, 1998–March 14, 1999. *

New York, Nolan-Eckman Gallery, *Gerhard Richter: Watercolors, Photographs and Drawings*, December 3, 1998–January 30, 1999.

Winterthur, Kunstmuseum Winterthur, *Ein Saal und ein Kabinett für die Sammlung*, March 7–November 15. *

1999

Aachen-Kornelimünster, Ehemalige Reichsabtei, *Werke von Gerhard Richter aus Aachener Samm-*

lungen, November 14, 1999–January 9, 2000. *

Barcelona, Consorci del Museu d'Art Contemporani de Barcelona, *Atlas*, April 23–July 4.

Berlin, Altes Museum, Neue Nationalgalerie, and Hamburger Bahnhof, *Das XX. Jahrhundert: ein Jahrhundert Kunst in Deutschland*, September 4, 1999–January 9, 2000. *

Essen, Galerie 20.21, *Gerhard Richter*, March 23–May 19.

Leverkusen, Schloss Morsbroich, Städtisches Museum Leverkusen, *Gerhard Richter: Aquarelle, Zeichnungen und Editionen aus Eigenbesitz*, March 17–August 29.

London, Anthony d'Offay Gallery, *The Complete Editions*, September 9–November 4.

Munich, Galerie Fred Jahn, *Gerhard Richter 855/1–64: Schwarz, Rot, Gold, 64 Hinterglasbilder, je 21,1 x 29,7 cm*, May 18–22.

Oslo, Astrup Fearnley Museum of Moderne Kunst, *Gerhard Richter: Det umuliges kunst, Malerier 1964–1998/The Art of the Impossible, Paintings 1964–1998*, January 17–April 1. *

Paris, Galerie Saint-Séverin, *Gerhard Richter, Art, Culture et Foi*, March 10–April 2.

Prato, Centro per l'Arte Contemporanea Luigi Pecci, *Retrospektive*, October 9, 1999–January 30, 2000. *

Stuttgart, Galerie Franke, *Gerhard Richter: Farbige Arbeiten auf Papier, Editionen*, February 13–April 10.

Winterthur, Kunstmuseum Winterthur, *Gerhard Richter: Zeichnungen und Aquarelle, 1964–1999*, September 4–November 21. Traveled to Staatliche Kunstsammlungen Dresden, Kupferstich-Kabinett, January 15–March 19, 2000; Kaiser Wilhelm Museum, Krefeld, April 9–June 18, 2000; De Pont Foundation for Contemporary Art, Tilburg, July 1–October 8, 2000. *

2000

Amsterdam, Kabinett Overholland in the Stedelijk Museum, *Gerhard Richter: Werken op papier*, July 1–September 3.

Dallas, Dallas Museum of Art, *Gerhard Richter in Dallas Collections*, February 12–April 16.

Frankfurt, Galerie Bernd Slutzky, *Gerhard Richter: Ausgewählte Druckgrafik 1966–1988*, December 1, 2000–February 15, 2001. *

Munich, Galerie Fred Jahn, *Gerhard Richter: Übermalte Fotografien*, October 5–27.

Prato, Museo Pecci, *Gerhard Richter*, October 10, 1999–January 9, 2000. *

New York, The Museum of Modern Art, *Gerhard Richter: October 18, 1977*, September 28, 2000–January 30, 2001. *

New York, Galerie Zwirner and Wirth, *Gerhard Richter: Early Works*, February 23–April 22.

Stuttgart, Institut für Auslandsbeziehungen e.V., *Gerhard Richter: Übersicht*, September 22–November 5. Traveled to Reykjavík National-museum, Iceland, January 20–February 18, 2001; Arken Modernes Museum für Kunst, Ishø (bei Kopenhagen), April 7–May 27, 2001; Bangkok Art Centre, Silpakorn University, Bangkok, July 22–August 10, 2001; National Art Gallery, Kuala Lumpur, Malaysia, September 14–October 14, 2001. *

2001

Friedrichshafen, Kunstverein Friedrichshafen in the Zeppelin Museum, *Gerhard Richter: Malerei 1966–1997*. Concurrently, *Gerhard Richter: Auflagen-Bilder, Fotoarbeiten, Druckgrafik*, Kunstverein Fried-richshafen, March 11–May 20. *

Friedrichshafen, Galerie Bernd Lutze, *Gerhard Richter: Editionen 1969–1998*, March 11–May 19.

Mendrisio, Switzerland, Massimo Martino Fine Arts and Projects, *Onkel Rudi, Onkel Rudi…in One Painting, Two Glasses, One Edition, One Show*, May 30–October 31. *

New York, Marian Goodman Gallery, *Gerhard Richter*, September 14–October 27. *

Tokyo, Wako Works of Art, *Gerhard Richter: New Oil on Photographs*, January 13–February 28. *

II. Group Exhibitions

1962

Fulda, Galerie Junge Kunst, *Manfred Kuttner/Gerd Richter, Düsseldorf*, September 8–30. *

1963

Düsseldorf, Ladengalerie, Kaiser-strasse, *Demonstrative Exhibition: Kuttner, Lueg, Polke, Richter*, May 11–26. *

Düsseldorf, Möbelhaus Berges, *Gerhard Richter/Konrad Lueg: Leben mit Pop, eine Demonstration für den Kapitalistischen Realismus*, October 11.

1964

Berlin, Galerie René Block, *Neodada, Pop, Décollage, Kapitalistischer Realismus*, September 15–November 5. *

Berlin, Akademie der Künste, *Neue Realisten & Pop Art*, November 20, 1964–November 3, 1965. *

Munich, Galerie Friedrich und Dahlem, *Uwe Lausen, Natai Morosov, Gerd Richter*, October 19–November 20.

Wuppertal-Elberfeld, Collectors Rudolf and Anneliese Jährling, Moltkestrasse 67, *Vorgarten-ausstellung*, November 5.

Wuppertal, Galerie Parnass, *Neue Realisten: Konrad Lueg, Sigmar Polke, Gerhard Richter*, November 20, 1964–January 1965. *

1965

Berlin, Galerie René Block, *Hommage à Berlin*, September 27–November 13.

The Hague, Galerie Orez, *Kapital-istisch Realisme: Richter, Lueg, and Polke*, July 10–August 5.

Reinbek, Rowohlt-Verlag, *Phänomene und Realitäten*. Traveled to Hochschule der bildenden Künste, Hamburg.

1966

Frankfurt, Galerie Patio, *Konrad Lueg, Gerhard Richter: Die beste Ausstellung Deutschlands*, September 9–30.

Hannover, Galerie h, *Polke/Richter*, March 1–26. *

1967

Berlin, Haus am Waldsee, *Neuer Realismus: 16 deutsche Maler*, January 6–February 19. *

Berlin, Galerie René Block,

Hommage à Lidice: 20. Ausstellung der Galerie René Block, October 22– November 18. *

Cologne, Galerie Heiner Friedrich, *Demonstrative 1967*, Cologne Art Fair, September 13–17.

San Marino, *Biennale 6*, July 10–September 30.

1968

Cologne, Galerie Rolf Ricke, *Querschnitt*, November 27, 1968–January 7, 1969.

Karlsruhe, Badischer Kunstverein, *V. Biennale Paris: Die jungen Deutschen*, January 21–February 25.

1969

Berlin, Galerie René Block, *Blockade '69: 5 Jahre Galerie René Block Berlin*, March–December.

Hamburg, Galerie von Loeper, *Neue Landschaften*, December 2, 1969–January 10, 1970. *

Lucerne, Kunstmuseum, *Düssel-dorfer Szene*, June 15–July 13. *

New York, Solomon R. Guggenheim Museum, *Nine Young Artists: Theodoron Awards*, May 24–June 29.

1970

Berlin, Galerie René Block, *Zeichnungen: Beuys, Brouwn, Polke, Richter, Hödicke, Vostell*, November 1–30.

Brussels, Palais des Beaux-Arts, *Gerhard Richter, Blinky Palermo, Günther Uecker*, February 12–March 1. *

Cologne, Kunsthalle Köln, *Jetzt: Künste in Deutschland heute*, February 14–May 18.

Hannover, Galerie Ernst, *Palermo/Richter: Für Salvador Dalí*, October 10–November 6.

Munich, Münchener Stadtmuseum, *Malerei nach Fotografie: Von der Camera Obscura bis zum Pop Art, eine Dokumentation*, September 8–November 8. *

1971

Berlin, Galerie René Block, *Grafik des Kapitalistischen Realismus*, January.

Cologne, Galerie Heiner Friedrich, *Palermo und Gerhard Richter (Wandmalerei und Skulptur)*, April 21–May 15.

Düsseldorf, Städtische Kunsthalle, *Prospekt 71: Projection*, October 8–17.

Zürich, Annemarie Verna Galerie, *Richter, Polke, Palermo*, April 6–May 16.

1972

Düsseldorf, Städtische Kunsthalle, *Musée d'Art Moderne, Département des Aigles, Section des Figures (Der Adler vom Oligozän bis Heute)*, May 16–July 9. [Richter painting included in Marcel Broodthaers exhibition.]

Essen, Gruga Hall, *Szene Rhein-Ruhr '72*, July 9–September 3. *

Kassel, Documenta 5, *Befragung der Realität: Bildwelten heute*, June 30–October 8. *

London, Anthony d'Offay Gallery, *Richard Long, Gerhard Richter, Lawrence Weiner: New Work on Paper*, closed March 8.

Venice, Biennale 36, German Pavilion, June 30–October 8. *

1973

Düsseldorf, Städtische Kunsthalle, *Prospect 73: Maler, Painters, Peintres*, September 28–October 7. *

Hamburg, Galerie von Loeper, *Mappenwerke*, February 16–March 16.

London, Gallery House, *Some 260 Miles from Here: Art from the Rhein/Ruhr, Germany 1973*, May 1–20.

Munich, Galerie Dorothea Leonhart, *Aquarelle und Handzeichnungen*, January 2–March 31.

1974

Berlin, Haus am Waldsee, *Landschaft: Gegenpol oder Fluchtraum*, October 29, 1974–January 12, 1975. *

Cologne, Wallraf-Richartz Museum, *Projekt '74*, July 5–September 10. *

Leverkusen, Städtisches Museum Leverkusen, Schloss Morsbroich, *Landschaft: Gegenpol oder Fluchtraum?* September 27–November 10.

New York, René Block Gallery, Ltd., *First Exhibition: Joseph Beuys, K.P. Brehmer, Stanley Brouwn, K.H. Hödicke, Palermo, Sigmar Polke, Gerhard Richter, Reiner Ruthenbeck*, opened May 29.

1975

Amsterdam, Stedelijk Museum, *Fundamentale Schilderkunst*, April 26–June 22. *

1976

Genoa, Galleria la Bertesca, *Gerhard Richter*, April.

1977

Berlin, Galerie René Block, *Durch, mit und nach Photographie*, opened September 11.

Chicago, The Art Institute of Chicago, *Europe in the Seventies: Aspects of Recent Art*, October 8–November 27. Traveled to Hirshhorn Museum and Sculpture Garden, Smithsonian Institution, Washington, D.C., March 16–May 7, 1978; San Francisco Museum of Modern Art, June 23–August 6, 1978; Fort Worth Art Museum, September 24–October 29, 1978; Contemporary Arts Center, Cincinnati, December 1, 1978–January 31, 1979. *

Humlebaeck, Denmark, Louisiana Museum, *21 Deutsche Künstler*, April.

Düsseldorf, Galerie Art in Progress, *Medium Malerei*, June 3–July 16.

Kassel, Documenta 6, June 24–November 11.

Munich, Galerie Art in Progress, *Maler auf Papier, Teil I*, June 3–July 6.

1978

Berlin, Nationalgalerie, *Aspekte der 60er Jahre: Sammlung Reinhard Onnasch*, February 2–April 23. *

Düsseldorf, Galerie Art in Progress, *Realität der Farbe: Beispiele für Malerei der Gegenwart*, December 1978–January 1979.

Zürich, InK–Halle für Internationale Kunst, *Poetische Aufklärung in der europäischen Kunst der Gegenwart: Beuys, Merz, Kounellis, Richter, Broodthaers, Buren, Geschichte von heute und morgen*, November 27, 1978–January 15, 1979.

1979

Düsseldorf, Galerie Konrad Fischer, *Gerhard Richter*, October 2–23.

Krefeld, Museum Haus Lange, *Wahrnehmung, Aufzeichnungen, Mitteilungen: die Erweiterung des Wirklichkeitsbegriffs in der Kunst der sechziger und siebziger Jahre*, January 21–March 18. *

London, Whitechapel Art Gallery, *Hamish Fulton and Gerhard Richter*, March 14–April 22. Traveled to Stedelijk Van Abbemuseum, Eindhoven.

1980

Cologne, Kölnischer Kunstverein, *Monumente–Denkmal*, March 18–April 20; Karlsruhe, Badischer Kunstverein, July 22–September 14. *

London, Hayward Gallery, *Pier+Ocean: Construction in European and American Art of the 70s*, closed June 22. Traveled to Rijksmuseum Kröller-Müller, Otterlo, July 12–September 8.

1981

Cologne, Rheinhallen, *Westkunst: Zeitgenössische Kunst seit 1939*, May 30–August 16. *

Düsseldorf, Kunsthalle Düsseldorf, *Georg Baselitz/Gerhard Richter*, May 30–July 5. *

London, Royal Academy of Arts, *A New Spirit in Painting*, January 15–March 18. *

Paris, Musée d'Art Moderne de la Ville de Paris, *Art Allemagne Aujourd'hui*, January 16–March 8. *

Stuttgart, Christian Brügge Stiftung, *Neue Abstraktion*, December 15, 1981–January 20, 1982.

1982

Berlin, Haus am Waldsee, *Spiegelbilder: Arbeiten von 70 Künstlern*, September 10–October 24. *

Kassel, Documenta 7, June 19–September 29. *

Munich, Galerie Fred Jahn, *Deutsche Zeichnungen der 60er und 70er Jahre*, February 2–20.

New Haven, Yale University Art Gallery, *Contemporary German Drawings: German Drawings of the Sixties*, January 27–March 28. Traveled to Art Gallery of Ontario, Toronto, February 2, 1982–March 19, 1983. *

New York, Metro Pictures, *Painting*, January 9–30.

Rome, Mura Aureliane, *Avanguardia, Transavanguardia 68, 77*, April 4–July 4. Organized by the Cultural Office of Rome.

1983

Bremerhaven, Das Kabinett für aktuelle Kunst, *Gerhard Richter*, February.

New York, Solomon R. Guggenheim Museum, *Acquisition Priorities: Aspects of Postwar Painting in Europe*. *

Rome, Galleria Mario Pieroni, *Isa Genzken/ Gerhard Richter*. *

1984

Düsseldorf, Städtische Kunsthalle, *Aufbrüche, Manifeste, Manifestationen: Positionen in der bildenden Kunst zu Beginn der sechziger Jahre in Berlin, Düsseldorf und München/ Upheavals, Manifestoes, Manifestations: Conceptions in the Arts at the Beginning of the Sixties, Berlin, Düsseldorf, and Munich*, October 12–November 25. *

Düsseldorf, Messegelände Halle 13, *Von hier aus, 2 Monate neue deutsche Kunst*, September 29–December 2. *

Kassel, Kasseler Kunstverein, *Aquarelle*, November 16, 1984–January 6, 1985.

New York, The Museum of Modern Art, *An International Survey of Recent Painting and Sculpture*, May 17–August 19. *

1985

Amsterdam, RAI, *Kunst RAI*, June 5–9.

Berlin, Neue Nationalgalerie, *1945–1985: Kunst in der Bundesrepublik Deutschland*, September 27, 1985–February 9, 1986. *

Cologne, Galerie Dieter Wilbrand, *Zwanzig Jahre Galerie Wilbrand 1965–1985: Deutsche Kunst drei Generationen*, March 12–April 24.

London, Royal Academy of Arts, *German Art in the Twentieth Century: Painting and Sculpture 1905–1985*, October 11–December 22. *

Munich, Staatsgalerie moderner Kunst, Bayerische Staatsgemälde-sammlungen, *Deutsche Kunst seit 1960: Sammlung Prinz Franz von Bayern*, June 20–September 15.

Pittsburgh, Carnegie Museum of Art, *Carnegie International*, November 9, 1985–January 5, 1986. *

Toronto, Art Gallery of Ontario, *The European Iceberg: Creativity in Germany and Italy Today*, February 8–April 7.

Turin, Palazzo della Societa Promotrice delle Belle Arti, *Rheingold: 40 Künstler aus Köln und Düsseldorf (40 artisti da Colonia e Düsseldorf)*, May 25–June 30.*

Wiesbaden, Museum Wiesbaden, *Modus Vivendi: Elf Deutsche Maler 1960–1985, Beispiele einer Sammlung*, September 8–October 13. Traveled to Landes-museum Oldenburg Augusteum, Oldenburg, October 27–December 8. *

1986

Nürnberg, Galerie Ursula Ehrhardt, *Meister Graphik*, November 16–December 23.

Berlin, Neuer Berliner Galerie im Alten Museum, *Positionen: Malerei aus der Bundesrepublik Deutschland*, October 31–November 30. Traveled to Staatliche Kunstsammlungen im Albertinum, Dresden, December 10, 1986–January 12, 1987.

1987

Berlin, Haus am Waldsee, *Auf der Spur—Sammlung Stober*, September 12–November 1. *

Düsseldorf, Kunstmuseum Düsseldorf, *Brennpunkt Düsseldorf, 1962–1987*, May 24–September 6.

Hamburg, Galerie Harald Behm, *Wasserfarben*, May 27–June 27.

Kassel, Documenta 8, June 12–September 20.

1988

Kassel, Neue Galerie, *Gerhard Richter*, October 4–November 29.

Paris, Galerie Liliane & Michel Durand-Dessert, *Les Chants de Maldoror–Lautréamont*, October 14–December 6. *

St. Gallen, Kunstverein St. Gallen im Kunstmuseum, *Rot Gelb Blau: Die Primärfarben in der Kunst des 20. Jahrhunderts*, March 19–May 21. Traveled to Museum Fridericianum, Kassel, June 12–September 18. *

Toledo Museum of Art, *Refigured Painting: The German Image, 1960–1988*, October 30, 1988–January 8, 1989. Traveled to Solomon R. Guggenheim Museum, New York, February 10–April 23, 1989; Williams College Museum of Art, Williamstown, Mass., February 11–March 26, 1989; as *Deutsche*

Malerei 1960–1988, Kunstmuseum Düsseldorf, Düsseldorf, May–July, 1989; Schirn Kunsthalle, Frankfurt, September–November 1989.

1989

Cologne, Kölnischer Kunstverein, *Aus meiner Sicht,* November 12, 1989–January 1, 1990.

Cologne, Rheinhallen der Kölner Messe, *Bilderstreit: Widerspruch, Einheit und fragment in der Kunst seit 1960,* April 8–June 28.

Mönchengladbach, Galerie Schröder, *Nebeneinander,* May 7–July 31.

New Haven, Yale University Art Gallery, *German and Austrian Contemporary Art from the Bareiss Collection,* February 2–March 19. *

Rome, Galleria Mario Pieroni, *Sol LeWitt/ Gerhard Richter.*

1990

Dresden, Albertinum, *Ausgebürgert: Künstler aus der DDR und aus dem sowjetischen Sektor Berlins 1949–1989,* October 7–December 12. Traveled to Kleine Deichtorhalle, Hamburg, January 10–March 1, 1991. *

Düsseldorf, Kunsthalle Düsseldorf, *Um 1968: Konkrete Utopien in Kunst und Gesellschaft,* May 27–July 8. Traveled to Museum für Gestaltung, Zürich, September–November. *

Cologne, Galerie Ernesto + Krips, *Multiple Objekte,* November 16–December 22.

Paris, Galerie Liliane & Michel Durand-Dessert, *Gerhard Richter,* December 8, 1990–February 2, 1991.

1991

Düsseldorf, Bayerische Hypo-Bank, September.

Paris, Galerie Liliane & Michel Durand-Dessert, *Novel Espace,* June 8–July 20

Vienna, Galerie Metropol, *Das Bild nach dem letzten Bild,* May–June. Traveled to Museum het Kruithuis, Netherlands, November 1991 January 5, 1992. *

1992

Duisburg, Wilhelm Lehmbruck Museum, *U-Bahn-Kunst in Duisburg: Isa Genzken, Yael Niemeyer, Gerhard Richter, Manfred Vogel,* July 11–August 2.

Frankfurt, Galerie Bernd Slutzky, *Grafik des Kapitalistischen Realismus,* September 29–November 25. *

Kassel, Documenta 9, June 13–September 20. *

London, Anthony d'Offay Gallery, *Richard Long, Gerhard Richter, Lawrence Weiner, New Work on Paper,* closed March 8.

Minneapolis, Walker Art Center, *Photography in Contemporary German Art: 1960 to the Present,* February 9–May 31. Traveled to Dallas Museum of Art and Modern Art Museum of Fort Worth, August 16–October 11; Solomon R. Guggenheim Museum, SoHo, New York, February 10–May 9, 1993. *

New York, The Museum of Modern Art, *Allegories of Modernism: Contemporary Drawing,* February 12–May 12. *

Vienna, Galerie nächst St. Stephan, *Abstrakte Malerei zwischen Analyse und Synthese,* January 24–March 18. *

1993

Vienna, Galerie nächst St. Stephan Rosemarie Schwarzwälder, *Works on Paper for exhibition, "Abstrakte Malerei zwischen Analyse und Synthese,"* March 4–27.

1994

Berlin, Martin-Gropius-Bau, *Der Riss im Raum,* November 26, 1994–February 5, 1995. Traveled to Galeria Zacheta, Warsaw, March 13– April 18, 1995; Galerie der Hauptstadt Prag, September 19–November 19, 1995. *

Edinburgh, Royal Scottish Academy and The FruitMarket Gallery, *The Romantic Spirit in German Art 1790–1990,* July 28–September 7. Traveled to Hayward Gallery, South Bank Centre, London, September 29, 1994–January 8, 1995; Haus der Kunst, Munich, February 4–May 1, 1995. *

New York, Marian Goodman Gallery, *A Painting Show,* April 15–May 28.

1995

Cologne, Museum Ludwig, *Unser Jahrhundert: MenschenBilder, BilderWelten,* July 9–October 8. *

1996

Berlin, Haus am Waldsee, *Der Diskurs findet hier statt: 50 Jahre Haus am Waldsee,* October 26–December 1.

New York, The Museum of Modern Art, *Beuys and After: Contemporary German Drawings from the Collection,* February 1–May 14.

1997

Essen, Museum Folkwang, *Die Maler und ihre Skulpturen: Von Edgar Degas bis Gerhard Richter,* October 12, 1997–January 4, 1998. *

Kassel, Documenta 10, June 21–September 28. *

Venice, Biennale 47, June 15–November 9. *

Prague, Ceské muzeum výtvarných umení, *Pro Lidice: 52 umelcu z Nemecka/Pro Lidice: 52 Künstler aus Deutschland,* March 9–April 6. *

Vienna, Galerie nächst St. Stephan, *Color and Paper,* April 8–May 10.

Berlin, Martin-Gropius-Bau, *Deutschlandbilder: Kunst aus einem geteilten Land,* September 7, 1997–January 11, 1998. *

1998

Paris, Galerie Liliane & Michel Durand-Dessert, *Dessins,* November 28, 1998–January 30, 1999.

Aachen, Neuer Aachener Kunstverein, *Jahresgaben 1998,* August 22–September 27.

Des Moines, Des Moines Art Center, *Shifting Visions: O'Keeffe, Guston, Richter,* October 10, 1998–January 24, 1999.

1999

Berlin, Martin-Gropius-Bau, *Gesammelte Räume, gesammelte Träume: Kunst aus Deutschland von 1960 bis 2000,* November 20, 1999–February 6, 2000.

Berlin, Neue Nationalgalerie, *Das XX. Jahrhundert, ein Blick zurück: Fünfzig ausgewählte Erwerbungen,* September 4, 1999–January 9, 2000. *

2000

Winterthur, Kunstmuseum Winterthur, *Von Edgar Degas bis Gerhard Richter: Arbeiten auf Papier aus der Graphischen Sammlung des Kunstmuseums Winterthur,* August 25–November 19. Traveled to Nationalgalerie Prag, Palais Kinsky, December 15, 2000–March 25, 2001; Rupertinum, Museum für Moderne und Zeitgenössische Kunst, Salzburg, April 7–May 20, 2001; Westfälisches Landesmuseum für Kunst und Kulturgeschichte, Münster, June 3–August 26, 2001; Neues Museum, Staatliches Museum für Kunst und Design, Nürnberg, December 7, 2001–February 24, 2002. *

Berlin, Haus am Waldsee, *Artistenmetaphysik: Friedrich Nietzsche in der Kunst der Nachmoderne,* December 9, 2000–March 18, 2001. *

Victoria, British Columbia, The Art Gallery of Greater Victoria, *Slippage: Taras Polataiko, Gerhard Richter, Lucio Fontana,* November 24, 2000–February 11, 2001. *

2001

Essen, Galerie 20.21, *Joseph Marioni, Gerhard Richter: The Flatness of Painting,* February 17–May 4.

Venice, Biennale 49, June 10–November 4.

LENDERS TO THE EXHIBITION

Fundació "la CAIXA," Barcelona

Staatliche Museen zu Berlin, Preußischer Kulturbesitz, Nationalgalerie Berlin

Kunstmuseum Bonn

The Art Institute of Chicago

Museum Ludwig, Cologne

Statens Museum for Kunst, Copenhagen

museum kunst palast, Düsseldorf

Museum Folkwang, Essen

Modern Art Museum, Fort Worth

Hamburger Kunsthalle, Hamburg

Stiftung zur Förderung der Hamburgischen Kunstsammlungen, Hamburg

The Museum of Fine Arts, Houston

Bayerische Staatsgemäldesammlungen, Munich

The Museum of Modern Art, New York

National Gallery of Canada, Ottawa

Museum of Contemporary Art, Pôrto

The Czech Museum of Fine Arts, Prague

Kunsthalle Recklinghausen

Museum Boijmans Van Beuningen, Rotterdam

The Saint Louis Art Museum

San Francisco Museum of Modern Art

Art Gallery of Ontario, Toronto

Hirshhorn Museum and Sculpture Garden, Smithsonian Institution, Washington, D.C.

Kunstmuseum Winterthur

Städtische Galerie Wolfsburg

Collection Martha and Bruce Atwater

Collection Frances and John Bowes

Collection Isabel and David Breskin

Collection Frieder Burda

Daros Collection, Switzerland

De Pont Foundation for Contemporary Art, Tilburg

Di Bennardo Collection

Stefan T. Edlis Collection

Flick Collection

Froehlich Collection, Stuttgart

Collection Peter Gidal and Thérèse Oulton

Joseph Hackmey Collection

Collection Gabriele Henkel

Collection Samuel and Ronnie Heyman, New York

Park Hyatt Chicago

Collection Jung

Collection Howard and Linda Karshan

Collection Robert Lehrman, Washington, D.C.

Collection Joshua Mack and Ron Warren

Collection Ron and Ann Pizzuti, Columbus, Ohio

Collection C. and J. Plum

The Rachofsky Collection

Collection Gilberto Sandretto

Collection Maria Rosa Sandretto

Collection Mr. and Mrs. Howard Stone

Collection Lise Spiegel Wilks

Anonymous private lenders

Marian Goodman Gallery, New York

Galerie Bernd Lutze, Friedrichshafen

Massimo Martino Fine Arts and Projects, Mendrisio

Barbara Mathes Gallery, New York

Galerie Neher, Essen

Zwirner and Wirth, New York

PHOTOGRAPH CREDITS

Photographs of works of art reproduced in this volume have been provided in most cases by the owners or custodians of the works, identified in the captions. Individual works of art appearing herein may be protected by copyright in the United States of America or elsewhere, and may thus not be reproduced in any form without the permission of the copyright owners. The following credits appear at the request of the artist or the artist's representatives and/or the owners of the individual works. For certain documentary photographs reproduced in this volume, we have been unable to trace the copyright holders. We would appreciate notification of such information for acknowledgement in future editions.

Michael Agee, Yale University Art Gallery, New Haven, 42
David Allison, 122, 159, 203
Jörg P. Anders, Staatliche Museen zu Berlin, Preussischer Kulturbesitz, Nationalgalerie, 154
© 2002 by Artists Rights Society (ARS), New York, 35 left, 50, 82
© 2002 by Artists Rights Society (ARS), New York/VG-Bild-Kunst, Bonn, 57
© 2002 by Georg Baselitz, 47
Jeff Bates, Columbus, Ohio, 188
Bayerische Staatsgemäldesammlungen, Munich, 109
Olaf Bergmann, Galerie Neher, Essen, 192
Ben Blackwell, San Francisco Museum of Modern Art, back cover, 107, 255
Blauel/Gnamm, Artothek, Peissenberg, 57
Jose Luis Braga, Filipe Braga, Serralves Foundation, Pôrto, 139
Courtesy Isabel and David Breskin, 256, 262
Courtesy Frieder Burda, 28, 34 top
A. Burger, courtesy Flick Collection, 177
Courtesy Hubertus Butin and August Haseke, 30 bottom
Javier Campano, Fundació "La Caixa," Barcelona, 204–205

Carlo Catenazzi, Art Gallery of Ontario, 186
The Czech Museum of Fine Arts, Prague, 121
Daros Collection, Switzerland, 131
Brenda Dereniuk, Art Gallery of Ontario, 133
Peter Dibke, 62
Thomas R. DuBrock, Museum of Fine Arts, Houston, 266–271
Fotostudio Faaber, courtesy Galerie Bernd Lutze, Friedrichshafen, 196
© by Galerie Konrad Fischer and Gerhard Richter, 32
Joachim Fliegner, 157, 224
Courtesy Marian Goodman, New York, 158, 238
Tom Griesel, The Museum of Modern Art, New York, 55, 87, 89
Mark Gulezian, 116
Reni Hansen, Kunstmuseum, Bonn, 48 left, 123, 146
Heinrich Heidersberger, Städtische Galerie, Wolfsburg, 117
Courtesy Helga Photo Studios, 148
Brigitte Hellgoth, back end papers
High Museum of Art, Atlanta, 80
ID.art, 179
Courtesy Galerie Fred Jahn, Munich, 197
Jung Collection, 173
Wolfgang Keseberg, 58 left
Paige Knight, The Museum of Modern Art, New York, 190–191, 259
Horst Kolberg, museum kunst palast, Düsseldorf, 132
Kasper König, 35 left
Jean-Pierre Kuhn, 260
Jean-Pierre Kuhn, Zurich, Kunstmuseum Winterthur, 127
© 2002 by The Roy Lichtenstein Foundation, 42
Salvatore Licitra, Milan, courtesy Massimo Martino, 96, 113, 126, 147, 149, 199, 200
Jochen Littkemann, 142, 152, 198
© 2002 by Museum Associates/ LACMA, 50
Courtesy Luhring Augustine Gallery, New York, 12, 110

Bernd Lutze, 70
Courtesy Galerie Bernd Lutze, Friedrichshafen, 140
Courtesy Joshua Mack and Ron Warren, 112
Courtesy Barbara Mathes Gallery, New York, 184
David Mathews, © by President and Fellows of Harvard College, Busch-Reisinger Museum, Harvard University Art Museums, 29
George Meister, 34 left
Modern Art Museum of Fort Worth, 125
Martin Müller, 95
Rudolf Nagel, Museum für Moderne Kunst, Frankfurt, 37
© by The National Gallery of Art, Washington D.C., 82
© by National Gallery of Canada, Ottawa, 153
Eduard Noack, 175
Jens Nober, Museum Folkwang, Essen, 151
Courtesy Anthony d'Offay Gallery, London, front cover, 83, 115, 261, 280
Mali Olatunji, The Museum of Modern Art, New York, 24 left
Frank Oleski, 47
Courtesy Pace Gallery, New York, 189
Courtesy Park Hyatt, Chicago, 145
Rolf Petersen, The Museum of Modern Art, New York, 49
Fritz Pitz, 128
Ian Reeves, 180–181
Rheinisches Bildarchiv, Cologne, 137
Courtesy Gerhard Richter, front end papers, frontispiece, 21, 22, 23, 25 left, 25 top, 30 top, 41 left, 41 right, 46, 48 right, 54, 58 left, 59 left, 62, 72, 83, 95, 155, 161, 162–169, 170, 171, 187, 193, 234, 236, 239, 241, 254, 265, 272, 273, 275, 286, 288, 291, 292, 294, 297, 299, 301, 302, 307, 310
© by Gerhard Richter, courtesy Anthony d'Offay Gallery, London, 87

Friedrich Rosenstiel, Cologne, 141, 174, 233, 245, 246–253, 257, 274, 276, 277, 279, 281, 284–285
Stefan Rötheli, Zurich, Kunstmuseum Winterthur, 134–135
Johnsen Røyneland, Oslo, 242, 243
Klaus Ruland, 263
© by Reiner Ruthenbeck, 26, 33
The Saint Louis Art Museum, 225, 226–227, 228–229, 230–231
San Francisco Museum of Modern Art, 283
Günter and Luise Scherer, 292
Axel Schneider, 111
Uwe H. Seyl, 119
SMK Foto, Statens Museum for Kunst, Copenhagen, 237
Courtesy Sperone Westwater, New York, 35 top, 235
Städtische Galerie im Lenbachhaus, Munich, 98–105
Lee Stalsworth, Hirshhorn Museum and Sculpture Garden, 183, 264
Daniela Steinfeld, Galerie Konrad Fischer, Düsseldorf, 31 top
Nic Tenwiggenhorn, courtesy Gabriele Henkel, 185
Michael Tropea, 202
Ferdinand Ullrich, Kunsthalle, Recklinghausen, 114
Elke Walford, Hamburger Kunsthalle, 67, 150
© 2002 by Andy Warhol Foundation for the Visual Arts/Artists Rights Society (ARS), New York, 37
Courtesy Michael Werner Gallery, Cologne and New York, 31 left, 63
Greg Williams, © 1999 byThe Art Institute of Chicago, 108
Greg Williams, © 2001 by The Art Institute of Chicago, 129, 232
John Wronn, The Museum of Modern Art, New York, 24 right, 52, 61, 201, 207–223
Zindman/Fremont, 59, 195
Courtesy David Zwirner Gallery, New York, 143
Courtesy Zwirner and Wirth Gallery, New York, 124

TRUSTEES OF THE MUSEUM OF MODERN ART